WORLD AGRICULTURE IN DISARRAY

World Agriculture in Disarray

D. Gale Johnson

Eliakim Hastings Moore Professor Emeritus of Economics
University of Chicago

Second Edition

M
MACMILLAN

for the
TRADE POLICY RESEARCH CENTRE
London

First edition 1973
Second edition 1991

Published by
MACMILLAN PRESS LTD
Houndmills, Basingstoke, Hampshire RG21 2XS
and London
Companies and representatives
throughout the world

British Library Cataloguing in Publication Data
Johnson, D. Gale (David Gale) *1916—*
World agriculture in disarray.—2nd. ed.
1. Developed countries. Agricultural industries
I. Title II. Trade Policy Research Centre
338.1091722

ISBN 0-333-54626-1
ISBN 0-333-54627-X pbk

Typeset by Latimer Trend & Company Ltd, Plymouth
Printed in Hong Kong

Trade Policy Research Centre

The Trade Policy Research Centre in London was established in 1968 to promote independent analysis and public discussion of international economic policy issues. As a non-profit organization, which is privately sponsored, the institute has been developed to work on an international

basis and serves as an entrepreneurial centre for a variety of activities, including the publication of a quarterly journal, *The World Economy*. In general, the Centre provides a focal point for those in business, the universities and public affairs who are interested in the problems of international economic relations.

The Centre is managed by a Council which represents a wide range of international experience and expertise.

The principal function of the Centre is the sponsorship of research programmes on policy problems of both national and international importance. Lectures, conferences, seminars and other meetings are also convened from time to time.

Publications are presented as professionally competent studies worthy of public consideration. The interpretations and conclusions in them are those of their respective authors and do not purport to represent the views of members of the Council, staff and associates of the Centre which, having general terms of reference, does not represent on any particular issue a consensus of opinion.

Contents

Dedicated
To the Memory of Helen
in recognition of her great devotion to her
community, friends and family.

Biographical Note

D. Gale Johnson is Eliakim Hastings Moore Professor Emeritus of Economics at the University of Chicago, Chairman of the Council of Academic Advisers at the American Enterprise Institute for Research on Public Policy, Washington, and Editor of the journal *Economic Development and Cultural Change*. Over the years, Professor Johnson has acted as an adviser, in various capacities, on agricultural policy and related issues in both the executive and legislative branches of the United States government. Besides *World Agriculture in Disarray*, first published in 1973, he has written extensively on agricultural issues in numerous books, professional journals, collections of essays, official reports, testimonies and monographs.

Professor Johnson graduated in 1938 from Iowa State College and obtained his master's degree at the University of Wisconsin. He returned to Iowa State College in 1941 as a research associate, becoming an assistant professor of economics a year later, obtaining his doctorate from there in 1945. In 1944, he joined the University of Chicago, becoming Professor of Economics in 1954 and serving in numerous other posts, including Dean of Social Sciences in 1960–70, Chairman of the Department of Economics in 1971–75 and 1980–84, Director of the Office of Economic Analysis in 1973–75, Vice President and Dean of Faculties in 1975 and Provost in 1976–80.

Regarding his advisory roles in the United States government, Professor Johnson was, from 1957 to 1969, a member of the Advisory Board of Policy Planning Council in the Department of State. In 1963–64 he was Agricultural Adviser to the President's Special Trade Representative; and in 1965–67 he was a key member of the President's National Commission on Food and Fiber. Then in 1970–72, he was a member of the President's National Commission on Population Growth and the American Future; and in 1972–75, a consultant to the President's Council on International Economic Policy.

In the 'think-tank' world of the United States, Professor Johnson was a member of the Social Science Research Council in 1954–67, President of the National Opinion Research Center, Chicago, in 1962–75 and 1978–85 and President of the American Farm Economic Association in 1964–65.

Professor Johnson is the author, *inter alia*, of *The Struggle against World Hunger* (1967), *Farm Commodity Programs: an Opportunity for Change* (1973), *The Sugar Program: Large Costs and Small Benefits* (1974), *World Food Problems and Prospects* (1976), *The Soviet Impact on the World Grain Trade* (1977), *Progress of Economic Reform in the People's Republic of China* (1982), *Prospects for Soviet Agriculture in the 1980s* (with Karen Brooks, 1983) and *The People's Republic of China: 1978–90* (1990). He is the editor, *inter alia*, of *The Politics of Food: Producing and Distributing the World's Food Supply* (1980), *The Role of Markets in the World's Food Economy* (with G. Edward Schuh, 1983), *Agricultural Policy and Trade* (with Kenzo Hemmi and Pierre Lardinois, 1985) and *Population Growth and Economic Development* (with R. D. Lee, 1987).

List of Tables

Foreword

In February 1987 I was honoured to present an invited lecture at the annual meeting of the Australian Agricultural Economics Society. The title of my lecture was 'World Agriculture in Disarray Revisited'. On what happened to the disarray, I generally concluded: 'Unfortunately it takes little more than casual observation to permit one to conclude that the disarray has not diminished in the intervening period. It is apparent that the disarray has, in fact, deepened.'

In revising and updating *World Agriculture in Disarray*, the basic analytical structure has remained essentially unchanged, for I believe that there is nothing in the experience of the intervening years that necessitated significant modification. Much of the empirical material is new, of course. But the basic view of the original edition that the numerous product market and trade interventions pursued by national governments had little or no effect on the welfare of farm people is, if anything, supported even more fully by the evidence accumulated over the years. The basis for the conclusion was a reasonably straightforward application of standard neo-classical economics to the conditions that influence agricultural activities in the industrialized countries.

The underlying ideas are simple ones. The starting point is that economic growth requires significant adjustments in agriculture and by farm people if farm people are to share in the benefits of economic growth in their economy. Most national policies try to cushion these adjustments by attempting to increase demand and product prices. Such policies are ineffective because they ignore the fact that the major adjustments occur in the factor markets. The primary determinants of the incomes and welfare of farm people are not the prices they receive for their products, but are the alternatives that are available for the use of their resources in the rest of the economy. The welfare of farm people is also a function of the resources that they own, especially their human capital. A serious defect of the agricultural policies of the industrial countries has been that the education of farm people has not been an important component of those policies.

There are two important omissions in the earlier edition of this book. One of these was the failure to recognize the significant impact of macro-economic variables on farming, farm people and the industries closely related to agriculture. I completely ignored the role of exchange

xv

rates and monetary and fiscal policies in influencing variables that have major consequences for agriculture. The role of interest rates in influencing the well-being of farm people in the industrial economies during the 1970s and 1980s cannot be exaggerated. It should by now be evident that macro-economic variables have an influence on farming equal to or greater than that of output prices or deficiency payments. I believe that I have corrected this significant shortcoming.

The other important omission was the failure to consider the price, income and trade policies for agriculture in the developing countries. I did not note the strong urban bias in the food price policies of developing countries that resulted in their keeping farm prices below world market prices and thus stifling the development of their agricultures. While the main focus is still industrial-country policies, note is taken of the quite different set of developing-country policies.

I have not attempted to present a detailed analysis of the farm price-support and income-support programmes of the major industrial countries as of the late 1980s. These programmes are enormously complex and are being subjected to gradual change and modification. But it should be clear from what is presented that for the major agricultural consuming and trading countries or entities – the United States, Japan and the European Community – the changes that have been made fall far short of what is required if the disarray which now exists is to be substantially eliminated.

The revision of this book has been under way far longer than I want to recall. In the long period of time I have benefited from the diligent and faithful efforts of several graduate students, especially Barbara Mace, William Goldstein, Anjini Kochar and Mansoora Rashid, who spent countless hours attempting to update tables and to find other relevant materials. Much of the difficult work of putting my mangled manuscript into reasonable order was done by one who had been my fellow worker and secretary for eighteen years and who had typed the manuscript for the original version, namely Alyce Monroe. Much to my regret, and I hope not because of this book, she retired before I was quite through. Barbara Belisle has successfully carried the effort forward. I owe each, as well as many others, a debt of gratitude.

D. GALE JOHNSON
Chicago

May 1989

Preface to the Second Edition

When the first edition of *World Agriculture in Disarray* was published in 1973, the world was experiencing a 'food crisis'. There were widespread shortages of supply, correspondingly buoyant commodity prices and terrible starvation in Africa and other parts of the world. The issue was high on political agendas in major capitals and, in the end, the United Nations convened a World Food Conference in Rome.

With so much instability in agricultural markets, it looked as if the architects of the European Community's common agricultural policy (CAP), which in the late 1960s was beginning to be attacked for its distortionary effects on international trade, had 'got it right' after all – notwithstanding the high-cost surpluses the CAP's various measures were generating. Indeed, to the casual reader, it might have looked as if, in his diagnosis of the disarray in world agriculture, D. Gale Johnson had got it wrong. Well, of course, Professor Johnson had done nothing of the sort. Nevertheless, the conditions in agricultural markets at the time meant that the book did not get, from the outset, the attention it should have got in public discussion and policy-making circles.

All the same, the book soon became a seminal work in the literature on the economics, and the politics, of agricultural-support policies in industrialized countries. Before long, efforts were being made at the Trade Policy Research Centre, in London, to persuade Professor Johnson to prepare a second edition. But there were lots of other demands on his time. Eventually the Alfred P. Sloan Foundation, in New York, made a grant which enabled the revision to be undertaken.

In revising the text, Professor Johnson has not had to modify the analysis and thrust of what he had to say in the early 1970s, for events since then have substantiated his arguments still further. His criticism of agricultural policies in the United States and the European Community, as well as in other industrialized countries, is therefore more trenchant than before in certain places.

During the 1970s another attempt was made, on the initiative of the United States (supported by other competitive agricultural-exporting countries), to tackle the distortions in agricultural production and trade during the course of the Tokyo Round of multilateral trade negotiations that were conducted in Geneva under the auspices of the General Agreement on Tariffs and Trade (GATT). As the negotiations got down to business in 1975, having been formally launched in September 1973, commodity prices were depressed and the commitment of the United States to liberalizing agricultural trade was strong. By the time the negotiations were concluded in 1979, however, commodity prices were again buoyant and American farm interests were relaxed. No longer was there a great deal of pressure at political level to reform agricultural-support policies and the trade restrictions associated with them.

At the beginning of the 1980s, pressure for reform of agricultural-support policies was again on the increase, so much so that it was acknowledged at the start of the Uruguay Round negotiations, launched in September 1986, that something fundamental had to be done to correct the disarray in world agriculture. Apart from yet another crisis in agricultural trade, with commodity prices at their lowest levels since the 1930s, there was a growing appreciation of the economy-wide costs of agricultural-support policies, of the costs imposed down the years on other sectors of the economy by the steady misallocation of resources caused by agricultural protectionism.

Whatever happens in the Uruguay Round negotiations, *World Agriculture in Disarray* will be a source of diagnosis and prescription for years to come, for nobody can be sanguine about the time it will take to put farm-support policies on a more rational basis – even supposing the readiness of governments to face up to what has to be done.

In his Foreword, Professor Johnson thanks those who helped him with this revised edition and, therefore, it only remains to thank the Sloan Foundation for so generously providing the financial support.

As usual, it has to be stressed that the views expressed in the book do not necessarily reflect the views of the Council or those of the staff and associates of the Trade Policy Research Centre which, having general terms of reference, does not represent a consensus of opinion on any particular issue. The purpose of the Centre is to promote independent research and public discussion of international economic policy issues.

HUGH CORBET
Director
Trade Policy Research Centre
London

July 1989

Explanatory Notes

Weights and measures

Unless specifically indicated to the contrary, all specific references to weights and measures are in the metric system. Some of the more important conversions from the system of weights used in the United Kingdom and the United States are:

$$1 \text{ kilogram} = 2.0246 \text{ pounds}$$
$$1 \text{ metric ton} = 2204.6 \text{ pounds}$$
$$1 \text{ hectare} = 2.471 \text{ acres}$$

Monetary units

Unless specifically indicated to the contrary, all prices or values indicated in dollars refer to the dollar of the United States. Conversions from other currencies have generally been made at the official IMF par values as of the date of the dollar estimate.

Dates

Statistics refer to calendar years unless otherwise indicated. Split years, such as 1987/8, refer to a fiscal or crop year generally beginning some time between 1 April and 1 October. When dates are separated by a hyphen, such as 1982–84, this means the average of the three years 1982, 1983, 1984.

Abbreviations

The initials below are used in the book to varying degrees:

CAP   common agricultural policy of the European Community, as distinct from the national agricultural policies of the member countries

c.i.f.   price including cost, insurance and freight
EC   European Community (see note below)
EFTA   European Free Trade Association
FAO   Food and Agriculture Organization, an agency of the
            United Nations, based in Rome
GATT   General Agreement on Tariffs and Trade, the secretariat of
            which is in Geneva
GDP   gross domestic product
GNP   gross national product
IMF   International Monetary Fund, based in Washington
IWC   International Wheat Council, based in London
MCA   monetary compensatory amount, a device of the European
            Community's common agricultural policy
MFN   most-favoured-nation
OECD   Organisation for Economic Cooperation and Development,
            based in Paris
OEEC   Organisation for European Economic Cooperation, re-
            placed in 1961 by the OECD
PL 480   Public Law 480 of the United States Congress, the Agricul-
            tural Trade Development and Assistance Act of 1954 (the
            Food for Peace programme), under which food shipments
            are made to developing countries on concessional terms.
USDA   United States Department of Agriculture
VER   voluntary export restraints

European Community

The original members of the European Community were Belgium,
France, Italy, Luxembourg, the Netherlands and the Federal Republic
of Germany. The Community was enlarged in 1973 to include Denmark, Ireland and the United Kingdom, again in 1981 to include
Greece and again in 1986 to include Portugal and Spain. The discussion
therefore refers when appropriate to the Community of Six (or the
original Six), the Community of Nine, Ten and Twelve. Throughout
the text the Federal Republic of Germany is referred to as West
Germany, although 'Germany' and 'German' are used on occasion.
  The term 'European Community' rather than 'European Communities' is used throughout the discussion. The former is used in popular
discussion, in the press and so on, and the latter is used in official
documents, but not always.

1 Politics and Economics and Farmers

Most short statements leave an impression that is partially untrue. The title *World Agriculture in Disarray* is no exception. Although most of the impression that it transmits is true, there is also an element of untruth, if the statement is taken too literally. Farm products are produced and sold at high cost in many parts of the world while elsewhere similar products that could be produced at low cost cannot be sold at all or only with great difficulty. The prices of farm products are manipulated by most governments and without any real knowledge of the consequences. In some countries consumers are forced to pay extremely high prices for many foods when comparable products could be available at much lower prices. Economic relations among friendly nations are soured by rigid adherence to economically unjustified restrictions on trade in farm products and by the use of large and variable export subsidies.

But it is not agriculture as a sector of the economy where resources are allocated and goods are produced that is in disarray. It is instead the policy setting in which agriculture finds itself that is in disarray. Farmers everywhere are capable of producing the right things in the right place in the right amounts and at low cost in terms of resources if they receive the proper economic signals. That farmers in the United States or France produce more wheat than there is a market for at a price that will cover the cost of producing that wheat is not due to shortcomings in the economic efficiency or rationality of farmers. It is due to the particular policies followed by their governments. The distinction between these two aspects of world agriculture is an important one and it should not be blurred by noting that the agricultural and trade policies followed by most governments are to some considerable degree intended to give farmers what it is believed they want or need.

In the major industrial countries the majority of the population has little or no contact with farming as such. The main sources of contact with agriculture are through the products available in the marketplace and the taxes that are levied to pay for the multitudinous and often conflicting farm programmes that have been devised.

1

There are a number of stereotypes about farm people that are all-too-widely held in most societies. Some of the stereotypes, such as the one that farmers are bound by tradition, are relatively free of derogatory connotation. Others, such as the one that farmers really are not as intelligent as the rest of us or that many farmers lack initiative, are not particularly pleasant in their connotations. It has been true in the past, although now much less common in the industrial countries, that the dress, speech and manners of farm people were different from those of the urban middle class. It may also have been true that farm people took a bath a little less frequently than did their better-off neighbours in the city. Particular categories of intellectuals, especially those strongly influenced by Marx, have tended to mistrust the peasant because of his attachment to individual property, especially land, and his petty-bourgeois social and political values. Farmers have all-too-often been either exploited or have had their most important needs, such as education, neglected. Except as the rest of society has decreed it through neglect or oppression, the farm people of the world are neither better nor worse, neither more nor less endowed with initiative, neither more nor less effective in using the resources that they have available to them than the rest of us. In fact, as the story unfolds it will become evident that farm people are more willing than many of the rest of us to change, to try the new and different and to accept risks.

It is rather surprising, given the type of stereotypes discussed above, that farm people have the political influence that they have displayed in the industrial countries. In the United Kingdom and the United States the agricultural labour forces are less than 2.5 per cent of the total. As of the mid-1980s, among the original members of the European Community, only Italy had a tenth of its labour force in agriculture; the next highest percentage was in France with about 8 per cent. In the Federal Republic of Germany, where the two major parties appear to be highly sensitive to, if not fearful of, the farm vote, only 5 per cent of the labour force was engaged in farming.[1] While in a later chapter I try to indicate why agriculture has been able to achieve so much political power with so 'few troops', at this point I only wish to point out the inconsistency between the all-too-frequent view that farm people really are not quite like the rest of us and the fact that, as politicians, they seem to have an uncommonly and unexpectedly large influence in the industrial countries.

All of the disarray in world agriculture cannot be attributed to the policies and programmes of the industrial market economies. The centrally-planned economies, especially the Soviet Union, have been and continue to be at least as irresponsible as the market economies in their pursuit of policies that impose substantial costs on other countries and their citizens. The centrally-planned economies have given high priority to maintaining stable nominal prices of most food products sold through their state store systems. Such policies have required very high rates of subsidies if reasonable prices are to be paid to the farms for their production. In at least one case, that of Poland, the magnitude of the subsidies became so large that the fiscal system could no longer manage them. To some significant degree, the civil and political crisis that engulfed Poland from 1981 onwards can be attributed to inappropriate food and agricultural policies.

Nor can one ignore the responsibility of most developing countries for the disarray in world agriculture. While the industrial market economies are generally engaged in heavily subsidizing agriculture, the developing countries are frequently guilty of exploiting their farmers.[2] The exploitation occurs both as a result of a low food-price policy for the benefit of urban consumers and by following import-substitution policies for industrial products that seriously reduce the capacity of agriculture to compete in world markets. Most developing countries have over-valued currencies; the effect is similar to an export tax. And all too many developing countries impose export taxes on the few farm products in which they have a comparative advantage.

If one surveys the agricultural policies of the market economies of the world, one finds what seems to contradict what one would expect. The larger the percentage of the population engaged in agriculture the more likely it is that farmers will be exploited by their governments through low consumer and procurement prices for one or more staple foods and export taxes. The lower the percentage of the population engaged in agriculture, the more likely it is that agriculture will be protected and consumer prices will be significantly higher than would prevail in the absence of the protection. Due to the strong negative correlation between the percentage of a country's population engaged in agriculture and the country's per capita real income, it is also true that farmers tend to be exploited in low-income countries and subsidized in high-income countries.

Since the Second World War there have been several examples that illustrate a changing pattern of governmental involvement in agricultural prices as the percentage of the population engaged in agriculture fell as a consequence of rapid economic growth. Three countries – Japan, the Republic of Korea and Taiwan – serve as examples of shifts from negative or nil protection of farm products during the 1950s and substantial protection by the mid-1970s. Each country had relatively low per capita incomes in the late 1940s or early 1950s and enjoyed remarkably rapid rates of growth from 1960 onwards. During the late 1950s the nominal protection of rice in Japan was 50 per cent, increasing to 100 per cent by the late 1960s and to more than 260 per cent for 1975–79.[3]

In South Korea the nominal protection of grains was a negative 15 per cent for 1950–59 and a decade later domestic and international prices were comparable. By 1975–79 the nominal protection of grains had increased to 125 per cent.[4] In Taiwan the nominal protection of rice, the only cereal produced in significant amounts, was nil or negative from 1955 through 1968 and then turned sharply positive, averaging a little more than 60 per cent for 1975–79 and 150 per cent for 1980.[5]

A cross-section of the countries of the world reveals that where agriculture accounts for a large percentage of total employment and of gross national product (GNP) the nominal protection of agriculture is negative. The same snapshot shows that in the industrial high-income countries the protection of agriculture is substantial, with nominal protection rates of 50 to 100 per cent or more being common.[6] And, as noted above, in countries with very rapid growth rates of per capita output between 1950 and 1980, the protection of agriculture has shifted from nil or negative to highly positive rates in a very brief period – the active life of many farmers.

If the general structure of farm policies in the industrial countries remains unchanged, the economic waste will grow rather than diminish. By any measure that one may choose, the costs of the farm programmes to taxpayers and consumers have trended upward since the late 1960s. Without significant policy reforms, the costs will continue to increase. It is also highly probable that the tensions in relations among countries will increase since almost certainly the flow of unsubsidized trade in farm products among the industrial countries will continue to decline. Nor will there be any significant progress towards the solutions of the farm problems that the present policies are supposed to alleviate. Whether stated explicitly or implicitly, the farm policies of the industrial countries are intended to reduce or eliminate the disparity in income between farm and non-farm people. This goal is to be achieved by higher prices or returns than would be realized if there were reasonably free trade in farm products and, too, by the payment of a wide range of subsidies, some associated with output and some associated with particular inputs. As I hope to show later, this approach requires an enormous and generally increasing cost and makes little contribution to the elimination of the income disparity referred to above.

Perhaps the most important reason why the negotiation process on agricultural trade has accomplished so little is that the industrial countries do not have a separate and identifiable trade policy for farm products. The trade measures that each country adopts are an adjunct of its domestic farm policies. In most cases, a specific trade restrictive or interfering device has been adopted, not for its particular direct benefits, but because it is a device that will make it possible for a domestic measure to function. If a country adopts a farm programme that establishes the domestic price for a product above the world market price, it must have some technique for preventing imports from entering its market and making it impossible to support the domestic price at the specified level. And if a country sets a support price for a product that it exports at a level above the world market price, it discovers that if no action is taken exports fall to zero. Thus in order to maintain its 'fair share' of the world market, or for some other equally transparent reason, it resorts to an export subsidy.

The United States, for example, did not resort to export subsidies and import quotas in the 1930s for entirely capricious reasons. In fact, such measures were strongly condemned by the policy-makers who were responsible for the shift from the high protectionist philosophy of the Smoot–Hawley Tariff to that expressed in the Reciprocal Trade Agreements Act of 1934, the first of a series of legislative authorities for the Administration to negotiate on the liberalization of international trade. Yet since that time, it has been necessary for the forces that favoured freer trade to accept the inconsistency of export subsidies and import quotas for farm products when such devices were required for the functioning of farm programmes. It was no accident that the United States Congress repeatedly attached to various pieces of trade legislation such limitations on the power of the President as the following: 'Nothing contained in this act shall be construed to affect in any way the provisions of Section 22 of the Agriculture Adjustment Act, or to apply to any import restrictions heretofore or hereafter imposed under such section' (Trade Expansion Act of 1962). Nor was it any accident that the General Agreement on Tariffs and Trade (GATT), the instrument which has governed the international trading system since the Second World War, includes various exceptions to the general principles for trade liberalization and conduct. Without such exceptions the GATT would not have been possible.

Nor did the European Community adopt variable import levies and export subsidies (euphemistically called restitutions) out of pique or stubbornness or ignorance of the major implications to other efforts to reduce trade barriers. But the Common Market found, as would anyone else, how enormously difficult it is for a group of countries to harmonize their agricultural policies and programmes. It is largely irrelevant to point out that more than two decades of the Community's common agricultural policy (CAP) have contributed almost nothing to the objectives of that policy. At the time, the continued development of the Common Market was probably impossible without agreement on a farm policy quite similar to what was adopted. It may be that the price that the Community's consumers and taxpayers are now paying for that decision is a higher price than is warranted by the other purely economic benefits from the Community. But, at the time, few envisaged the high costs that are now so apparent, and little can be gained at this stage by lamenting that general lack of foresight.

But it is not only the United States and the European Community who have been willing to live with the glaring inconsistencies between their general trade principles and the particular restrictive devices that affect trade in farm products. In 1964 the United Kingdom, before joining the Community, decided that it no longer wanted the Treasury to bear the full costs of its price-support measures. The burden was conveniently shifted by setting minimum import prices on grains (this in addition to existing restrictions on bacon and butter imports). And Japan, which has to export to live, has probably had the most restrictive trade policies of any major industrial country (except the Soviet Union) for farm products; only in recent years has there been a significant reduction in the use of import licences and state trading in the importation of farm products.

The general trend in trade interferences by the industrial countries has been towards liberalization. Over the past three decades major reductions in tariff levels have been negotiated and many non-tariff barriers have been eliminated. The elimination of most exchange controls also operated to permit an increase in the flow of investment funds and trade. Unfortunately the above statements apply primarily to non-agricultural products. The degree of governmental intervention in the trade of agricultural products has increased since the late 1950s (see Chapter 5). The trade negotiations that resulted in significant changes in the restraints to trade in industrial products had on minimal positive effects where agricultural products were involved. In fact, during the Dillon, Kennedy and Tokyo rounds of multilateral trade negotiations, under the GATT's auspices, agricultural trade was considered quite separately from the remainder of trade.

The primary reason for the difference in results with respect to agricultural and industrial trade is that the countries engaging in the negotiations view their interferences with agricultural trade as an adjunct to their domestic agricultural policies and programmes and the countries have generally been unwilling to negotiate about matters that they consider to be primarily of domestic concern. Agriculture is not, of course, the sole such instance in which compelling domestic or national interests are used to justify trade interferences. But agriculture surely stands out as the most important single case in which the governments of most industrial countries are willing to permit domestic policy considerations to override so completely their interests in achieving the advantages from increased international specialization in production.

What is the evidence that world agriculture is in disarray? In general it is seen in the lost opportunities for producing farm products under lowest-cost conditions and in the fact that much of the growth in world farm output has been – and is – occurring in countries where policies are encouraging output expansion with little or no consideration of the long-run effects on either their own citizens or the interests of agricultural producers in other countries. In short, a significant amount of world farm output is being produced in the wrong place. If important benefits of a permanent nature were being derived from the distortions in location of output, there might be a reasonable basis for such interferences. But the benefits that have been, and are being, derived are minimal; and the costs to consumers and taxpayers in many industrial countries, and the forgone possibilities for developing countries to use their own resources to best advantage and to earn foreign exchange required for rapid economic growth, far outweigh any possible gains.

More specifically, several points that illustrate and define the nature of the disarray can be briefly noted. First, there are wide variations in the prices received by producers for each of the major farm products in the major industrial countries. It is not uncommon to find differences of 100 per cent between the producer price and the import cost of a particular commodity and much larger differences can be found in a few cases. These variations in producer prices are one of the important causes of output being produced in the wrong places. Second, taxpayers and consumers are faced with large and increasing costs by the efforts of the industrial countries to achieve certain objectives in their agricultural policies. Third, the farm policies in the industrial countries are resulting in a growth of output of farm products that is greater than the growth in consumption of those products within the industrial countries.

This last effect of the efforts to solve domestic farm problems has wide and serious implications to the developing countries that depend on their exports of farm products for such a large share of their export earnings. The low-income countries find themselves competing with the subsidized production and exports of the industrial countries and the result is what one would expect in such an uneven encounter. The exports of farm products from the developing countries to the industrial countries are increasing at a much slower pace than the exports from the industrial countries either to other industrial countries or to the developing countries. In practice, the industrial countries view the control of imports as an adjunct of their domestic farm policies and of no reasonable concern to other countries; and they consider international markets as an outlet for unwanted production that is encouraged by such domestic programmes. The only measure of the absorptive capacity of international markets that seems significant to policymakers in some industrial countries is the cost of the export subsidies.

The above are some of the reasons why it can be said that world agriculture is in disarray. The basic element common to the farm policies of the industrial countries is that each encourages the expansion of output of some or all farm products. Seldom is there adequate concern about the prospective market for the additional output. Until output expands to the level requiring subsidized sale abroad, it is probably correct to say that there is no concern about the market for the output that has been encouraged by high prices and subsidies. Not so long ago this lack of concern for the interests of countries for whom the export of farm products was important was justified on the grounds that starvation and famine were imminent in major areas of the world and the excess production could be put to a useful purpose. While there cannot be a certainty that the same pressure on food grain supplies that emerged in the mid-1960s and early 1970s will not occur again, it is clear that there are other means of meeting such difficulties that are much more efficient and viable from an economic standpoint (see Chapter 8). In fact, the emphasis given to stable farm prices in many countries was responsible for a considerable part of the large international grain price increases that occurred in 1973 and 1974. When stable domestic farm prices are achieved by varying exports and imports, the effects of world demand and supply variability are concentrated in the international markets and in those countries that permit their domestic prices to vary with international prices.[7]

The disarray in world agriculture is clearly significant because of (i) the distortions in prices and trade, (ii) the large costs imposed on taxpayers and consumers and (iii) the uneconomic expansion of farm output in the industrial countries and the associated effects on the developing countries. But these serious consequences may be of secondary importance, being far outweighed by the possibilities for protection and intransigence that persist in agriculture to erode, and perhaps destroy, the basis for liberal trade policies generally. How sad it would be if this should be the case, since the present farm policies have been largely ineffective, except in the very short run, in achieving their avowed objectives.

As noted earlier, the Tokyo Round negotiations, completed in 1979, made very little contribution to the reduction or modification of barriers to trade in agricultural products. In fact, several critical issues related to agricultural trade were not resolved during the formal negotiations, but were to be left for subsequent discussions. Subsequent discussions and negotiations made little or no progress on any of the issues. Perhaps the most important issue of all was to devise a subsidies code that would make Article XVI of the GATT meaningful, but nothing was accomplished. Other issues included trade in dairy products and health and sanitary regulations, labelling regulations and standards that serve to restrict imports in a significant way. These issues remained as the Uruguay Round negotiations began in 1987.

The responsibility is widely distributed for recent and past failures to achieve a significant degree of liberalization of agricultural trade. As will become clear later, the policies and practices of the United States bear a large share of the responsibility for the current disarray in international trade in farm products. In the periods before and after the Second World War the United States largely ignored its responsibilities for the development of sound world trade policies for farm products. In fact, it lent its power and prestige to the distortion of the principles of liberal trade as applied to agricultural products in the establishment of the GATT. I refer to the special rules or exceptions to general GATT principles that were applied to trade in agricultural products at the insistence of the United States.

It was unfortunate that the Tokyo Round negotiations achieved so little with respect to agricultural trade. American agricultural interests remain as one of the important forces supporting liberal trade. While a great deal has been achieved during the post-Second World War period in liberalizing trade in industrial products, the various barriers to such trade that were imposed by the United States and the European Community during the latter half of the 1970s and the early 1980s indicate the fragility of support for liberal trade. Failure to make some progress during the 1980s in reducing barriers to trade in agricultural products may erode an important source of support for liberal trade in the United States.

2 Farm and Trade Policies of the Industrial Countries

It is neither possible nor necessary to give a detailed review of the farm and trade policies of each of the major industrial countries. Excellent summaries, with major emphasis on farm policies, already exist.[1] While there are differences in detail, general patterns can be delineated. In any case, the detailed features of the farm policies are not of primary interest to us; our concern is with the effects of the farm policies on prices, production and trade.

Objectives of Farm Policies

In most democratic countries one has considerable difficulty in determining the objectives of policies and programmes. With few exceptions, this is true of the agricultural policies of the industrial countries. When objectives are stated, the level of generality is often very great. This is understandable since, if the objectives are stated clearly and with considerable specificity, the politicians would provide too obvious a guide for determining the relationships between promise and performance. But the lack of specificity makes sense on grounds that are more reasonable or significant than protecting the credibility of politicians and the political process.

The outcome of any given policy is subject to many factors beyond the control of government and this is particularly true in agriculture. Output is subject to considerable variation, either domestically or in foreign areas important as sources of supply or as an outlet for exports. Compared with most other goods and services, the demand for farm products, especially food products, is relatively stable over time. But the low short-run price elasticities of demand and supply can result in significant price variability or, if price variability is prevented, in rapid accumulation or drawing down of stocks. Furthermore, the linkage between the actions that may be taken, such as higher prices, and the objectives desired is often quite indirect. Thus if the objective is

11

something other than the means used, say higher farm prices or a limitation on output, the final impact on the objectives desired is subject to responses by farmers, consumers, marketing firms and the policies of other governments.

Historically, the objectives of farm policies have included one or more of four major concerns: (i) national self-sufficiency or autarky for food or some raw material that is considered to be of critical importance; (ii) reducing balance-of-payments difficulties; (iii) benefits for the farm population in terms of higher incomes, stable prices or expanded employment opportunities; and (iv) benefits to consumers in the form of an assured source of supply and stable and reasonable prices. I have excluded a fifth category of objectives, namely the maintenance of a large and prosperous agriculture because such an agriculture is essential to the country's prosperity. Agricultural fundamentalism is often attributed to the Physiocrats, but its origins are much older. More though on this later.

The first of the concerns, self-sufficiency in food, had its origin in the vulnerability of a nation in time of war, especially a nation that imported a significant part of its food supply. The use of agricultural programmes to solve balance-of-payments difficulties is either quite old or quite new; quite old if one considers it a feature of mercantilist policy, quite new if one relates it to the monetary difficulties dating from the early 1930s. British agricultural policy after the Second World War was strongly influenced by the fear that the immense amount of foreign exchange required to import about half of the food supply would create continuing and not readily solvable balance-of-payments problems. The severe restrictions on imports of farm products by several of the major West European countries during the 1950s were both justified and excused on the grounds of balance-of-payments difficulties.

The frequently-stated objective of benefiting the consumer through an assured source of supply and stable and reasonable prices can seldom be taken seriously so far as recent experience in the industrial countries is concerned. Prior to entry into the European Community, this objective was met for a major part of the British food supply. There were exceptions, but in the main the British consumer had reasonable access to most of his food at prices that approximately reflected world market conditions. When one reads that one of the main objectives of the sugar programme of the United States during the period from 1936 through 1974 was to 'assure United States consumers of a plentiful and stable supply of sugar at reasonable prices', or that one of the objectives of the agricultural policy of the European Community – as stated in the Treaty of Rome – is 'to ensure reasonable prices in supplies to consumers', one can easily imagine that he is accompanying Alice through Wonderland.

This brief summary of objectives will conclude with the discussion of the benefits that are to accrue to the farm population. Three benefits were specified: stable prices, higher incomes and employment opportunities. In the United States, the emphasis on stable prices as an objective of farm policy grew out of the trauma of price gyrations during and following the First World War and in the Great Depression. Farmers, who are often more heavily in debt than the rest of us, fear price declines; and the emphasis on price stability as an objective was evident in the policies adopted both before and after the Second World War in Canada, Australia, New Zealand and the United Kingdom as well as in the United States. Price stability is a reasonable and a manageable goal, unless it is also tied to the objective of higher average farm prices. It has proven difficult for governments to pursue a reasonable degree of price stability without being forced to undertake measures to increase the price for some or all of the output. In all-too-many cases the objective has become stable *and* high prices, and measures have had to become much more complex than stockholding, or minor use of taxes and subsidies, in order partially to insulate producer prices from variations in market prices. But as will be shown in Chapter 9, stable prices do not provide for stable incomes for farm-operator families. Other variables, such as interest rates and the importance of debt, have much greater influence upon income stability than do output prices.

Until the Second World War farm policies were primarily concerned with price objectives. The idea of a 'fair price' has a long history. In the United States the concept of 'parity price' gradually emerged out of the numerous efforts to create farm programmes during the 1920s. When the Agricultural Adjustment Act of 1933 was enacted, it included the concept of parity price as a measurement of the price objective to be achieved. The parity price was simply a price that would achieve a constant real price relative to some past period. The parity price was calculated for each farm product. The base period was 1910–14 for most products. This period was chosen because it was one that was considered satisfactory in terms of price relationships and because it was the only period not affected by the First World War and its aftermath for which the necessary data for the calculation of indices of prices paid by farmers were available.

It was soon discovered that, even if one accepted the general concept of parity price, numerous difficulties were involved in the use of such prices to guide farm price programmes. Both demand and cost conditions change and, by the end of the Second World War, it became obvious that the relationships of three decades earlier were no longer viable. Enormous changes had occurred in the intervening period and attempting to maintain the same relative price relationships became an impossibility. While efforts to modernize parity relationships were made, these were insufficient to make parity price a viable policy objective. The current use of parity price is minimal and it plays largely a symbolic role.

In recent years there has been a trend towards a general consensus that the primary objective of national farm policies should be to improve the income status of the farm population. As I shall argue later, the emergence of income objectives represents a significant departure in the development of agricultural policies. It has also brought with it a number of problems, few of which were anticipated.

In its highly useful summary, *Agricultural Policies in 1966*, the staff of the Organisation for Economic Cooperation and Development (OECD) states the following:[2]

> The main objectives of most governments in their agricultural policies continue to be to support farm incomes, adjust production to outlets and ensure supplies at reasonable prices to consumers. ... The aim of improving farm income levels is set out in legislation, or in official statements of policy, in the majority of countries. The income level aimed at is defined in various ways, often by reference to incomes in other sectors. Thus the aim may be to ensure for those engaged in agriculture a 'fair' or 'proper' remuneration (as in the Netherlands, the United Kingdom and the Treaty of Rome), to enable them to participate in the general improvement of incomes or living standards (Austria, Germany, Sweden), to reduce the income gap between agriculture and other sectors (Italy), or to ensure farm incomes comparable with those in other occupations (Finland, France, Iceland, Japan, Luxembourg, Norway, Switzerland).[3]

This statement of objectives is as relevant for the 1980s as when written two decades earlier.

The general acceptance of an income objective for farm policies has much in it to commend. The income objectives described in the above quotation are, in general, consistent with the broad national objectives of most democratic nations. We do want equal opportunities for all our citizens; opportunities to earn should not be dictated by birth, whether this is reflected in race, religion or being born on a farm or in a city. Each individual should have the opportunity to use his native talents to the fullest extent. And in an imperfect way, this is what the income objectives of farm policies are all about.

An income objective, if defined appropriately, is not only consistent with the broad objective of equal opportunity, but is also consistent with an efficient use of resources. One of the criteria for efficient use of resources is that comparable resources should earn equivalent return in alternative uses.

There are a number of serious problems involved, however, in the various efforts to achieve approximate equality between the returns to farm and non-farm people. Some of the problems are due to difficulties of measurement – how do you accurately measure returns to resources in agriculture and what would these resources earn if engaged elsewhere in the economy? A related problem is that the return to farmland is directly affected by the level of farm prices or the magnitude of subsidies. Consequently, if the rate at which future returns to farmland are discounted differs from the rate at which the returns from other assets are discounted, it may not be possible to determine when equality of return has been achieved. But these are problems that could probably be resolved if enough thought and effort were given to the measurement problems; unfortunately I know of no government that has made a reasonable attempt to resolve these issues despite the costly nature of the programmes seeking to achieve income objectives.

But there are other issues that are far more important. Having a reasonable and appropriate objective is far from assuring the proper policy. If the methods used are not appropriate, a highly meritorious objective will not prevent wasted resources. The types of farm policies now prevalent in the industrial countries are wasteful primarily because an effort is made to attack the problem of low farm incomes through higher prices or subsidies that are related to output or size of farm. Such policies induce unwanted production. They also result in widening income differentials within agriculture, or would if market forces did not operate to offset some or most of the distribution effects.

The incomes of farm people can be low for two reasons: (i) they own fewer resources per family than the rest of the population; and/or (ii) ney receive lower returns for each of the resources that they own. High farm prices or subsidies will do little to correct the first deficiency, except as they make larger investment in non-human capital possible. If the adult farm population has less education than the rest of the population, as is true almost everywhere, higher farm prices are not going to correct this disability. And as I will argue in greater detail later, attempting to achieve higher incomes by higher prices assumes that incomes are primarily determined by demand. But, at least in the case of agriculture, this is certainly a fallacious idea. The price or return to farm resources is a function of both supply and demand conditions. And given the large and continuing flow of labour out of agriculture in industrial countries, the conditions of supply become exceedingly important in determining the return to farm labour. It is only land for which it can be said that its return is largely determined by demand, given that for the short and intermediate runs the supply of land changes very little. But few would argue that consumers and taxpayers should be taxed as heavily as they are in industrial countries for the primary benefit of landowners.

There is a final reason why income objectives must be used with great caution in the establishment of farm programmes. Agriculture is a declining industry when economic growth occurs. This is inevitable and desirable. The percentage of a country's labour force engaged in agriculture declines and eventually the absolute size of the farm labour force falls, as it has in Western Europe in recent decades. Unless workers are to be denied the right of free choice with respect to their jobs, it follows that the current return to farm workers will be less than what comparable labour earns in other jobs. This will be true even if full and accurate adjustment is made for differences in the cost of living and the non-pecuniary benefits that farm people may derive from variety of work, clean air, being their own boss or not having to commute. Some positive differential in earnings must remain to induce individuals to leave jobs in agriculture and to take other positions. Thus complete equality in current returns to resources is impossible to achieve unless we are willing to forgo the gains from the transfer of labour from declining to expanding sectors of the economy and are willing to pay the enormous costs that such a programme would incur.

The objective of equal returns for comparable resources is a much more subtle and complicated objective than is recognized in the farm policies of the industrial nations. It is a meaningful and appropriate objective, but only if its subtleties are recognized and the means used are effective in achieving it.

Forms of Intervention Directly
Affecting Prices

Governments can influence prices received by farmers in four ways: (i) by price supports enforced by purchases, either directly or through an intermediary, or by loans to sellers; (ii) by limiting output; (iii) by payment of a subsidy to equal the difference between a market price and some specified price; and (iv) by controlling or influencing imports and exports. There are other ways of influencing farm incomes, or attempting to, and these will be considered later.

Several of these techniques, if not all, may be used simultaneously. In the United States the Agricultural Adjustment Act of 1933 authorized the use of all of the techniques; subsequent changes largely added refinements. For example, the original Act permitted the discretionary use of import taxes to prevent imports from interfering with price supports; Section 22, an amendment that is known throughout trade circles all over the world, provided for import quotas as a more certain device. The 1933 Act also provided authorization and funds for export subsidies (dumping); two years later Section 32 was added and it spelled out in greater detail the authority for export subsidies and provided that 30 per cent of all receipts from customs duties could be used for encouragement of exports and domestic surplus disposal.[4]

The details of the procedures for enforcing price supports are of little relevance to our task. The introduction, however, of the non-recourse loan (discussed below) in the 1933 Act merits notice because of its ingenuity and novelty. I do not know if the non-recourse loan was the product of some populist or a Wall Street lawyer, but wherever it came from it merits a low bow. Partly because it was quite uncertain where a specific lot of grain or cotton would be finally marketed and partly because there had long been substantial storage of farm products on the farms where production occurred, a direct purchase programme at specified prices would have involved a tremendous problem of storage and numerous mistakes in the location of that storage as well as the creation of a large bureaucracy. It was also generally agreed in early 1933 that action had to be taken by the autumn of that year in order to prevent further economic distress. A measure for supporting prices that could be put promptly into effect was needed. In addition, the Federal Farm Board, which had functioned between 1929 and 1933, had operated by making loans to cooperatives.

The populist background of the non-recourse loan is implied by the terms of the loan. The non-recourse feature meant that a farmer who obtained one of the loans had a choice of two alternatives: to deliver the farm product (the security for the loan) in lieu of payment or to pay off the loan in cash with accumulated interest and storage costs, if any. The loans were made on sealed corn stored on farms – the term 'sealed' was used because corn pledged as security was put in a special bin and a seal was placed on the bin to indicate that the grain had not been tampered with or removed. If a farmer later decided to feed the grain that he used as collateral, he simply paid off the loan and used the grain. This technique eliminated the need for transporting the grain to a central location and then returning it. If the market price rose above the loan rate, obviously it was in the interest of the farmer to pay off the loan and sell the grain. But if at the date the loan was to be repaid the market price was below the loan value, the farmer would deliver the grain to the Commodity Credit Corporation and the loan would be cancelled. The loan programme was applied to products other than grain, such as cotton, flaxseed and peanuts; in the case of cotton the product was generally not stored on farms but in public warehouses.

For a country the size of the United States with its varying conditions, the loan programme functioned very well. It did not place an absolute floor under prices but permitted some variation seasonally as well as regionally. The government was not forced to make an enormous number of purchases if the market price dropped slightly below the loan level; and since farmers generally had the alternative of obtaining a non-recourse loan or of selling in the market, this left the onus of the functioning of the system partly on the actions of the farmers. In addition, a price-support loan was one of the benefits that was held out to farmers for participating in some of the acreage-limitation programmes; if too few farmers participated, the market price might fall significantly below the loan value. And if participation were great enough, or so the theory went, market prices would be at or above the loan value.

While a number of countries have used limitations on acreage or output for individual products as a means of maintaining or increasing prices, the United States was probably the first to attempt output control for a major part of its crop output. By 1932 it was generally agreed that the government was largely powerless to influence the level of farm prices unless it could influence the output of farm products. A government faced with more or less stable output and declining demand could do little more than delay the inevitable – accumulated stocks must generally be disposed of.

Because of the year-to-year variability in crop yields, efforts to limit crop output have generally emphasized control of the area planted or seeded to the crop and the area harvested. In other words, output is to be influenced by control of one input – land. While there are many reasons to doubt the effectiveness of this approach, it is the approach that has been followed by the United States since 1933. While there has been considerable variation in the features of particular programmes from year to year, efforts to limit acreage have been applied to wheat, cotton, feed grains, peanuts, rice, sugar and tobacco. In recent years, Canada and Australia have adopted similar programmes to reduce the area devoted to wheat production.

The purpose of production controls is to increase prices; and it is generally assumed that since the price elasticity of demand for crop products is low, then relatively small reductions in output would result in much larger price increases. The United States, however, was in the unfortunate position of being a significant exporter of its major crop products – wheat, cotton and tobacco. As it turned out, the price elasticity of export demand for American production was not nearly as low as the price elasticity for domestic use. Because the United States restricted its output of a product while other countries were increasing theirs, the gain to farmers was small. One consequence of such efforts was the loss of export markets, both because the United States' price was higher than the prices offered by other sellers and because other countries increased their output because of the actual or anticipated effectiveness of the American efforts at limiting output. Thus it is almost inevitable that a country that attempts to limit the output of a crop or product that it normally exports, and uses price supports as the primary means for transferring benefits to farmers, will sooner or later resort to export subsidies. As noted earlier, provision for export subsidies was included in the same act that established acreage limitation programmes.

The United States used direct payments to make up the difference between a price objective and market prices during the latter part of the 1930s for cotton, wheat, corn and rice. Since the 1960s, the United Kingdom was the only other country that used such deficiency payments as the major component of its price-support programme for a large part of its farm output. Deficiency payments, equal to the difference between guaranteed prices and actual market prices, were authorized in the Agricultural Act of 1947. Since, for the products included in the price guarantee scheme, Britain had few barriers to

imports, the market prices that prevailed were generally those resulting
from the availability of imported supplies at approximately world
market prices. Not all British farm products were included in the
scheme – horticultural products were fairly heavily protected by import
duties and sugar imports were controlled. But, on balance, the deficiency-payments scheme made it possible for the British Government
to maintain the world's most open market for food products and still
achieve guaranteed prices for its farmers.

As the combination of heavily subsidized exports by some suppliers,
actual or potential, resulted in rising costs of maintaining the guaranteed price scheme, the United Kingdom resorted to import controls for
butter, voluntary agreements on cheese imports and minimum import
prices for cereals. From 1 July 1971, Britain began a full-scale transition to a variable import-levy system, in anticipation of membership in
the European Community. The deficiency-payments scheme was
phased out as the CAP was applied to British agriculture, starting in
1973. Thus this large-scale experiment that, despite its defects, represented one of the most, if not the most, rational approach to guaranteed prices for farmers in any of the industrial countries came to an end.

The variety of price supports and methods of realizing them in the
mid-1950s was indicated by the following summary of the Organisation
for European Economic Cooperation.[5]

> *Fixed prices* were implemented either through administrative price
> control under which, for example, the ex-farm price of milk was
> announced and no sales could take place above or below that price
> (Austria) or through purchase at a fixed price and subsequent
> resale by a government agency as was commonly the case for
> breadgrains (Austria, Greece, Norway, Portugal, Spain, Switzer-
> land and Turkey). In the former case, sale of the supported
> commodity at later distributive stages might take place either at
> prices corresponding to the fixed ex-farm price or at lower prices.
> Subsequent sales took place at lower prices if output subsidies
> (sometimes regarded as 'consumer' subsidies) were injected into
> the pricing arrangements. If subsequent sales took place at prices
> corresponding to the fixed producer price, then producers received
> a national subsidy from consumers.
>
> *Target prices* were pursued (and if possible implemented)
> through the intervention in the market either of a government
> agency (Belgium) or of an organization representing producers,
> distributors and consumers, operating on behalf of the state (meat

in Switzerland), which endeavoured to cover its costs by storing the commodities it had purchased until it could sell them when prices were higher. Usually, however, such stock operators resulted in a net loss to the stabilization agency. Sometimes such trading or stockholding activities were partly or wholly replaced by storage subsidies paid directly to producers (Austria).

Minimum prices were generally implemented through a governmental or producers' price supporting agency that either took the produce off the market when market prices fell to the prescribed level (Netherlands) or accepted offers by producers to sell it at the prescribed minimum price (Canada) or extended 'non-recourse' loans to producers (USA).

Guaranteed average prices were implemented through output subsidies in the form of deficiency payments. The guarantee was either to producers themselves (Canada, Netherlands, United Kingdom) or to a marketing board representing them (United Kingdom).

Since the above was written, changes have occurred in price-support measures involving the European Community and the United States. The important change in the United States involved lowering price supports to levels that would permit the major export products to move directly into international markets and making up the loss of income by various payments associated with the efforts to limit acreage. As will be noted later, the role of export subsidies was reduced, in fact eliminated from 1973 to 1981, but they were reintroduced in 1982.

So much has been said and written about the European Community's common agricultural policy that only its broadest outlines need to be described. The major elements of the CAP are free trade in farm products within the Community, common prices (with variations by regions to reflect usual price differentials due to location) in the form of threshold, target and intervention prices, variable import levies reflecting the differences between threshold and import prices and the establishment of the European Agricultural Guidance and Guarantee Fund (Fonds Européen d'Orientation et de Garantie Agricole [FEOGA]) drawing resources from the import levies and national treasuries. There is no consistent relationship between the target prices and the intervention prices. For the grains, except rice, the intervention or support price was 70 to 80 per cent of the target price in the late 1980s, while for rice it was less than 60 per cent of the target price. In the first years of the CAP (late 1960s) the intervention prices for grains other than rice were about 93 per cent of the target price. There are target prices for milk, but no support price; for butter, cheese and non-fat dry milk there are no target prices, but there are intervention prices.

Threshold prices exist, of course, for all products covered by variable import levies – grains, eggs, poultry, beef, pork and milk products. The threshold prices are required for the calculation of the variable import levies even though there may be no target or intervention prices. The variable levies represent the difference between the threshold price and the import price and thus fluctuate with the import price. The variable levies, however, have not completely replaced import duties on imports from 'outside' countries. Customs duties are still charged for beef, veal and pork and will probably continue to be charged regardless of world prices. The variable import levies may be suspended if the domestic prices go above an established level. The Common Market prices for livestock products must take into account the substantial competitive disadvantage resulting from high internal grain prices. The CAP for pork specifically recognizes the additional costs of the high feed prices.

As protective as the CAP appears to agricultural interests of such countries as the United States, Canada, Australia and Denmark, it should be noted that the variable import levies replaced a whole host of other trade restrictions, including many quantitative restrictions. Import quotas and licences, state trading and mixing regulations were used in many cases prior to the adoption of the CAP and are still used for products not covered by the CAP. Was the CAP more restrictive of trade than the measures that it replaced? The available evidence indicates that the degree of protection increased with the CAP. One study obtained an estimate of the average level of nominal protection in 1956 for the Original Six of 16 per cent; a second study using comparable methods of estimation found an average level of 52 per cent for 1965–67.[6] A study by the Australian and Japanese economists, Kym Anderson and Yujiro Hayami, determined a level of nominal protection in 1955 of 30.7 per cent, increasing to 40.3 per cent in 1965 and 47.1 per cent in 1970. While the extent of the increase in protection may be in dispute, there seems little doubt that the CAP resulted in more rather than less protection.

The description of price-support measures has been quite general and has ignored a number of details and actual departures from original intentions. While there has been a significant degree of continuity in price-support policies in the United States, the farm legislation enacted in 1977 gave much less emphasis to price stability than had previously been the case.[7] From 1960 through 1971 the price-support programmes for grains had resulted in a remarkable degree of price stability. Prices were supported primarily through the acquisition of stocks by the Commodity Credit Corporation. Since the Commodity Credit Corporation released or sold grain from its stock at prices of only 10 to 15 per cent above the current price-support level, prices of the grains moved within very narrow limits until the stocks were largely disposed of in 1972.

Farmers had long argued that the price-support system set maximum as well as minimum prices. The 1977 legislation established a farmer-held reserve for the grains designed so that most of the stocks required to hold market prices at or above the support levels would be held by farmers. If the Commodity Credit Corporation acquired any grain, it could not sell it at less than 150 per cent of the support level. The government paid storage costs and loans were provided for holding the grain at low or nil interest rates. Consequently the storing of grain under this programme was heavily subsidized.

If the farmer withdrew grain from the reserve at less than the release price specified in the legislation or by the Secretary of Agriculture (125 per cent of the loan rate for corn and 140–150 per cent for wheat), he had to repay the storage payments that he had received and could be required to pay for any foregone interest. The 1981 and 1985 agricultural acts continued the farmer-held reserve programme. With the introduction of payment-in-kind (PIK) in 1983, however, the farmer-held reserve programme has been significantly de-emphasized. Under the PIK programmes farmers who participate in the supply-management programme and are eligible to receive deficiency payments and participate in the price support programmes receive a significant part (approximately half) of their deficiency payments in kind, either through the release to the farmer of any commodities that he has used as security for a price-support loan or by receipt of a certificate that can be exchanged for a given amount of grain or cotton. During the Reagan Administration an important objective was to reduce the stocks of farm commodities in order to eliminate the price-depressing effects of those stocks.

The earlier description of the operation of the CAP was in terms of how it was expected to function, with uniform prices (except for transport costs) and free trade in farm products within the European Community. The CAP operated with common intervention or guaranteed prices for only two years, from approximately mid-1967 through mid-1969.[8] The maintenance of uniform prices rested on one of two assumptions, either that exchange rates within the Community would remain unchanged or that when exchange rates changed relative to the Community's unit of account (UA), intervention prices in domestic currencies would reflect the new exchange rate.

Neither of these assumptions proved to be valid. In 1969 the French franc was devalued and soon thereafter the German Deutschmark was revalued. With the devaluation of the franc by about 11 per cent, the maintenance of common prices would have required that the French intervention prices for farm products be increased by the amount of the devaluation. Later the Deutschmark was revalued by 9 per cent and farm prices in Deutschmarks should have been reduced by an equivalent amount. The French did not want to increase their consumer prices for food and the Germans did not want to lower farm prices. The two problems were solved by the simple expedient of introducing a new exchange rate, the green exchange rate, which was applied to transactions involving most agricultural commodities. The green exchange rate was the market rate of exchange prior to the devaluation of the franc and the revaluation of the Deutschmark. As is true of so many agricultural policy measures, at the time of writing two decades after the introduction of the green rates, they still differ from the actual exchange rates in spite of numerous efforts to eliminate the differences.

The disparity in farm prices across countries due to the differences between the green and actual exchange rates required control over exports and imports of farm products within the European Community. Thus, contrary to the rhetoric, there has hardly ever been free trade in farm products under the CAP. The disparity required the introduction of border taxes or subsidies, called monetary compensation amounts (MCAs), within the Community. Imports into a country whose currency was appreciating relative to the average for the Community, such as Germany, were subject to a tax while exports from Germany to other countries within the Community required a subsidy. In a country whose currency had depreciated relative to the average, such as the United Kingdom, imports had to be subsidized and exports taxed. The disparities in internal prices increased substantially with the currency disturbances in 1973.

The magnitudes of the MCAs reached very high levels by the end of 1976. On that date the MCA for the United Kingdom was −40.6, for France it was −41.9 and for Germany 9.3. For the year as a whole, the discrepancies among the MCAs were significantly lower. Yet for 1976 producer prices in Germany for soft wheat averaged 40 per cent higher than in the United Kingdom and 30 per cent higher than in France. Over time, the disparities in the MCAs have been reduced, but at the end of 1988 the MCAs still existed.

Trade Policies

Foreign trade, particularly as regards imports, is in most cases of a residual character and is the corollary, if not the consequence of the production price and income objectives of the country.[9]

How long will it be possible to consider the international market for *any* unwanted production, with the consequential increasing discrepancy between domestic and international prices?[10]

If the objective of price supports is more than a modest degree of price stability, it is impossible to have price supports without interference with international trade, either with exports or imports or both. This is true of even the least distortive of the methods of achieving price guarantees, namely deficiency payments. The guaranteed prices, if they require deficiency payments to be made, encourage the expansion of local production and either reduce imports or expand exports as a consequence. Thus free trade plus deficiency payments to meet guaranteed prices in a given country has the effect of reducing export opportunities in farm products for all other countries. The difference between such a system and one dependent on achieving the guaranteed prices through market prices, and for some though not all products it is an important difference, is that the deficiency-payments system does not restrict consumption, while the higher market prices (wholesale and retail) do.

For a given level of guaranteed prices the relative advantage of deficiency payments in maintaining trade is a function of the price elasticity of supply of domestic production and the price elasticity of domestic demand for the products involved; it is also a function of the degree of self-sufficiency. But if the elasticity of supply is larger than the elasticity of demand, the reduction in imports with the deficiency-payments scheme could be more than half as large as would the reduction with guaranteed market prices. Obviously this is an important difference, but not so important that the trade-distorting effects of deficiency payments should be ignored.

If a country has been an exporter of a product and wishes to increase the market prices received by its producers, it must either face the loss of export markets or offer export subsidies to make up the difference between the internal and external prices. And it may well find that it must also impose import quotas to protect the export subsidy! This was true in the past in the United States for cotton and wheat, although it was obvious that, without the price-support programmes as they operated before 1965, there would have been no imports, because the United States would have continued to export both products.

Life is a little simpler for a government with a price-support programme for an import commodity, unless such support eventually leads to an export surplus through reducing consumption and expanding production. It needs to engage in only one type of trade-disruptive activity – namely limiting imports either by higher tariffs, import quotas, licensing or variable levies. When the European Community was formed, it was a net importer of most agricultural products and variable levies were a technique for supporting domestic prices that appeared to be both effective and with no government cost.

Put simply, international trade is a dangerous nuisance to domestic price-support programmes. Either surpluses must be disposed of or imports must be kept out. In either case your competitors or suppliers have grounds for complaint and recrimination and, occasionally, for retaliation. But retaliation, as in the 'chicken war' of the early 1960s (when the United States imposed a duty on cognac because the European Community foreclosed on imports of American canned chicken), is seldom good for anything except the soul.

As a later chapter will indicate, the amount of protection provided has reached very high levels in many cases. Nominal protection rates of 100 per cent or more are not uncommon. In terms of effects on the volume of trade over a period of time, it is the average degree of protection that is important, whether that protection is achieved by variable import levies, variable export subsidies or import quotas. Widely fluctuating rates of protection, however, such as the European Community's variable import-levy system in 1972 through 1975, had an important impact on the stability of prices in international markets. Variable levels of protection have significant short-run effects on the stability of prices and these effects have been assiduously ignored by the Community and other governments, such as Japan.

The domestic programmes of the industrial countries have had a major impact on the amount and distribution of foreign trade in farm products. These effects have derived directly from the domestic programmes; and while many of the industrial governments appear to show little concern for the effects of their actions on others, it is not correct to assume that these trade effects are the result of deliberate intent. This does not make them any less damaging nor unfortunately does it make it any easier to remove them.

Other Policies and Programmes

The governments of the industrial countries have a host of special agricultural programmes not directly related to price supports or the control of international trade. Most, if not all, industrial countries have special credit institutions to serve agriculture. Governments conduct or support research and provide farmers with free advisory or extension services. Input subsidies are numerous as are subsidies for investment in buildings and machinery. The improvement of farm structures has been a commonplace slogan in Western Europe. Adding and consolidating land to create more efficient farms is one of the major objectives of the European Community and other countries as well. Most governments subsidize land reclamation and improvement schemes ranging from irrigation to drainage and from land levelling to contouring.

Whatever such measures as those described above may contribute to higher farm incomes, it is clear that they result in increased output. Each acts to hold or induce more resources in agriculture. Thus such measures act to reinforce the undesirable consequences of high price supports and subsidies related directly to output. It is true that such measures make it possible for the farmers of a given country to compete more effectively with producers in a low-cost country, but it is extremely doubtful if there has been any case where such subsidized efforts have resulted in lowering costs to a level consistent with world market prices. In other words, if the alternative of obtaining farm products at world market prices were considered, few if any of the measures would have a benefit–cost ratio approximating one.

The farm programmes of the industrial nations have a clear bias in favour of measures dealing with things – land, grain, livestock, buildings, tractors, fertilizer – or prices. Until recently, policy measures that directly deal with the circumstances of farm people – their education, their capacity to shift from farm to non-farm jobs, the social and health services available to them – have been noticeable by their absence. I have no doubt that the most important single cause of the disparity between farm and non-farm incomes in the industrial countries has been the failure to provide farm people with the same educational opportunities as are available to urban people. Yet in all of the industrial countries, until recently, the educational opportunities available to farm people were distinctly inferior to those available elsewhere in the society. It should not have been too surprising that, in addition to the disability of poor-quality education, farm people have had many fewer years of schooling than their urban counterparts.[11]

Governments have seldom done anything to assist farm people to migrate to non-farm communities or specifically train farm adults for non-farm occupations. Only recently has there been some progress in these directions. Modest efforts at training farm people for non-farm jobs have been undertaken in France, the Netherlands, Norway, Sweden, West Germany and the United States. In some cases, part of the actual cost of relocation is subsidized. But such efforts are generally pitifully limited when compared with the magnitude of the adjustments that farm people must make through migration and occupational change. Despite the recent attention to such problems, the level of expenditure is only a small fraction of that spent on price supports.

The gradual extension of social-security measures to the farm population in most industrial countries has contributed significantly to the well-being of older farm people. In some countries – Belgium, France, the Netherlands and West Germany – special programmes exist for payments to induce farmers to retire early. As applied, these measures probably contribute little to the solution of the problem of excess resources in agriculture, for the land and other non-labour resources become available to other farmers. Fortunately, the measures contribute to the alleviation of poverty among older farm people who have not found it possible to adjust to rapidly changing agricultural conditions.

Trade Conflicts not Resolved

During the 1980s the continuing and growing discord between agricultural policy-makers in the European Community and the United States weakened the support for trade liberalization. As will be clear later, there was no willingness on either side of the Atlantic to give serious consideration to reasonable and appropriate modifications of agricultural policies that would facilitate the growth of international trade and the realization of some of the benefits of comparative advantage. Tensions grew with the failure of the GATT ministerial meeting in late 1982 and with the payment of a huge export subsidy by the United

States to obtain a sale of flour to Egypt. The United States claimed, of course, that its export subsidy was nothing more than an effort to offset the export subsidies paid by the European Community. The latter, in turn, denied that it had used export restitutions to increase its share of the world's exports of flour and wheat. Similarly, actions and reactions continued for the next several years, with export subsidies equalling or exceeding the farm prices for wheat in both the Community and the United States on occasion.

The export subsidy war between the United States and the European Community reached the silly stage by 1987 and 1988. A major beneficiary of this conflict was the Soviet Union. During 1987 the Soviet Union obtained wheat from both the Community and the United States for approximately $80 per ton. In the United States the deficiency payment plus the direct export subsidy amounted to $117 per ton; the farm price of wheat was approximately $88 per ton. In the Community in early 1987 the export rebate for wheat sold to the Soviet Union was $150 per ton when the intervention price was approximately $192. Either figure is indicative of the lengths to which the excess productive capacity of the Community and the United States, created by unrealistically high price-incentives, has driven policy-makers to go.

During 1982 to 1985 the United States farm price supports for grains, even with the limited use of export subsidies, were effective in increasing world market prices of grains and cotton. In spite of significant efforts to reduce grain production, stocks of grain increased to high levels and the United States lost its share of the world export market for grains and cotton. The 1985 farm legislation permitted the Secretary of Agriculture to lower the price supports by 20 per cent without a change in target prices. Thus the potential deficiency payment increased from $40 per ton in 1985/86 to $73 per ton in 1986/87 for wheat. The potential deficiency payment for maize increased from $19 to $44 per ton. Market prices immediately responded and fell by the amount of the decline in the price supports for wheat and the feed grains.

The market and export prices declined even more for both cotton and rice, farm products that are produced primarily by developing countries. The United States and the Soviet Union are the only industrial countries that are significant producers of cotton. The greater declines in cotton and rice prices resulted from the introduction of marketing loans for cotton and rice. The idea of the marketing loan can perhaps be best visualized through the use of rice as an example. The reduced price support for rice was $158 per ton. A farmer could obtain a price support for his rice in that amount. He was permitted, though, to repay the loan at an amount that the Secretary of Agriculture determined was the world market price. For a period of time in 1986/87 the rice producer could repay his price support loan for $79 or almost exactly half of the amount he had borrowed. Overall, the subsidy to the rice producer was the difference between the target price of $262 per ton and the marketing loan of $79 per ton or $183 per ton. To receive the payment, the producer was required to reduce rice acreage by 35 per cent of his base area. By late 1987 the world price of rice had approximately doubled from its low point following the United States introduction of the marketing loan, but this price improvement was primarily due to a poor crop in Thailand, a country whose farmers had been very adversely affected by the change in United States rice price policy.

Unfortunately export subsidies were but one source of tension and conflict that affected the efforts to liberalize agricultural trade. The continued use of import quotas on dairy products to achieve milk prices in the United States that exceeded those in the European Community in the early 1980s, plus substantial deficiency payments on major crop products, were viewed by Europeans as evidence of lack of sincerity by American policy-makers. In turn, United States policy-makers saw Community efforts to tax soyabeans or soyabean products and corn gluten meal as clear violations of trade concessions that were given some two decades earlier. Domestic politics prevented any consideration by the United States of the fact that the free entry of soyabeans and nearly free entry of numerous non-grain feeding materials occurred at the expense of Community imports of feed grains and resulted in larger Community exports of grain with the aid of export restitutions.

The late 1970s and the 1980s saw at least an interruption in the trend towards general trade liberalization that had persisted for almost four decades. If the trend interruption becomes a long-run trend, it will be so to some considerable degree, for no progress is being made to reduce the barriers to trade in agricultural products. World agriculture is in disarray. It is not improbable that, unless serious efforts are made to moderate the sources of disarray, the extent of the disarray will increase to a significant degree. And it will not be only trade in agricultural products that will suffer. The isolationism that has surrounded so much of agricultural policy-making was extended to many industrial products during the first years of the 1980s. While it can be hoped that a world economic recovery will stem the tide of protectionism for industrial products, it will take much more than economic recovery to prevent further disorientation in world trade in farm products.

Some General Comments

Except for measures described in the previous sections, the farm measures of the industrial countries are designed to increase farm incomes by affecting demand for the resources owned by farm people. This is accomplished by higher output prices or by subsidizing certain inputs. The only significant exception to this statement has been the efforts to limit output by controlling the area devoted to various crops in the United States and, on occasion, in Canada and Australia; and in the mid-1980s, the European Community applied quotas to limit milk output. But it is still basically correct to say that the programmes have been demand-oriented. Little has been done to affect the conditions under which farm people supply their services – primarily their own labour – to agriculture and little has been done to influence favourably and positively the quality and thus the basic earning power of these services. As noted earlier, farm incomes are lower than non-farm incomes for two reasons: the ownership of fewer resources and lower prices for those resources. Farm policies have done little to increase the amount of labour services possessed by the average farm resident. They attempt to influence the returns to farm resources by operating only on demand, largely neglecting the conditions of supply of resources to agriculture. Thus it is perhaps not surprising that so much has been expended to accomplish so little.

3 Present State of Disarray

In the first chapter several indications of the disarray in world agriculture were briefly noted – the large costs of the recent farm policies of the industrial countries, the enormous differences in prices received by farmers in the industrial countries, the more rapid growth of output than of consumption and the consequent disruptive effects on trade in farm products. More fundamentally, the disarray is evidenced by the ineffectiveness of the farm and trade policies to accomplish their avowed purposes, namely that of significantly improving the income position of farm families. Instead, as will be argued at length later, these policies are primarily responsible for too many resources being engaged in agriculture, encouraging too large a farm output and impeding changes that are inevitable and cannot be significantly mitigated by the policies being followed. In most cases, the policies being followed are an exercise in futility, albeit a very expensive exercise. And as noted earlier, the stubbornness of policy-makers in the industrial countries with respect to agricultural trade policies may well destroy some significant part of the gains in trade liberalization that have been achieved over the past three decades.

Costs of Farm Policies in Industrial Countries

In a sophisticated analysis of the costs of farm programmes, one would attempt to distribute the total costs between (i) the part that represented a transfer of income from consumers and taxpayers to farmers, (ii) the part that represented the increase in real resources used as a result of the programmes and (iii) the part that represented the loss in consumer welfare due to consumption alternatives that they must forgo because the prices they face do not represent the real cost alternatives.

Such an analysis is not presented at this point, but will be later.[1] For the purpose of demonstrating the state of disarray in the agricultural and trade arrangements of the industrial countries it is sufficient to consider only the obvious and directly measurable costs of the programmes, namely those costs borne by taxpayers and consumers. As will be shown later, most of the costs of the policies consist of income transfers to agriculture from consumers and taxpayers. These costs are larger than the costs due to excess resources being kept in agriculture or the loss of consumer welfare due to the high prices of farm products in most industrial countries. Economists usually emphasize only the wastage of resources or the loss in consumer welfare due to price distortions and give less emphasis to income transfers since such transfers represent primarily a redistribution of income within an economy.

Why, then, do I emphasize costs that are largely income transfers? If consumers and taxpayers, in their roles as citizens, are to have a basis for deciding if the income transfers to agriculture are desirable, they require information concerning the cost of the transfers. The cost of the transfers is certainly one of the bases for deciding if the social or other objectives of the transfers are sufficiently worthy to justify them. If the transfers go in significant amounts to persons with higher incomes than the incomes of those who pay the cost of the transfers, it may be decided that such transfers are inconsistent with other objectives the country is attempting to achieve. Or if the transfers fail to achieve the stated objective of improving the relative income position of farm families, it is reasonable to emphasize the cost of making the transfers. A purist might argue that if the transfers are ineffective, the transfers should be abandoned, regardless of their cost. But the ineffectiveness cannot be proven beyond the proverbial shadow of a doubt and knowledge about the magnitude of the costs may have a significant influence on public decisions.

It must be said that until the early 1980s there was remarkably little knowledge about the cost of the domestic farm policies of the industrial countries. Policy-makers, either in the legislatures or in the ministries of agriculture, showed a remarkable lack of interest in obtaining reliable measures of costs. Alas, most agricultural economists failed to pursue the topic with any degree of vigour. When policy-makers did show some interest in costs, it was generally only the costs to their treasury; consumer costs were largely ignored. Fortunately, in the 1980s efforts have been made to obtain estimates of the costs of farm price and income policies to both consumers and taxpayers.

The first edition of this book presented estimates of the consumer and taxpayer cost of the CAP of the original Six and of the agricultural programmes of the United States. The estimate of the cost of the CAP for the late 1960s was $13 billion and farm policies in the United States a cost of $9.6 billion. Rough approximations of the excess consumer costs of food in Japan and other West European countries and governmental costs in Canada and Australia put the total of the consumer and taxpayer costs for the industrial market economies at somewhat more than $40 billion. If one added to this total the estimated budgetary costs of the meat, dairy and other food-price subsidies in the Soviet Union of $7 billion for 1968, the total was approximately $47 billion.[2] In 1985 American dollars this would be approximately $145 billion. What has happened to the consumer and taxpayer costs since 1973? No attempt has been made to duplicate the detailed estimates presented in the first edition for the European Community and the United States. While there were only a few estimates of such costs for the earlier period, numerous estimates of such costs are now available for the late 1970s and the 1980s.

The state of the disarray can be revealed from recent studies by Rodney Tyers and Kym Anderson, at the University of Adelaide, of the effects of trade liberalization on domestic and international market prices and on producer incomes, consumer expenditures on foods and economic welfare. One of the set of estimates was for 1980–82 when levels of protection in the industrial market economies were at relatively low levels compared with the late 1970s and in the years that followed, especially in 1986–88. Another set was for 1988 protection levels with projections for 1995.[3]

The estimates presented in the first edition could be criticized because the costs were based on the actual prevailing international market prices. These prices were not the equilibrium prices that would prevail if there were free trade in agricultural products. Thus, it was argued, such estimates exaggerate the true costs of the farm programmes. For most farm products, this criticism was primarily a debating point, for the international market prices in the late 1960s were only moderately lower than they might have been under free trade. As is shown in Chapter 7, prices for dairy and beef products were significantly depressed, but for the grains, oilseeds, cotton and meat other than beef the error caused by basing the cost estimates on international market prices was relatively small.

In several of the recent studies referred to above, including the one that will be summarized, the basis for comparisons between domestic and world prices are not actual world market prices but the estimates of prices that would prevail if there were trade liberalization, either for all market economies or some large sub-set of such countries.

The costs of recent and current farm price and income programmes in the OECD countries have been estimated by Dr Tyers and Dr Anderson. Their estimates are based on a large model that simulates the effects of trade liberalization on international market prices,

exports and imports and domestic market prices. From this information it is possible to estimate the effects of current farm price and
income policies and the associated trade interventions on producer
incomes, consumer food costs and welfare losses for the economy. The
model has been revised and extended a number of times. The results
reported here are based on analyses done for the World Bank in
preparation for the *World Development Report 1986*. Seven commodity
groups were included – wheat, rice, coarse grains, ruminant meat, non-
ruminant meat, sugar and dairy products.

It is important to note in interpreting the results from such exercises
that the estimated effects depend to a significant degree on the base
period. Trade liberalization is assumed to occur relative to the actual
levels of protection prevailing in a given period of time. The degree of
protection, as measured by the difference between domestic prices plus
any deficiency payments and world market prices, has varied markedly
from year to year over the past two decades or so. Rates of protection
in the European Community and the United States declined from the
late 1960s and early 1970s to the mid-1970s, then returned to the earlier
levels by the late 1970s and then declined again in the early 1980s. The
decline was especially significant in the Community during 1980–85 due
to the increases in international market prices during those years. The
increases occurred due to a variety of factors, including the increase in
the foreign-exchange value of the American dollar and certain supply
factors that were important in 1980 and 1983. Since the Tyers–
Anderson results that will be summarized here are based on protection
rates for 1980–82 and 1988, Table 3.1 shows the nominal rates of
protection for seven commodity groups for the European Community,
the European Free Trade Association (EFTA), Japan and the United
States. It is not surprising that estimates of the effects of trade
liberalization starting from these two periods give significantly different
results.

The increases in nominal rates of protection, as measured by the
ratio of producer to border prices, during 1980–82, and the projected
1988 levels, are substantial for each of the industrial market areas or
countries. The studies based on 1980–82 protection rates reveal modest
effects of trade liberalization for sugar. The reason is fairly obvious.
Due to the relatively high international market prices of sugar during
these years, the producer prices in the European Community and the
United States were 50 and 40 per cent, respectively, in excess of
international market prices. In 1986 and 1987 the domestic sugar prices
were occasionally as much as five times the world price. The price

Table 3.1 Producer-to-border price ratios for various commodities and industrial market economies, estimated 1980–82 and projected 1988 and 1995[a]

	Wheat	*Coarse grain*	*Rice*	*Rumi-nant meat*	*Non-ru-minant meat*	*Dairy products*	*Sugar*	*Weighted average*
EC-12								
1980–82	1.40	1.40	1.35	1.95	1.25	1.75	1.50	1.55
1988	3.40	2.40	2.40	2.75	1.60	2.50	2.80	2.25
1995	2.60	1.75	2.20	2.50	1.35	2.50	3.00	2.05
EFTA-5								
1980–82	1.65	1.55	1.00	2.30	1.40	2.45	1.55	1.90
1988	3.90	2.85	1.00	4.25	1.90	3.90	3.20	3.15
1995	2.05	1.55	1.00	4.35	1.65	4.40	3.90	3.35
Japan								
1980–82	3.90	4.30	3.35	2.80	1.50	2.90	3.00	2.35
1988	8.00	11.65	8.20	5.40	1.90	5.55	7.10	3.80
1995	3.90	9.30	9.30	5.15	1.90	6.45	8.55	3.65
United States								
1980–82	1.15	1.00	1.30	1.10	1.00	2.00	1.40	1.20
1988	2.20	1.60	1.85	1.30	1.00	2.20	2.05	1.50
1995	1.30	1.00	1.60	1.30	1.00	2.30	1.95	1.25
All industrial market economies								
1980–82	1.25	1.15	2.50	1.50	1.20	1.90	1.50	1.40
1988	2.45	1.75	5.65	2.05	1.40	2.55	2.60	2.00
1995	1.75	1.20	6.15	1.95	1.30	2.70	2.80	1.80

[a] The projected ratios are taken from the reference projection.
Source: Rodney Tyers and Kym Anderson, 'Global Interactions and Trade Liberalisation in Agriculture', mimeograph, Department of Economics, University of Adelaide, April 1987, p. 60.

differences projected for 1988 for sugar were about the same as those actually prevailing in 1987, but significantly smaller than in 1985 when Community and United States producer prices of sugar were five times world market prices. The projected 1995 protection levels are relevant because they are used to estimate the effects of trade liberalization as of 1995. It was assumed that with some modest changes in price and income policies, and with some recovery in international prices resulting from the disposal of the large stocks that overhung markets in the mid-1980s, protection levels would decline from their high 1988 positions. Thus for all industrial market economies, the weighted average of domestic to border prices was estimated to be 1.4 for 1980–82, 2.0 for 1988 and 1.8 for 1995. The price projections are presented in Chapter 7. Our interest here in the projections is in terms of the consumer and taxpayer costs.

The domestic costs of the farm programmes in 1985 American dollars based on the 1980–82 protection rates are presented in Table 3.2

for the European Community, EFTA, Japan, the United States and Canada. The costs are the difference between actual expenditures by consumers and taxpayers and what the expenditures would have been if there had been trade liberalization in the industrial market economies. Even at the relatively low levels of protection in the Community, the United States and Canada in 1980–82, the consumer costs come to nearly $123 billion (1985 American dollars), according to the estimates in Table 3.3. Taxpayer costs were modest since expenditures were largely offset by either levies or, as in the case of Japan, selling low-priced imports into the high-price domestic market. If one adds in the price subsidies that were paid in the Soviet Union in 1980–82 of 37 billion roubles and assumes an exchange rate of 1:1 for the American dollar instead of the official rate of exchange of about $1.25 per rouble, the total in 1985 United States dollars was approximately $160 billion.

Similar estimates for the 1995 projection indicate that the costs to consumers and taxpayers in OECD countries would be $160 billion, an increase of 30 per cent. If current subsidies in the Soviet Union of 60 billion roubles are maintained, the total might be $220 billion, a significant increase compared with the late 1960s.

These results reflect the inefficiency of the price and income policies of the industrial countries in achieving one of their major objectives, namely increasing the income of farmers. The net domestic cost in column 4 of Table 3.2 is a measure for 1980–82 of the excess of consumer and taxpayer costs over the increase in net agricultural incomes. For the European Community, the consumer and taxpayer costs exceed the income transferred to farmers by $8.9 billion. This means that it cost consumers and taxpayers $1.19 for each dollar retained by farmers. The same relationship prevailed in North America. In Japan the cost of increasing farm income by $1 was $1.44. These costs do not include the adverse effects on other countries, but are the losses the countries suffered from not taking full advantage of their comparative-advantage situation. This is known as shooting yourself in the foot.

The 1995 estimates indicate that the cost of transferring $1 to farmers would increase significantly compared with the early 1980s – from approximately $1.20 to $1.40.

If one compares the total consumer and taxpayer costs for the industrial market economies and the Soviet Union of the farm price and income programmes for 1980–82 with the costs for the late 1960s, the difference appears to be relatively small – $160 billion compared with $145 billion. Two points merit note. First, the late 1960s estimates are over-estimated relative to those for 1980–82, for the cost estimates assumed that international market prices that actually existed were appropriate bases for the cost estimates. If trade liberalization would have increased international market prices by 10 per cent, the cost estimates may have been over-estimated by at least a fourth. Second, the farm population in the early 1980s was hardly more than half what it was in the late 1960s. Thus the real cost per farmer or member of the farm population in the early 1980s was more than double the cost in the late 1960s. Since real per capita incomes in the industrial market economies increased by about 60 to 70 per cent, however, the cost to consumers and taxpayers of the transfers to farmers as a percentage of their incomes did not increase over that fifteen-year period. One factor in the continued viability of the farm price and income programmes may well be that their cost as a percentage of gross national product has not increased significantly over the period. It follows from the above that the increase in the cost of the transfers per farm worker has increased relatively little compared with the change in real per capita incomes in the industrial economies.

The estimates of the costs of the income transfers to agriculture do not provide any indication of the increase in net farm income that is realized. In the long run the increase in the net income of farm families for their labour and capital can be only a minor fraction of the cost of the transfers. The transfers primarily pay for increased output and higher land values while the increase in the return to farm labour is very small.

Prices of Farm Products: National Differences

The consumer costs of the farm price programmes as presented in Table 3.2 reflect the national differences in farm prices. The measures of the ratios of domestic-to-border price ratios in Table 3.1 directly reflect national differences in prices received by farmers. These measures reflect differences due to transport costs as well as product quality. In other words, higher prices in an importing region that reflect the costs of transport and marketing from the exporting area are appropriately not reflected in the price ratios. The data in Table 3.1 reveal very sharp differences in domestic farm prices for the same product. For example, in 1980–82 the price of wheat in Japan was more than three times what it was in the United States and nearly three times the price in the European Community.

Table 3.2   Domestic costs and benefits of grain, livestock and sugar policies of various industrial countries, 1980–82 (columns 1–4 in 1985 US$ billions per year; column 5 in US$ per year)

	Domestic consumer cost (1)	Domestic producer benefit (2)	Taxpayer cost (3)	Net domestic cost	
				Total[a] (4)	Per capita (5)
EC-12	55.0	47.3	1.2	8.9	25
EFTA-5	11.7	9.6	0.6	2.7	85
Japan	35.6	20.6	− 6.0	9.0	75
United States	17.5	16.9	2.6	3.2	14
Canada	3.0	3.3	0.3	0.6	24
TOTAL	122.8	97.7	− 1.3	24.4	

[a]Column (1) minus column (2) plus (3) minus stock profits. That is, it does not include costs of raising and dispersing government tax revenue and of lobbying by farm groups, nor does it include the costs to the rest of the world.
Source: Rodney Tyers and Kym Anderson, 'Global Interactions and Trade Liberalisation in Agriculture', mimeograph, Department of Economics, University of Adelaide, April 1987, p. 49.

But the distortions and disarray created by price differences are due at least as much to the wide differentials in the degree of protection within countries as to national differences in the average level of protection. The European Community provided little protection for hogs and poultry, but high rates of protection for beef and dairy products. The price in the Community for hogs has been above the import cost of hogs, but almost all of the difference appears to have been due to higher feed costs imposed by the protection of grains. The level of nominal protection for grains since the formation of the CAP has generally been much higher than was the case in 1980–82.

Similar disparities in the protection levels exist in the United States. Until recently coarse grains received relatively little protection, but dairy and sugar had high rates. In many years during the past two decades the nominal protection of sugar has exceeded 100 per cent and in the late 1980s was generally 200 per cent or more.

The elasticities of supply for individual farm products are substantially higher than the supply elasticity for all farm products in a country or region. The supply functions for individual products reflect the possibility of resource substitution within agriculture such as a shift from feed-grains to wheat or vice versa. Thus if wheat receives a greater degree of protection than feed-grains, there will be a shift of resources to wheat production with the consequent effects on trade in wheat. Therefore it is important to look not only at average differences in prices of all farm products from country to country, but also to consider international differences for individual farm products.

Before presenting information on the magnitude of price differences among countries, a caveat must be asserted. It is extremely difficult to make comparisons of prices received by farmers across national boundaries and eliminate all elements of non-comparability. While we generally think of many farm products as being reasonably uniform in quality, the differences in prices resulting from quality factors are large compared with, say, the cost of transporting a product from North America to Western Europe. Price spreads in the wholesale prices of the different types of wheat (excluding durum wheat) among mid-western markets in the United States were $25 to $30 per ton in the late 1980s.

Even if there were free trade in farm products there would be differences in prices received by farmers in various countries. In general, the importing countries would have higher prices than the exporting countries with the differential covering approximately the costs of loading, unloading, transportation, insurance and interest costs. One can observe differences in the price of, say, wheat between the Gulf ports in the United States and Rotterdam that approximate the enumerated costs. In the late 1980s, the difference was approximately $30 per ton, about 25 per cent of the United States export price and 30 per cent of the price received by American farmers. Thus compared with the United States it could be said that farmers in Western Europe have a 'natural' nominal rate protection of perhaps 30 per cent due to transport and related costs. When nominal prices were higher, as they were in the mid-1970s, the 'natural' protection was significantly lower, often no more than 15 per cent.

Price Differences

It does not follow, however, that if there were free trade the prices received by all farmers in an importing region, such as Western Europe, would exceed the Canadian or American prices by 25 per cent, even after adjustment were made for differences in quality of the product. Internal transport costs can be substantial and there may be important differences in marketing costs other than transport. For example, in 1968/69 (before the currency flotations which followed the 1971 'dollar' crisis) the German farmer received $6.70 per ton less than the threshold price for barley, while the French farmer received $19.05 less. In spite of a French threshold price that was $1.70 per ton higher than in West Germany, the French farmer received $10.70 per ton less than the German farmer.[4]

Thus if the French and German barley were of the same quality, the difference in prices between the two countries was almost the same as the cost of shipping barley from the Great Lakes to the United Kingdom. The difference in the French and German producer prices was probably due to several factors, but most important was that, within the European Community, France is a major exporter and West Germany is a major importer and considerable quantities of barley move physically from France to West Germany. Land transport costs are high relative to water transport. Thus in a free trade situation, the price received by French barley producers might exceed that received by Canadian or American producers by only $5 per ton.

To illustrate some of the complexities of price formation for farm products I repeat two tables of price comparisons from the original edition. While these tables provide data for 1968/69, they represent price patterns with far fewer abnormalities than is true today where price patterns have been affected by exchange-rate variations, deficiency payments and other market interventions. While no year can be called a normal year, exchange rates had been subject to relatively few changes in the years before 1968 and, while the United States had some direct payments, they were modest compared with the payments made during the 1980s.

Table 3.3 reveals a rather complex price pattern for barley.[5] It appears that the cost of moving barley from the wholesale markets in the United States (Minneapolis) and Canada (Fort William) to the United Kingdom was approximately $10 per ton in 1968/69. In the United States farmers received approximately $4 per ton less than the wholesale price, although some quality differential may be involved. The threshold price for barley in the European Community was about $95 per ton and import cost was about $49; however, producer prices in the Community were significantly less than the threshold price, especially in France which exports barley to other Common Market countries.

Table 3.3   Barley prices in 1968/69

	US$ per ton
Producer price – exporters	
United States	41.70
Canada	45.90
Australia	37.50
Wholesale prices	
United States	46.00
Canada	46.00
Import price	
United Kingdom	56.00
European Community	51.00
Variable levy	
European Community	46.05
Producer price	
France	78.52
Germany (feed barley)	92.45
Netherlands (feed barley)	89.64

Sources: *Grain in the European Community* (Washington: United States Department of Agriculture, 1970); and Presidential Commission on International Trade and Investment Policy, *United States International Economic Policy in an Interdependent World*, Williams Report (Washington: US Government Printing Office, 1971).

A further illustration of the complex nature of pricing patterns in farm products may be appropriate. The purpose is to show the fairly wide range of prices that can coexist within a single but large country, the United States. The commodity chosen for illustration is hard red winter wheat and all data are for the 1968/69 marketing year; the wheat produced in Kansas and Colorado is primarily hard red winter. Selected prices of hard red winter wheat in 1968/69 are given in Table 3.4.[6]

The Rotterdam price was included to show that price differences within the United States are greater than from major American ports to Western Europe. The margin between Kansas City and the ports on the Gulf of Mexico is almost identical to the margin between the Gulf ports and Rotterdam, while the margin between the price received by the Colorado farmer and the domestic price at the Gulf ports was almost three times the Gulf ports–Rotterdam margin. The United Kingdom price was approximately $5 per ton above the Rotterdam price.

The first edition of this book included a long table that gave approximate prices for several farm products for a dozen or so

Table 3.4   Hard red winter wheat prices in 1968/69 (US$ per ton)

Average price received by farmers	
Colorado	41.10
Kansas	44.80
Kansas City	50.65
Domestic price, Gulf ports	56.15
Export price, Gulf ports[a]	62.75
Rotterdam, c.i.f.[b]	67.15
United Kingdom, c.i.f.[bc]	72.10

[a]During 1968/69 the United States imposed an export tax on hard red winter wheat which averaged about $6.50 per ton; the objective was to keep the US export price at the floor specified in the ill-fated International Grains Agreement. In the absence of the export tax (and without an export subsidy) the average price received by Kansas and Colorado farmers would have been about $47.70 and $51.40, respectively. Export price is the cost to the foreign buyer.
[b]c.i.f. relates to a price that covers cost, insurance and freight.
[c]The United Kingdom price has been reduced by $1.15 to reflect protein content comparable with Rotterdam (12 per cent).
Sources: *Wheat Situation and Outlook Report*, United States Department of Agriculture, Washington, July 1969, pp. 21, 22 and 24; and *Review of the World Grains Situation, 1968/69* (London: International Wheat Council, 1969), p. 77.

countries for the late 1960s. The differences in producer prices were very large since for each product the highest price was four or five times the lowest. Due to the changes in farm price and income support policies and the increased complexity of protection simple comparisons of the prices that producers received during the 1980s could be misleading. For example, for some grains, the farm price in the United States in 1986 and 1987 represented little more than half of the total returns, including deficiency and diversion payments.

What we would like to compare across countries are the differences in the returns to producers, including subsidies on both output and inputs and reflecting the effects of currency misalignments on real farm prices. It would be even better if we could compare the returns to producers, including subsidies, with the border prices that would prevail under free trade and an equilibrium exchange rate, with the border prices adjusted back to the farm level by reflecting transport and with marketing costs within the country. Table 3.5 is an approximation of this ideal comparison. It is based on estimates of producer subsidy equivalents (PSEs) made by the United States Department of Agriculture. Unfortunately, the PSEs reflect the costs of providing protection and not the actual benefits received by farmers. For example, the PSE calculation includes, for both the European Community and the

Table 3.5 Approximate ratio of producer returns to adjusted border prices, commodities by country, 1982–84[a]

Ratio[b]	United States	Australia	Canada	New Zealand	European Community	Japan
<0.50						
0.50 to 0.75						Citrus
0.76 to 0.89						
0.90 to 0.99						
1.00 to 1.10	Beef Pork Poultry meat* Soyabeans*	Barley* Beef* Cotton* Pork* Poultry meat* Sheep meat* Wheat* Wool*	Beef Corn Oats* Pork* Soyabeans	Barley* Wheat	Corn	
1.11 to 1.31	Barley*	Cane sugar* Manu. milk* Rice*	Barley* Flaxseed* Poultry meat Rapeseed* Rye* Wheat*	Beef* Fluid milk Manu. milk Wool*	Barley* Common wheat* Pork*	
1.32 to 1.96	Corn* Cotton* Dairy* Rice* Sorghum* Wheat*	Fluid milk	Sugar	Sheep meat	Dairy* Durum wheat* Poultry meat Rapeseed Rice Sheep meat Soyabeans Sugar*	Poultry meat
2.00 to 3.85	Sugar		Dairy*		Beef*	Beef Pork Soyabeans Sugar
4.00 and over						Barley Fluid milk Manu. milk Rice Wheat

Note An asterisk denotes a net exporter during 1982–84.
[a]Some products lack data for some years.
[b]Ratio of gross domestic value of production, including direct payments, to adjusted border price, approximately.
[c]Impacts of input subsidies are not included.

Taiwan[c]	South Korea[c]	India	Argentina	Nigeria	Mexico	Brazil
				Cocoa*		
				Sugar		
		Cotton (LS)*	Wheat*			
		Wheat				
		Cotton (MS)*	Corn*			
		Peanut meal	Sorghum*			
		Rice	Soyabeans*			
		Rapeseed meal		Rice		Soyabeans*
		Soyabeans		Cotton		Corn
						Beef*
Pork*				Corn		Manu. milk
						Poultry meat*
Corn	Poultry meat	Peanuts*			Cotton*	
Soyabeans		Rapeseed				
Sugar*						
Beef	Pork	Peanut oil		Wheat	Sorghum	Cotton*
Dairy		Rape oil			Soyabeans	Rice
Poultry meat		Soya oil			Wheat	
Rice*						
Tobacco						
Sorghum	Barley				Corn	Wheat
Wheat	Beef					
	Corn					
	Fluid milk					
	Rice					
	Soyabeans					
	Wheat					

Source: Derived from *Government Intervention in Agriculture: Measurement and Implications for Trade Negotiations*, Foreign Agricultural Economic Report No. 229 (Washington: Economic Research Service, United States Department of Agriculture, [April] 1987), p. 29, by converting producer subsidy equivalents to the ratio of producer returns, including policy transfers, to border prices. The ratio is equal to $1 + [PSE/(1 - PSE)]$ for all positive PSEs. Where there is a tax, the ratio is $1 -$ the tax ratio.

United States, the costs of storage of excess products generated by the incentives given to farmers and the costs of administering the programmes. The farmers do not benefit directly from the several billion dollars spent annually on storage and administration, but such costs are included as a part of the costs of protection. Thus the PSE measure is affected by the efficiency with which government policies transfer incomes to farmers. But even with this defect, the other advantages are such as to warrant the use of the PSEs to compare differences in returns with farmers across countries.

Table 3.5 has not been taken directly from the estimates of PSEs. The conventional method of assigning a value to PSEs, adopted by the OECD and the United States Department of Agriculture, is the ratio of the policy transfers to the total value of domestic production, including direct payments. This has the effect, in my opinion, of giving a misleading impression to the unsophisticated observer of the difference between domestic producer returns and the adjusted border prices. A PSE of 0.50 doesn't seem so unreasonable until it is understood that the domestic returns are double the adjusted border price. A PSE of 0.50 means that policy transfers, a euphemism for subsidies, equals the returns received from the market. But there is also a distortion in perception for the unwary – a PSE of 0.75 does not seem that much larger than one of 0.50, yet if all the transfer were made by border protection (a variable levy, for example), in the one case domestic prices would be double the world price and in the other case four times it. A PSE of 0.80 increases the ratio of domestic to border prices to five. Consequently, the PSEs are converted to a ratio of the policy transfers to gross domestic value of production minus the transfers. If all of the policy transfers consisted of deficiency payments or border measures on output, this ratio would be the ratio of domestic prices or returns to adjusted border prices.

Production, Use and Trade

Between 1961/63 and 1979–81 the developed regions of the world increased their export volume of agricultural products by 160 per cent while their imports increased by only 65 per cent. Exports from Western Europe increased by 232 per cent while imports increased by 60 per cent; North American exports increased 158 per cent and imports by only 36 per cent. On the other hand, the developing regions increased exports by only 40 per cent and imports increased by 202 per cent.[7]

World trade in agricultural products stagnated in the 1980s, in terms of volume and value through 1986. The only noticeable change was the emergence of China as a significant net exporter of agricultural products during the mid-1980s. Thus the disparities in export and import growth between the developing and developed market economies that prevailed in the two previous regions was a result of a more rapid growth of production than consumption within those regions. In the absence of other evidence, it could be argued that the excess of production over consumption was due either to the increasing comparative advantage of agriculture in the developed regions or to the need to meet the shortfall in production relative to consumption in the developing regions. But as noted later, the first argument is not valid. As for the second, it is true that during the 1960s and 1970s much of the excess agricultural production of the developed regions was used to improve the food situation in the developing regions. This result, however, was not intended when the policies that led to the excess production were inaugurated; nor was the flow of highly subsidized exports to the developing countries of the 1960s available during the 1970s in like degree as international market prices increased.

The pattern of more rapid increase in production than consumption is not just a recent phenomenon. Compared with the last half of the 1930s, exports of agricultural products from Western Europe increased 54 per cent by 1957–59 while imports into Western Europe increased only 14 per cent. While the North American situation is complicated by the drought conditions of the period that resulted in net imports of wheat by the United States, it may be noted that exports increased by 108 per cent and imports by 75 per cent.[8]

In the first edition data on the growth of imports and exports of agricultural products were presented for the OECD countries for the 1960s. It was noted that while the value of agricultural exports increased by 93 per cent between the late 1950s and 1968 and the value of agricultural imports increased by just 68 per cent, the value of net agricultural imports increased by about a third.[9] The obvious conclusion was drawn: If the trends in growth of exports and imports of agricultural products continued, net imports must eventually decline.

This conclusion was illustrated by a table that showed how the annual growth of production and consumption of agricultural products in the OECD countries must result in a decline in net agricultural imports, if those trends continued. The table showed how a small difference in growth rates for production and consumption of agricultural products would result in a decline in the annual rate of growth of net imports. The approximate data were for the OECD countries in the mid-1960s (Australia and New Zealand were not then members) and are reproduced in Table 3.6.

Table 3.6   Production, imports and consumption of agricultural products in OECD countries in the mid-1960s (annual levels of rates) (in US$ millions)

Value of gross output of farm products	100 000
Net imports of farm products	8 000
Consumption of farm products	108 000
Annual growth of output	2 per cent
Annual growth of consumption	1.5 per cent
Value of output growth	2 000
Value of consumption growth	1 620
Potential decline in net imports annually	380

Sources: The growth rates for agricultural production and consumption are based on *Agricultural Statistics, 1955–1968* (Paris: OECD, 1969), pp. 106–9. The net imports of agricultural products are from the same source and are an average for several years around the mid-1960s. The value of agricultural output for OECD countries is the author's estimate based on agriculture's share of gross domestic product adjusted to account for intermediate inputs.

The trends did continue and the value of net agricultural imports by the developed market economies declined during the 1970s and approached zero. For these economies the value of agricultural imports in current prices increased from $40 460 million in 1970 to $157 700 million in 1980. The value of exports increased from $29 300 million to $150 500 million; and the value of net imports declined from $11 160 million to $7200 million in current prices and to about $2400 million in 1970 prices. In real terms, however, the value of net imports of the developed market economies increased during the 1980s, though by 1986 was still less than in 1970.

The result that could be projected from the data in Table 3.6 actually occurred, namely that the value of net imports of agricultural products by the developed market economies did decline during the 1970s. In 1970 the net imports of agricultural products by the developed market economies (nearly synonymous with the OECD countries) was $11 121 million; the net import surplus in 1980 in 1970 prices was $3000 million. This meant that, in terms of 1970 prices, the net agricultural imports declined at an annual rate of $800 million, approximately double the projection in the last line of Table 3.6. While output growth in the developed market economies during the 1970s was very close to an annual rate of 2 per cent, the annual growth of consumption was significantly less than 1.5 per cent. Consumption growth appears to have declined to about 1.0 per cent. Consequently the gap between output and consumption growth increased and the decline in the value of net agricultural imports was significantly greater during the 1970s than would have been the case if the trends of the 1960s had persisted. Table 3.7 indicates the significant changes in the degree of self-sufficiency and world import and export shares that occurred between 1961–64 and 1980–83 for major farm products. These data are an alternative way of presenting the trends in world agricultural trade.

Table 3.7   Food self-sufficiency and world trade shares of developed market, centrally-planned and developing economies, 1961–64 and 1980–83 (per cent)

Industrial market economies	Wheat	Coarse grain	Rice	Ruminant meat	Non-ruminant meat	Dairy products	Sugar
Self-sufficiency							
1961–64	146	98	105	97	100	104	63
1980–83	195	110	112	102	100	109	95
Share of world exports							
1961–64	83	65	20	56	78	90	12
1980–83	91	79	36	70	72	94	29
Share of world imports							
1961–64	26	77	12	80	61	64	58
1980–83	17	48	11	60	63	53	33

Source: Rodney Tyers and Kym Anderson, 'Distortions in World Food Markets: a Quantitative Assessment', a background paper for the World Bank's *World Development Report 1986*, January 1986, p. 16.

There is abundant evidence that the capacity of agriculture of the industrial countries is such as to permit more rapid expansion of output than the anticipated increases in demand if current farm policies are maintained. Furthermore, there are currently too many resources engaged in agriculture in the industrial countries, and it is one of the major premises of this study that such excess resources are maintained in agriculture because of the farm policies that have been and are being pursued.

The previous paragraph has been taken without change from the first edition. There were those who interpreted the sharp increase in real grain and other food prices in international markets that occurred in

1973 and 1974 as forerunners of scarcity and high prices for food. It is now clear, as it should have been then, that the sharp increases in real prices of food and other farm products in those years did not represent a long-run trend towards higher real prices of agricultural products. The brief but sharp increase in the price of grain was due to several factors – a small reduction in world grain production in 1972 of 3 per cent, a nearly equal increase in grain use as a result of demand growth in the high income countries, some excessive speculation, and the effects of domestic price stabilization of farm and food prices on instability in international market prices.

As noted in a paper that I wrote in 1975, perhaps as much as half of the sharp increase in real grain prices from 1972 to 1974 was due to governmental policies of domestic price stabilization.[10] These policies operated by varying the amount of imports and exports as the means of equating domestic supply and demand at fixed prices. In regions or countries that consumed a significant percentage of the world's grain, neither domestic producers nor consumers reacted to the large increase in international market prices, because their governments varied imports and exports to keep prices stable. Taken together, the Soviet Union, China, the European Community and the rest of Europe consumed approximately half of the world's grain in the early 1970s. In these countries and regions the internal prices were prevented from reflecting the changes in world supply and demand for grain. Consequently all of the adjustment to the shocks to demand and supply that occurred in 1972 to 1974 were concentrated on the international markets and those countries that permitted their domestic prices to vary with international prices. In the Community the real prices of grain were permitted to decline between 1971 and 1974, thus discouraging output expansion and encouraging increased consumption.

Another factor that contributed to the grain price increases was the export pricing policy followed by the United States during the spring and summer of 1972. This policy, which involved a commitment by the United States to hold the price of wheat at Gulf ports at approximately $65 per ton, made it possible for the Soviet Union to import more than 20 million tons of grain in 1972/73 at a very low price and with almost no effect on international wheat and grain prices until after the purchases were completed.[11] Consequently, the Soviet Union imported more grain than it would have, had export prices been permitted to reflect the large purchases that were made. The United States maintained the export market price by assuring exporters that an export subsidy would be paid, reflecting the difference between domestic market prices and the export price. This policy helped the Soviet Union to conceal the massiveness of its purchases since the United States exporters had no need to buy grain, either cash or futures, to protect their positions since an export subsidy was to be paid representing the difference between the domestic market price and the export price at the time the subsidy was requested.

In Chapter 7 results of several studies of the effects of the form of protection on international price instability will be summarized. These studies support the view that a major source of international market price instability is found in domestic price-stabilization measures. It will also be shown that there are forms of agricultural protection that would not cause increased international price instability.

The unwillingness to recognize that a large part of the price increases that occurred during the early 1970s was the result of deliberate governmental policies, meant that many looked for underlying shifts in real factors affecting world supply and demand for food that could explain the short-run price increases and would justify the view that the increases were likely to be long-run in nature. Some held the view that there had been a fundamental change in the world supply and demand balance for food from one of relative ease and low prices to one of relative tightness and high and increasing prices. These beliefs were held in spite of several authoritative studies that were available in 1972 that supported the view that the world's productive capacity was likely to grow more rapidly than demand from the early 1970s to 1980 or 1985. Three such studies were summarized in the first edition of this book.

Martin E. Abel and Anthony S. Rojko, in a study for the United States Department of Agriculture, concluded: 'The combined excess food production capacity of all of the developed countries in 1980 will be more than adequate to provide for the increased food import needs of the Third World. This is likely even if the less developed countries do not improve their rates of growth in grain production.'[12] Later they noted: 'The rate of improvement in agricultural production in Eastern Europe, the USSR, and other developed importing countries – particularly the countries of Western Europe which have highly protective agricultural policies – probably will not be influenced very much by what happens to food production in the developing world.'[13]

In its *Provisional Indicative World Plan for Agricultural Development*, the United Nations Food and Agriculture Organization (FAO) was not concerned about rising real food prices but about the sharp differences in the rates of growth of agricultural exports from the developing and developed countries and the failure of the developed countries to open their markets for agricultural imports from the developing countries. It was noted that the self-sufficiency ratios for most agricultural products in the industrial countries had increased significantly from the mid-1950s to the mid-1960s. The following important conclusion was presented: 'A reversal in the trends of increasing self-sufficiency in the high-income countries as a group can be brought about only if their domestic farm policies and trade policies for the relevant commodities are modified considerably. The essence of the modification in farm policies would consist of ensuring that total resources used for current agricultural production ... were smaller than they otherwise would be.'[14]

In 1968 the OECD Secretariat completed projections of agricultural output and consumption for the major industrial market economies.[15] Two of the major conclusions bear repeating: 'Agriculture in the OECD area has the potential to expand output faster than the growth in requirements within the area. ... These increased availabilities can be achieved without any stimulus to output beyond those given by current policies.' These projections, which were for the period ending in 1985, have clearly not been contradicted by experience. But it is also obvious that these projections were ignored by policy-makers in the industrial countries.

The industrial market economies followed agricultural policies that increased their degree of self-sufficiency in all major categories of food and increased their share of world exports in all categories except meat between 1961–64 and 1980–83.[16] Table 3.7 indicates the changes in food self-sufficiency and shares of world trade. In 1961–64 the industrial market economies were net importers of coarse grains, ruminant meat and sugar. By 1980–83 they were net exporters of each of these commodity groups except sugar and in this case its self-sufficiency percentage had increased from 63 to 95 per cent. By the mid-1980s the industrial market economies were net exporters of sugar.

In every category the industrial market economies increased their share of world exports and simultaneously reduced their share of world imports. These shifts in self-sufficiency and trade patterns are the direct consequence of a more rapid growth of production than of internal consumption. If the shifts in self-sufficiency and trading patterns had resulted from competitive factors – had been based on the prevailing comparative advantages – there could be no objection to these outcomes. It is abundantly clear, however, from the data and argument presented above, that these shifts were generated in large part by governmental policies that encouraged farmers to produce more than they would have produced if faced with world market prices.

The price increases that occurred during 1973 and 1974 had a short life. The price declines in international markets were as rapid and sharp as were the price increases. As measured by the real export prices of wheat and maize from the United States, the prices had returned to the 1972 levels by 1977. The long-run downward trend in real grain prices reasserted itself by the late 1970s. These trends are given in Table 3.8.

For most of the years since 1960 the real export prices of wheat and maize, as represented by American export prices, have been at or below the real prices during the Great Depression of the 1930s. The exceptions were in the 1973–76 period. In 1986, partly as a result of changes in American price-support policy, the real export prices had fallen to less than half the levels of the 1930s, to hardly more than a third in the case of maize.

Table 3.8   Real export prices for wheat and maize in the United States, selected years 1910 to 1988[a] (1967 $ per ton)

Calendar year	Wheat	Maize	Calendar year	Wheat	Maize
1910–14	100	74	1971	54	50
1925–29	103	76	1972	54	46
1930–34	79	85	1973	80	63
1935–39	79	85	1974	110	79
1945–49	122	94	1975	95	76
1950–54	95	80	1976	80	64
1955–59	69	61	1977	58	52
1960	65	53	1978	61	50
1961	69	52	1979	67	50
1962	70	52	1980	66	50
1963	69	56	1981	62	50
1964	69	57	1982	56	39
1965	62	57	1983	53	44
1966	62	56	1984	50	46
1967	64	54	1985	47	38
1968	60	48	1986	40	32
1969	57	48	1987	32	25
1970	53	52	1988	37	33

[a]The export prices are export unit values; the price deflator is the United States wholesale price index.

The price trends in Table 3.8 do not by themselves prove that there are excess resources in agriculture in the industrial countries. But the

World Agriculture in Disarray

price trends viewed against the background of the increased degrees of self-sufficiency in these countries are consistent with the conclusion that supply has been growing more rapidly than demand in the industrial countries. Given the protection that is provided to agriculture, it is also clear that in North America and Western Europe farmers are not producing these crops in response to the prices displayed in the last years in Table 3.8.

4 Agricultural Change

The agriculture of the industrial countries has changed significantly and rapidly over the past half century. Farming is not what it used to be. Mechanical power has replaced animal power almost everywhere. This transition was completed during the 1970s. The self-contained farm is a thing of the past in the industrial regions of the world; in a number of countries the value of purchased inputs (other than labour) exceeds half of the gross value of output. Farming has become a highly sophisticated production process, depending on fertilizers, tractors, electric motors, hydraulic devices, air conditioning, pesticides, herbicides, vitamins, antibiotics, synthetic proteins and, to an increasing degree, computers. The management of such enterprises requires a high degree of flexibility and intelligence and a great deal of detailed knowledge of prices and production alternatives.

In the space of this chapter it is not possible to portray fully how agriculture has changed in the recent past. Yet one can summarize some of the major changes that have occurred and leave it to the reader to imagine other and much more subtle adjustments and modifications that must have occurred. But the primary purpose of this chapter is not that of displaying change in agriculture, interesting as that topic may be in itself. My purpose is to make it clear that agriculture is a highly dynamic industry that has adjusted to changing conditions and will continue to do so. Government policies that ignore this significant characteristic of agriculture will be thwarted and distorted; and costs of the programmes under them can rise above almost any level that may be imagined. To some considerable degree we have already witnessed this outcome. To be successful, government policies must anticipate and facilitate changes that are under way, rather than to assume that agriculture is sluggish and slow to adapt to changing circumstances. Unfortunately, policy-makers have not been able to adjust government policies speedily and to react effectively to the rapid changes in agriculture. This failure helps to explain the enormous costs the farm programmes of the 1980s have imposed on consumers and taxpayers.

**Changes in Average Product per
Worker – Agriculture and the Rest of
Us**

In an economy in which real income per capita is increasing, the average product per worker will also be increasing. The latter measure has many limitations for most purposes for which it is used. It is not a reasonable measure of the extent of technological changes in an economy or industry; if one industry has a much higher rate of change in average product per worker than another this can be due, for example, to a higher rate of investment or a greater increase in purchased inputs. Nor does it measure what changes are occurring in real wages in an industry or economy.

But the growth of average product per worker is a good measure of change. It does not directly indicate what changes are occurring, but it does highlight when rapid and/or differential change is occurring. And it is in this sense that changes in average product per worker is being used here – as an indication of changes in methods of production, including substitution of other inputs for labour.

There are various measures of average product per worker, including average total output or sales and average gross domestic product (GDP). It is difficult to use the first for comparison of agriculture with other sectors of the economy since total output or sales is affected over time by the way an industry or sector is defined. Total sales includes the value of current inputs or materials purchased from other parts of the economy, from abroad or from other farmers. Thus the comparisons between sectors made below are based on gross domestic product. This measure is an indication of the returns for labour and all capital used in the industry per worker. It includes depreciation on capital as well as the current return to capital, including interest paid, and any return to land. The average product per worker is thus a measure of the average value added per worker in a given sector of an economy, although no inference should be drawn that it is a measure of the contribution of labour to the product of any sector.

Table 4.1 presents data for most OECD countries on the annual percentage growth rates of gross domestic product per employed worker for two periods of time – namely 1957–58 to 1967–68 and 1967–68 to 1983–84. There are a number of notable features of the data on annual rates of change in real gross domestic product per worker in agriculture and in the rest of the economy. One is that in almost 90 per cent of the comparisons the rate of growth in agriculture is the larger.

In the first period, agriculture's growth rate lagged behind that of the rest of the economy in three relatively low-income countries (Spain, Greece and Turkey) and one high-income industrial economy (Norway). The three relatively low-income countries had rather high percentages of their labour forces engaged in agriculture in 1970, ranging from 31 per cent in Spain to more than 70 per cent in Turkey. In the second period, in only one country (Portugal) did the growth of average labour product in agriculture lag behind that of the rest of the economy.

Table 4.1 Gross domestic product in constant prices per employed person: annual percentage growth rates, 1957–58 to 1967–68 and 1967–68 to 1983–84

| | 1957–58 to 1967–68 | | 1967–68 to 1983–84 | |
	Agriculture	Other sectors	Agriculture	Other sectors
Canada	4.8	1.4	2.5	1.0
United States	5.5	2.4	2.1	0.3
Japan	–	–	4.4	3.0
Australia	–	–	3.3	2.5
Austria	5.0	4.2	6.6	5.8
Belgium	3.9	3.4	5.7	2.9
Denmark	6.1	3.0	5.4	1.7
Finland	3.9	2.1	5.0	2.3
France	6.5	4.2	5.3	2.6
West Germany	6.9	4.8	5.2	2.7
Greece	3.6	4.0	2.2	1.6
Ireland	4.0	3.0	–	–
Italy	7.8	4.9	5.0	1.8
Luxembourg	4.7	1.5	6.6	1.5
Netherlands	6.4	3.9	–	–
Norway	2.8	3.8	4.4	1.7
Portugal	5.2	5.0	− 2.7	3.8
Spain	5.4	5.9	6.5	3.4
Sweden	5.6	3.8	3.4	1.3
Turkey	2.5	4.1	2.9	2.7
United Kingdom	6.0	2.4	–	–

Sources: *Labour Force Statistics*, OECD, Paris, for 1956–67 and 1964–84; and *National Accounts*, OECD, Paris, for 1950–58 and 1964–84.

A further notable feature of the data is that for the first period the median rate of growth of labour product in agriculture was somewhat more than 5 per cent and this implies a doubling in fourteen years. In the second period, the median growth rate was 4.4 per cent, somewhat lower than the first period. It may be noted that the decline in the growth of labour productivity in agriculture between the two periods was significantly less than for the rest of the economy, where the decline in the median growth rates was from 3.4 to 2.3 per cent. The final feature worthy of note is the number of instances in the two periods in which the annual rate of growth in agriculture exceeded 6 per cent; there were nine such instances or approximately one out of four. The differences that are shown for agriculture and other sectors also hold generally for a comparison of agriculture and industry.[1]

A comparison of changes in output and gross domestic product of agriculture is indicative of change in agriculture, as reflected in increased reliance on purchased inputs as well as on additional capital inputs per worker. Table 4.2 presents data on the increase in farm production between 1969–71 and 1984–85, the compound annual growth rate of production, the compound annual rate of decline of the farm labour force, and the annual rate of increase in output or production per worker in agriculture. In a clear majority of the countries, the increase in output or production per worker was greater than the increase in gross domestic product per worker. It is reasonable to conclude from this relationship that purchased inputs, either from domestic or imported sources, increased more than gross domestic product.

The data in Tables 4.1 and 4.2 give a general picture of agriculture as an industry in which rapid changes are occurring. Output is growing, the labour input is declining and other inputs are being employed to replace, and more than offset, the downward trend in labour. We shall now turn to a discussion of some of the important changes that have been associated with these rapid adjustments in agriculture in the industrial countries.

Current Purchased Inputs

An important source of the growth of labour productivity in agriculture has been the increase in the importance of inputs purchased from the rest of the economy. These inputs have been of two sorts – current purchased inputs (intermediate consumption) and capital items. The first includes such items as fertilizer, feeding materials, medicines and fuel while the second includes buildings, land improvements and machinery.

A major change in agriculture in the industrial countries since the Second World War has been the rapid increase in current purchased

Table 4.2 Indices of agricultural production and annual rates of change of production, labour and production per worker in agriculture, 1969–71 to 1984–85

Country	*Agricultural production 1984–85* (1969–71 = 100)	*Production growth* (annual % rate)	*Labour*[a] (annual % rate)	*Production per worker* (annual % rate)
Canada	130	1.8	−0.4	2.2
United States	133	2.0	−0.3	2.3
Norway	137	2.3	−3.0	5.3
Finland	127	1.7	−6.2	8.3
Sweden	134	2.0	−2.5	4.7
Denmark	146	2.6	−3.4	6.2
United Kingdom	135	2.1	−1.6	3.8
Ireland	146	2.6	−3.1	6.0
Netherlands	145	2.8	−2.0	4.7
Belgium–Lux.	110	0.7	−3.1	3.9
France	136	2.1	−3.6	5.9
West Germany	120	1.3	−3.4	4.9
Austria	120	1.3	−4.2	5.7
Italy	122	1.4	−3.5	5.0
Portugal	76	1.9	−0.1	1.8
Spain	150	2.8	−4.7	7.9
Greece	134	2.0	–	–
Turkey	152	2.9	+0.2	2.8
Japan	109	0.6	−3.8	4.6
Australia	133	2.0	−0.4	2.4
New Zealand	126	1.6	+0.5	1.2
Switzerland	133	2.0	−1.7	3.8
Iceland	125	1.6	−1.8	3.4

[a]1985 imputed from 1969–71 to 1984 average rate.
Sources: *Labour Force Statistics*, OECD, Paris, for 1964–84; and *Production Yearbook*, FAO, Rome, for 1979, 1980, 1981 and 1985.

inputs. A substantial part of the increase occurred in the first two decades after the war in north-western Europe. Between 1950–52 and 1963–65 agricultural output in the region increased by 37 per cent while current operating expenses (in constant prices) increased by 73 per cent or almost exactly twice as fast.[2] This meant that these inputs were increasing in importance relative to agricultural output.

Table 4.3 gives data on the relationship between intermediate consumption and gross agricultural output for several member countries of the European Community and the United States. Intermediate consumption does not include payments for labour, depreciation, interest or rent. It is primarily purchases from the non-farm sector for current operations, although purchased feed materials are included. The table covers the period from 1950–52 to 1986. Except for Italy and France, in 1986 nearly half or more of gross agricultural output was required to pay for intermediate consumption. In France the relative importance of intermediate consumption had more than doubled in the 35 years and had increased to 43 per cent of the value of gross farm output. Only in Italy was intermediate consumption less than 30 per cent of the value of output. In the United States the relative importance of current purchased inputs was large from 1950–52 to the present, essentially paralleling the experience of Denmark.

Table 4.3 Intermediate consumption as a percentage of gross agricultural output at current prices in the European Community and the United States

Country	1950–52	1958	1968	1977	1986
Belgium	21.6	33.3	42.3	58.5	57.8
Denmark	37.3	–	–	51.0	49.7
France	18.5	23.4	29.1	39.0	43.0
West Germany	27.2	33.1	43.8	51.4	52.3
Ireland	–	–	–	35.7	47.8
Netherlands	32.8	40.7	45.2	50.0	48.9
United Kingdom	–	–	–	57.2	54.0
Italy	13.2	15.1	23.3	28.6	28.0
United States	39.4	44.8	49.5	51.0	47.4

Note United States data are for cash income and expenditures only and exclude dwellings.
Sources: For 1950–52, *Output, Expenses and Income of Agriculture in European Countries*, Sixth Report (New York: United Nations, for the Economic Commission for Europe and the FAO, 1969); for other years, *Agriculture Statistical Yearbook*, Statistical Office of the European Community, Luxembourg, various issues; and *Economic Indicators of the Farm Sector: National Financial Summary 1986* (Washington: United States Department of Agriculture, 1987).

But the increasing importance of purchased inputs is not the only indication of the growing dependence of agriculture on inputs acquired from the rest of the economy. As agriculture has modernized, the traditional agricultural inputs of land and labour have become relatively less important, both as factors contributing to production and as income recipients from the total value of agricultural output. There is all too little recognition in the formulation of agricultural policy that the labour and land supplied by farm-operator families receive a minority of the value of farm output.

Current purchases or intermediate consumption exclude two important non-farm inputs – depreciation of equipment and buildings and interest paid. In 1986 in the European Community of Ten the depreciation was 14 per cent of the gross value of output and interest was 6.2 per cent for a total of approximately 20 per cent. These two inputs were nearly half as large as intermediate consumption at 43 per cent. In the United States, for the same year, depreciation was 10 per cent of gross cash income and interest was 11 per cent of gross product.[3] Thus total expenditures on non-farm inputs for both the Community and the United States exceeded three-fifths of the gross value of output in 1986.

There are several reasons for emphasizing the increasing importance of purchased inputs in agriculture. As current inputs become more important relative to output, it is obvious that a smaller fraction of the value of output is available for payment for the resources owned by the farmers themselves – labour, management, land and capital – and for interest on borrowed funds. When almost all of the value of sales is retained by the agricultural sector, as was the case in Italy during 1950–52, a given absolute increase in the value of sales will result in nearly the same increase in the incomes accruing to farmer-owned resources. Agriculture in the United States was apparently commercialized earlier than in Western Europe. In 1925–29, current purchased inputs were equal to 27 per cent of gross output, about the same as in 1950–52 for several of the countries included in Table 4.3.

A related point is that the elasticity of supply of farm products increases as the relative importance of purchased inputs increases. In an agriculture that has few purchased inputs, output can be increased primarily by cultivating more land or working longer hours. In fairly densely populated regions, the possibilities of expanding output by cultivating more land are limited. The same is true of working longer hours in most agricultural settings, although it is possible to employ more workers. But either or both of these types of adjustments will permit only a limited response to higher output prices. In other words, the elasticity of supply with respect to price is low. But when purchased inputs amount to a third to a half of the value of output, the potential for increasing output in response to increased incentives is much greater. More fertilizer, pesticides, herbicides, high protein feeds and tractor fuel can be added to the production process as needed and desired.

The implication of the larger elasticity of supply in agricultures with the greater percentages of current operating expenses to the value of output is that higher output prices will be a relatively ineffective device for increasing the returns to farmer-owned resources, as noted above, but will be effective, whether desired or not, in increasing output.

As will be discussed at greater length in Chapter 6, the trend towards greater importance of purchased inputs can result in an increase in the degree of effective protection for agriculture, even if real output prices remain unchanged. This result occurs if the degree of nominal protection for agricultural output is greater than the nominal protection for the inputs that agriculture purchases from the rest of the economy or from imported sources. The importance of purchased inputs increases and the value added falls and the rate of effective protection increases.

Data for the United States that separate total inputs into non-purchased and purchased indicate how much change has occurred in a period of four decades. From 1950–52 to 1986 the index of all inputs used in farm production actually decreased from 106 to 87 (1977 = 100). Non-purchased inputs, which includes operator and unpaid family labour and operator-owned real estate and capital, declined from 159 to 83, but purchased inputs increased from an index of 66 to 91. Non-purchased inputs decreased by 48 per cent while purchased inputs increased by 38 per cent. Hired labour, which was included in purchased inputs, declined by more than 50 per cent for the period; thus inputs purchased from the rest of the economy increased even more than the increase in purchased inputs as measured.[4] In this comparison, purchased inputs included capital items as well as interest paid and rent to non-farmers. The non-purchased inputs were those supplied by the farm operator and his family.

Power: Animal and Mechanical

The modernization of agriculture in the industrial countries has depended on an enormous increase in the amount of power available for the farm production process. Man alone or man plus animal draft power can cultivate only a limited area. The United States achieved a high level of agricultural technology and mechanization based on horse power in the 1910–19 decade. During that decade there were approximately 2.5 horses for each farm worker (about 25 million horses and mules and about 11.5 million farm workers). The total harvested crop area was a little less than 140 million hectares or 13 hectares per farm worker with associated power and machinery. The output from 31 million hectares of harvested land was required to provide feed for the animal power; a substantial area of pastureland was also required for the draft animals.[5] The horse has now disappeared from the American commercial farms. In 1977 there were 3.2 million farm workers; they harvested a total of 130 million hectares of crops, or an average of 40 hectares per worker or three times the pre-First World War average.

In the transition from the use of animal to mechanical power, the output of farm products available for human use increases more rapidly than the value added by agriculture or the equivalent gross domestic product. The feed used by horses as a source of energy is replaced by other forms of energy, principally petroleum products for tractors, but increasingly by whatever sources of energy are used to produce electricity.

One consequence of the substitution of mechanical sources of power for animal power is that the potential amount of power that can be utilized is so much greater than is possible when primary reliance is on animal power. If one assumes that a horse delivers one horsepower, this means that during the 1910s American agriculture had a maximum of 25 million horsepower available from this source. By 1950, when horses were no longer an important source of power, the horsepower available from tractors was 93 million; by 1985 it was in excess of 300 million.[6] If *all* of the crop output of American agriculture had been used to provide feed for horses, the maximum amount of horsepower that would have been available in 1985 would have been about 200 million. There are other major sources of power now available on farms, such as trucks and electric motors, that add significantly to the total power supply.

The shift from animal to mechanical sources of power is an important source of the apparent inherent capacity of agriculture in the industrial countries to expand output for sale or use more rapidly than demand during the transition since the Second World War. Some part of the relatively rapid growth of marketable farm output in the industrial countries since the 1950s has resulted from the displacement of horses by tractors and other sources of power.

This shift is documented in Table 4.4 for Western Europe, the United States and Britain since 1955. The rapid adoption of tractors in Western Europe had resulted, by 1970, in more tractors per 1000 hectares of arable land than in the United States. In 1970 the European Community (original Six) had 89 tractors per 1000 hectares compared with 24 in the United States. By 1986 there were 123 tractors per 1000 hectares in the Community, 25 in the United States and 76 in the

United Kingdom. Not only were there more tractors, they were more powerful.

Table 4.4   Horses and tractors in agriculture, 1955, 1970, 1980 and 1986 (horses and tractors are in thousands)

	1955	1970	1980	1986
United States				
Horses[a]	4309	–	–	–
Tractors	4480	4584	4775	4670
Tractors/1000 Farm Workers	667	1285	1353	1476
Tractors/1000 HA of Arable Land	24[b]	24	25	25
European Community (EC-6)				
Horses	4443[c]	1420	1123	–
Tractors	1067	3445	4333	4418
Tractors/1000 Farm Workers	59[d]	364	647	806
Tractors/1000 HA of Arable Land	22[b]	89	122	123
United Kingdom				
Horses	274[c]	144	140	–
Tractors	422	447	502	515
Tractors/1000 Farm Workers	367	572	693	699
Tractors/1000 HA of Arable Land	59	63	74	76

[a]Data for 1970, 1980 and 1986 not available. Horses that remain on farms are not used for tractive power.
[b]Arable land data for Luxembourg and the United States are for 1954 rather than 1955.
[c]October–September 1954/55.
[d]Employment data for the Netherlands and Luxembourg are for 1956 rather than 1955.
Sources: *Production Yearbook*, FAO, Rome, for 1956, 1957, 1958, 1972, 1976, 1981 and 1986; *Statistical Yearbook 1979–80* (New York: United Nations, 1981); *The Agricultural Situation in the Community*, Commission of the European Community, Brussels, reports for 1981 and 1987; *Labour Force Statistics*, OECD, Paris, for 1955–66 and 1969–80; and *Manpower Statistics, 1954–1964* (Paris: OECD, 1965).

The number of tractors per 1000 farm workers has also grown to an impressive figure in the European Community, in the original Six (806), and in the United Kingdom (699). These compare with 1476 per 1000 workers in the United States in 1986.

When a farmer buys a tractor, he finds himself in much the same situation as the lady who buys a new dress and, much to the distress of her husband, discovers she needs new shoes, a handbag and hat, at a minimum. The tractor requires, for its efficient use, a complement of machinery rather different than that used with horses. While tractors can generally pull the same machinery formerly used with horses, the labour-saving potential of the tractor is enhanced by machines designed for use with the tractor. These machines incorporate such features as hydraulic attachments and are generally designed to operate at greater speeds than can be maintained by horses. As a consequence, the farmers of the industrial countries now have very substantial investments in machinery and equipment.

The agriculture of the industrial countries has become, or is becoming, highly capital intensive. While similar data do not appear to be available for other countries, it is worth noting that total investment per worker in American agriculture is greater than in manufacturing. In 1986 the total investment in production assets, excluding farm land and buildings, per farm worker was $46 000. If land and buildings are included, it is $205 000. This compares with capital per production worker in manufacturing of $35 200.[7]

Reduction in Farm Employment

The most important adjustment that has occurred in the agricultures of the industrial market economies since the Second World War has been the large decline in farm employment. While detailed national data on annual rates of decline in farm employment for periods starting with 1960 are given in Table 11.4, here it is sufficient to note the large magnitude of the decline over a period of two or three decades. In the European Community (of Nine), farm employment declined by half from 1965 to 1985 – from somewhat more than 15 million to less than 7.5 million. In the United States, in the two decades from 1950 to 1970, farm employment also declined by a half or slightly more – from 7.2 million to 3.5 million. While in Japan the farm population declined very slowly over the past three decades, between 1960 and 1980 farm employment fell by more than 55 per cent. The annual compound rates of decline were very large – from 3.4 to 4.2 per cent.

Based on past experience, I doubt if most readers have gained an adequate conception of the magnitude of the adjustments that have been involved in the reductions of farm employment and the transfers of labour out of agriculture. Thus, even at the expense of what may appear to be some repetition, certain additional information will be presented on this important topic.

When it is said that farm employment has declined by about 3.5 per cent annually, this does not give a full picture of the amount of migration that has to occur from farm to non-farm areas or occupations. Consider a concrete example. The annual rate of decline in farm employment in the United States between 1955 and 1968 was 4.1 per cent. In 1955 the United States farm population was 19.1 million; and it was 10.5 million in 1968, a reduction of 8.6 million. Employment in agriculture was 6.4 million in 1955 and 3.8 million in 1968; thus the absolute reduction in farm population was more than 3.5 times as great as the reduction in employment. The first point that needs to be recognized is that a reduction of employment by one person involves two to three additional persons transferring out of the farm population.

Furthermore, the number of persons who migrated from farm to non-farm areas was greater than the reduction in the farm population. The farm population is subject to natural increase and an amount of migration equal to the natural increase must occur before there is a decline in farm population or employment. In order to achieve a reduction of the farm population of 8.6 million a total of 10.7 million persons had to migrate from farm to town or city.[8]

From 1950 to 1968, based on data for five-year periods except for 1965–68, the annual net migration from farms to non-farm areas in the United States ranged from 5.2 to 6.3 per cent.[9] Thus, on the average, each year more than one-twentieth of the farm population moved from a farm to a town or city during this period. Similar data do not seem to be available for Western European countries, but it appears that the same rates of migration off the farm occurred in several of the countries, at least until 1980.

Between 1968 and 1980 farm employment in the European Community (original Six) declined from 12.1 million to 7.6 million; the reduction was 36 per cent.[10] In 1970 the agricultural population in the Six was 2.4 times the labour force engaged in agriculture.[11] Thus the individuals involved in the reduction of farm employment during the period was not 4.5 million, but nearly 11 million. This means that almost a million persons were involved each year in the process that resulted in a 37 per cent reduction in the farm labour force over a twelve-year period.

The data on the large number of individuals who have left farms in certain industrial countries have been emphasized to illustrate what is required to achieve a 3 to 4 per cent annual reduction in farm employment. The data also give an indication of how high the mobility of the farm population actually has been and continues to be in some countries. Annually in the Western industrial countries the number of farm people who voluntarily chose not to be farmers has been in the millions. Each year millions reacted positively to opportunities that they consider to be preferable to remaining in agriculture, although as of the late 1980s the absolute level of migration is much smaller than earlier because the farm population has been reduced by the migration. The necessity for making this choice is both one of the costs of economic growth and an indication that the non-farm sectors of these economies are providing opportunities for people reared on farms. While one can be impressed by the difficulties and sadness that may be involved in leaving one's home community, one should not forget how much greater the poverty and disappointment would be if the millions who have moved had been forced to remain in agricultural occupations because there were no opportunities elsewhere.

While this point will be emphasized in Chapter 11, the cost of the labour adjustment process in the industrial countries was substantially less in the late 1980s than in the previous decades. There are several reasons for this – the improvement in communications (telephones, radio and television), the reduction in the costs of transport due to all-weather rural roads and the availability of car and bus transport, and the rapid growth of off-farm employment for farm people. Increasingly the transfer of labour out of agriculture has occurred by one or more family members accepting non-farm employment while retaining their farm residence. In the United States in 1986, the off-farm income of farm-operator families at $45 billion exceeded the net farm income of $38 billion; the latter figure included nearly $12 billion in government payments.[12]

Fertilizer

The use of chemical fertilizers is not a recent development in Western Europe. Before the Second World War, Western Europe used half or more of the major plant nutrients applied as commercial fertilizer in the world. But since the early 1950s the use of fertilizer in the major industrial countries has grown 'by leaps and bounds'. The increased use of fertilizer made a major contribution to the increase in grain yields in the developed countries from an average level of 1.26 tons per hectare in 1948–52 to 2.63 tons in 1979–81 and to 2.83 tons in 1983–85.[13] Other changes that contributed to higher yields also occurred, such as improved seeds, more timely seeding and harvesting due to mechanization and the use of pesticides and herbicides, but the increase in yields would have been much smaller if the huge increase in fertilizer use had not occurred. For the grain yield levels now prevalent in Western Europe, the United States and Japan, chemical fertilizers are a necessary condition; any significant reduction in the use of fertilizer would result in lower yields.

In the OECD countries the total use of plant nutrients derived from commercial fertilizer increased by 89 per cent between 1955–59 and 1965–69; this was an annual rate of increase of seven per cent. The growth in nitrogen use was the largest at 147 per cent. Very high rates of fertilizer application per hectare of arable land were achieved by 1965–69, with the Netherlands having the highest use rate for nitrogen and Belgium for phosphate and potash among OECD members at the time.[14] The use of fertilizer per hectare in Canada and the United States was modest in both 1970 and 1984 compared to Western Europe and Japan. Fertilizer use increased between 1970 and 1984 but at the much slower rate of about 1.5 per cent annually in the OECD countries.[15]

Between 1955–59 and 1965–69 the increase in the use of nitrogen in the OECD countries was 8.1 million tons. If one uses the rough approximation that the average productivity of a ton of nitrogen is 10 tons of grain, the increase in the use of nitrogen would have been associated with an increase of grain production of 81 million tons. Not all of the nitrogen was applied to grain crops but it is not altogether inappropriate to note that, over the same period of time, grain production increased by approximately 95 million tons.[16] The marginal product of nitrogen is clearly less than 10; perhaps half that. Obviously other inputs besides nitrogen are required to produce the additional grain. To achieve the average product of nitrogen of 10 units of grain requires appropriate changes in other inputs, such as seed varieties, rates of seeding, and application of insecticides and herbicides.

Agriculture Today and Yesterday

It is difficult for many who can now observe the highly complex and productive agriculture of Western Europe and North America to realize that as late as the early part of the nineteenth century the agriculture of these regions would have been hardly distinguishable from what one can observe today in the developing areas of the world, such as South Asia. Except for the United Kingdom, the percentage of the population dependent on agriculture was in the range of 60 to 80 per cent throughout Western Europe and North America; this is approximately the situation today in the developing regions. Thus in terms of the total history of man, modern agriculture is a recent phenomenon with a period of development of only a little more than a century. Even as late as the 1930s grain yields in the industrial countries were at the same level as in the developing regions. As recently as a half century or so ago, the sources of power used in agriculture were the same as those now used in developing countries.

Comparing the amount of farm land per farm worker in India in the 1960s with the amount in the (now) industrial regions at the end of the nineteenth century, we find these differences are not as great as many might expect. As late as 1880 there was about 7 hectares of agricultural land per male farm worker in France compared with about 2 hectares in India in 1965. Total agricultural output per hectare of agricultural land in France in 1880 and in India in 1965 were the same. Agricultural output per farm worker in France in 1880 was only 3.5 times as large as in India in 1965, but by 1965 farm output per worker was about 20 times as large in France as in India in that year. Denmark, which today has one of the most technically advanced agricultures in the world, had in 1880 about five times as much land per male worker and five times as much output per worker as India in 1965. By 1965, Denmark still had only about five times as much agricultural land per farm worker as India, but output per male farm worker had increased to 25 times that of India. Both in 1880 and in 1970 Japan had less farm land per agricultural worker than India. In 1880, its output per farm worker was about the same as India's in 1965, but by 1970 its output per farm worker was six times that of India's and its output per hectare of farm land was seven times.[17]

Throughout its history, from the beginning of European settlement, the United States has had a favourable land-to-labour ratio. Output per worker has been high and output per unit of land has been relatively low compared with either industrial or developing countries. As of 1880 there was about fifteen times more land per farm worker in the United States than there was in India in 1965; output per worker was about six times greater in the United States in 1880 than in India in 1965. By 1980 in the United States there was approximately 247 hectares of farm land per worker, or about 123 times the amount per worker in India. Output per worker in the United States was more than 90 times greater than in India in 1980.

A striking indication of how much change occurred over the century ending in 1960 is provided by Table 4.5. It provides a comparison of critical features of the agriculture of the United States, Japan and India as of 1960 and 1980. There is an amazing difference in the quantities of important inputs associated with a farm worker among the three countries.

Table 4.5 Agricultural output per male farm worker and per hectare, inputs per male farm worker and levels of education and research and extension in the United States, Japan and India, 1960 and 1980

	United States		Japan		India		United States Japan		United States India	
	1960	1980	1960	1980	1960	1980	1960	1980	1960	1980
Agricultural output (wheat units/worker)	93.8	285	10.3	27.8	2.20	3.1	9.1	10.3	42.6	91.9
Agricultural output (wheat units/hectare)	0.80	1.16	8.64	12.23	1.06	1.58	0.1	0.095	0.75	0.73
Agricultural land (hectares/worker)	117	247	1.2	2.3	2.0	2.0	97.5	107.4	58.5	123.5
Fertilizer (metric tons/worker)	1.9	11.0	0.3	0.9	0.004	0.018	6.3	12.2	475	611
Machinery[a] (horsepower/worker)	41.4	151.8	1.0	17.7	0.008	0.148	41.4	8.6	5175	1026
Education[b] (school enrolment ratios)	99	100	8.8	9.4	28	51	1.12	1.06	3.5	2.0
Research and extension (graduates from agricultural colleges per 10 000 workers)	21	135	13	58	0.4	1.0	1.6	2.4	52.5	1350

[a] Horsepower of tractors only.
[b] Percentage of children in primary and secondary schools.
Source: Yujiro Hayami and Vernon W. Ruttan, *Agricultural Development: an International Perspective*, revised edition (Baltimore: Johns Hopkins Press, 1985), pp. 120 and 457–59.

The differences in the factors that cooperate with labour and the amount of education of farm workers explain virtually all of the differences in output per worker. Thus it cannot be said that the Indian farm operator and worker is less efficient or effective than the farm operator and worker in the United States or Japan; the Indian farm operator and worker functions in a much less affluent setting.[18]

The purpose of the above comparisons is not to show the superiority of the agriculture of the industrial countries over that of the developing countries. The objective is quite the contrary, namely that if you move

back into history by a century the agricultures of the now industrial
countries were not all that different from the agricultures of the Indian
subcontinent today. The rapid change in agriculture in the industrial
countries over the century has not been due primarily to conditions
over which farmers had control, but rather to the rapid general
development of such economies. Unfortunately, the agriculture of the
developing countries still depends primarily upon land and labour for
its productivity, although the 1960s through the 1980s brought forth
some significant changes through new seeds, fertilizer and irrigation.
While grain yields in the developing countries are lower than in the
industrial countries, between 1969–71 and 1983–85, grain yields in the
developing market economies increased by 34 per cent, while in the
industrial market economies the increase was 24 per cent. In 1983–85,
however, the developing countries' grain yields were 1661 kilograms
per hectare compared with 3577 kilograms for the developed country.[19]

Agriculture Must Change

In the previous chapter a few of the recent changes in agriculture in the industrial countries were described. The purpose was primarily to emphasize the rapidity with which agriculture has adjusted in the period since the Second World War. It was shown that the organization of agriculture in Western Europe, North America, Japan and Oceania was capable of large and numerous adjustments to changing conditions and that many of these adjustments were made with remarkable speed. The chapter was also intended to make clear that policy-makers who fail to recognize the speed of adjustment that is possible in modern agriculture do so at considerable risk. Policies that are based on the assumption that agriculture is relatively static and subject to slow rates of change will have a series of effects that are largely unintended and undesired; and such policies will become far more costly than anticipated.

The ability of modern agriculture to adjust to changing conditions is a highly desirable characteristic despite the fact that it is this ability that negates most of the efforts of governments to improve farm incomes by such sector-specific measures as price supports and deficiency payments. The reason why this ability is a desirable characteristic is that an economy with increasing per capita incomes requires that agriculture undergo continuous change and adjustment. Unfortunately for farm people, the necessary adjustments to the changing conditions of a growing economy all lead in one direction – agriculture becomes a declining industry at an early point in economic growth if growth is defined in terms of increases in per capita income. A declining industry is defined as one whose share of national output and national employment declines as real per capita incomes increase. When per capita real incomes are low but increasing and population growth is occurring, the number of workers employed in agriculture may increase absolutely while declining as a percentage of national employment. But in all of the major industrial countries a time came when employment in agriculture declined absolutely as well as relatively.

A necessary condition for the decline of agriculture is that as the income of a person or family increases, that person or family spends a smaller percentage of the increased income on food, than was true of the previous increase in income. Or stated slightly differently, the larger is a family's income, the smaller is the percentage of that income spent on food. This relationship between income level and expenditures on

72

food was discovered by a German civil servant and statistician, Ernst Engel, who published his results in 1857. He based his conclusion on the study of family budgets. His discovery was one of the earliest empirically-based generalizations in economics and ranks in importance with the much earlier empirical verification of the inverse relationship between the price of a commodity and the quantity demanded for all products following the normal law of demand. The implications of Engel's Law are clear: the more income people have, the smaller percentage of it will they spend on food.

Income Elasticity of Demand for Food

In more modern terminology we would say that the income elasticity of demand for food is less than unity. The income elasticity of demand for a commodity or service is defined as

$$\frac{\text{percentage increase in expenditure}}{\text{percentage increase in income}} \text{ or } \frac{\dfrac{\Delta E}{E}}{\dfrac{\Delta Y}{Y}}$$

where E is the expenditure on a given commodity, Y is income, ΔY is the change in income and ΔE is the change in expenditure associated with the change in income or Y. Stated somewhat more elegantly, the income elasticity of demand is

$$\frac{d \log E}{d \log Y} \text{ or } \frac{dE}{dY}\frac{Y}{E}.$$

To illustrate the calculation of the income elasticity of demand for food, assume a family with a per capita income of $1000 and a per capita expenditure on food of $300. The per capita income of the family increases by $20 and its per capita expenditures on food increase by $3. The increase in food expenditures is 1 per cent and the increase in income is 2 per cent; the income elasticity of demand is 0.5. One of the implications of an income elasticity of demand of less than unity is that the percentage of income spent on food at the margin is less than the average percentage of income spent on food. Before the increase in income, 30 per cent of our assumed family's income was spent on food; of the increase in income of $20, only 15 per cent is spent on food. In this example, the average propensity to consume food is 0.3 while the marginal propensity is 0.15, just half of the average.

Engel's Law, when stated in terms of income elasticity of demand, is very simple. The income elasticity of demand for food is less than unity if Engel's Law is valid. And a vast amount of empirical research has indicated that except under very unusual circumstances, such as a period immediately after a famine, Engel's Law is valid. It appears to be valid at all levels of per capita annual income of $150 or more (as of the mid-1980s). The reason for the validity of Engel's Law as applied to food is a simple one, although it may at first appear to be somewhat paradoxical.

Food is a necessity; like water and air, food is a necessary condition for the maintenance of life. Life is not possible, except for a few days, without food. Thus at very low income levels people are primarily concerned with obtaining enough food to maintain life and sustain the required body functions for some level of work.[1] At very low levels of income, as much as 70 per cent of all income will be used to obtain food. As income increases, people can make more choices concerning their expenditures. More food may be desired to increase the number of calories available or to add variety or to provide certain nutrients in more adequate quantities. But as increased incomes make possible consumption choices among a wider range of goods and services, people will choose new goods and services as well as more of the goods and services now being consumed, such as housing, clothing, fuel and similar items that contribute to health and comfort. But having already more nearly satisfied their desires for food than for any other item of consumption, a smaller fraction of the additional income will be spent on food than was true of the average expenditure percentage prior to the increase in income.

The fact that food is a necessity has influenced governmental policies towards agriculture and has frequently resulted in an argument made by farmers that they deserve particular care and attention from society because their production is essential to life. During a war, or in a period in which there is a serious threat of war, no government likes to be in a position in which it may face the loss of a significant part of the country's food supply due to an embargo or blockade. Thus it has been fairly common in the history of man to find governments following a policy to expand domestic production of food in order to strengthen its position during an actual or possible war. This posture on the part of governments has or, probably more correctly, had a certain validity.

But the view of farmers that their position should be a special one in a modern industrial society because their main products are necessities has little merit or persuasive power. There are two reasons for this conclusion. First, in high-income countries, consumers want to and do spend most of their additional income on goods and services other than food. In a high-income country, producing a necessity does not grant one any special favours or blessings if governments act rationally. Second, in high-income countries most of the foods consumed do not fall in the category of necessities. Nutritionally adequate diets could be provided for the populations of the industrial countries with only a fraction of the total calories now utilized to provide for both direct and indirect consumption. The indirect consumption refers to the calories used as feed to produce livestock and poultry products. Most of the food consumed by most consumers in Western Europe, for example, is consumed because people 'want' to consume it and not because it is required for a diet that is nutritionally adequate for the maintenance of life, good health and physical vigour.

More than half of the original calories produced on farms in the industrial countries is used to feed livestock and not for direct consumption by people. The amount of livestock products required for a nutritionally adequate diet is only a small fraction of the amount actually consumed in the industrial countries. While this fact largely negates any presumption that agriculture in the industrial countries warrants special favours because food is a necessity, were it not the preference of high-income consumers to consume additional amounts of livestock products as their incomes increase, agricultural employment would be an even smaller fraction of total employment than it is now.

Declining Relative Demand for Food

As long as the income elasticity of demand for food is greater than zero, an increase in per capita income will result in some increase in the amount of food demanded, assuming constant prices. So why is an income elasticity of demand of less than unity of such critical importance in requiring change in agriculture? The reason is that the income elasticity of demand for all goods and services produced in an economy is unity under conditions of full employment and departs from unity only slightly during periods of moving away from or back towards full employment. If the income elasticity of demand for food is less than unity, the income elasticity of demand for all other goods and services is greater than unity. When per capita real income increases, the demand for food will increase by less, proportionately, than the increase in income; and the demand for everything else will increase proportionately more than the increase in income. Put another way, the rate of increase in the demand for food will be less than the rate of increase in the demand for everything else.

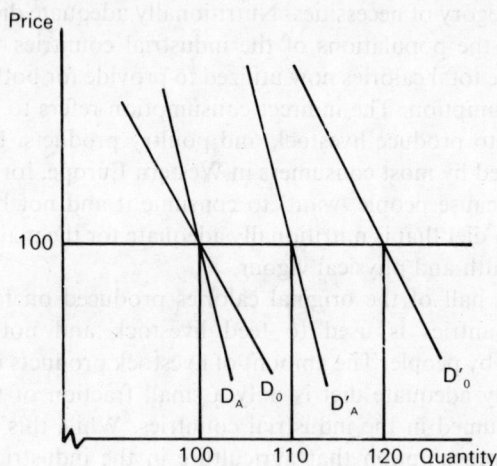

Price

100

D_A D_0 D'_A D'_0

100   110   120   Quantity

Figure 5.1

Figure 5.1 illustrates how the demand for food (D_A) and for all other goods and services (D_0) might change over time as real per capita incomes increase. For the period involved, it is assumed that real per capita incomes increase by 20 per cent, that at the beginning of the period half of all expenditures are for food, and that the income elasticity of demand for food is 0.5 and 1.5 for all other goods and services. Since half of all expenditures are for food, this means that the income elasticity of demand for all goods and services is unity at the beginning of the period and will be unity at the end of the period, by definition.

As indicated in Figure 5.1 the 20 per cent increase in per capita income increases the quantity of food demanded at constant prices by 10 per cent during the period; however, the increase in the quantity demanded for all other goods and services is 30 per cent or three times as great. For illustrative purposes, the demand curves for food and all other goods and services have been drawn through the same quantity and price point at the beginning of the period. Partly to facilitate comparison, the price elasticity of demand for food at the price and quantity circumstances at the beginning of the period is smaller than the price elasticity of demand for all other goods and services. It is generally assumed, and probably rightly so, that the price elasticity of demand for food is lower than for all other goods and services.

Shifts in Demand and Supply

Figure 5.2 (in two parts for clarity) indicates what would happen over the same period of time if the supply functions for agricultural products (S_A) and all other goods and services (S_0) shifted in exactly the same degree. In the diagram it is assumed that at constant relative prices the supply of both agricultural and all other products and services would increase by 20 per cent between period t_0 and period t_1; in other words, both supply functions would shift to the right by 20 per cent if the prices of period t_0 were maintained. It is clear that if the demand and supply curves shifted as depicted in Figure 5.2a, agricultural prices would fall, as in Figures 5.2a and 5.2b here and all other prices would rise. Figure 5.3 depicts what must happen if there is to be no change in the relative price of agricultural products. In this case the supply function for agricultural products can shift by only 10 per cent while the other supply function must shift by 30 per cent.

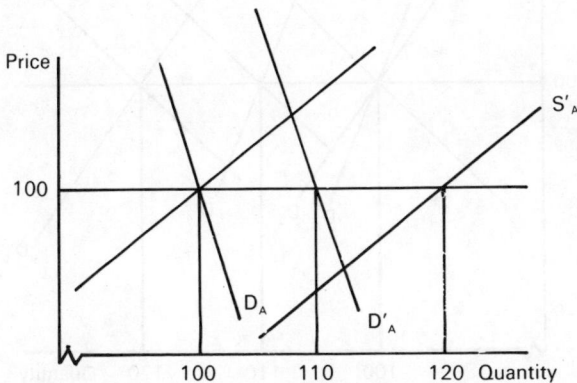

Figure 5.2a

These simple diagrams illustrate why agriculture is a declining industry when per capita incomes increase. In the first period agriculture was responsible for 50 per cent of the total output of the economy;

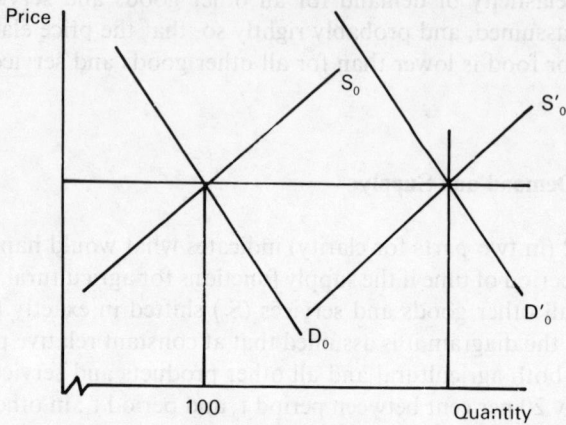

Figure 5.2b

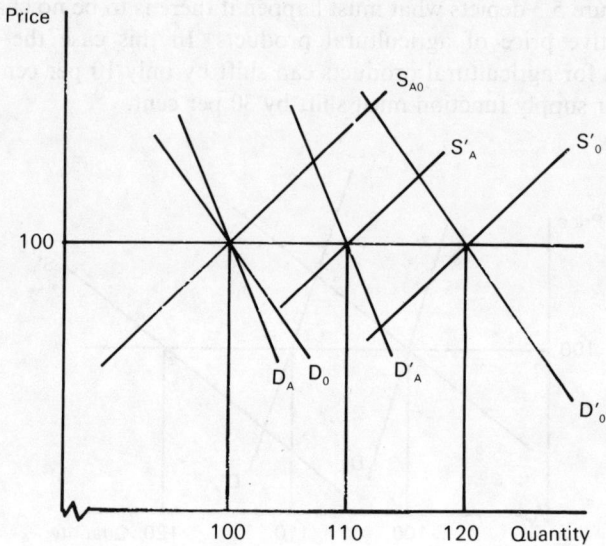

Figure 5.3

at the end of the period it was responsible for only 46 per cent. If at the beginning of the period 50 per cent of the labour force were engaged in agriculture, at the end it would be 46 per cent. Thus agriculture must decline relatively because the demand growth for its output is slower than for the output of the rest of the economy.

Zero or Negative Income Elasticities

Up to this point in the discussion it has been noted that the income elasticity of demand for food is less than unity. The possibility that the income elasticity of demand for some individual foods may be zero or negative cannot be ruled out. A zero income elasticity means that changes in per capita income will not result in an increase in demand or consumption at constant prices. A negative income elasticity means that quantity demanded will actually decline as per capita income increases; in other words, the demand curve will shift to the left when income grows. After a country reaches a particular per capita income level, the per capita consumption of some food products does decline. The main candidates for declining demand due to income growth are rye, wheat and potatoes. In the United States the per capita consumption of wheat as a food has declined since 1909 from about 98 kilograms per capita to 56 kilograms in 1980. Potato consumption per capita was about 82–86 kilograms in the second decade of this century and declined to a low of 47 kilograms in 1956; since that date with the further development of potato chips, frozen potato products and 'instant' mashed potatoes, per capita consumption increased to 54 kilograms by 1980.[2]

That the American experience is not unique is indicated by the simple tabulations in Table 5.1 for developments in per capita consumption between 1960 and 1985/86 for three members of the European Community for wheat, rye and potatoes. Between the late 1950s and 1985/86 there were significant declines in the per capita consumption of the two cereals and potatoes in both West Germany and France. Italy, which had a significantly lower per capita income than the other two countries during this period, did not have a decline in per capita consumption of wheat by the mid-1960s, but wheat consumption declined with the much higher per capita incomes.

The general order of income elasticities of demand for food products is given in Table 5.2. These are estimates published by the Food and Agriculture Organization in 1971 and were used for projections for 1980. There are several aspects of Table 5.2 that are worthy of note. First, none of the income elasticities of demand for North America,

World Agriculture in Disarray

Table 5.1 Per capita consumption of wheat, rye and potatoes in West Germany, France and Italy, 1960, 1965 and 1985/86

	Per capita use as food (in kilograms)		
	1960	1965	1985/86
West Germany			
Wheat	72	66	52
Rye	29	23	14
Potatoes	133	113	78
France			
Wheat	130	116	70
Rye	1	1	–
Potatoes	118	102	75
Italy			
Wheat	160	166	107
Rye	2	1	–
Potatoes	44	42	35

Source: *Agriculture Statistical Yearbook 1988* (Luxembourg: Statistical Office of the European Community, 1988).

Oceania and Western Europe exceed unity; the highest is 0.5 for Ireland for cheese. Second, the income elasticities of demand for cereals are negative for all of the industrial countries and, if one excludes Japan, are 0.15 or less for fats and oils and dairy products. Third, of the commodities included in the table only meat and eggs have elasticities that are approximately 0.5, and even for these commodities there are examples of income elasticities that approximate to zero. As expected, the lower income countries or regions do have higher income elasticities of demand than the industrial countries.

Income Elasticities of Demand for Food Decline with Economic Growth

The fourth important relationship that can be derived from Table 5.2 is that the size of income elasticities is inversely related to the level of per capita income. The last column of the table is a measure of the income elasticity of demand for food at the farm level and is an average of the income elasticities of the various food products. If one tabulates the gross national product per capita and the income elasticities as

Table 5.2   Income elasticities of demand for food products

	Cereals	Sugar	Fats and oils[a]	Whole milk	Butter	Cheese	Meat	Eggs	Farm value
North America	−0.25	0.10	−0.01	−0.47	−0.45	0.43	0.26	−0.10	0.05
European Community[b]	−0.29	0.31	0.13	0.08	0.17	0.42	0.48	0.32	0.25
Oceania	−0.10	−0.09	0.04	−0.01	−0.09	0.39	0.05	0.00	0.09
Denmark	−0.32	0.00	−0.09	−0.10	−0.30	0.30	0.19	0.30	0.15
Ireland	−0.29	0.10	−0.05	−0.10	−0.20	0.50	0.33	−0.10	0.10
United Kingdom	−0.19	0.00	0.04	−0.10	0.00	0.20	0.18	0.00	0.09
Greece	−0.26	0.70	0.10	0.40	0.20	0.30	0.59	0.60	0.28
Sweden	−0.31	0.00	0.09	−0.20	−0.20	0.30	0.17	0.10	0.09
Japan	−0.07	0.39	0.40	0.50	1.20	1.00	0.79	0.50	0.28
Africa	−0.25	3.23	0.23	1.20	1.44	3.71	1.44	0.32	0.42
Near East	−0.02	0.43	0.44	0.68	0.32	0.41	0.59	0.57	0.29
Asia and Far East	0.25	0.79	0.70	1.03	0.61	0.46	1.06	1.15	0.51
South Asia	0.25	0.91	0.83	1.18	0.69	0.54	1.20	1.15	0.59
Latin America	0.05	0.20	0.50	0.53	0.55	0.45	0.33	0.62	0.29

[a]Includes butter.
[b]Original six members.
Source: *Agricultural Commodity Projections, 1970–1980* (Rome: FAO, 1971) Vol. II, Table 13.

measured by farm value, the relationship shown in Table 5.3 is obtained.

Thus it is not only that income elasticities of demand for food are low in the industrial countries, but the income elasticities decline as real per capita incomes increase. Not only does the demand for food grow more slowly than the demand for all other goods and services but the relative discrepancies between the growth rates increase as real incomes rise. The above tabulation can be used to illustrate this statement. If the income elasticity of demand for food is 0.5 and food constituted about a third of total expenditures, the income elasticity of demand for all other goods and services would be about 1.3; an income elasticity of 0.15 is associated with about a fifth of total expenditures being for food and an income elasticity of demand for all other goods and services of about 1.05. At the income level of $2000 to $3000 per capita, the growth in demand for food due to an increase in per capita income would be about 10 per cent as great as the growth in demand for all other goods and services. At a per capita income level of $4000, the

Table 5.3   Relationships between per capita national incomes and income
              elasticities of demand at farm values

	1970 per capita national income	Farm value elasticity
North America	4200	0.05
Sweden	3721	0.09
Denmark	2992	0.15
European Community[a]	2250	0.25
Oceania	2110	0.09
United Kingdom	2037	0.09
Japan	1690	0.28
Ireland	1230	0.08
Greece	1090	0.28
Latin America	550[b]	0.29
Africa	190	0.42
Asia and Far East[c]	120	0.51

[a]Income elasticity is for the original six members, while national income is for the Nine.
[b]Includes the Caribbean.
[c]Excludes Japan.
Source: *Statistical Yearbook 1979–80* (New York: United Nations, 1981) and Table 5.2.

growth in demand for food would be only 5 per cent as great as for all other goods and services. The income figures are in 1970 dollars.

I have used food and agricultural products more or less interchangeably in the discussion of demand growth as a result of increasing per capita incomes. Would the specific recognition of fibres, primarily cotton and wool, change the conclusions that have been reached? The income elasticities for textile fibres are of roughly the same order of magnitude as for food products as a whole. According to FAO estimates, as of the late 1950s, the income elasticity of demand for cotton and wool was 0.5 in the European Community, 0.15 in Canada, 0.0 in the United States, 0.3 in Oceania and generally from 0.9 to 1.1 in the developing countries.[3] These estimates do not reflect the continuing inroads that were made into the markets for wool and cotton by the synthetic fibres since they were made under the assumption of constant shares of the market for natural and man-made fibres.

The high-income industrial countries have now reached the stage where further increases in per capita income will have little effect on the level of demand for all farm products – because the income elasticities are negative. Further increases in per capita incomes will reduce the per capita consumption of several food products – the cereals, sugar, fats and oils and some dairy products. Some food products do have positive income elasticities at the highest level of per capita income yet achieved. But it is clear that in the aggregate further increases in per capita income in the major industrial countries will absorb only a small part of further farm output increases.

The above discussion has ignored an important element affecting the growth in demand for food and other products, although the introduction of population growth does not negate any of the relations in the patterns of demand growth. Aside from the introduction of new products, the two primary variables that affect demand growth are income and population changes. Population growth does not have a differential effect on demand growth, if we assume that all other important variables (such as per capita income, age distribution and relative prices) remain unchanged. In other words, the population elasticity of demand is unity for all goods and services. It is true that an increase in density of population may have a modest effect on relative demands for garbage disposal or elevators, but these effects seem small enough to be safely ignored for present purposes.

Population and Growth of Demand

If relative prices are constant, the growth in demand for any commodity or service can be depicted as follows: $\dot{D} = e \cdot \dot{Y} + \dot{P}$. where $\dot{D}$, $\dot{Y}$ and $\dot{P}$ are growth rates of quantity demanded, per capita income and population, respectively, and e is the income elasticity of demand for a particular commodity or group of commodities. If the income elasticity of demand is 0.5, $\dot{Y}$ is 3 per cent and $\dot{P}$ is 1 per cent, $\dot{D}$ will be 2.5 per cent. For given growth rates of income and population, the relative importance of population as a demand shifter is larger the smaller is the income elasticity of demand. But in no case can population growth completely offset the effect of an income elasticity of demand of less than unity on the growth of demand relative to demand growth for the rest of the economy.

In the early stages of urbanization and industrial development, population growth rates tend to increase; and in the 1970s and 1980s they were 3 per cent or more in some developing countries. As per capita income increases, however, there is a clear tendency for population growth rates to decline. These rates have now declined to 1 per cent or less in most of the high-income industrial countries. Economic growth appears to have inherent in it a limitation on the increase of the one variable that shifts the demand for food products at the same rate as for all other goods and services. In the industrial countries, demand for food and other farm products grows slowly, and then more slowly, and then more slowly still.

The relatively slow growth of demand for farm products in industrial countries necessitates that agriculture be a declining industry. Output growth in agriculture at the same rate as in the rest of the economy cannot be sustained unless exports increase very rapidly or governments stockpile or destroy increasingly large amounts of agricultural output.

Relative Growth of Supply and Demand

I have said that the structure of demand for food and farm products is such that demand grows more slowly than for all other goods and services and, too, that the relatively slow growth of demand is a necessary condition for agriculture to be a declining industry. Is it also a sufficient condition? Can one imagine no set of circumstances in which agriculture's relative importance as a source of employment or output would not decline in an economy with increasing per capita real incomes? The answer to this question is in the affirmative.

An increase in real per capita incomes means that both aggregate supply and aggregate demand are increasing and that the demand for farm products is increasing, albeit more slowly than the demand for all other goods and services. But if farm output increases more slowly than output in the rest of the economy *and* more slowly than the demand for farm products, the relative price of farm products will increase. Whether the slower growth of supply than of demand for farm products will result in an increase in the proportion of the country's labour engaged in agriculture depends on a number of factors, such as the price elasticity of demand for farm products and the inelasticity of the supply of farm products.[4]

The considerations that would result in a slow growth in the supply of farm products are also likely to result in a rather inelastic supply. The slow growth could result from a fixed quantity of land that is already well and intensively cultivated in terms of the technology and knowledge of the times. An increase in real product prices could bring forth some increase in output by encouraging additional employment of labour and other inputs. But if there are no new inputs to introduce, the law of diminishing returns will apply and the growth of output will be less than proportional to the increase in total inputs.

In these circumstances labour would not leave agriculture and it would be possible for labour to be attracted to farming from other types of employment. Relative earnings or wages would be increasing in agriculture and the increase might be enough to reverse the flow of migration that occurs generally in an economy that is growing in real per capita income.

Effects of Slow Growth of Agricultural Output on Farm Incomes

These hypothetical circumstances would appear to be beneficial to farm people. The return to land would surely increase and for persons of comparable abilities and education, wages would be as high in agriculture as elsewhere. But such gains would be largely illusory. A very real cost of such gains would be that the rate of growth of real per capita income in the economy would be less than if agriculture were a declining industry – were losing labour through migration.

Another way of putting the point of the previous paragraph is that agriculture would be making little or no contribution to economic growth in these circumstances and thus the rate of economic growth, as measured by the rise in real per capita income, would be lower than it would be if output per worker increased more rapidly. The slower rate of economic growth will result in a lower level of return to labour over a period of time. In the long run the slow rate of increase in return to labour in the economy as a whole will be reflected in the return to labour in agriculture.

While the set of circumstances postulated in this discussion has probably never prevailed in Western industrial countries, the United States has tried to create a similar situation by reducing the amount of land that could be devoted to crop production. Other factors, such as the introduction of new inputs and increased education of the farm labour force, has largely offset the effect of the land restriction. It has not been possible to reduce the rate of growth of supply below the growth of domestic demand in the United States or Western Europe.

Barring direct efforts by governments to interfere with the use of resources in agriculture, there should be no expectation that the growth of supply of farm products should lag significantly behind the growth of demand. As economic growth occurs, the forces that result in such growth are as likely to affect agriculture as the rest of the economy. One common aspect of economic growth is that agriculture becomes more like the industrial sector of the economy. The importance of land as a factor of production and as a restraint on the expansion of output declines as mechanical power replaces animal power (made possible by industrial development), as fertilizers substitute for land, and as feeding efficiency increases due to better control of disease and improved knowledge of nutrition. While the concern of the classical economists about the limited amount of land and the effect of diminishing returns as a restraint on the expansion of food production had considerable validity during the late eighteenth and early nineteenth century, the very processes that resulted in economic growth greatly reduced the significance of land as a factor of production.

As the previous chapter has made clear, agriculture can change and has changed to an amazing degree in recent decades. Land has not been a significant restraint on increasing output, and agriculture has adopted new inputs at a rate at least equivalent to the rate of adoption in the rest of the economy. Whatever hopes there may be that there are special restraints, other than the absence of incentives, to control output growth in agriculture, they have near-zero probability of being realized.

It may be more difficult to increase the output of agricultural products at the same or slightly higher cost than to increase the output of automobiles or steel or cotton textiles. But the growth of demand for food products in industrial countries is so slow that only a moderate expansion of output is required in order to maintain stable farm prices. And this moderate output expansion does not require an increase in the number of farm workers in the circumstances that prevail in such economies.

One part of the circumstances of industrial economies that is often lost sight of in the development of agricultural policy is that the objective of achieving comparable returns for non-farm and farm workers involves a moving target – rising real wages in the non-farm part of the economy. If farm workers are to retain the same relative earnings position, returns to labour in agriculture must increase year after year. The increase in the value of farm labour induces farm managers to seek substitutes for it, even when the labour is that of the farm manager. The increase in average product per farm worker described in the previous chapter can be viewed in one of two ways: (i) It is the result of using more inputs per farm worker because the cost of labour is increasing relative to all other inputs, or (ii) it is necessary to achieve an increase in the marginal productivity of farm labour equal to the increase in farm wages or other returns to farm labour. The first is a description of what is required to minimize production costs given the existing input prices, including that of labour; the second is a description of what is required if agriculture is to provide a return for labour that will induce some given number of workers to remain in agriculture. They are two different but equivalent ways of describing the same phenomenon – how agriculture adjusts to continuously rising real returns to labour.

Have the changes in the returns to labour been large relative to the prices of purchased inputs? Data for the United States illustrate the magnitude of the difference. Between 1950 and 1987 farm wage rates increased by 759 per cent while the prices paid for production inputs increased by only 350 per cent.[5] It is not surprising that farmers combined a much larger volume of other inputs with each farm worker. Without the large increase in cooperating factors, labour productivity could not have risen so much.

Decline of Agriculture will Persist

Will there be a point in the history of agriculture in the industrial countries when the need for change and the decline of farm employment will come to a halt? Short of the complete disappearance of agriculture from a country or region, there is no theoretical basis for assuming that the decline of employment opportunities in agriculture will come to an end. There is no particular magic percentage of a country's labour force that represents the minimum 'needed' in agriculture. The forces that have resulted in a declining relative demand for labour in agriculture will continue to operate in the future. The income elasticity of demand for food products will continue to decline and there is no reason why it cannot approach zero. As a consequence the discrepancy between the income elasticity of demand for food and for all other goods and services will continue to widen.

Is the conclusion that agriculture's relative importance must decline as economic growth occurs valid for a small economy whose exports and imports do not influence world market prices? In this situation the low income elasticity of demand for farm products is irrelevant or nearly so. The demand for the small country's exports is perfectly elastic and is influenced by the low income elasticity of demand only because for the world as a whole the real prices of farm products may decline over time. But even if real prices of farm products remained constant, agriculture in a small country will decline as real per capita incomes increase in that country. This would be the case even in a country that exported only agricultural and other primary products and imported only manufactured products. During the 1960s both Australia and New Zealand came very close to meeting these criteria. And neither New Zealand nor Australia have escaped the relative decline of agriculture. In 1980 agricultural employment in New Zealand was 11 per cent of national employment and in Australia it was 7 per cent.

Why does the decline occur? Farm people, it can be said, are responsible for their declining relative importance due to their behaviour as consumers and producers. As consumers, they devote a declining percentage of their incomes on food and an increasing percentage on non-traded goods and services. These vary from the services of barber shops and beauty parlours to movie theatres, educational services and transport services. Further, their increased demands for imported manufactured products require non-traded and domestically provided services to make the products available to them.

But it is primarily farm people's behaviour as producers that causes their relative decline. As is clear from Chapter 4, increases in agricultural productivity are associated with increased purchases from the non-farm economy. These purchases, again, have significant non-traded components consisting of both services and locally produced products such as farm machines, fertilizer and energy. Even when the tractor is imported, it requires locally provided maintenance and repair services. Consequently, being a small country with a comparative advantage in agriculture is not enough to avoid the relative decline of its agriculture.

There is no reason to anticipate that the sources of new inputs for agriculture will diminish as time goes by. While agriculture may decline relatively in a country's economy, its absolute size, as measured appropriately in this case by the value of its output, is likely to continue to increase. This has certainly occurred during the 1980s in Western Europe and North America. Thus the absolute gains from new inputs that reduce costs will increase in magnitude rather than diminish over time and the incentive to create the new inputs will rise rather than fall even though the relative importance of agriculture continues to decline.

New inputs for agriculture do not just happen by accident. Such inputs, and the research that makes them possible, become available in response to economic incentives. For too long we have tended to assume that discovery and invention were primarily due to idle curiosity. It is becoming quite clear that the primary causative factor is the benefit that would be derived from solving a particular problem. This causative factor seems to be as relevant whether the research and development occurs in the private or the public sector, whether the research is undertaken by Shell or by the Agricultural Experiment Station of the University of Minnesota. The one responds to direct profit possibilities; the other responds to the gains to the citizens of the state and nation that support the institution.

In their excellent study of agricultural development, Yujiro Hayami and the American economist Vernon Ruttan showed how the research organizations and input industries responded to the very different circumstances of agriculture in Japan and the United States. In Japan the scarce factor was land, while in the United States it was labour. In the one case the primary emphasis was upon finding substitutes for land; in the other, research and development activities were designed to save labour. They conclude:

> the history of agricultural innovation in Japan and the United States is consistent with the proposition that innovative efforts in both the private sector and the public sector have been directed toward saving the relatively scarce factors of production. In both countries advances in mechanical and biological technology responded to changing relative factor prices and the prices of factors relative to products to ease the constraints imposed by inelastic supplies of land and labour.[6]

As in the past, so will it be in the future. The flow of innovations available to agriculture will not diminish so long as such innovations offer prospects for profit. Since it is inevitable that farm labour will continue to become more expensive relative to output prices, there will be a continuing incentive for the creation of innovations that will provide effective substitutes for labour. And if current farm policies of the industrial countries are continued, with most of the benefits going to land and resulting in higher land prices, there will be a permanent incentive to search for innovations that will substitute for land. Innovation and change are inevitable. Some change, however, may be counter-productive if it is change induced by farm policies that are already inducing too many resources to enter agriculture.

6 Agricultural Prices and the Use of Resources

As noted in Chapter 2, many governments attempt to use prices as a means of achieving income objectives for their farmers. It is hoped that higher output prices would result in higher and more satisfactory farm incomes. As argued later (Chapter 9), such an expectation has little realism. The aim in this chapter is to illustrate some of the effects of distortions in prices on the use of farm resources.

As has already been shown, there are wide differences in the level of farm product prices among the various industrial nations. If farmers did not respond to prices of outputs and inputs, these wide differences would primarily reflect differing degrees of income transfers to the various producer groups within agriculture. On the other hand, if farmers do respond to changes in prices, the use of prices as a means of increasing income has effects on the way the resources of a nation are used. The effects impinge not only on what are commonly thought of as strictly farm resources, such as land and farm labour, but also on the inputs that farmers purchase from the rest of the economy.

The first part of the chapter presents a striking illustration of price effects on decisions made in feeding livestock. Because of high variable import levies on feed-grains and the absence of such levies on feeds that are high in protein as well as on certain other types of feed, farmers in the European Community have made significant adjustments in their feeding decisions since the Community's common agricultural policy was adopted. Next, the effects of a seemingly modest adjustment in soyabean price supports in the United States are shown. The final part of the chapter presents some of the available information on the elasticity of supply of farm output – the responsiveness of farmers to changes in relative prices, either of individual commodities or farm products generally.

Feed Prices and Relative Feed Use

In an efficient pricing system, prices serve as guides to decisions for the use of a product. If the system is functioning properly, a product will yield the same relative return in every use to which it is put. Thus the wheat that goes into bread and that which is used for biscuits should have the same marginal value, at least for all those persons who consume both bread and biscuits. Similarly, when a given purpose can be served by more than one product or input, the function of the price system is to assist in meeting that purpose at the lowest cost. A final consumer who chooses a diet with specified nutritional requirements is guided by the prices in the markets that are readily available to him; the same is true of the manager of a feed-mixing plant whose objective is to produce a mixed feed with given specifications at the lowest possible cost. But if the prices that the consumer or the manager of the mixed feed enterprise faces have been seriously distorted by differential taxes or subsidies, the final decisions made will have little correspondence to those that would be required if the real costs of production under efficient conditions were to be minimized. Use and trade patterns can be affected in quite surprising ways.

The European Community subjects certain feed materials to substantial variable import levies; this is true for corn (maize), barley and sorghum. Other feed materials, especially the oilseeds and oilmeals, pulses, corn gluten feed and manioc products, enter the Common Market without a variable import levy and a zero or low import duty. Thus some types of feeds are available at world prices while others enter subject to duties of 50 to 100 per cent. The relative prices that prevail within the Community for these two broad categories of feeding materials have not reflected the relative costs of production in the major exporting areas of the world.

While some feeds that are primarily used for their carbohydrate content are imported without duty or with a modest duty (manioc products, for example), the major group of feeds so imported are those that are high in protein, such as the oilmeals. It is generally true that the real costs per unit of weight of producing a feed product that is high in protein are substantially higher than costs of producing a product that is high in carbohydrates and low in protein. In the United States, where soyabeans and corn generally compete for the same land and require roughly similar amounts of non-land resources (except fertilizer), the price of soyabeans has been about 2.5 times that of corn per ton. The cost of a soyabean oilmeal, at the consuming farm, in 1985 was $227 per ton compared with $93 for corn. The costs of transporting corn or soyabeans from the United States to Western Europe are approximately the same. But in the European Community soyabeans were admitted without import duty while corn was subject to a variable import levy of about 70 per cent in 1968/69 and more than 100 per cent in 1978/79 and in 1986.[1] (See Table 6.1.) The variable levy on maize resulted in farmers in the Community paying nearly the same prices for maize and soyabean oilmeal even though the production cost of the oilmeal was about 2.5 times that of maize.

Table 6.1   Prices paid by farmers for maize and soyabean oilmeal, 1968/69, 1978/79 and 1986

	Maize (US$ per ton)			Soyabean oilmeal[a] (US$ per ton)		
	1968/69	*1978/79*	*1986*	*1968/69*	*1978/79*	*1986*
France	97	218	217[d]	129	280[c]	336[d]
West Germany	116	294	257	116	280	271
Netherlands	112	314	241	122	306	205
United Kingdom	70	250	282	122	304	277
United States	41[b]	84[b]	93[bd]	119	258	227[d]

[a]Protein content of meal or cake probably varies from country to country; could affect price comparisons by up to 10 per cent.
[b]Price received by farmers in the United States.
[c]Estimated by the author.
[d]1985.
Sources: *Prices of Agricultural Products and Fertilizers in Europe, 1968–69* (New York: United Nations, for the Economic Commission for Europe and the FAO, 1969), pp. 48 and 50; *Agricultural Statistics*, United States Department of Agriculture, Washington, various issues; and *Agriculture Statistical Yearbook 1988* (Luxembourg: Statistical Office of the European Community, 1988), pp. 200–201.

The effect of artificially determined price relationships among competitive products is well illustrated by developments in the mixed feed industry in the Netherlands. In that country as early as the mid-1960s more than 80 per cent of all feed concentrates (feeds other than roughage and pasture) were fed as mixed feeds. Thus the decisions of the mixed-feed industry concerning the composition of feeds have reflected quite fully the total concentrate feed market in the Netherlands for the last two decades. In 1960/61, prior to the imposition of the European Community's variable import levies on grain, grain accounted for 68 per cent of all concentrates fed in the Netherlands. By 1967/68 the percentage had fallen to 45 per cent; the decline in the importance of cereals continued and in 1985 accounted for just 15 per cent of the output of the compound feedstuff industry and an even smaller percentage of total concentrates fed.[2]

The displacement of grain resulted from the increase in its absolute and relative price due to the imposition of variable import levies in July 1962 and the payment of large subsidies to divert certain products from food to feed use. A number of feed sources have entered and continue to enter the European Community without duty or levy or with nominal duty. In addition to soyabeans and the oilmeals, corn gluten feed, fish meal, meat meal, beet pulp and dehydrated alfalfa enter free of duty. Manioc products are subject to a duty of 6 per cent, a minor fraction of the levy on maize.[3] In addition to the competition from imported feeding materials, the coarse grains compete with denatured wheat, sugar and non-fat dry milk and, on occasion, butter, products available for livestock feed due to large subsidies.

Table 6.2 provides data on the declining share of grain in compound feeds in the European Community from 1974 to 1985. The mixed or

Table 6.2   Use of cereals by the compound feedstuff industry

	% of production of compound feedstuffs			1000 tons		
	1974	1984	1985	1974	1984	1985
1	*2*	*3*	*4*	*5*	*6*	*7*
European Community (12)[a]	46.9	39.4	38.8	30 366	37 486	36 617
Belgium–Luxembourg	42.8	29.9	29.0	2 142	1 494	1 456
Denmark	51.9	40.5	39.3	1 400	1 700	1 700
Germany, FR	39.6	23.4	24.6	4 238	4 028	4 102
Greece	–	–	–	–	–	–
Spain	65.0	65.0	66.0	3 432	7 634	7 715
France	49.1	48.1	46.8	5 449	7 213	6 890
Ireland	63.7	45.6	46.8	700	913	936
Italy	54.7	55.1	56.6	3 500	6 000	6 000
Netherlands	31.9	16.2	15.2	3 349	2 597	2 470
Portugal	55.0	52.4	45.0	840	1 360	1 160
United Kingdom	51.6	42.1	40.0	5 316	4 547	4 188
European Community (10)[a]	45.2	35.2	34.6	26 094	28 492	27 742

[a]Greece and Luxembourg are not included.
Source: *The Agricultural Situation in the Community: 1987 Report* (Brussels: Commission of the European Community, 1988), p. T/246.

compound feed industry was more fully developed at the time of the formation of the European Community in the Netherlands than in the other countries in the Community. The types of substitutions described above have gone further in the Netherlands than in the other Community members. In 1985, for the Community of Ten, grain accounted for 35 per cent of the output of the mixed feed industry, down from 45 per cent in 1974, but in the Netherlands the change was from 32 per cent to 15 per cent. During the 1970s the mixed-feed industry expanded significantly in the Ten. In 1985 the total output of compound feeds in the Ten was 80 million tons, up from 58 million tons in 1974. Over the same years the production in the Netherlands grew from 10 million to 16.2 million tons, a significantly higher rate than in the rest of the Ten.

Although the volume of international trade has been reduced by the variable import levies on feed-grains, that is not the major point here. A number of the products substituted for feed-grains are imported, such as manioc meal, corn gluten feed and oilmeal and alfalfa meal. The primary point is that having levies that average about 65–70 per cent of the import value of the feed-grains and no levies on a number of substitute feeds has induced substitutions for reasons that have nothing to do with the relative costs of producing the various products. The cost of producing corn gluten feed has not suddenly fallen relative to the cost of producing corn or grain sorghum; but the price signals that the Common Market farmer receives implies that such is the case. One of the effects of these policies is a waste of resources for the world as a whole – more of some products and less of others are being fed than would be the case if differential degrees of protection did not prevail. The consequence is that more resources are used to produce a given tonnage of equivalent feed than is necessary.

While a number of factors other than changes in relative prices of feed-grains and protein feeds will affect trends in the use of these products, it is of interest to note the changes that occurred within the original Six after the European Community's formation. Before July 1962 tariffs or levies on feed-grains were rather modest, especially in France and the Netherlands. After mid-1962 the price relationships between feed-grains and oilmeals changed substantially due to the increased prices of feed-grains. Table 6.3 indicates the changes in feed-grain and oilmeal used for feed in the original Community and the United States.

An unintended and unanticipated effect of the differential treatment of high protein feeds and the coarse grains has been the encouragement of livestock production, especially milk production. The intervention

Table 6.3   Changes in the use of cereals and oilmeal in the European
Community and the United States (million tons)

	Period	EC-6	EC-9	United States
Cereals fed	1960/61–1961/62	33.7	49.0	123.7
	1970/71–1971/72	46.7	67.1	137.9
	1978/79–1979/80	51.8	70.5	139.6
	1984/85–1985/86	51.2	68.3	145.2
Oilmeal fed	1960/61–1961/62	4.2	6.6	11.0
	1970/71–1971/72	15.4	17.8	14.2
	1978/79–1979/80	17.8	22.4	18.6
	1984/85–1985/86	19.0	24.2	20.4
Ratio of oilmeal fed to grain fed (%)	1960/61–1961/62	12.5	13.5	8.9
	1970/71–1971/72	33.0	26.5	10.3
	1978/79–1979/80	34.4	31.8	13.3
	1984/85–1985/86	37.0	35.4	14.1

Sources: *The Agricultural Situation in the Community*, Commission of the
European Community, Brussels, various issues; *Agriculture Statistical Yearbook 1988* (Luxembourg: Statistical Office of the European Community, 1988);
and *Agricultural Statistics*, United States Department of Agriculture, Washington, various issues.

prices for milk were established in terms of an 'appropriate degree of
protection' for milk production in the European Community plus an
amount to compensate for the variable levies on the feed-grains. In
other words, the milk producer was to receive a high enough price to
permit him to pay for feed-grains at prices substantially above the
world market level. Since farmers could purchase high protein feeds
without the imposition of any duty, their use of such products
increased substantially. One effect that has been attributed to the
increased use of high protein feeds has been an increase in milk yields
per cow. For several years the Common Market has been plagued by a
surplus of milk; in other words, it has produced more than can be sold
at the artificially inflated domestic prices. The Community has resorted
to a variety of devices to reduce the surplus – export subsidies,
denaturing of butter, payments for the slaughter of cows and national
and individual milk quotas. While not all of the responsibility for the
excess production of milk can be attributed to the relatively low prices
of high protein feeds, some part of the output effect has been due to the
farmers and the feed industry working for farmers overcoming some of
the effects that were desired from the policies by those who had

promulgated them. This is not the first time, nor will it be the last, that farmers have found ways of negating the anticipated outcomes of programmes designed to influence their behaviour.

Output Effects

I have so far emphasized only a limited aspect of the effects of distortions in price relationships resulting from domestic farm programmes, namely the substitution effects among a limited category of farm inputs. The first part of this chapter was intended to illustrate some quite striking effects of tinkering with prices not so much because of the importance of the effects, but as a transition to the much more important output and consumption effects of high farm prices. The view that farm people are insensitive to price incentives is still so prevalent, despite the evidence to the contrary, that I felt it desirable to try to weaken somewhat the basis for such an irrational view. If we assume that farmers are rational and calculating entrepreneurs, we will make far fewer mistakes than if we cling to our stereotypes of the peasant bound by tradition and family ties or the family farmer who looks on farming as a way of life rather than primarily as an economic activity.

Soyabeans: Prices, Production and Stocks

A near-classic example of the dislocations that can occur as a result of governmental intervention was provided by the price-support programme for soyabeans in the United States during the late 1960s. Soyabeans have been the most dynamic of the major farm crops. Acreage and production almost doubled during the 1950s and did double during the 1960s. The only farm programme that has been in effect for soyabeans has been price supports and, from 1949 to 1988, the average price received by farmers exceeded the support price in all but six years.

By contrast to most crop products the end-of-year stocks of soyabeans were very low – often less than 10 per cent of annual production. During the period of relatively stable soyabean prices during the 1960s, a modest 10 per cent increase ($9.17 per ton) in the price support resulted in an increase of stocks of 1.5 million tons in 1966/67. The average price for the year was above the support level, but during the latter third of the year prices fell to near the support price. In each of the next two years prices averaged below the support price and stocks increased by 2.0 million tons in 1967/68 and 4.4 million tons the following year. Total stocks increased to 8.9 million tons in 1968/69 compared with production in that year of 30 million tons. The price-support level was reduced by $11 per ton in 1969/70 and stocks declined 2.3 million tons that year and a further 3.9 million tons the following year.

The substantial changes in production and stocks were in response to price-support changes of approximately 10 per cent. Because the elasticities of supply and demand for soyabeans are quite large, even in the short run, price changes of the magnitude implied by the changes in price supports can have important effects on the amount produced and consumed. One study of the supply function for soyabeans in the United States indicated that the short-run elasticity of acreage is 0.43 with respect to the price-support level and 0.84 to the lagged price of soyabeans.[4] The long-run elasticities may be as much as five times the short run. Table 6.4 clearly shows the output responsiveness in soyabean area.

Table 6.4 Responsiveness of soyabean acreage to price-support levels

	Hectares harvested (millions)	Support price ($ per ton)	Market price, lagged one year ($ per ton)	Stocks of soyabeans, end of year (million tons)
1964/65	12.8	82.58	92.12	0.81
1965/66	14.3	82.58	96.15	0.97
1966/67	15.1	91.75	93.13	2.46
1967/68	16.5	91.75	100.92	4.53
1968/69	17.0	91.75	91.38	8.91
1969/70	17.1	80.74	89.18	6.26
1970/71	17.5	80.74	86.24	2.69
1971/72	18.8	80.74	103.49	1.96

Source: *Agricultural Statistics, 1980* (Washington: United States Department of Agriculture, 1981).

While the trend in soyabean area has been an increasing one in recent decades, most of the change in area between 1965 and 1973 can be largely explained by changes in price supports and the lagged price of soyabeans and competing crops. The increase in harvested area of 0.8

million hectares between 1965 and 1966 is almost exactly explained by
the response to an increase in soyabean price support of 11 per cent, a
decline in lagged price of soyabeans of 4 per cent and declines in the
effective price supports for corn and oats. The decrease in the price
support for soyabeans in 1969/70 halted the increase in harvested area;
the substantial increase in area in 1973/74 was due to the 45 per cent
increase in lagged soyabean prices offset in part by the significant
increase in the price of corn in 1972/73.

The main purpose for this brief discussion of soyabeans is to indicate
that there are instances when governmental actions, taken primarily for
political reasons, can create surpluses and stock accumulations where
none existed before. Furthermore, the example indicates that when the
mistake – the increase in price support – was corrected, the market
made the appropriate adjustments.

A basic assumption of the farm policies of the industrial countries is
that farmers do not increase output significantly in response to higher
output prices. This assumption is held – perhaps it would be more
accurate to say that it is hoped that it is true – because a large part of
the desired income effects from higher prices will only be realized if
output changes very little in response to higher prices. Furthermore, the
larger the increase in output from a given percentage increase in prices,
the greater will be the costs of the kinds of farm policies now existing in
the European Community, the United States or Sweden. Thus these
policies would be more viable, both in terms of meeting their primary
objective of increasing farm incomes and of keeping costs to consumers
and taxpayers at manageable levels, the smaller is the response of
output to price changes.

Measurement of Supply Response

If we are to know how farmers will change the output of a given
commodity in response to a change in the price of that commodity, we
need to know the supply function. The supply function, in the
economics textbook, shows the relationship between the output price
and the quantity of the product produced. Such a supply function
assumes that all other relevant prices remain unchanged. In effect, the
output price is a relative price for the product, although it may be
expressed in terms of a specific amount of money. The relative price is a
very complicated one; it is the price of the particular product relative to

the prices of all other products that could compete for the use of the same resources and to the prices of all the inputs used in the production of the product. Thus if we are interested in the supply function for wheat, and if the resources that are used to produce wheat could be used to produce corn, barley and grain sorghums, the wheat price should be the price of wheat relative to the prices of the other three products. Similarly, if land, labour, tractors and petrol are required to produce the wheat, the price of wheat must reflect its relationship to the prices of these inputs. The reason for this is obvious since the amount of wheat that will be produced at a price of \$20 per 100 kilograms will be quite different if an hour of labour costs \$4 or \$8.

Analytically, no particular problem arises because the amount of wheat produced is a function of many other prices. Assuming that the output reaction to any price change is instantaneous, the supply function for wheat can be written as follows:

$$W = f(Pw, Pa, Pi)$$

where W is the output of wheat, Pw is the price of wheat, Pa is the price of other products that could be produced with the same resources and Pi is the price of each of the inputs.

Unfortunately there are a number of very good reasons why the supply function as given above cannot be actually determined or estimated.

First, if there is a time lag between the making of a decision that affects output and the culmination of the process that results in an output, the decision must be made on the basis of expected rather than actual prices. The decision to produce wheat occurs from four to nine months prior to the completion of the production process. Time lags of varying lengths, ranging up to several years for tree crops, are involved in the production process for farm products. Expected prices cannot be directly observed; thus it is necessary to introduce into the estimation process price variables that are estimates themselves.

Second, it is not possible for a farmer to react instantaneously and fully to a change in circumstances. If a farmer is fully confident that the price of wheat relative to the prices of competing products and inputs has risen by 10 per cent and will maintain that relationship into the indefinite future, the output level in the first year will be less than in the second year, less in the second year than in the third year and so on. There are many reasons why a complete response cannot be made at once to such a change. The farmer may not be able to change immediately to the most profitable input combinations without incurring substantially greater costs than would be involved if he adjusted more slowly. Expanding the area devoted to wheat might require destroying a stand of hay that would be productive for two or three years more, although if he had known about the increase in wheat price he would never have invested in the hay. It could require some change in the type of machinery that he uses and it may pay to wait a year or so before making the change. Thus if after complete adjustment to the higher price of wheat he would increase wheat production by 20 per cent, it is quite possible that in the first year he would increase by only half this much, 10 per cent, and gradually approach the 20 per cent increase over a number of years. Essentially what has been described is the distinction between long-run and short-run supply curves.

Third, in the case of agriculture there is not a unique relationship between output and the quantities of inputs used. To a greater extent than in most other types of productive activity, the outcome of the agricultural production process is subject to conditions over which the farmer has little or no control. The amount of rainfall, variations in temperature, the amount of sunshine and the incidence of diseases and insects affect the production outcome and their specific occurrence cannot be predicted in advance. Consequently it is not only that the prices that influence output decisions are expected prices, but the output variable is an expected variable at the time production decisions are made. Actual output can be greater or less than expected output depending upon the distribution of the variables over which the decision-maker has no control.

There are some other reasons why the supply function described above cannot be estimated from data on the actual behaviour of farmers, but the reasons given are sufficient for our purposes. Let us turn briefly to a discussion of the types of supply functions that can be and are estimated.

When supply functions are being estimated for crops one simplification that is often made is to estimate acreage response rather than output response. The farmer can control or determine the acreage devoted to a crop, while factors beyond his control can significantly influence the amount of output per unit of land. Since the expected yield can be influenced by conscious decisions, such as the amount of fertilizer used, in recent years some attempts have been made to estimate a yield response function. Thus the elasticity of output with respect to price is (approximately) the sum of the elasticities of acreage and yield responses.

As noted above, expected prices cannot be observed. In response studies the price variables are usually last year's prices, the average of prices for the last several years or prices for each of the last several years. The assumption is that farmers must rely on such information in determining their expected prices. If farmers have more sophisticated and accurate methods of determining expected prices, these empirical methods will result in an under-estimate of the response elasticity.

The analysis of supply response is thus complicated in two ways: the problems involved in determining expected prices and the fact that adjustments to changes in expected prices take time. Perhaps the most common method for dealing with the problem of price expectations has been to assume that the expected price for this year is the actual price received in the immediate past year. This would mean that the following function would be estimated: $O_t = a + bP_{t-1} + u_t$. But as Marc Nerlove, now at the University of Pennsylvania, has shown in his pioneering work, *The Dynamics of Supply*, this equation assumes that farmers only take into account the price of the immediate past year in determining price expectations for the current year.[5] But it is reasonable to assume that farmers take into account information that can be learned from past prices in addition to the immediately preceding year. This is particularly true since each farmer has found that the expected price based entirely on last year's price has turned out to be in error. Thus it may be reasonable to assume that farmers base their expectations on a weighted moving average of past prices, with the weights being based on the error made in predicting price in the immediate past year.

After a hiatus during the 1970s when there were very few new empirical studies of agricultural supply response, the several analyses of the effects of agricultural protection on production, trade and prices have produced some new estimates of supply response. Two important sets of recent supply response estimates are included in Table 6.5. Most elasticities reported in the original edition are also included, for reasons indicated below.

Table 6.5 reports estimates of short-run and/or long-run elasticities of supply based on a model developed by Professor Nerlove. In this model it is assumed that the primary reason for the differences between actual behaviour and expected behaviour is the lag in adjustment rather than errors in expectations. In other words, given the expected price, farmers are unable to adjust fully to the desired position in one unit of time. The amount of time required for nearly full adjustment is dependent on the particular conditions of production and the availability

Table 6.5 Price elasticities of supply of farm products in industrial countries

Country and commodity	Dependent variable	Time period	Short-run	Intermediate-run	Long-run
United States					
Crops	O	1926–59	0.17		1.56
	A	1926–59	0.04		0.10
	Y	1926–59	0.15		1.50
Livestock	O	1926–59	0.38		2.90
	N	1926–59	0.12		1.80
	Y	1926–59	0.26		1.10
Total	O	1926–59	0.25		1.79
Farm output	O	1952–61	0.46	0.84	2.96
Wheat	A	1909–32	0.48		0.93
	O	1960–77	0.45		0.8
Corn	A	1909–32	0.10		0.18
Coarse grain	O	1960–77	0.40		0.75
Cotton	A	1909–32	0.27		0.67
Hogs, spring	N	1949–60	0.82		
Hogs, fall	N	1949–60	0.56		
Ruminant meat	O	1960–77	0.10	0.10	0.50
Non-ruminant meat	O	1960–77	0.27		0.80
Australia					
Wheat	O	1947–65	0.18	0.82	3.82
Coarse grains	O	1947–65	0.21	0.81	1.54
Beef and veal	O	1947–65	0.16	–	–
Lamb	O	1947–65	0.21	0.94	3.20
Wool	O	1947–65	0.05	0.25	3.59
Dairy	O	1947–63	0.20	0.43	0.46
Netherlands					
Calf production	N	1955–65	0.43		
Broilers	O	1957–65	0.79		
Sows	N	1956–62	0.12		
West Germany					
Wheat	O				0.85
Coarse grain	O				0.55
Oil fruits, protein feeds, industrial crops	O				1.53
Fruits and vegetables	O				0.33
Pork, poultry and eggs	O				2.23
Bovine and ovine meat	O				0.94
Milk	O				1.22
Wool	O				0.06

Country and commodity	Dependent variable	Time period	Short-run	Intermediate-run	Long-run
United Kingdom					
Crop products	O				0.44
Livestock products	O				
Feed prices fixed absolutely					0.84
Feed prices fixed relatively					0.37
Agricultural output	O				
Feed prices fixed absolutely					1.07
Feed prices fixed relatively					0.34
Cereals, all	O				0.9
Grain, all	A	1924–39	0.12		0.52
Grain, all	A	1946–58	0.17		0.30
Wheat	A	1924–39	0.33		0.46
Barley	A	1924–39	0.63		1.75
European Community					
Agricultural output	O	1953–66		0.2–0.5	
Crop production	O	1953–66	0.37		0.5
Coarse grain	O	1960–77	0.5		0.9
Rice	O	1960–77	0.2		0.4
Wheat	O	1960–77	0.3		0.9
Beef	N	1953–66	0.2–0.7		0.7–1.8
Livestock (except beef and dairy)	O	1953–66	0.33		2.6–4.2
Ruminant meat	O	1960–77	0.12	0.12	0.68
Non-ruminant meat	O	1960–77	0.35	–	0.70
Japan					
Rice	O	1961–83	0.20	–	0.50
Wheat	O	1961–83	0.30	–	0.60
Dairy	O	1961–83	0.05	0.30	0.80
Ruminant meat	O	1961–83	0.10	0.20	0.80
Non-ruminant meat	O	1961–83	0.33		0.99

Sources: Anthony H. Chisholm and Rodney Tyers, *Food Security and Agricultural Policy in Asia and the Pacific* (Honolulu: East–West Center, 1981) Table A2; and Klaus Frohberg, Hartwig de Haen, Michel Keyzer and Stefan Tangermann, 'Towards an Agricultural Sector Model of the European Community: Model Structure and Preliminary Results', a paper presented at the Second European Conference of Agricultural Economists, Dijon, France, 4–8 September 1978.

of inputs, if an increase in inputs is required, or the ease of releasing inputs if a decrease in one or more inputs is needed to move to the most profitable position. The simplest form of the equation that is estimated statistically is the following: $O_t = a + bP_{t-1} + BO_{t-1} + u_t$. Here O_{t-1} is the dependent variable lagged one year. If the value of B is very small, this means that output adjustments can be made almost completely in one time period. But if B is large (theoretically it should fall between zero and unity), it means that several production periods are required to carry out all of the production adjustments. The short-run elasticities of supply are determined by the coefficient P_{t-1}, while the long-run elasticities of supply are estimated by calculating

$$\frac{b}{(1-B)}.$$

While the state of analysis of supply response for farm products is still less robust than one might like, there has been considerable attention to the empirical estimation of supply or acreage functions.

Tables 6.5, 6.6, 6.7 and 6.8 present representative examples of the estimates of acreage or supply responses for crops and livestock products. Numerous additional estimates may be found in the sources listed for the tables. Tables 6.5, 6.6 and 6.7 are for the industrial countries while Table 6.8 presents similar estimates for the developing countries. The latter elasticity of supply estimates show clearly that prices received by farmers in developing countries have a significant effect on production. The supply elasticities for industrial and developing countries are similar in size, a point policy-makers in industrial countries should bear in mind when the actions of those countries depress prices on international markets.

All of the supply estimates that were included in the original edition have been retained; these were estimates that were available to policy-makers during the 1960s. A small number of more recent estimates have been added. These estimates were based on data through the mid-1980s and are consistent with the earlier studies. The supply elasticities available during the 1960s were large enough that policy-makers should have known that even quite modest increases in real product prices would generate significant output increases. The later supply elasticity estimates both confirm the general level of the earlier estimates and are consistent with the actual output experience that has occurred where output prices have increased.

Table 6.6   Price elasticities of supply for wheat

Country	Dependent variable	Time period	Short-run	Long-run
European Community	O		1.70	–
	O	1960–77	0.30	0.90
	A		–	0.70
	Y		–	0.25
France	A		0.05	0.11
	A		0.60	–
	O		0.9–1.1	–
West Germany	A		0.20	–
Italy	A		0.10	0.40
United Kingdom	A	1924–39	0.33	0.46
	A	1955–70	0.11	–
	O		0.19	–
United States	A	1909–32	0.48	0.93
	O	1960–77	0.45	0.80
	A		–	2.5[a]
	Y		–	0.05[a]
Canada	A		0.56	1.2–1.4
	O	1951–67	1.40	–
	A	1951–57	0.50	–
	A		–	0.50
Argentina	A		0.7–1.3	–
	A	1951–57	0.40	–
	O	1951–57	0.90	–
	A		–	0.40
	Y		–	0.10
Australia	O	1947–65	0.18	3.82
Australia and New Zealand	A		–	0.40
	Y		–	0.15
Japan	A		0.20	–
	Y		–	0.30
Brazil	A		–	0.70
	Y		–	0.05

[a]Trade price instead of supply price.
Sources: John E. Hutchinson, James J. Naive and Sheldon K. Tsu, *World Demand Prospects for Wheat in 1980 with Emphasis on Trade by Less Developed Countries* (Washington: United States Department of Agriculture, 1970); and Table 6.5 above.

The first column of Tables 6.5 and 6.6 indicates the country or region and the product; the third column gives the period used in the analysis where this is obvious from the published material. The second column gives the dependent variable – the variable for which the elasticity of supply is calculated. This variable differs from study to study. In some cases the dependent variable is the area planted or harvested (A). These elasticities do not reflect the total response to price since any effects on yield per unit area are not included. In other cases the dependent variable is total output (O), and presumably the effects of both area and yield (Y) are reflected for crops or both livestock numbers (N) and yield of livestock product per head.

The last three columns are the lengths of run to which the elasticities apply. The short run is one production period, generally a year; the intermediate run is arbitrarily specified to be five years; and the long run is for an infinite period, although in almost all cases nearly full adjustment would be reached in a decade. Almost certainly the area response functions under-estimate the total output response to changes in prices. These types of functions are used where it is not feasible to reflect the effects of weather and other variables outside the control of man on year-to-year changes in yields. Thus the comment that the acreage-response function gives an under-estimate of the output elasticity is not meant as a criticism of those who undertook the research but only to warn the reader that such elasticities are on the low side.

The supply elasticities given in the tables include several for individual farm products, such as wheat or beef, and for major groupings of farm products, such as all crops, all grains or all livestock, as well as for agricultural output as a whole. In general, one should expect a higher elasticity of supply response for individual commodities than for agricultural output as a whole. The reason for this expectation is simply that when the price of an individual product changes, the output of that product can change by shifting resources from other farm products. For agricultural output as a whole, however, the resource changes will involve at least shifting resources away from, or to, the rest of the economy. It has often been argued that the supply elasticities for individual commodities have only limited relevance in the evaluation of the kinds of agricultural policies now operated by the industrial countries. Such policies, so the argument goes, are primarily concerned with adjusting the general level of farm prices and, so long as the aggregate supply elasticity is low, the output effects will be minimal. The supply elasticities included in Table 6.5 indicate that the assumption of low long-run elasticities is in error; but it is also important to remember that in most countries there are rather different degrees of protection for various farm products. The United States, for example, gives much more protection to dairy products, sugar and peanuts than it does for feed-grains or beef. The European Community provides a much higher rate of protection for grains and dairy products than it does for beef and pork. The United Kingdom, before joining the Community, was rather more solicitous of horticultural products than it was of eggs or pork.

The OECD study *National Policies and Agricultural Trade* estimated supply elasticities for aggregate agricultural output for most of the industrial economies. The aggregate supply elasticities were estimated under two assumptions: (i) response to increase in all production prices except livestock feed prices and (ii) response to increase in all production prices including livestock feed prices. These elasticities are presented in Table 6.7. The elasticities are defined as medium term or for about five years. A comparison of the elasticities with those in Table 6.5 indicates a high degree of similarity. Table 6.7 also includes the demand elasticities estimated by the OECD.

It is difficult to understand why policy-makers have not recognized the consequences for domestic production and consumption of increasing support prices or returns for farm products. For the range of supply elasticities given in Table 6.8, a 10 per cent increase in real prices would increase production by 2.2 to 5.1 per cent while, given the demand elasticities, would reduce consumption by 2.4 to 6.0 per cent. Thus the combined change in exports or imports, measured as a percentage of domestic production, could be as high as 9 per cent (Canada) and no lower than 6.6 per cent (United States).

The individual product supply elasticities in Table 6.5 and the several supply or acreage elasticities for wheat in Table 6.6 indicate that significant differences in the degree of protection by commodities can have important effects on resource allocation. The elasticities are generally sufficiently high that policy-makers should not ignore the actual or potential effects of different protection levels. The brief discussion of soyabeans in the United States presented earlier in this chapter indicates that problems can arise if it is assumed that the supply elasticities for individual crops are so low that they can be ignored.

The individual crop supply elasticities for Australia indicate long-run elasticities of three or more for wheat, lamb and wool and greater than unity for coarse grains. Only in the case of dairy products is the long-run price elasticity of supply less than unity. The acreage elasticities for individual crops for the United States and the United Kingdom for the years before the Second World War are generally much lower than the

Table 6.7 Supply and demand elasticities for agricultural output, selected countries

	Aggregate supply elasticities (per cent)		Aggregate final demand elasticities (per cent)
	Response to increase in all production prices except livestock feed prices[a]	*Response to increase in all production prices including livestock feed prices*[b]	*Response to increase all consumption prices (excludes changes in livestock feed quantities)*
Canada	0.32	0.28	−0.60
Australia	0.28	0.22	−0.46
European Community	0.68	0.38	−0.41
United States	0.38	0.26	−0.40
Austria	0.57	0.36	−0.35
New Zealand	0.55	0.49	−0.38
Japan	0.69	0.51	−0.24
Nordic	0.42	0.30	−0.49
Mediterranean	0.51	0.33	−0.38
OECD	0.48	0.31	−0.40

[a]Elasticity measures the effect on total agricultural output of a 1 per cent increase in all agricultural prices, holding feed prices constant.
[b]Elasticity measures the effect on total agricultural output of a 1 per cent increase in all agricultural prices.
Source: *National Policies and Agricultural Trade* (Paris: OECD, 1987), p. 141.

estimates for Australia. Even the acreage-response functions, however, with long-run elasticities ranging from 0.18 to 0.93 (ignoring the higher elasticity for barley in the United Kingdom) indicate that a 10 per cent increase in relative output price would increase acreage by a significant amount. Such elasticities ignore the effect of prices on yields per unit of land. The estimates made by Luther Tweeten, now of Ohio State University, for the United States for all crops indicate that the elasticity of yield to price is significantly greater than the elasticity of acreage to price.[6] Thus the crop acreage elasticities for Britain and the United States are clearly under-estimates of the output elasticities for the period involved.

While it is true that there is considerable variability in the elasticities of supply for the crop products included in Table 6.5, the long-run elasticities are of a magnitude to indicate that prices do have significant effect on output in the industrial countries. The full long-run effect of prices on output is a sizeable one when prices are 30 to 100 per cent above import prices, even when the elasticity of supply is as low as 0.2. But one can infer from the results presented in Table 6.5 that in the long run the supply elasticities may be significantly greater than 0.2.

The results for major groups of commodities for the United Kingdom are especially important. The long-run elasticity of supply for all crop products is estimated to be 0.44, while it is 0.9 for all cereals. The estimates for agricultural output as a whole are worthy of note; two estimates are presented and the distinction between holding feed prices fixed absolutely and relatively to all output prices is an important one for an agriculture that has depended to a considerable extent on imported feeds. When feed prices are fixed in an absolute sense, an increase of 1 per cent in the average price of all agricultural output would increase that output by 0.84 per cent. If feed prices are fixed at the same relative position to all output prices, the elasticity of supply is 0.37. This is a very reasonable result for the United Kingdom since over 70 per cent of the final output of British agriculture consists of livestock products. If profitable, the output of livestock products can be increased significantly, so long as feed is available and feed can be imported in the necessary quantities with little or no long-run effect on the price of feed.

The results given in Table 6.5 for the European Community indicate relatively high elasticities of supply, especially for livestock products. The elasticity of supply of beef production, as measured by numbers, may well be at least unity in the long run. The supply function for other livestock (primarily pork) is very high, but expanding pork production is probably the easiest of all livestock products. The short-run elasticity of supply for crop production is estimated to be 0.37 while the long-run elasticity is estimated to be greater than 0.50. George Jones, of the University of Oxford, estimated that the intermediate-run elasticity of supply of agricultural output is in the general range of 0.2 to 0.5.

The short-run elasticities that have been estimated for the Netherlands are only for livestock. The short-run elasticities may be compared with those found for similar products in Australia.

The data in Tables 6.5 and 6.6 indicate that the supply elasticities for farm products in several major industrial countries are clearly too high to be ignored by policy-makers. The substantial long-run supply elasticities are also cause for concern even if no further increases are

Table 6.8   Price elasticities of supply of farm products, developing countries

Commodity and area	Dependent variable	Time period	Elasticities Short-run	Elasticities Long-run
Rice				
Punjab	A	1914–45	0.31	0.59
	A	1960–69	0.19–0.24	0.64–0.68
Philippines	A	1954–64	0.13–0.22	0.15–0.62
	O	1960–77	0.16	0.26
Indonesia	A	1951–62	0.30	–
	A		–	0.20
	Y		–	0.10
Thailand	A	1940–63	0.18	0.31
	O	1960–77	0.05	0.15
	A		–	0.05
	Y		–	0.10
India	A		–	0.25
	Y		–	0.07
South Korea	O	1960–77	0.25	0.35
Wheat				
Punjab	A	1914–43	0.08	0.14
	A	1960–69	0.02–0.08	0.15–0.58
India	A		–	0.30
	Y		–	0.08
Maize				
Punjab	A	1960–69	0.11–0.13	0.14–0.16
Thailand	A	1950–63	1.03	2.29
Coarse grains				
Philippines	O	1960–77	0.20	0.40
Thailand	O	1960–77	0.12	0.22
	A		–	0.10
	Y		–	0.10
India	A		–	0.17
	Y		–	0.04
Indonesia	A		–	0.14
	Y		–	0.05
Oilseeds				
India	A		–	0.20
	Y		–	0.15
Indonesia	A		–	0.30
	Y		–	0.02
Cassava				
Thailand	A	1954–63	1.09	1.09

Commodity and area	Dependent variable	Time period	Elasticities	
			Short-run	Long-run
Groundnuts				
Punjab	A	1960–69	0.51–0.78	3.05–3.25
Sugar				
Punjab	A	1915–43	0.34	0.60
	A	1951–64	0.09	0.73
Philippines	A	1914–64	0.08–0.13	0.13–0.16
Cotton				
India	A	1922–23	0.59	1.08
	A	1948–61	0.64	1.33
Egypt	A	1913–37	0.40	–
	A	1944–66	0.28	0.51
Punjab	A	1960–69	0.45–0.68	0.79–1.17
Jute				
India	A	1911–38	0.46	0.73
Bangladesh	A	1948–66	0.35	0.83
Kenaf				
Thailand	A	1954–63	2.70	5.75
Non-ruminant meat				
Korea	O	1961–83	0.43	0.86
Philippines	O	1961–83	0.62	1.03
Taiwan	O	1961–83	0.47	0.94
Brazil	O	1961–83	0.30	0.90
Mexico	O	1961–83	0.30	0.90

Sources: Raj Krishna, 'Agricultural Price Policy and Economic Development', in Herman M. Southworth and Bruce F. Johnston (eds), *Agricultural Development and Economic Growth* (Ithaca, New York: Cornell University Press, 1967), pp. 506–7 (based on a summary made by Dr Krishna of research done by him and others); *Alternative Futures for World Food in 1985*: Vol. I, *World GOL [grain–oilseed–livestock] Model – Analytical Report*, Foreign Agricultural Economic Report No. 146 (Washington: United States Department of Agriculture, 1978); Hosseini Askari and John T. Cummings, *Agricultural Supply Response: a Survey of the Econometric Evidence* (New York: Praeger, 1976); Jere R. Behrman, *Supply Response in Underdeveloped Agriculture: a Case Study of Four Major Annual Crops in Thailand, 1937–63* (Amsterdam: North-Holland, 1968); J. L. Kaul and D. S. Sidhu, 'Acreage Response to Prices for Major Crops in Punjab: an Econometric Study', *Indian Journal of Agricultural Economics*, Bombay, October–December 1971; Mokhlis Y. Zaki, 'Egyptian Cotton Producers' Response to Price: a Regional Analysis', *Journal of Developing Areas*, Macomb, Illinois, October 1976, pp. 39–57; Anthony H. Chisholm and Rodney Tyers, *Food Security and Agricultural Policy in Asia and the Pacific* (Honolulu: East–West Center, 1981) Table A2; and Rodney Tyers, Kym Anderson, Prue Phillips and Eric Saxon, *The Anatomy of World Food Markets: Trends in and a Model for Grains, Livestock Products and Sugar* (Washington: World Bank, 1986).

made in product prices. It may well be that farmers have not yet completed their adjustment to price increases made five or perhaps ten years earlier.

There is another set of estimates of supply elasticities that merit attention. These are the estimates for developing countries and are given in Table 6.8. While by now it should be apparent that farmers in the developing countries are responsive to economic opportunities, as evidenced by the rapid adoption of high yielding varieties of rice and wheat, the sharp increase in fertilizer usage, and the great expansion of tube-well irrigation, it is appropriate to include some of the available estimates of the elasticities of supply for farm products. These elasticities are important because they show that the lowering of international market prices by the farm policies of the industrial market economies have consequences and they have adverse effects on some of the poorest people in the world. The estimate of supply elasticities for the developing countries are of the same order of magnitude as in the industrial market economies. As a consequence, to the degree that the lower international market prices are passed through to farmers in the developing countries, such farmers find themselves in competition with the treasuries of the high-income countries. While policy-makers in the industrial countries want the credit for their economics and food aid for the poor people of the developing world, they are unwilling to modify their domestic farm policies to eliminate the adverse effects on the same poor people that result from the depressed world prices.

Illustrations of Trade Effects

Let us assume a country that would be 80 per cent self-sufficient in a farm product if there were no import restrictions. How much effect would an increase in real farm product prices of 25 per cent have on the degree of self-sufficiency? Obviously this will depend on the price elasticities of supply and demand. In Table 6.9 some calculations have been made for both the short run and the long run; the supply elasticities have been taken from Table 6.5. Three different price elasticities of demand have been chosen. The lowest price elasticity of demand (-0.16) is probably reasonable for grain products used for direct consumption in the industrial countries, while the highest elasticity (-0.65) is an approximation for meat products.

Since the estimates in Table 6.9 do not include any shifts in either the supply or demand functions, the estimates should not be taken too literally. These estimates would validly describe what would happen in

Table 6.9   Degree of self-sufficiency resulting from a 25 per cent increase in real farm prices in the short run and long run for a country 80 per cent self-sufficient under free trade

Supply elasticities	Price elasticities of demand		
	−0.16	−0.40	−0.65
	% self-sufficient		
Short-run			
0.10	86.50	92.50	98.75
0.20	89.00	95.00	101.25
0.60	99.00	105.00	111.25
Long-run			
0.50	96.50	102.50	108.75
1.00	109.00	115.00	121.25
1.50	121.50	127.50	133.75

a real situation only if demand and supply curves shifted to the right at exactly the same rate, say 2 per cent per annum. Even the lowest of the two elasticities indicates that a 25 per cent increase in output prices would increase the self-sufficiency ratio by a substantial margin – from 80 to 86.5 per cent. In this instance imports would fall by 6.5/20 or 32.5 per cent. The intermediate short-run supply elasticity combined with the highest of the demand elasticities would result in the complete elimination of imports and a small amount available for export – with a subsidy, of course. If the demand curve shifts at a slower annual rate than the supply curve, then the increase in self-sufficiency would be greater than indicated in Table 6.9.

The lowest of the long-run supply elasticities combined with the lowest demand elasticity would nearly eliminate imports if farm product prices were increased by 25 per cent while any of the higher long-run supply elasticities would result in export surpluses.

The reader might well ask: 'Are the illustrated changes in self-sufficiency given in Table 6.9 at all valid? Has the degree of self-sufficiency in the industrial countries significantly changed?' As indicated in Chapter 3 of the first edition, the self-sufficiency ratio for the industrial market economies changed only moderately between 1956 and 1965, except for sugar and fats and oils. There was a small increase in the degree of self-sufficiency for the grains during the decade. This small increase was the forerunner for a very large increase in the degree of self-sufficiency, especially for the European Community and the United States that occurred during the 1970s.

Rodney Tyers and Kym Anderson have estimated the change in the degree of self-sufficiency for the industrial market economies for 1961–64 and 1981–83.[7] Their estimates include the grains, meats, milk products and sugar and consequently are primarily representative of foods and not of the fibres. During the first period the industrial market economies were very small net importers – consumption exceeded production by about 1 per cent. In the latter period, however, production exceeded consumption by 10 per cent.

The same economists have also estimated the change in the net trade position for the same groups of farm commodities for North America and Australasia, Western Europe and Japan. The change in position is measured in terms of the share of world trade in these particular agricultural products. Between 1961–64 and 1981–84, North America and Australasia increased their share of world trade from 48 to 53 per cent. Japan's position changed very little; in the earlier period she accounted for 10 per cent of world imports of the group of products and in the later period the share was 12 per cent. But Western Europe's shift in its trading position was substantial. In 1961–64 Western Europe was a large net importer of food products. Its net imports accounted for 39 per cent of world trade in food products. By 1980–83, however, Western Europe had become a net exporter of food products and its net exports equalled 9 per cent of world trade in those products.[8]

These data are clearly consistent with what could be inferred from the simple model presented earlier. A small excess of the rate of growth of supply over that of domestic demand generates a much larger percentage change in trade. And this is exactly what has occurred. During the 1970s, the rate of growth supply of agricultural products in the European Community was approximately 2 per cent, while demand grew at 1 per cent. The excess supply was primarily exported, although some was stored and some was recycled, so to speak, by feeding butter to cows and using large quantities of dried skim milk as feed.

Changes in Real Farm Prices

The increase in self-sufficiency in agricultural products in the industrial market economies could have been even greater had it been possible to either increase or hold constant real farm output prices. From 1960 to the mid-1980s only Japan was able to achieve a significant increase in real farm output prices, achieving an increase of about 40 per cent by 1970. Since 1970, however, real output prices have either been constant or have fallen slightly.

France was the only major exporter of agricultural products that achieved an increase in real output prices during the 1960s, presumably as a consequence of aligning her farm prices with those of the newly formed European Community. The increase for France was about 10 per cent during the 1960s, but after the mid-1970s there set in a small but gradual decline in real prices, a decline that continued through the mid-1980s.

The United States has much more variable real output prices than the European Community or Japan. Real farm output prices increased sharply in 1973 and 1974, perhaps creating over-optimistic expectations among both farmers and policy-makers. But starting with 1980, real farm prices declined by more than 25 per cent by 1986, although part of this decline was offset by deficiency payments.

What is very clear is that the modest declines in real output prices were insufficient to restrict output growth to the demand growth in the industrial market economies. Had policy-makers been successful in increasing real output prices, the disequilibrium in world markets for farm products would have been even greater.

Price Response and Costs of Farm Programmes

The evidence is now overwhelming that farmers in both industrial and developing countries do respond significantly to price incentives. The response to changes in the price of an individual product is greater than for changes in the prices of all agricultural products. And this is what economic theory would lead us to expect. But the response to changes in the average level of farm prices, if sufficient time is given for adjustment, is large enough to create a number of adverse effects as a consequence of a significant degree of agricultural protection. One of these effects is that the cost of farm policies based on high levels of farm prices will increase over time, since all of the output adjustment does not occur in the first two or three years of the increased prices. Another is the effect on trade. Output expansion results in a reduction in the level of imports and in some cases has resulted in an export surplus

Table 6.10   Prices received and paid by farmers and ratio of prices received to prices paid, selected industrial countries (1970 = 100)

Country and index		1960	1965	1970	1980	1985
Japan	PR	51.2	76.4	100.0	220.6	227.4
	PP[a]	57.3	81.4	100.0	228.4	246.6
	R(%)	89.4	93.7	100.0	96.6	92.2
France	PR	70.4	83.5	100.0	219.7	314.3
	PP[a]	76.9	85.5	100.0	267.4	411.5
	R(%)	91.5	97.7	100.0	82.2	76.4
Netherlands	PR	71.8	86.7	100.0	145.6	167.4
	PP[a]	70.9	90.2	100.0	172.3	201.7
	R(%)	101.3	96.1	100.0	84.5	83.0
United States	PR	85.1	88.6	100.0	223.0	213.2
	PP[a]	77.2	82.3	100.0	250.9	296.9
	R(%)	110.2	107.7	100.0	88.0	71.8
West Germany	PR	96.9	116.3	100.0	147.5	151.9
	PP[a]	84.5	97.2	100.0	166.9	191.9
	R(%)	114.7	119.6	100.0	88.4	79.2
Canada	PR	85.4	92.9	100.0	279.8	289.1
	PP	75.3	85.3	100.0	267.1	324.2
	R(%)	113.4	108.9	100.0	104.8	89.2
Australia	PR	109.1	114.4	100.0	298.8	358.8
	PP	78.2	86.5	100.0	329.4	527.1
	R(%)	139.5	132.3	100.0	90.7	68.1
Belgium	PR	79.3	95.7	100.0	139.4	183.4
	PP	65.8	84.7	100.0	161.5	219.2
	R(%)	120.5	112.9	100.0	86.3	83.7
Sweden	PR	75.7	94.0	100.0	226.5	321.6
	PP	72.5	89.8	100.0	245.9	425.4
	R(%)	104.4	104.7	100.0	92.1	75.6
United Kingdom	PR	80.6	85.8	100.0	360.1	446.0
	PP	71.3	77.4	100.0	496.0	654.8
	R(%)	113.0	110.9	100.0	72.6	68.1

Note   PR = prices received; PP = prices paid; and R = ratio of prices received to prices paid.
[a]All items including household production expenditures; other prices paid indexes are for production items only.
Source: *Production Yearbook*, FAO, Rome, various issues.

where none existed before. As the European Community has found, when the degree of protection exceeds 50 per cent, the costs of export disposal can become very large indeed.

It has been shown that only two of the industrial countries were able to increase the relative prices of farm products during the 1960s. But even if relative output prices were held constant, there is a trend underway in all of the industrial countries that will increase the degree of effective protection of agricultural production over time. And this increase in effective protection will almost certainly induce further expansion of output.

As indicated in Chapter 4, agriculture in the industrial countries is undergoing a number of important structural changes. The decrease in employment of labour and the enlargement of farm size, combined with the availability of new and improved inputs at prices that are falling relative to land rent or the returns to farm labour, has resulted in a trend towards the greater use of purchased inputs. It is clear that the relative and absolute importance of purchased inputs will become even greater in the years ahead. There is no indication that these have run their course.

Why are these changes important to understanding agricultural protection? They are significant for two reasons. First, the effective protection of the farm production activity is now much greater than is indicated by the comparison of domestic and import or export prices of farm products. Second, as purchased inputs become more important, the degree of effective protection will increase over time, even though the difference between domestic output prices and world prices for each farm product remains unchanged. What has been called effective protection is a measure of the difference between the industry's value added under protection and under free trade conditions expressed as a percentage of the value added under free trade. In other words, it is a measure of the protection provided to a particular industry, to the resources that are normally considered to be agriculture in the present case. Effective protection for agriculture is the protection of the land, labour and capital engaged in producing farm products, but not the protection of the inputs that farmers purchase from the rest of the economy or by importation. Nominal protection is the usual measure of protection as indicated by the relative or percentage size of tariffs or where quantitative restrictions are used by the percentage excess of domestic price over the import price. Nominal protection is a measure of the protection afforded a commodity, while effective protection is a measure of the protection afforded the industry that combines various resources and inputs to produce the commodity.

If agriculture purchased no inputs from the rest of the economy, the degree of protection of agricultural activity could be measured by a calculation of tariff rates or of the discrepancy between domestic and world market prices for the output of each country. But this type of calculation, which is quite common, is almost certain to under-estimate the effective protection for a given activity when a significant fraction of total inputs is purchased from outside a given sector.

A simple example may be used to illustrate this point. Most industrial countries permit certain raw materials to be imported free of duty, but place a tariff on products at the first stage of processing. The tariff may appear to be quite nominal, say 10 per cent, on the first processed products. Assume that there is no tariff on soyabeans, but soyabean oil and soyabean cake or meal have a 10 per cent tariff. The cost of processing soyabeans into oil and meal is approximately 10 per cent of the value of the soyabeans. Thus the activity which is protected by the 10 per cent tariff – the processing of soyabeans – does not have an effective protection of 10 per cent, but has in fact a degree of protection of 100 per cent.

If a significant fraction of the inputs used by agriculture are purchased from either domestic or foreign sources, a seemingly modest difference in the tariffs on output and inputs will mean that the degree of protection of the farming activity is much greater than the nominal protection as conventionally measured. The following simple example is designed to show two things: first, the difference between the effective and nominal rates of protection and, second, the effects of an increase in the importance of purchased inputs on the rate of effective protection for given nominal rates of protection. In Chapter 4 it was noted that one effect of the increased relative importance of inputs purchased from the non-farm sector was to increase the degree of protection even when the difference between domestic and world prices was unchanged.

Assume a country in which the average difference between domestic farm output and world prices is 40 per cent and the tariff on all inputs purchased by farmers is 10 per cent. In one part of the example, purchased inputs are equal to 25 per cent of the value of output, the situation in a number of countries in the 1950s. In the other part of the example, purchased inputs are 45 per cent of output value. The effective protection of agricultural production may be calculated as shown in Table 6.11.

The degree of effective protection of farm production in the first case is not 40 per cent, but considerably greater, or 54 per cent. In other words, the domestic farm inputs in this country receive a return that is 54 per cent greater than it would be if there were no tariffs on either inputs or output. The second part shows the sharp increase in the degree of effective protection due solely to the increase in the relative importance of purchased inputs. The nominal rates of protection are the same in Part I and Part II; all that has changed is the substitution of

Table 6.11   Calculation of effective protection of agricultural production

		Part I	Part II
A.	In domestic prices		
	Value of total output	100	100
	Value of purchased inputs	25	45
	Value of farm inputs[a]	75	55
B.	In world prices		
	Value of total output	71.4	71.4
	Value of purchased inputs	22.7	40.9
	Value of farm inputs[a]	48.7	30.5
C.	Farm inputs at domestic prices[b] divided by		
	Farm inputs at world prices	1.54	1.80
D.	Rate of effective protection (%)	54	80

[a]Farm inputs include the inputs not purchased from other sectors of the economy and thus consist primarily of labour and land.
[b]The value of farm inputs represents the value added by agriculture.

purchased inputs for farmer-owned inputs to approximately the same extent as has occurred in several industrial countries over the past quarter-century. The increase in the effective rate of protection is from 54 to 80 per cent. It should be no surprise that surpluses have been generated by the farm price policies.

To my knowledge, policy-makers in the industrial countries have not taken this type of effect into account in the establishment of subsidies and price supports. Because they have not done so, the effective degree of protection to agriculture has become substantially greater than what was originally intended. Since the major policy objective, however, is some concept of income parity and such income parity is seldom if ever achieved, there is always an excuse for not reducing the nominal rates of protection even when this means that the effective rate is increasing.

It can also occur, of course, that the effective rate of protection may be substantially less than the nominal rate of protection. As noted in the next chapter, this may have been the situation with respect to pork in the European Community, at least for certain periods. The very high rate of nominal protection is not much more than is required to offset the high prices for feed-grains and the high land prices that have resulted from the high feed and food grains prices. Thus, with respect to pork, Common Market protection is responsible for high prices to consumers and little else.

7 World Prices for Farm Products – Real or Fictitious?

Three main lines of arguments are now used to support the protection of agriculture. One is that the farmers of the country or region have some particular disadvantage, such as small farms, poor land or bad weather, that increases their costs compared with those who farm under more satisfactory conditions.

A second argument is that the world market prices for most farm products are significantly distorted and fail to reflect real cost conditions due to the use of export subsidies, production subsidies and import restrictions.[1] Thus the argument is made that no single country or region can afford to open its market to imports or it will be deluged with products that are priced unfairly and unreasonably low.

A third argument is that international market prices are highly variable and it would be unreasonable to subject either domestic consumers or producers to so much variability of prices for the major food products. This third line of argument for protection is a relatively recent innovation. Since the Second World War agricultural protection has been assigned the added objective of achieving a high degree of price stability for domestic producers and consumers of farm products. Consequently the form of protection has become important since different protective measures do not provide the same degree of domestic price stability. The argument for a form of protection that provides a high degree of domestic price stability, such as variable import levies, is that international market prices are highly unstable and that domestic producers and consumers should not be subjected to any degree of price instability.

The presumed shortcomings of international market prices are thus used to justify a significant degree of protection for agriculture and particular forms of protection, namely those forms that stabilize domestic prices. When the arguments for particular restraints on trade become self-fulfilling, high rates of protection imposed by major importers induce exporters to subsidize their producers. And vice versa: export subsidies justify the imposition of import restraints.

It is now quite clear that one effect of achieving domestic price stability is to increase price instability in international markets and in countries whose domestic prices vary with export and import prices. It is more than a little ironical that one of the claimed benefits for the European Community's common agricultural policy in 1974 and 1975 was that it prevented the high international market prices for grain from being imposed on the consumers in the Community since an important source of the high prices was the price stability provided by the CAP. Due to that price stability, the Community failed to adjust in any way to the shortfalls in world grain production in 1972 or 1974, neither consuming less nor providing its farmers with an incentive to produce more. The Community was not alone in this behaviour; among its companions were most other countries of Western and Eastern Europe, the Soviet Union, Japan and China. As will be noted later, Australia and Canada followed domestic price policies that contributed to the sharp increase in world grain prices in 1973 and 1974. It is worth noting that several countries that give great emphasis to domestic price stability for consumers have done so by establishing consumer prices that are substantially below those paid to their farmers. The policies of these countries, primarily the centrally-planned economies of Europe and Asia, have not only contributed to international price instability but have added to world import demand for grains, feeding materials and meat. Consequently it should not be assumed that all interventions depress international market prices; some have significantly increased such prices.

Arguments for Trade Interventions

The view that world prices of agricultural products were not adequate guides to real costs was reflected in an anonymous but apparently official French source in 1963 as the CAP was evolving:[2]

> The variable levy applied by the EEC to agricultural imports from non-member countries is aimed at making up the difference between the abnormally low world prices at which products are usually sold and prices within the Community. It is therefore nothing more than the counterpart of the export subsidies used by these non-member countries; these subsidies also vary in relation to world prices so that products may be marketed below domestic

prices. While this variable levy presents an effective counter to the disturbing effects of dumping foreign surpluses, it is not intended to prevent the entry of products that meet a need on the Community market, either because of their quality or the services provided.

A rather more restrained and accurate statement was made by a group of experts brought together by the Atlantic Institute of International Affairs in Paris in 1970:[3]

The meaningfulness of world prices may be questioned in the light of the present distorted nature of the world market. One method of determining world prices is to examine the prices paid by the largest importing country, Great Britain. Such an examination shows that for cereals this price is about the same as the prices received by producers in the main exporting countries, the United States and Canada. Even under the favourable conditions of production in Canada, there is an element of subsidy in the prices. Moreover, the similarity of the world price to prices received by producers in exporting countries disappeared when the International Wheat Agreement was broken. As a result prices in world markets fell below those paid to producers in exporting countries . . .

The agricultural policies of the industrialized countries are increasingly caught up in a vicious circle: they all contribute to the collapse of world prices and at the same time they are all condemned to protect themselves from the effects of low world prices in an even more uncompromising manner. Butter is the most extreme example. Under a regime of free competition the world market price would be established at a level that would just cover the costs of production of the highest cost producer whose output was still needed to meet the demands. What happens is the very opposite. The costs of production of the producer most favoured by climate and technological advance, New Zealand, should provide the basis for world prices. However, the Community being unable to find other outlets for its butter, subsidizes its export to the point of selling *below* the New Zealand price and thereby continually forces the New Zealand price to decline. The price for one hundred kilos of butter in London once went as low as $47.25; today it is $68 whilst the internal price of the Community exceeds $187.

Spokesmen for the United States have made similar arguments to justify the use of various forms of export subsidies. For example, in early 1983, John R. Block, as Secretary of Agriculture, said the following in testimony before a Congressional committee:[4]

> The practices of some foreign governments pose extremely difficult issues for US trade policy. The European Economic Community now engages in massive subsidized export action of agricultural products to dispose of the surpluses created by its high internal price-support program. Other countries, such as Japan, severely limit market access. These measures depress world prices of agricultural products, imposing substantial costs on US producers in a sector where the United States holds a clear comparative advantage.

In the same testimony, Mr Block referred to the successes that had been achieved through the use of export credit subsidies in increasing agricultural exports. He also referred to the highly subsidized export of 1 million tons of flour to Egypt. The low delivered price to Egypt, a price that did not even cover the cost of the wheat used to produce the flour, was apparently justified by the use of export subsidies by others: 'In the past few years, the Egyptian market for flour imports has been dominated by the European Community through its use of export subsidies.'

An argument to justify protectionism not specifically included in the three already noted is that the world demand for food will outpace the world supply of food in the years ahead and, therefore, countries must maintain a high degree of food self-sufficiency. While one occasionally finds such a view expressed by a spokesman for the European Community, the view is most readily identified with Japan. In a report issued in June 1982 by the Japanese Ministry of Agriculture, Forestry and Fisheries there was included, in a section headed 'The Necessity for Maintenance of Domestic Agricultural Production', projections of world food demand–supply balances and of international market prices for 2000. From the viewpoint of Japan, the projections of the world food supply situation for the rest of this century presented a gloomy picture of shortages and high prices.

Briefly, in the year 2000, the world will be short of grain if prices remain constant: 'a grain shortage of 53 million tons will occur in the case of normal crop and a shortage of 198 million tons in case both the United States and the Soviet Union are simultaneously hit by crop failures. There will also be considerable shortage of livestock products.'5 The price adjustments that would be required to equilibrate import demand with export supply were projected for 2000. The prices of grains and soyabeans were projected to increase by 70 to 80 per cent in real terms compared with 1978 while the prices of meat were projected to increase 30 per cent. If the United States and the Soviet Union were hit by two years of simultaneous crop failures, grain and soyabean prices would increase by from three to four times, except that rice prices would only double.

As I will indicate later (Chapter 8), the world has not entered a period when the demand for agricultural products will grow more rapidly than the supply. The evidence for that view seems to me to be overwhelming, yet there continue to be projections of food shortages made both by private individuals or groups and governmental agencies. Among the most striking, and thus most misleading and wrongheaded, set of such projections were included in *The Global 2000 Report to the President*, prepared at the end of the Carter Administration in the United States.

This chapter consists of three major parts. The first two parts address the issue of whether the average level of world prices of major farm products have been significantly affected by the numerous interventions in domestic prices and international trade. The first of the two parts will be largely historical and will consist of a summary of the results presented in Chapter 7 of the original edition of *World Agriculture in Disarray*. The second part will present the results of several recent and more sophisticated studies of the effects of domestic policies and trade restrictions upon the level of international market prices for farm products. These studies were all published after 1973. The summary of my earlier work assumes that the price effects of trade interventions during the 1960s and early 1970s still have relevance for the future. Can one generalize from that period to what may occur in the late 1980s and early 1990s? Obviously I believe that the period before the early 1970s does have relevance to the future, if for no other reason than that many of the protectionist policies that now plague world trade in farm products were formulated and perfected in the 1960s under the assumption that world market prices were seriously distorted. But there is also an empirical relevance, as will be seen from the general conformity of the estimates of the price effects during the 1960s and early 1970s and those estimated for more recent years. With the exceptions of dairy products, sugar and rice, the international market prices were depressed by such small percentages, at least until the mid-

1980s, that nominal protection rates of 50 to 100 per cent are difficult to justify on the ground of distorted international prices.

The third part of the chapter considers the sources of international price instability. The interrelationships between national agricultural policies, including both their domestic and trade implications, and instability of prices in international markets is explored. As is shown, governmental policies influence not only the average level but also the instability of international prices. The evidence indicates that the net effect of national agricultural policies is significantly greater in inducing price instability than in changing the average level of world market prices. In the 1980s international price instability was significantly greater than during the 1960s and about the same as it was in the 1970s.

Market Price Distortions – 1960s and Early 1970s

The following discussion of market price distortions is either taken directly (with some editorial but no substantive change) from the original edition or is a summary of the material presented there. As I noted, my estimates of how much the trade and agricultural policies of the industrial countries depressed world prices of major agricultural products was not based on systematic econometric investigation of supply and demand. The somewhat impressionistic conclusions were made on the basis of the available evidence on elasticities of supply such as those presented in Table 6.5 and some general ideas of demand elasticities.

Wheat

During the 1960s and early 1970s the three major wheat exporters made efforts to increase wheat prices in the commercial international market. This was reflected by numerous actions, such as large food-aid shipments by the United States, restriction of wheat acreage in the United States in every year from 1961 through 1972, a striking reduction of wheat acreage by half in Canada in 1970, the imposition of delivery quotas in Australia in 1970 and 1971 and the accumulation of large carry-over stocks at various times by the United States and Canada. In addition, the United States, Canada and Australia used pressure to establish a relatively high minimum price for wheat in the International Grains Arrangement of 1967.

Intention and achievement, of course, are not the same. Each of the three countries did some things that encourage expansion of wheat production. In Canada, the federal government paid the storage costs on carry-over stocks held by the Canadian Wheat Board in excess of 5 million tons; Canada also had a freight-rate structure that involved substantial subsidy to wheat exports. Australia maintained support prices and guaranteed returns on all domestically consumed wheat plus 5.4 million tons of exports.

What was generally ignored, however, was that the fourth largest exporter of wheat – Argentina – permitted her farmers a price that was significantly *below* the world price. This was not a new development. It had been true for almost a quarter of a century. Because of the use of multiple exchange rates and the over-valuation of the Argentine peso, it was difficult to measure the extent of the difference between the proceeds to domestic producers and the international price, but in the summer of 1970 wheat was subject to an export tax of approximately 20 per cent plus a discriminatory exchange rate of about 17 per cent; in effect, the farmers were at that time receiving about two-thirds of the price at which Argentine wheat was sold in international markets. In addition, the policy of import substitution increased input costs for farming to a not-insignificant degree. To some extent the restraints on wheat production in Argentina offset the more aggressive actions of its export competitors, although there is no implication that the offset was complete.

The United States had a series of programmes affecting wheat, some intended to restrict production and some to encourage it. Unfortunately, the research has not been undertaken that indicates the net output effects of the programmes. The cropland devoted to wheat was limited by governmental action and in 1970–72 was a third below the peak of 30 million hectares reached in 1947 when wheat prices were high and no governmental programmes were in effect. It is not known to what degree the reduction in wheat area was due primarily to the lower real returns from wheat production or to acreage restrictions that have been imposed. The official position of the United States Department of Agriculture was that the programmes reduced wheat area and output.

It is probable that some of the effects of the area restrictions were offset by the higher average return per ton that was realized during the period. Under the land regulations that were in effect, wheat producers were given individual allotments specifying permitted harvested area. Two types of payments are made: one called a price-support payment on approximately 45 per cent of anticipated production and the other a payment for diversion of additional land. Most of the payments were of the first kind and the second type of payment was not available in 1967 and 1968. The price-support payments were large, being the difference between the loan rate and the parity price of wheat which was approximately $102 per ton in 1969. The support payment was financed by a marketing certificate of about $27 per ton for all wheat used for food, with the remainder being paid from the Treasury. For several years during the period the market price received by farmers for their wheat approximated the export price; in some years there were export taxes and in other years there have been export subsidies.

An unresolved question concerning the wheat programme is whether farmers respond to *average* returns or *marginal* returns. The marginal returns – the amount received for an additional ton of wheat produced – is the market price while the average return is the market price plus the total payments from the programme divided by total production. If farmers respond to the marginal returns in their decisions concerning inputs, then the wheat programme certainly reduced production; if they respond to the average returns, then yields have undoubtedly been increased because of the payments. The situation was complicated by the fact that the yield used to allocate the marketing certificates or price-support payments was the average yield of (approximately) the previous three years. Thus decisions that influence yields in a given year would be affected by the changes in prospective payments under the programme. An additional yield of 50 kilograms per hectare was worth more than the market price for that year; the higher yield had some probability of increasing payments received under the programme in future years. The effect on output was almost certainly small compared with the area reductions that were achieved, but the method of payment still represented an anomaly in a programme designed to reduce output. But no one should be surprised at anomalies in agricultural programmes!

Table 7.1 provides certain measures of the effect of various features of the wheat programme on the return to wheat producers in the United States for the period 1964 to 1974. The first column gives the average prices received by farmers for 1964/65 and after. This was the market price and it was the actual return per unit of output for about 15 per cent of the total wheat area, since some farmers chose not to participate in the wheat programme. Prior to 1964/65 the wheat programme was mandatory, but after that date farmers were able to choose participation or not. Thus about a sixth of the wheat was produced by farmers who each year decided that the market price alone offered greater opportunity for profit than meeting the requirements of the wheat programme. The majority of farmers who participated in the wheat programme received a marketing certificate payment on that part of their individual acreage allotment that, on the average, was used for domestic food. The second column gives the value of these certificates per ton of wheat produced on participating farms. In order to receive the certificate payment, farmers restricted their acreage to the amount of their allotment. Additional payments were earned in some years by diverting a larger area than required, but such additional diversion was unimportant for the period covered by Table 7.1. The third column is the sum of the prices received and the average value of the marketing certificate and is thus the average return received by participants in the programme.

Table 7.1　Market prices, supplementary payments and export subsidies for wheat in the United States, 1964/65 to 1973/74

Crop year	Price received by farmers	Marketing certificates and payment[a] ($ per ton)	Average return, programme participants	Export subsidy ($ per ton exported)
1964/65	50.85	15.78	66.06	8.44
1965/66	49.54	16.15	65.69	17.25
1966/67	59.82	21.55	81.47	8.44
1967/68	51.01	17.51	68.63	2.90
1968/69	45.51	20.18	65.69	–[b]
1969/70	45.88	23.49	69.36	5.10
1970/71	48.81	27.42	71.34	8.00
1971/72	49.18	19.82	69.00	5.14
1972/73	64.59	17.25	81.84	9.38
1973/74	145.33	8.44	155.03	1.41[c]

[a]For programme participants only.
[b]No export subsidy was paid.
[c]The wheat export subsidy programme was suspended in August 1972 and no new wheat export subsidy commitments were made until the 1980s. The subsidy payments made in 1973/74 were made on wheat exports for which a commitment had been made prior to the suspension in August 1972.
Source: *1974 Feed Grain, Wheat and Upland Cotton Programs* (Washington: Agricultural Stabilization and Conservation Service, United States Department of Agriculture, 1975) pp. 67–88.

The last column of the table is the average export subsidy on American wheat. Export subsidies were relatively unimportant in three crop years – 1967/68, 1968/69 and 1969/70 – but increased during the first half of 1970/71 and were then entirely eliminated on some types and classes of wheat for the next several months. Later the export subsidies were reinstated. None were paid after 1973/74 until 1982.

Prior to 1973/74 the market price remained fairly stable, as did the average return to programme participants.

As noted earlier, it is not clear which of the various measures of returns influence farmers' decisions with respect to output, especially that part of output due to yield. For at least a sixth of the total output – for wheat produced outside the programme – it was the market price or average price received by farmers.

It is clear that the wheat programme had some effect on the area seeded to wheat. Changes in the programme, such as in 1967/68 and 1968/69 when the wheat allotment was increased very substantially and then reduced but not to the level in 1966/67, were followed by significant changes in the area seeded. In 1967/68 the area seeded to wheat increased by about 20 per cent in response to a 35 per cent increase in allotments and other changes in the programme. In the following year the allotment was reduced by about 3.5 million hectares and the area harvested by 1.4 million hectares. What is not known, unfortunately, is what the wheat area would have been in the absence of the wheat programme. The relatively large area in 1967/68 was due, probably, not only to the changes in the wheat programme but the relatively favourable price of wheat in the previous year and the general, but mistaken, impression that the world was in for a period of stringency in the food grains.

The extent of subsidization of wheat production by the other two major wheat exporters – Australia and Canada – has been modest, certainly modest compared with the level implied by the quotation from the anonymous French source. Australia subsidized wheat production by setting a minimum price for domestic food use of wheat and by operating a price-stabilization pool with a guaranteed price for a specific quantity of exports. Throughout the 1960s the price-stabilization pool lost money; the average loss per ton of wheat exported from 1965/66 through 1968/69 was $4.80 per ton compared with an average wheat export value of $59 per ton. The price for home food consumption ($70 in 1968/69) applied to only a tenth of total output in most years.[6] The higher price for domestic food-use added about $1 to the average return received by farmers. Thus the combination of subsidy to exports and the price discrimination against domestic food users of wheat amounted to a subsidy rate of about 10 per cent during the latter half of the 1960s.

With this wheat policy Australian wheat area almost doubled to about 10 million hectares during the 1960s. Thus with a farm price that was not more than 10 per cent in excess of export returns there was a substantial expansion of wheat production. This experience indicates that even if there had been no subsidy to wheat production in Australia there would have been a substantial expansion of wheat production in one of the major wheat exporting countries, although such expansion would have been smaller than what actually occurred.

In 1969/70 and again in 1970/71, due to the accumulation of substantial stocks of wheat by the end of the 1968/69 crop year, a wheat delivery quota was established. The purpose of the quota was to reduce stocks while permitting the Wheat Board to maintain its export price. The accumulation of wheat stocks in Australia, as well as in Canada, from 1966 through 1968 clearly held world wheat prices at a higher level than would have prevailed if these stocks had been disposed of in international markets.

As noted earlier in this chapter, Canada subsidized wheat production through the government bearing the costs of all stocks in excess of 5 million tons held by the Canadian Wheat Board and by favourable freight rates on exported wheat. The combined effect of these two measures could have increased the return to farmers by about 20 per cent or no more than $12 per ton. Canada may have encouraged the expansion of wheat production by accumulating substantial stocks of wheat, but in 1970 Canada undertook a programme to limit wheat production through acreage limitations and succeeded in reducing the wheat area by more than 50 per cent. By 1971 the planted wheat area in Canada was fully a third below the peak reached in 1968. In both Canada and Australia the governments were partly responsible for the expansion in wheat area after 1965 due to their unwarranted optimism about the future level of world wheat prices. Both governments increased their price guarantees to farmers, which only added to the optimism that the general increase in wheat prices in 1966 and 1967 had engendered. But both countries later took steps to reduce the wheat area and both were quite successful, especially Canada.

It is not clear how much protection there was of wheat production in the major exporting countries. As estimated earlier, Argentina taxed wheat, while the degree of nominal protection in Australia and Canada was estimated at 10 to 20 per cent. As noted above, it is unclear whether the combination of subsidies and acreage restrictions significantly reduced American wheat production. A minority of farmers chose to forgo the subsidies, but their situations were obviously somewhat atypical. The subsidies were very large and it is not unreasonable to assume that acreage was reduced somewhat by allotments. If the effect of the payments on yields just offset the acreage reduction, this would imply that American wheat output was approximately the same with the wheat programme as it would have been without it, although there is some probability that the programme reduced wheat production. In any case, it is unlikely that the policies of the four major exporters increased wheat production by more than 7 million tons or an amount that would result from an increase of wheat prices of 10 per cent if the supply elasticity were unity.

We can be reasonably certain that the degree of protection for the European Community and the West European importers was greater than 15 per cent.[7] If it had been that low, which it was not, then the absolute contribution to wheat output would have been about 7 or 8 million tons (15 per cent of 50 million tons).[8]

If the excess production of wheat had been of the order of 15 million tons, it does not follow that the world wheat price was lower than it would have been under free trade in wheat. Partially or entirely the additional output was offset by the denaturing of wheat for livestock feed in the European Community and the concessional sales made to the developing countries by the United States, Australia, Canada and the Community. There were also some subsidized exports of wheat for feed.[9] In the United States the change in market price policy for wheat, which brought the price of wheat close to the price of feed-grains, resulted in a substantial increase in the amount of wheat fed. The additional quantities of wheat fed by the end of the 1960s, compared with the beginning of the 1960s, was about 10 million tons annually in the Community and the United States.[10] In 1967/68 Australia, Canada, the Community and the United States exported 16.2 million tons of wheat under government-assisted programmes; in 1968/69 the amount was 12.7 million tons.[11] Some of the wheat and flour involved only limited concessional terms, while some undoubtedly replaced wheat that would have been purchased on regular commercial terms if the concessional terms had not been available. No one really knows how much wheat and flour the developing countries would have purchased in regular markets if food-aid had not been available. It appears quite reasonable to assume, however, that at least half of the wheat and flour exported under special terms was additional to what would otherwise have been purchased by the developing countries.[12] If only half of the

1968/69 concessional sales were counted as sales over and above what would have moved under free trade, the total of additional wheat fed and extra export disposals would exceed the estimate of additional wheat output due to protection. I do not want to say that the two effects exactly offset, but it is not unreasonable to assume that the discrepancy has been relatively small.

There is another reason why one can conclude that in the last half of the 1960s the world wheat price was approximately what it would have been under free trade. In the United States and in international markets the prices of several types and qualities of wheat have been very close to the feeding value of wheat given the market prices of feed-grains. The output of feed-grains in the industrial countries was more than twice the output of wheat. While the use of wheat for feeding in substantial quantities had some adverse effects on feed-grain prices, the effect was modest because of the much larger volume of feed-grains involved. It was highly probable that under a free trade situation wheat prices, except for certain wheats with special milling qualities, would be close to feed-grain prices.

In the above discussion the price elasticity of demand for wheat as food has been ignored. Lower market prices for wheat would result in some increased consumption, but the effect would be small. It would certainly be too small to divorce wheat prices from feed-grain under free trade. The reason is that the price elasticity of demand for wheat is very low in all of the industrial countries, except Japan where there is substitution of wheat for rice.

While world wheat prices were certainly not free of substantial interference and departure from the conditions of free trade, it apparently should not be concluded that levels of world market prices were significantly lower than the prices that would have prevailed under something approximating free trade prior to 1973. While wheat production was increased in Australia, Canada, the European Community and other Western European countries by protectionist policies, it is not clear what wheat output would have been in the United States in the absence of acreage restrictions and subsidies. With respect to the United States, the most reasonable conclusion is that wheat output was little affected and if there had been an effect, it was to reduce output somewhat. Argentina clearly discouraged wheat production by pricing policy. Offsetting all or most of the expansion of output was the increased use of wheat for feed and the increase in imports by developing countries over and above what their imports would have been in the absence of food-aid programmes. While there was some restriction of wheat use as food because of high domestic prices in most industrial countries, this effect was small because of the low price elasticity of demand.

On balance, it would be very difficult to support the view that world market prices of wheat would have differed by more than 10 per cent from free trade levels and it is not certain whether the difference would have been positive or negative. In any case, much of the downward pressure that existed was due to high prices paid to producers in Western Europe. Thus even if world wheat prices had been depressed, such depression can hardly stand as justification for variable import levies that ranged up to 90 per cent during the 1960s and early 1970s.

Feed-grains

During the 1960s the United States supplied half of world feed-grain exports, Argentina about 13 per cent, France almost 10 per cent, South Africa about 4 per cent, Canada only 2 per cent and the Soviet Union about 3 per cent. A group of other countries, including Thailand, provided about a fifth of the total. Of the major exporters it can be alleged that three engaged in some degree of protection of feed-grain production – the United States, the Soviet Union and France. The feed-grain price was depressed during the 1960s by the subsidization of wheat for feed purposes, especially in the European Community for both internal use and export.

Because of its importance in the international feed-grain market, the situation in the United States merits the most attention. As in the case of wheat, the United States had a programme designed to limit the production of feed-grains. It was a voluntary programme in the sense that each farmer could decide to participate or not as he desired. If he participated, he agreed to limit the area devoted to one or more of the feed-grains. In return he received payments of two types – one for diversion of land into non-productive use and one as a price-support payment based on projected production on a specified amount of land. To receive the price-support payment some land diversion was originally required, generally 20 per cent of the farm base. In later years, however, no explicit payment was made for the required 20 per cent diversion and diversion payments could be earned only if additional land were diverted. In most years small farmers (with 10 hectares or less of feed-grain base) could divert their entire acreage and receive diversion payments, although no price-support payments.

In some years the total payments under the programme were very large – $1664 million in 1969/70. The average payment per ton was about $10.45 in that year, or about 22 per cent of the average farm price of feed-grains. After 1963 there were no export subsidies on corn and oats, and relatively modest subsidies on grain sorghums and barley.[13] Except for the period of food scarcity in India in the mid-1960s, only 5 to 7 per cent of American feed-grain exports were due to Public Law 480 shipments (sold on concessional terms – in the currencies of recipient countries – under the Food for Peace programme) during the 1960s and early 1970s.

Table 7.2 gives certain data on prices received by farmers and the amount of payments per ton of feed-grain produced both for total payments and for price-support payments only. The price-support payment ranged from $2.32 to $4.60 per ton or generally of the order of 6 to 11 per cent of the price received by farmers for corn. Total payments ranged from $5.43 to $10.45 per ton or 12 to 25 per cent of the price of corn.

Table 7.2   Market prices, supplementary payments and export subsidies for feed-grains in the United States, 1962/63 to 1972/73

Crop year	Prices received by farmers for corn ($ per ton)	Average programme payments ($ per ton of all feed-grains)	Export subsidy ($ per ton exported)
1962/63	44.02	6.56	—
1963/64	43.62	6.06	—
1964/65	45.98	9.61	0.75
1965/66	45.59	9.68	1.46
1966/67	48.73	9.06	0.38
1967/68	40.48	5.43	—
1968/69	42.50		—
1969/70	45.65	10.30	0.83
1970/71	52.34	5.62	0.55
1971/72	42.50	10.27	—
1972/73	61.78	6.28	—

Sources: *Agricultural Statistics*, United States Department of Agriculture, Washington, various issues; and *Feed Situation and Outlook Report*, United States Department of Agriculture, Washington, various issues.

But it should be noted that part or all of the price-support payment was required to induce farmers to participate in the acreage-restriction programme. It is in large part an administrative decision, although also partially political, how the payments are divided between acreage diversion and price support. Despite the seemingly high level of payments in the period covered by the table, the maximum percentage of the seeded area of feed-grains grown on participating farms was 44 per cent in 1969; in 1966 it was only 39 per cent. Thus from 56 to 62 per cent of the feed-grain planted area was on farms where the decision was made not to participate in the programmes and receive the payments.

If the feed-grain programme had an output increasing effect, it was only through providing incentives for higher yields on the participating farms. This effect was surely at least offset by a reduction in the planted area of feed-grains from about 61 million hectares in 1959 to 47–49 million hectares in 1965–70. There is no proof that all of the reduction was due to the acreage restriction programme, but some part was.

Because such a large fraction of the feed-grain producers elected to remain outside the programme and forgo the payments that would have been available, I conclude that from 1962 through 1972 the feed-grain programme did not put downward pressure on the market price of such grains. In the long run it is possible that the payments induced some farms and some land to stay in production that would otherwise have gone out of production with the land used much less intensively. But it may be noted that for the 1969 crop year a third of the payments were made to farmers who virtually gave up the production of feed-grains, entirely on some farms and nearly so on others. The two groups included 850 000 farms out of a total number of 3.2 million with a history of feed-grain production.[14] It is true that these farms were small, but together they accounted for about 10 per cent of the national feed-grain base.[15] The total base of these farms was about 5 million hectares and the planted area of feed-grains in 1969 was only 440 000 hectares.[16] Thus it would appear that many of the probable high-cost producers had been bribed to give up feed-grain production, either entirely or in large part.

Three of the major feed-grain exporters – Argentina, South Africa and Canada – did not significantly subsidize except through preferential freight rates in South Africa and Canada while Argentina imposed export taxes on the feed-grains as it did on wheat. The other two major exporters engaged in heavy subsidization of feed-grains. In 1967, for example, the average export unit value for barley sold by the Soviet Union was $63 per ton while the average procurement price was $84. All of the Common Market feed-grain exports, originating primarily in France, that went outside of the Community were subsidized. The size of the subsidy was approximately equal to the import cost for feed-grains. In 1968/69 the Community exported approximately 2.7 million tons of feed-grain to countries outside the Community.[17]

Another source of downward pressure on world feed-grain prices was the subsidization of wheat for feed-grain use. In the late 1960s the European Community denatured and subsidized about 4 million tons of wheat for feed use.[18] This amounted to about 9 per cent of total feed use in the Community.[19] Wheat for use as feed was also exported and the quantity of such wheat rose towards the end of the 1960s.[20]

During the last half of the 1960s world feed-grain exports averaged about 42 million tons.[21] The 4 million tons of denatured wheat plus the more than 3 million tons of heavily subsidized feed-grains and feed wheat from the European Community were large relative to world exports, although small compared with world feed-grain production of 450 million tons.[22] Since two-thirds of the feed-grains were produced in North America and Western Europe, the more relevant comparison of the subsidized quantities is to total production rather than to exports.

During the 1960s the most important source of downward pressure on feed-grain prices was the restriction on feed-grain use caused by high prices of feed-grains in most of Western Europe. Excepting only the United Kingdom and Denmark, the protection of feed-grains limited livestock production. If protection of feed-grains had been at moderate levels during the latter part of the 1960s, meat prices could have been reduced by 30 per cent in all of Western Europe excluding the United Kingdom and Denmark. What effect would the reduction in meat prices have had upon the demand for feed-grains? Assuming a price elasticity of demand for meat of -0.6, the increase in meat consumption would have been about 20 per cent. Excluding the United Kingdom and Denmark, grain consumption by livestock in Western Europe in the late 1960s was estimated to be 60 million tons. A 20 per cent increase in meat consumption would have required about 12 million tons of feed-grains to feed the additional livestock.

On balance, world feed-grain prices during the 1960s and early 1970s were only a little lower than they would have been in the absence of the price and subsidy programmes that encouraged production and prices that discouraged consumption. The high prices for feed-grains in Western Europe were offset, in considerable part, by the United States' efforts to restrict output and the adverse price conditions confronting farmers in Argentina. The consumption restrictions that resulted from high livestock prices were probably not offset by other factors, but such adverse effects on world feed-grain prices should not have been used as an argument against freer trade in grains by the nations responsible for the high domestic feed-grain prices. A reasonable estimate of the effects of all the interventions affecting the production and consumption of feed-grains was that during the late 1960s and early 1970s the price of maize at Rotterdam was reduced by approximately 10 per cent. In summary, it was not unreasonable to conclude that international prices of the feed-grains during the late 1960s and early 1970s were depressed by 10 per cent or less by the actual farm policies and trade interventions compared with what the prices would have been if there had been free trade in grains in the industrial countries.

Soyabeans

While the soyabean is only one source of high-protein animal feeds and vegetable oil, by the mid-1960s it was the most important source. In 1968 world production of the major vegetable oilseeds (soyabean, cottonseed, groundnut, sunflower and flaxseed) was 95.5 million tons.[23] Soyabean production was 43.6 million tons, or 46 per cent of the total. Approximately two-thirds of all soyabeans were produced in the United States. Cottonseed is a secondary joint product with cotton lint and its output is influenced more by the price of cotton than by the price of products derived from cottonseed.[24]

The emphasis on soyabean prices is relevant for two reasons. First, expansion in soyabean production was very great and two-thirds of the increase in world production of the major oilseeds between 1952–56 and 1968 was due to the increase in soyabeans.[25] Second, the soyabean was grown primarily in temperate zones and the largest producer was an industrial country, while most of the other major oilseeds (except sunflower and rape) are grown primarily in tropical or semi-tropical zones or in the warmer areas of the temperate zone.

During the 1960s acreage and production of soyabeans approximately doubled in the United States. The only direct governmental programme for soyabeans was a price-support programme. The price support had little effect, however, on the average level of soyabean prices since year-end stocks were generally small, ranging from about one to six weeks' supply, except at the end of the 1968 crop year when stocks increased to fifteen weeks' supply as a result of support prices that were too high in 1967 and 1968. Price supports were lowered in

1969 and 1970 and, by the end of 1971, stocks were back to minimal levels.

While there have been no direct subsidies for soyabean production, it could be argued that acreage limitations on cotton and the grains induced a shift of land from these crops into soyabeans, since soya-beans have not been subject to any acreage limitations. The land diverted under the major farm programmes, however, could not be used (legally) for soyabean production, although other resources (labour and machinery) could be. The relationship between changes in the land devoted to wheat, feed-grains and cotton, on the one hand, and soyabeans, on the other hand, do not appear to have been very close in the 1960s. In other words, when the combined area of the controlled crops increased, the area devoted to soyabean did not decline. For example, between 1966 and 1969 the increase in land harvested for the three major crops was 900 000 hectares; during the same period, the area devoted to soyabeans also increased by 1.8 million hectares.

There were two considerations on the demand side that had a positive effect on soyabean prices. One was the importation of soya-beans and soyabean meal into the European Community without duty or levy and the resulting distortion in price relationships due to the high rate of protection of feed-grains (see Chapter 6). The relative price situation encouraged the use of high-protein feeds, although this encouragement was partially offset by the effects of high grain prices restricting the consumption, and thus the production, of livestock products within the Community. The other factor was the disposal of a substantial quantity of soyabean and other vegetable oils under United States PL 480 enacted after the Second World War. From 1955 through 1969 about two-thirds of all American exports of soyabean oil was made under government-financed programmes, primarily sales for foreign currencies.[26] By the end of the 1960s soyabean oil exports, including both commercial and government sales, involved about 15 per cent of all American soyabean oil production.[27] The effect of the subsidized exports of soyabean oil, as well as PL 480 exports of cottonseed oil, was probably to increase the domestic and world price of vegetable oils.[28]

The primary determinants, though, of the price of soyabeans were the price of maize and the relative costs of producing maize and soyabeans in the United States. Soyabeans and maize are substitutes in both use and production. During the 1950s and 1960s the price of soyabeans gradually increased relative to the price of maize due to changes in relative costs of production. Farmers were much more successful in increasing maize than soyabean yields. These changes, it may be noted, continued during the 1970s. Thus during the 1950s soyabean prices were somewhat less than twice maize prices while by the end of the 1960s the soyabean price was about 2.2 times that of maize. From year-to-year soyabean prices followed closely the changes in maize prices. Either under the policies that prevailed during the 1960s and early 1970s or free trade, the prices of soyabeans would have been determined primarily by maize prices. Thus soyabean prices during the period were probably depressed by up to 10 per cent compared with the prices that would have prevailed with free trade.

Meats

The discussion of the effects of domestic policies and trade restrictions on meats was inconclusive, except for the direction. It was noted that, as of the early 1970s, there was general agreement among the various projection exercises that the meats, especially beef and veal, had excellent prospects for expanded world trade. The income elasticities of demand were positive and high, at least compared with other food products. The price elasticities of demand for meat were also relatively high. Consequently the reduction in consumer prices of meat that would result from free trade would result in a significant increase in consumption in several high-income countries and a large increase in world trade in meats.

It is almost true to say that the restraints on importation of meat are primarily to protect grain prices or to reduce the cost of maintaining a particular support or intervention price. This statement was illustrated by comparing the total returns from producing a ton of pork (liveweight) and the cost of feed in the European Community and the United States. In 1968 the price of hogs (liveweight) received by the European Community's farmers was $662 per ton compared with approximately $400 per ton in the United States. Assuming that 600 kilograms of feed was used to produce 100 kilograms of liveweight, the margin between the value of the hogs and the feed cost was $134 in the Community and $148 in the United States.[29]

Except for the effects of high dairy product prices, there was no evidence that the production of meats was significantly encouraged by governments during the 1960s and early 1970s. In Argentina, as with the grains, domestic prices of beef were below export prices. In the United States, tariff duties and the quotas on beef and veal did not result in a beef price more than 10 per cent higher than it would have been if the United States permitted free imports. But the elimination of the high rates of protection of milk production in Western Europe, the United States and Canada would have a positive effect on the price of beef since an important source of beef in the industrial countries is as a joint product with milk.

The other important factor depressing world market prices for beef was the effect of high beef prices on the consumption of beef in Western Europe. The price elasticity of demand was estimated to be −0.6. If the Common Market retail prices of beef had been increased by a third, the per capita consumption of beef was reduced by 20 per cent. In 1969 beef and veal consumption totalled 4.6 million tons in the original Six members of the Community.[30] If the prices had been similar to those then prevailing in the United Kingdom, consumption would have increased to 5.5 million tons. The increase in consumption of a million tons compared with total beef and veal exports from Australia and New Zealand in 1961–65 of 559 000 tons.[31] It in fact exceeded the net imports of OECD countries of 815 000 tons from all sources.

While it was clear that meat prices in international markets would have been higher under free trade than with the then existing trade restrictions in the industrial countries, no estimate was made of the magnitude of the price distortion.

Dairy Products

No projection was made of the price effects of the numerous interventions that affected the world market price of dairy products in the late 1960s and early 1970s. It was true then, as now, that all of the industrial countries protected their dairy industry by providing high price supports. And in the United States, by contrast to the farm programmes for grain and cotton, no effort was made to limit the output response to the relatively high dairy product prices. But none of the other industrial countries took any measures to prevent the production of milk from growing more rapidly than demand.

Of the industrial countries that produced dairy products in significant quantities, only New Zealand exported at essentially the same price that was paid to farmers. New Zealand had a price-stabilization scheme, but it remained that for the period under consideration rather than a disguised technique for increasing returns to producers. Over three decades the export trading operations for butter and cheese resulted in nil gain or loss to the government.

Among them the United States, Canada and the original Six members of the European Community produced about 40 per cent of the world's estimated 400 million-ton milk output in the late 1960s. And they were responsible for at least that large a percentage of the underlying disarray in the world's market for dairy products. The United States vigorously defended the sanctity of its borders (as it does now) against the importation of more than a negligible amount of dairy products. Its internal price for butter was approximately double the world price as of the early 1970s. Yet the United States utilized export subsidies and PL 480 shipments to dispose of significant quantities of dried milk, butter and condensed and evaporated products. Since the United States did not make any efforts to limit the production of milk, it had to obtain a GATT waiver for its import quotas on manufactured dairy products. The existence of a GATT waiver clearly weakened the bargaining position of the United States in its efforts to reduce other forms of interference with trade in agricultural products.

During the period Canada followed dairy price policies quite similar to those in the United States. Prices were similar and import licences were used to control imports of butter, skim milk powder, cheddar and colby cheeses.[32] Dairy products were included in the European Community's common agricultural policy and during the early 1970s it had high import levies on butter and cheese (generally 150 per cent or more of the import cost) and equal or greater export premiums or subsidies.

The world market prices of manufactured dairy products were clearly far below those that would have prevailed in a free trade situation. But given the validity of this statement, it was not a valid argument in support of the dairy policies followed by the industrial countries. It was not a valid argument because the wide differences between the domestic and world market prices were largely due to the policies that the industrial countries were following. If all of the industrial countries had simultaneously adopted free or liberal trade in dairy products as of 1970, producer prices would have fallen throughout most of Western Europe and North America, but the declines would have been a rather small fraction of the differences between domestic and world prices that then existed. There simply was not enough capacity to expand production in the low-cost dairy regions to have a significant impact on world milk supplies. Thus the increased consumption that would have resulted from some lowering of consumer prices of dairy products would have offset some of the price effects of increased production in New Zealand and Australia.

Cotton

The United States and the Soviet Union were both major industrial countries and major producers of cotton. Together they produced 50 per cent of world output in the late 1960s and their production was approximately equal. Both countries subsidized producers of cotton, although in the United States an effort was made, through acreage limitations, to keep cotton production at a reasonable level. In the United States cotton production declined by about a third during the 1960s. For the same period cotton output in the Soviet Union increased about 50 per cent.[33] Since the 1920s the Soviet Union had followed a policy of encouraging cotton production and in the late 1960s the procurement price was at least double the world price.[34]

Outside the United States and the Soviet Union, most cotton is grown in countries that are too poor to manipulate the price of cotton, except all-too-frequently to depress it by taxation or by over-valuation of its currency. From 1954 through the early 1970s there were acreage allotments for cotton in the United States. When there were no allotments in the years 1951–53 the harvested area of cotton was about 10 million hectares. The harvested area was gradually reduced to a little more than 5 million hectares in 1965. As cotton stocks continued to accumulate, the harvested area fell to a low of 3.2 million hectares in 1967. By 1970 the cotton area had increased to 4.3 million hectares. In the mid-1950s cotton production averaged 14–15 million bales. Production was reduced to 9.5 million bales in 1966 and to 7.5 million bales in 1967, then gradually increased to slightly more than 10 million by 1972.

In 1947–49 the United States produced almost half of the world's cotton; by 1969 its share had been reduced to 20 per cent. The decline in the United States share of world cotton production was due to a number of factors, but efforts to increase world cotton prices during the 1950s by reducing American production encouraged production in other regions of the world. The loss of export markets during the 1950s resulted in the introduction of export subsidies in 1956. While exports increased, output expansion outside the United States was not deterred. The export subsidy was abandoned in 1965, in part because

American mills found themselves faced with substantially higher raw-material costs than foreign mills that purchased American cotton at the subsidized price and then exported the finished product to the United States. The average price received by farmers for cotton declined from 31–32 cents per pound in 1961–63 to about 21–22 cents in 1969–70. There is evidence that the changes in cotton production during the 1960s occurred primarily in response to the prices received by farmers and, except for 1966 and 1967, the various features of the farm programme other than price supports had little effect on production.[35] And in the two years indicated the effect of the programme was to reduce substantially the harvested area.

The cotton programme during the 1960s and early 1970s appeared to have had at most a modest effect on the cotton area and apparently the same conclusion held for yields. It was concluded that for the period under review the cotton programme had not depressed world cotton prices; it may have had a very modest influence in raising the level of such prices.[36]

Price Distortions in the 1970s and 1980s

In my approximations of the price effects of trade liberalization I assumed that such liberalization would occur only in the OECD countries and that the price and other agricultural policies of the centrally-planned economies and the developing countries would remain unchanged. For each of the studies that will be summarized the degree of liberalization and the country coverage will be described.

Alberto Valdés and Joachim Zietz, in a study published by the International Food Policy Research Institute in Washington,[37] estimated the effects of a 50 per cent reduction in both tariff and non-tariff barriers for agricultural products by the OECD countries. The reduction in non-tariff barriers, such as import quotas, was measured by the change in the difference between the domestic and import price for each affected commodity. In other words, if a non-tariff barrier resulted in a domestic price double the import price, a 50 per cent reduction in protection would be achieved when the domestic price was 50 per cent greater than the import cost.

The objective of the Valdés–Zietz study was to provide a projection of the increase in the value of exports of agricultural products for the

World Agriculture in Disarray

world as a whole and for the less developed countries in particular. At this point my primary interest is in the world price effects of trade liberalization. The study included 99 commodities; the price increases associated with trade liberalization were presented for 47 of them. The estimates were based on the degree of protection prevailing in 1975–77. For some important commodities, especially sugar, nominal protection during these years was significantly less than during the 1960s or after 1978.

Table 7.3 Projected world price increases from a 50 per cent reduction in trade barriers in OECD countries

0–5%	5.1–7.5%	7.5–10%	>10%
Green coffee	Refined sugar	Cocoa butter oil	Roast coffee
Tobacco	Beef and veal	Pork	Cocoa paste
Maize	Olive oil	Molasses	Cocoa powder
Wheat	Potatoes	Apples	Malt
Soyabean cake	Barley	Copra cake	Wine
Tea	Coffee extracts	Sugar confectionery	
Palm oil	Groundnut oil	Oats	
Cocoa beans	Grapes		
Copra oil	Wheat flour		
Soyabeans	Sunflower cake		
Soyabean oil			
Bananas			
Milled rice			
Groundnut cake			
Beef preparations			
Mutton and lamb			
Oranges			
Beans, dry			
Groundnuts, shelled			
Chicken			
Castor oil			
Lemons and limes			
Sorghum			
Copra			

Source: Alberto Valdés and Joachim Zietz, *Agricultural Protection in OECD Countries: Its Costs to Less-developed Countries*, Research Report No. 21 (Washington: International Food Policy Research Institute, 1980), p. 46.

For the commodities that I analyzed above, the range in world price increases due to the 50 per cent reduction in the degree of protection was less than 1 per cent for rice to a high of nearly 9 per cent for pork. The increases projected for the remaining commodities were 7 per cent for beef and veal, 8 per cent for raw sugar, 2 per cent for maize and 4 per cent for wheat. For other important farm products, the projected price increases were well within the ranges indicated (see Table 7.3). Only five products had projected increases greater than 10 per cent and wine at 16 per cent was the largest. The other products with increases greater than 10 per cent were processed from raw products that are generally imported freely, but are products for which the processing is heavily protected, such as roast coffee and cocoa powder.

In a subsequent paper, Dr Valdés presented slightly revised estimates of the price gains from liberalization.[38] The revision reflected some changes in the rates of protection that occurred after 1975–77. The largest price increase in the revised study was less than 20 per cent and seven products had projected price increases of between 10 and 20 per cent – pork, olive oil, wine, cocoa powder, malt, roasted coffee and cocoa paste cake. Note that except for pork and wine, the other products are processed or refined and thus subject to protection provided for the processing industries and not for agriculture in the countries imposing the protection.

From a very ambitious undertaking, Rodney Tyers estimated the effects of full trade liberalization for five commodities – rice, wheat, coarse grains, ruminant meat (beef, veal and lamb) and non-ruminant meat (pork and poultry) – for three lengths of runs.[39] The three periods were for three, eight and thirteen years. The three-year period represented the short run and the thirteen years a long run in which there was full adjustment to free trade.

Dr Tyers assumed full free trade – the abolition of all measures that separated domestic and world prices – for the large OECD countries and a number of important developing market economies. The study included five of the six ASEAN countries (Indonesia, Malaysia, Thailand, Singapore and the Philippines, but not Brunei) plus India, the Republic of Korea, Pakistan and Sri Lanka. Trade liberalization was not assumed for the centrally-planned economies, Western Europe outside the European Community nor for any other developing economies except those named above. International market prices were projected for the three lengths of run for (i) continuation of the agricultural and trade policies of the late 1970s and (ii) free trade. The levels of protection assumed in the projections were for 1975–77; the base year for the economic data other than protection levels was 1977. The price projections are presented in Table 7.4. The reference price is the projected price assuming continuation of the degree of protection and domestic policies that existed in 1975–77. The prices are in 1970 American dollars and thus changes in the prices reflect changes in real values.

Table 7.4 Effects of multilateral agricultural liberalization in the principal market economies and ASEAN on international trading prices

		1980	1985	1990
Trading prices, $(1970)/ton				
Rice	Reference[a]	138	148	175
	Liberalization[b]	115	134	139
Wheat	Reference	64	57	61
	Liberalization	51	63	65
Coarse grain	Reference	49	49	53
	Liberalization	47	54	55
Ruminant meat	Reference	411	448	532
	Liberalization	735	769	799
Non-ruminant meat	Reference	597	589	636
	Liberalization	627	650	675

[a]Projections based on continuation of agricultural policies as of late 1970s.
[b]Free trade, both internationally and domestically, assumed to prevail in Australia, Bangladesh, Canada, India, Indonesia, Japan, Republic of Korea, Malaysia, Pakistan, Philippines, Singapore, Sri Lanka, Thailand, United States and European Community.
Source: Rodney Tyers, 'Effects on ASEAN of Food Trade Liberalization in Industrial Countries', a paper presented to the Second Western Pacific Food Trade Workshop, Jakarta, 22–23 August 1982.

The projected effect of free trade on rice prices may surprise many. Dr Tyers explains the result: 'Rice prices fall, relative to the reference projection, as the effect of the removal of protectionism in the industrialized importing countries is outweighed by the removal of negative protection in South Asia, Indonesia and Thailand. The decline in excess rice demand in the developing countries thus exceeds its increase in industrialized countries.'[40] What his results indicate is that the countries that have prices for consumers and producers that are lower than world market prices place upward pressure on world market prices. The upward price pressure exists because low national prices discourage production and encourage consumption. Such countries either import more or export less than they would if their domestic consumer and producer prices were the same as world market prices. And the net effect is to increase world market prices.

The price projections for wheat and the coarse grains reflect very modest long-run effects of trade liberalization. The projected lower prices under free trade in the short run reflect a release of government stocks and recognition of the existence of some degree of excess productive capacity that would be eliminated under free trade. To some degree the small price effects of free trade on grain prices reflect the historically low rates of nominal protection for the European Community during 1975–77. Nominal protection for the grains averaged about 25 per cent compared with the more usual 50 to 100 per cent. Had a different period been used, the price effects of free trade would have been somewhat larger.

Free trade was projected to have a large impact on the prices of ruminant meat, resulting in a long-run price increase attributed to free trade of 50 per cent. Dr Tyers attributes this primarily to the effects of Japanese trade liberalization. For pork and poultry the long-run price effect of free trade was estimated to be quite modest at just a 6 per cent increase.[41]

Ulrich Koester, of the University of Kiel, using the model and data bases developed in the Valdés–Zietz study, estimated the effect of removing the grain protection by the European Community on the level of international market prices for grain. The projected increases in world grain market prices ranged from less than 1 per cent for millet and sorghum to almost 20 per cent for oats. For wheat the projected increase was 9.6 per cent; and for maize, 2.2 per cent. The price increase for barley was projected at 14.3 per cent. If the grains are weighted by the value of world exports in 1975–77, the average increase in price would have been 6.7 per cent.[42]

Maurice Schiff, in a study for the United States Department of Agriculture, estimated a model of the world wheat market, based on econometric estimates of his own.[43] Free trade was assumed for the European Community, the United States, Canada, Australia, Japan and Argentina. The model included estimates of the wheat trade functions of the Soviet Union and the rest of the world for continuation of existing policies. He estimates that if there had been free trade in wheat in the designated countries from 1964 to 1978 the average increase in world wheat price would have been 15 per cent. He also estimates that if there had been free trade in the Community only, with all other countries continuing their actual policies, the world market price of wheat for the same period would have been 17 per cent higher. This result may seem somewhat surprising until it is remembered that during most of the years included in the analysis the major exporters, especially the United States and Canada, had limited the output of wheat by domestic supply management programmes. If there had been universal free trade, exports of wheat by the major exporters would have been somewhat higher than they actually were.

Stefan Tangermann and Wolfgang Krostitz, of the University of Göttingen, estimated the effects of trade liberalization on the beef sector.[44] They estimated the implicit tariff equivalent of the restraints on trade that existed during 1977–79. Elasticities of supply and demand were also estimated. With this information plus the actual levels of production and consumption of beef in each country or region, changes in production, consumption and net trade were made for reductions in the implicit tariffs of 25, 50 and 100 per cent. They estimate that with full trade liberalization the international market price for beef would increase by 47 per cent; this is almost identical to the 50 per cent increase projected by Rodney Tyers.

One very interesting result is that no one of the three degrees of reduction of the implicit tariffs would have any noticeable effect on domestic prices of beef in the United States or Canada. The reason for this rather striking result is that the increase in world market prices would be approximately equal to the reduction in the implicit tariff for each of the three cases – 25, 50 or 100 per cent. For example, if the United States reduced its implicit tariff by 50 per cent, this would have amounted to a decrease in the tariff by $230 per ton (slaughter weight). If, however, all countries reduced their implicit tariffs by 50 per cent, the world price would increase by $220 per ton. For the European Community a reduction of its implicit tariff of 118 per cent by 50 per cent would have resulted in a decrease in the domestic price of 15 per cent or $50 per ton. The decline in the domestic price in Japan was projected to be 28 per cent or $163 per ton.

Roy Allen, Claudia Dodge and Andrew Schmitz, in a study undertaken at the University of California at Berkeley, arrive at a much more modest estimate of the effect of the voluntary export restraints for beef that have been caused by the existence of United States beef.[45] For 1976/77, when there were voluntary restraints on beef exports to the United States, the United States price of frozen boneless beef was increased by about $85 per ton or about 8 per cent of the free trade price. The price increase for all United States beef, however, would be significantly smaller than the estimated 8 per cent, since beef of the quality that is imported accounts for no more than a quarter of United States beef consumption. An interesting result of the study was that the average price received by the exporters was slightly higher than it would have been under free trade. Under the voluntary quotas the exporters realized the price gain from the reduced level of United States imports. It may be noted that there were no voluntary restraints in effect during 1980, 1981 and 1982, although such restraints were imposed for the second half of 1983.

The various studies make it quite clear that the European Community could not justify its policies of the late 1970s and early 1980s on the grounds that international market prices are seriously distorted.[46] There was some distortion, true. But a considerable part of the departure of current prices from what they would have been in the absence of market interventions was due to the interventions by the European Community. Dr Tyers and Kym Anderson estimated what the international price changes would be if only the Community grain and meat trade barriers were eliminated.[47] The price effects of this change can then be compared with the price effects when all developed market economies liberalize grain and meat trade. According to their projections, the Community's barriers account for two-thirds of the wheat price distortion, all of the coarse grain, a third of the rice and two-thirds of the ruminant meat price distortions resulting from trade barriers in all developed market economies.

Alexander Sarris and John Freebairn, in another study at Berkeley, analyzed the effects of governmental interventions on the world wheat market.[48] The empirical analysis was for the average of 1978/79 and 1979/80. Free trade was assumed for all countries except the centrally-planned ones. Their results indicated that world wheat price under free trade would have been 11 per cent higher than with the existing policies for the time period involved. As did Dr Schiff, Professors Sarris and Freebairn projected the effect on world prices if only the European Community had free trade and all other countries continued their policies. This simulation resulted in an increase in world prices of somewhat more than 9 per cent. The authors conclude that 'the EC(9) policies alone account for more than 80% of the decline in average world wheat prices from their free-trade levels . . .'.[49]

Other similar studies have made estimates of the effects of trade liberalization on world market prices[50] and the results are similar to those reviewed above. While there are differences among the studies reviewed, the results for years since the mid-1970s seem to me to be consistent with the view that for the grains, pork and poultry the price effects of protectionist policies were relatively small for the early 1980s as well as for the late 1960s and early 1970s. The effect of trade liberalization on beef and veal prices has been projected as very substantial.

The extent that domestic farm price and income programmes of the OECD countries depress international market prices varies from period to period. The variation in the international market price effects depends on the degree of protection existing in the years used to derive the estimates. The nominal rates of protection in the last half of the 1970s and 1980–82 were relatively low compared with protection levels in either the late 1960s or the mid-1980s. The sharp increase in protection levels between 1980–82 and the late 1980s is shown in Table 3.6. The rates of nominal protection increased from a weighted average for the industrial market economies of 1.4 in 1980–82 to an estimated 2.0 in 1988, an increase of well over 40 per cent. The increase in protection levels in countries other than the United States were due, in considerable part, to the decline in the foreign-exchange value of the dollar as well as to American efforts to dispose of large stocks and to expand its share of world trade in grains, cotton and soyabeans through the use of increased deficiency payments and export subsidies.

Dr Tyers and Dr Anderson estimated that if there were phased liberalization of agricultural trade in the industrial market economies, international market prices would have been increased by 16 per cent with the protection levels of 1980–82 and by 30 per cent if there were a phased liberalization from the 1988 levels of protection.[51] Thus the level of agricultural protection that prevailed in the late 1980s did have a significant effect on international market prices. But this large effect was a consequence of the protectionist policies, not their cause.

National Price Stability and International Instability

In a brief article that I wrote in 1974, I argued that when countries stabilize their domestic prices they do so at the expense of increasing price instability in the rest of the world.[52] After noting that the United States export price for wheat increased from $60 per ton in 1971/72 to $130 per ton in early 1973, I wrote that it

> had no effect on the consumer or producer in the EEC. When wheat prices increased even further, the EEC imposed export taxes and export licensing to discourage sales in foreign markets. As a result, grain prices in local currencies increased by no more than 10

per cent between 1971 and early 1974 in the Six, except for Italy. During the same period international prices of grain (in dollars) were doubling and trebling. But within the EEC (except for the new members) grain became a bargain during a period of real food stringency in the world. The same nationalistic approach has been followed in Japan and the Soviet Union.

The consequences of these policies were delineated as follows:[53]

Consequently, virtually all required price adjustments have been imposed on a limited part of the world – the major grain exporters and a number of developing countries which rely heavily on food imports. There is no doubt that if there had been something approximating free trade in grains and other foods over the past few years price increases would have been significantly smaller than they have in fact been.

In an article published a year later, I estimated that approximately half of the increase in international market prices of grain that occurred between 1972 and 1974 was due to national price policies of demand stabilization and not to variations in world grain production.[54] This is a conclusion that is strongly resisted by policy-makers in countries that follow domestic price-stabilization programmes. It is particularly difficult, as it should be, for policy-makers in high-income countries to admit that their efforts to protect their own high-income consumers from the vagaries of international supply and demand might result in millions of poor people being exposed to hunger due to the high-income country not adjusting its consumption and production at all.

In the late 1970s and early 1980s the results of numerous empirical and theoretical studies of the effects of national price-stabilization schemes on international price instability were published. The results of some of the studies are summarized here; references to others are provided in a note. Maurice Schiff modelled the world wheat market for 1960–80.[55] He estimated that the effect of the domestic price support and trade policies increased the variability of international market prices of wheat by more than 40 per cent. This estimate was based on the reduction in the standard deviation of world market prices with existing policies and with free trade in the market economies. The actual standard deviation of world wheat prices for 1963/64 to 1977/78 was $42 per ton; under free trade the standard deviation was projected to be $25 per ton. Since the world market price under free trade would have been $104 instead of the actual $91, the reduction in the coefficient of variation would have been from 46 to 24 per cent, a reduction of 48 per cent.

At Purdue University, Shei Shen-Yi and Robert Thompson, using a model in which empirical estimates were made of excess demand functions for importing countries and excess supply functions for exporting countries, estimated the effects of various trade restrictions on the international price of wheat in 1972/73. They conclude:[56] 'The most significant result of this study is the demonstration that greater world market price variability results as more countries prevent world price signals from being reflected across their borders into the domestic market through some form of trade control.'

Paul Johnson, Thomas Grennes and Marie Thursby, in a study at North Carolina State University, estimated the effect of national wheat price policies of Canada, Australia, Argentina, Europe and Japan on the increase in the international and American price of wheat between 1972/73 and 1973/74.[57] In their estimate they assumed that wheat exports to the rest of the world were exogenous. Between 1972/73 and 1973/74 the increase in the real price of wheat in the United States was 49.1 per cent. If 1972/73 policies, such as the size of the European Community's variable import levy, had remained unchanged, the estimated real price of wheat would have increased 19.9 per cent. The actual policy changes in the countries specified were responsible for an additional increase in the price of wheat of 20.9 per cent or somewhat more than a third of the actual increase between 1972/73 and 1973/74. Approximately a third of the price increase was not explained by their model.

It can be concluded now, as it was a decade ago, that either world market prices have not been seriously distorted by trade interventions or that where there exists significant distortion it is primarily due to the policies of those industrial countries that complain most stridently about the low level of the international prices. Consequently it is not now the case, nor was it so in the past, that the distortions in international market prices are a reasonable basis for maintaining current trade interventions and failing to achieve any significant degree of trade liberalization.

Concluding Comments

As of the late 1980s the intervention in agricultural markets by the governments of industrial countries can only be described as massive.

What the interventions have caused is a higher level of farm production in the industrial countries than represents an economic use of their national resources. The programmes have also reduced international market prices to some degree, thus imposing costs on developing countries that have a comparative advantage in farm products. The programmes have also made international market prices more unstable than would be the case either under a liberal trade regime or a protectionist system that used instruments other than variable import levies, variable export subsidies or quantitative import quotas. The form of protection as well as its extent does matter.

8 World Food Adequacy and Security

In the first edition this chapter had a different title – 'Food Surpluses of the Industrial Countries and Food Needs of the Developing Regions'. While a great many things have changed since then, I find little reason to modify the major points made in that chapter. But since changes have occurred, it seemed best to completely recast it rather than revise and update.

A brief review, however, of the major points of the original Chapter 8 seems in order. The major objective of the chapter was to argue that food aid would not provide an ever-expanding outlet for the surplus production of the industrial countries. It was noted that food prospects in the developing countries had improved significantly due to the new seeds and cultural practices, commonly known as the Green Revolution. Thus the demand for food aid was likely to diminish over time. But the important point given the greatest emphasis was that large-scale food aid, such as the United States provided in the 1960s to South Asia, did not provide a long-run solution to inadequacy of food supplies. The superior alternative to such food aid was to assist the developing countries to increase their own productive capacity. The Green Revolution, combined with large-scale investments in irrigation in Asia, did provide for some of the most densely populated areas of the world a superior alternative to food aid.

I did not then argue, though, that all food aid had negative effects. I believed then, as I do now, that there are roles for limited amounts of directed food aid. One role is to provide supplementary food for certain vulnerable groups in low-income populations. In particular, food programmes for pregnant and nursing mothers and for children can have positive health effects with minimal disincentive effects for either farmers or the recipients. Another role is to use food aid for school lunch programmes, as much as an inducement for school attendance and to improve school performance as for contributions to health. A third role is to assist in meeting emergency food needs due to some natural catastrophe, such as earthquakes, typhoons and floods. In such cases it may save time to bring food and other products from outside the country rather than from within it. Drought is also a natural disaster and its occurrence may warrant food aid. I say 'may' because the major cause of food insufficiency among rural people in case of a drought is the loss of income. If income is made available, in most developing countries food will become available in the market. But there may be instances in which the infrastructure is so primitive that the usual market forces cannot react in time. In such cases, provision of food aid may have positive consequences for those who have lost their source of income and do little harm to other farmers. It must be recognized, however, that where the lack of infrastructure – roads, railroads, storage facilities – makes market responses inadequate, it also makes the delivery of food aid difficult and subject to significant delays.

Some would argue, and this is certainly the position taken by the International Food Policy Research Institute in Washington, that food aid could be used in more substantial ways than indicated here.[1] Such ways could include food for work programmes used in conjunction with improving the rural infrastructure, including water and sanitation facilities as well as roads, irrigation and communication facilities. The presumption is that the food aid leaves a positive residue in terms of the work output and has had little or no adverse effect on the demand for locally-produced food since the work programme increased the overall demand for food. Even if such food for work programmes have the effects attributed to them, it is difficult to imagine that the administrative capacity exists in developing countries to devise and manage enough such programmes to use large quantities of food aid.

Food aid may have other objectives than improving food security. Food aid may be a means for increasing the total flow of aid since it may be easier to obtain the necessary political support for food aid than for additional general aid. One study of food aid in the 1960s and the early 1970s indicated that about two-thirds of food aid was provided as income support in the sense that the food was delivered to the government of the recipient country and it was sold in the domestic market and the receipt from the sale was a part of the government revenue.[2]

A World Food System

The twentieth century has seen remarkable progress in mankind's effort to reduce the horror of famine. In fact, this century could go down as the one in which famine due to production shortfalls had been eliminated. Much of this book presents a negative picture of the functioning of the world agricultural system – too much production, much of it produced in the wrong places at high costs with efficient producers losing their market to subsidized competitors. Yet not everything is bleak and negative. The costs of producing the major sources of calories have fallen significantly over the past half-century and food output has increased more than population even though, since 1950, world population growth has been at unprecedented rates. Per capita food consumption, almost everywhere, is greater than ever before. Instead of the 5 billion people, as of the late 1980s, being more insecure than the 3 billion just a little more than a quarter century earlier, or the 1.6 billion at the beginning of the century, the 5 billion are in fact much less subject to famine and food insufficiency.

World economic growth and its associated technological changes have greatly increased international food security during this century. Substantial, perhaps even revolutionary, improvements in the speed of communication, the near-universal availability of low-cost forms of communication and, too, the reductions in the costs of and time required for transportation have significantly decreased the hardships and suffering resulting from shortfalls in food production in specific geographic areas. These dramatic changes in communication and transportation have enormously expanded the extent of the market from which food supplies could be drawn for almost any local community in the world. For many parts of the world only a century ago food stored 100 miles away was inaccessible. There remain but a few areas in the world that are so isolated that food relief need be delayed due to limited communication and high transport costs. Such areas involve but a small fraction of the world's population. And even in these areas, if their governments cooperate with an early warning system, most of the suffering from food insufficiency due to natural causes could be avoided. Of course, when governments are insensitive to human suffering or actually use famine as a tool to achieve political objectives, famine remains and will remain.

A world food system has been created in which almost anyone in the world, if he or she has the means to do so, can have access to the world's supply of food if his or her government permits such access. Under these conditions, individuals almost anywhere can obtain wheat produced in France or Australia, corn produced in the United States or Argentina or rice from Thailand. The volume of trade in the cereals, which remains the major source of calories for over half the world's population, has increased dramatically during the twentieth century. Before the First World War just 11 per cent of the world's wheat and feed-grains moved in international trade. In the early 1960s just 10 per cent moved across national borders and by the late 1980s, even with the weak international markets for grain, a little more than 15 per cent of these grains were exported. The volume of grain trade reached enormous quantities by the 1980s, in most years exceeding 200 million tons. Only the United States and China consistently produce more than 200 million tons of grain annually; a third country – the Soviet Union – exceeded that figure less than half the time during the 1980s.

The significance of the growth of trade in cereals was illustrated by large imports by the Soviet Union in 1984/85 of 55 million tons of grain, very nearly the total world trade in wheat and feed-grains during the 1950s, and yet international grain prices declined in real terms.

Another factor that has increased food security has been a consequence of the increase in per capita incomes of a considerable fraction of the world's population. The growth of per capita incomes has created reserves of food that could be and have been drawn upon. The substantial increase in the amount of cereals fed to livestock, other than draft animals, has occurred primarily over the past half century. In the 1980s more than a third of the world's grain production was fed to livestock and poultry.[3] If farmers receive the appropriate price signals, some of the grain usually fed to livestock will be made available for human consumption. This is exactly what occurred in the United States in 1974/75 when the feed use of grain declined by a quarter.

In 1974/75, United States supplies of grain were 50 million tons less than in the previous year; stocks had been reduced by 17 million tons during 1973/74 in response to the price increases and production was down by 33 million tons. Significant adjustments were made to the changed supply and price situation in the United States. In nominal terms the Chicago price of corn was almost 60 per cent higher in October 1974 than a year earlier. Most of the weather-induced production shortfall in the United States was in corn and other feed-grains. The adjustments to the supply reduction consisted of a decline of 36 million tons in domestic use, a decline of 10 million tons in exports and a decline of 4 million tons in stocks to the lowest level in two decades. In other industrial economies there was no significant reduction in grain use. This was true of the European Community (of Nine) and Japan as well as Australia. Canada reduced domestic use by less than

10 per cent, approximately half of the reduction that occurred in the United States.

The reason that United States utilization of its grain supply changed sharply in 1974 differed so much by contrast to little or no change in other market economies or for the centrally-planned economies was a very simple one, namely that in the United States, by contrast to the European Community (of Nine), Japan and the Soviet Union, domestic market prices reflected the underlying world demand and supply situation and farmers reacted by feeding substantially less grain to livestock. By cutting such use drastically, it was possible to hold the reduction in United States exports to just 10 million tons or by less than 15 per cent. Had United States market prices not increased – had domestic producer and consumer prices remained fixed at the prior year's level – exports would have fallen by at least the amount of the absolute reduction in production or by nearly 45 per cent. Such a large reduction in American grain exports would have very serious consequences for low-income grain importers.

The previous paragraphs have been intended to make a simple point and nothing more, namely that the price system, when it is permitted to function, can contribute to world food security by shifting available supplies from one use to another, namely from feed to food. The experience cited indicates that when prices are permitted to play a role, the existence of a large livestock sector in the industrial economies can serve to improve food security. But if domestic prices do not react to changes in world market prices, the livestock sector is not permitted to play this important role.

Causes of International Food Insecurity

The primary cause of food insecurity at the household or individual level is poverty or lack of income. When one has very little income or loses one's income source, food insufficiency is a likely outcome. If one has an income equal to that achieved by most who live in the industrial market economies, food insecurity does not exist because food in adequate quantities can be obtained even if prices increase substantially. Food is available virtually everywhere if one has the income to buy it. Our discussion of the methods of reducing food insecurity, like virtually all approaches to the subject, does not address the issue of poverty or temporary loss of income due to whatever cause. What is intended is to address those aspects of food security that are involved in making food supplies generally available at prices not significantly different than the prices prevailing in the world market and in reducing the variations in prices on international markets. Both are important in reducing food insecurity.

Failure to achieve the degree of world food security that is now possible is not due to nature but to man. The aspect of man that is responsible for that failure is not man as a farmer or scientist or extension worker or grain marketer or food retailer, but man as a politician. I use the term politician very broadly to all those who influence decisions that affect production, prices and trade in food. In other words, it is those among us who use the political process to protect their own interests with little regard to how others may be affected.

Why do I say that nature bears none of the responsibility for international food insecurity? It is because if we view the world as a unit, we find that the variability in world food production from year to year is very small, far too small to be a significant source of instability of food supplies. If variability in grain production is used as an approximate indication of variability of world food production, the variation of production around the trend is quite small. This is particularly true for negative deviations. For the years from 1970/71 through 1986/87 the maximum negative deviation from trend was 6.6 per cent in 1983/84. This was due to shortfalls in the United States feed-grain crop resulting from a combination of a large reduction in planted area as a part of the supply management programme and bad weather. But United States stocks of grains were so large in mid-1983 that United States feed-grain exports were larger in 1983/84 than in the prior year. World grain exports were also larger than in 1982/83. The next largest shortfall was 3.3 per cent in 1975/76. For the period under study, there appear to be more negative deviations from trend than positive ones, but the negative deviations are smaller than the positive ones.[4]

With any reasonable assumption concerning the price elasticity of demand for grain for all uses, the negative deviations from trend cannot be considered to be large. A negative deviation of 3 per cent, which has occurred infrequently since 1960, and a price elasticity of demand of -0.1 would result in a price increase of 30 per cent – assuming that stocks remained unchanged.

A production shortfall can and is offset in part by a reduction in stocks. Year-end stocks reached a low for the world, as estimated by the United States Department of Agriculture, in 1974/75 at 10.8 per cent of use. In the mid-1980s year-end stocks reached 22 to 24 per cent of use.

As shown in Chapter 7, a major source of instability in international market prices is the national policies of price stability in which the stability is achieved by varying imports and/or exports. Such policies insulate the producers and consumers in the particular country or economic unit from both their own variations in supply and demand and from the variations that occur in the rest of the world. The consequence of many countries following such policies is that international market prices are far more unstable than would be true if there were free trade in farm products or if protection were achieved by methods (for example, either specific or *ad valorem* tariff duties) that required domestic prices to vary with international market prices.

The study of the effects of various trade restrictions on international wheat prices in 1972/73 by Shei Shun-Yi and Robert Thompson was referred to in Chapter 7. They concluded: 'The most significant result of this study is the demonstration that greater world market price variability results as more countries prevent world price signals from being reflected across their borders into the domestic market through some form of trade control.'

There is great resistance to accepting the view that it was man and not nature that was responsible for as much as half of the substantial increases in international grain prices that occurred after mid-1972. To accept such a conclusion is to admit that much of the human suffering that occurred in the world's low-income countries was due to actions taken by man and not the inevitable consequence of adversities imposed by nature. It is not claimed that the adversities imposed on poor people were intended to be the effects of the policies followed. In other words, decision-makers in the Soviet Union or the European Community did not intend to reduce the food supplies available to South Asia or Central Africa. But one can hope that the point has been made that national policies that insulate domestic prices and consumption from the effects of world variations in demand and supply have inevitable and, at times, serious adverse effects on others. And generally those who are adversely affected are much less capable of coping with the consequences than those who are being protected by the policies. It is time to recognize that policies of national price stability that depend on variations in trade are 'beggar thy neighbour' policies.

Alternatives for International Food Security

There are numerous approaches that could contribute to improved food security. Three approaches merit consideration and analysis: (i) liberalization of barriers to trade in agricultural products, (ii) grain and food reserves and (iii) insurance schemes for developing countries. These approaches should not be considered to be competitive. It can and will be shown that, if trade were liberalized, the size of national grain reserves required for a given degree of food security would be greatly reduced. Further, if international trade were conducted on more liberal terms than is now the case, any of the proposals for insurance that emerged during the 1970s would be less costly than with the current trade policies affecting agriculture. It is not too surprising that I shall give primary emphasis to a proposal that I developed, although other insurance proposals will be described briefly.

Trade Liberalization

The conventional argument for a grain or food reserve is to offset variations in production resulting from natural causes. This argument may be valid for an individual country that either does not engage in international trade in food or holds its trade at quite constant levels from year to year. Is this a valid explanation for holding reserves for the world as a whole or for a country that permits its citizens to import and export without significant governmental intervention? Estimates were made of optimal reserves of grain for regions and for the world as a whole and these estimates can be used to indicate the effect of free trade on the appropriate size of grain reserves.[5]

Since the results depend on the assumptions that were made, these assumptions are now indicated. Optimal grain reserves are defined according to a storage rule in which the expected gain from adding a small amount to reserves equals the expected cost of holding that amount of grain until it would, on average, be withdrawn.[6] In other words, the amount of storage is determined by the expectation that investment in holding reserves would yield a normal or usual rate of return on the investment involved. As with any other investment, there is no certainty that when grain is added to a reserve the investment will yield the expected return, but that over a period of time, with repeated applications of the rule, the actual return should be approximately the expected return.

The estimates of optimal grain reserves presented here are intended to show the effects of self-sufficiency on the amount of storage that would be optimal. In turn, it then becomes clear that trade is a highly efficient substitute for storage, for storage is costly in terms of both physical and financial resources. The optimal grain reserve estimates are based on two assumptions that must be borne in mind. One is that only production variability has been taken into account; demand variability also affects the size of optimal reserves. For food grains, however, demand variability by final consumers is very small and would have little effect on the estimates, although the same is not true for feed-grains. But for the low-income countries grains are primarily for direct human consumption. The second assumption is that for the country and region estimates it is assumed there is free trade in grain within the country or region, but net grain trade among countries or among regions was held at the 1970 level. The estimates of optimal reserves are over and above working stocks or the stocks that are required at year-end to provide a smooth transition from one crop year to another. Depending on the adequacy of transport and communication facilities working stocks may range from 10 to 12 per cent of annual use. The estimates of storage costs and grain prices were in constant 1970 prices and a real interest rate of 5 per cent was used in the estimates of optimal storage presented below, although other interest rates were used in the study.

Table 8.1 provides illustrative estimates of optimal grain reserves, centred on 1975 trend production, based on the distribution of grain production for 1950 to 1974 for each country or group of countries. The estimates of optimal carry-overs are given at three levels of probability. The optimal carry-over level for a given year is a function of the carry-in and the actual production for that year. There is a distribution of the sum of these two quantities and the cumulative probability levels indicate the maximum optimum storage levels for the three probability levels. The optimal levels of storage for India in Part A of the table would not exceed 6.5 million tons more than 50 per cent of the time or would exceed 13.5 million tons 5 per cent of the time. Another example, 50 per cent of the time the optimal level of storage for Indonesia would have been less than 1.6 million tons and 95 per cent of the time less than 4.4 million tons.

The estimates of the optimal storage levels in Part A of Table 8.1 assume that net international trade in grains is held constant for each country or region from year to year. In other words, trade is not permitted to adjust to changes in the domestic or regional supply

Table 8.1   Optimal carry-overs for selected countries and regions, 1975

Country or region	1975 trend production	Cumulative probability levels		
		0.50	0.75	0.95
	(million tons)[a]			
	A. Demand elasticity n = −0.10			
Burma	6	0.3	0.7	1.2
India	100	6.5	9.5	13.5
Indonesia	16	1.6	2.9	4.4
Pakistan–Bangladesh	23	1.4	2.4	4.2
Philippines	6	0.1	0.2	0.3
Thailand	13	3.5	4.7	6.2
Other Far East	19	1.4	2.1	3.1
Africa	46	1.5	3.0	5.0
Far East	184	3.0	7.5	12.5
Latin America	78	2.5	5.0	8.5
Near East	48	2.5	4.5	8.5
All developing regions	353	2.5	7.5	15.0
Europe	231	1.3	5.5	9.5
North America	270	10.0	18.0	33.0
Oceania	18	8.0	10.5	15.4
Soviet Union	199	28.0	41.0	49.0
World	1304	0.0	2.0	18.0
	B. Demand elasticity n = −0.20			
India		2.0	4.0	7.5
Africa		0.0	0.5	2.5
Far East		0.0	1.0	7.0
Developing regions		0.0	1.0	7.0
North America		1.5	8.5	22.0
Soviet Union		13.0	24.0	37.0
World		0.0	0.0	7.0

[a]In estimating optimal reserves, a real interest rate of 5 per cent and an annual storage cost of $7.50 per ton were used. The general price level assumed that of 1967. Estimations of optimal carry-overs assume that there is free trade within a country or region but that the level of trade in grain between a country or region is held at a constant level of net imports or net exports.

situation. Under this assumption, the sum of the optimal carry-over levels for six individual countries and all other developing countries in the Far East (excluding China) at the 0.50 probability level is 14.8 million tons. If there were free trade within the Far East, however, the optimal carry-over levels at the same probability levels is 3.0 million tons. It should be noted that it is free trade within the Far East that is assumed, not worldwide free trade. If all countries in the developing regions had free trade among themselves, but not with the rest of the world, at both the 0.50 and 0.75 probability levels the optimal storage levels would be less than for India alone; only at the 0.95 probability level would the optimal storage for all developing countries exceed that for India alone under the assumption of constant net trade with the rest of the world.

Attention is called to the estimated optimal storage levels for the world under the assumption of free trade assuming a price elasticity of demand of -0.1. At least half the time the optimal level of carry-over of grain would be zero or nil; only working stocks would be carried from one year to the next. Only 5 per cent of the time would it be expected that world stocks over and above working stocks would exceed 18 million tons. This level is less than half again as large as India's optimal amount at the same probability level.

Part B of Table 8.1 provides optimal storage estimates for a limited number of cases assuming a price elasticity of demand for grain of -0.2. As expected, the optimal carry-over levels decline significantly. The reason why this is true is that a given percentage shortfall in supplies below trend level will have only half as much effect on grain prices with the higher price elasticity of demand than it would with the lower elasticity. This means that the expected gain from adding to any given level of stocks is less with the higher than the lower elasticity. It is equally true that a given percentage excess of supplies over the trend level will have less effect on prices with the higher than the lower elasticity.

The estimates of optimal carry-over levels for the world indicate the striking effects of free trade on food security. Costs of storage are substantial, as will be shown below. Free trade involves few resource costs and thus provides for a high degree of food security at low cost.

How much price stability would be achieved under free trade and optimal storage for the world? The prices used in the estimates were 1967 real prices, assuming that a year of grain storage cost $7.50 plus 5 per cent interest. Assuming a grain price of $100 per ton, the expected price increase would be less than 12.5 per cent half the time since for the world optimal carry-over levels would be nil at least half the time. There can be no guarantee, though, that under free trade or national storage programmes that price changes from one year to another can be held to less than a given percentage. There is some very small probability that a series of below-trend output levels could exhaust available stocks. In such an instance, a 5 per cent reduction in production could result in a price that was 50 per cent above the level with trend supplies if the price elasticity of demand were − 0.1 or 25 per cent with the − 0.2 elasticity. But the probability of a 5 per cent output reduction following exhaustion of stocks is exceedingly low – there has been but one reduction below trend levels for world grain of this magnitude during the past 40 years, the period for which we have reasonably reliable data for world grain production. And a record reduction in grain production following exhaustion of grain reserves in excess of working stocks is even less probable than the occurrence of the maximum production reduction.

Grain Reserves

There is no question that grain reserves could be managed to virtually eliminate the variability in international market prices for the major grains. This result was in fact achieved from the late 1950s through the early 1970s. The remarkable price stability for these years was due primarily to the large stocks held by the major grain exporters, primarily the United States and Canada, as an unwanted consequence of their domestic price policies. Achieving domestic price stability does not result in international market instability if governments hold large enough stocks so that they can sell any amount that may be demanded at the fixed price or are willing to acquire any amount that may be offered at that price. This was basically the position of the governments of Canada and the United States during this period of more than a decade. The rates of return on stockholding, however, were negative and large; the stocks were not held in response to an investment criterion. The high costs of holding the stocks led to the two governments undertaking radical steps to reduce the level of stocks after 1969 and the willingness of the United States to permit the export of a large share of its grain stocks in 1972. And it was these decisions that were partly responsible for the sharp price-increases that followed and continued through 1974/75.

India has the distinction of being one of a very few countries, perhaps the only one, to have followed a conscious grain storage policy starting in 1974. India not only accumulated reserves from domestic production, but also imported large quantities of grain in 1974–76 – a total of more than 18 million tons. Unfortunately for India these were years of high prices and the grain remained in the stocks for several years. Estimates have been made of the costs of the policy actually followed for 1974/75 through 1979/80. A primary objective of the buffer stocks was to assure the supply of grain for the domestic distribution programme through the fair-price shops. The costs of storage for these years of the actual stocks accumulated was 11 billion rupees of constant 1970/71 value. The costs were those actually incurred by the Food Corporation of India, including interest costs and storage operations but not including the cost of the stocks.

The Indian Government could have followed an alternative policy of not holding stocks but relying on international trade to make up the difference, either positive or negative, between domestic procurement and domestic distribution through the fair-price shops. In this exercise it was assumed that neither procurement nor distribution were affected by using international trade to balance the two operations rather than using changes in stocks. Using international trade in this way would have actually generated net gains of 9 billion rupees (1970/71 constant value). These gains would have been in foreign exchange.[7]

At the end of the period (mid-1980) the Government of India had approximately 20 million tons of grain for which it had paid (in constant prices) 24 billion rupees. Adding the costs of carrying the grain during the period the total investment was 33 billion rupees and the salvage value was, at most, 24 billion rupees. The true real cost of the storage programme could be put at 20 billion rupees. The actual loss to the Indian Government was much higher than this since the prices at which the 18 million tons of grain were imported in 1974–76 was much greater in real rupees than the international market prices in mid-1980. The decline in real international prices of wheat, the most important grain import, was a third.

This example, of course, does not prove that a domestic storage programme will always suffer such large losses. The size of the stocks were permitted to grow to unrealistically and unnecessarily high levels. But at least for this period no storage programme could have competed on a cost basis with using international trade as the means for balancing domestic procurement and distribution.

Grain Insurance

As noted at the beginning of this chapter, the food-aid bureaucracies emphasize the need for a constant flow of food aid. FAO has for some years sought commitments from donor countries to provide 10 million tons of cereals annually. While some part of this aid would be distributed on the basis of anticipated variations in local supplies, most would be forthcoming without regard to any variations in nutritional status of the recipient populations.[8]

A number of insurance proposals were made during the 1970s that would have related the amount of food aid or financial assistance to meet food import needs as a result of variations in either local production or in food import costs due to variations in international market prices. For a number of reasons I shall give primary emphasis to a proposal, which I made first in 1975, that the United States or any group of industrial nations offer to provide food aid to offset any reduction in grain production in a developing country that exceeded a given percentage of the trend level of production. This was to be the primary form of food aid and was designed to assure that the reduction in national consumption of cereals would not fall below a minimum level. The proposal was called a grain insurance proposal and estimates were made of the grain shipments that would be required if shortfalls in production greater than 6, 5 or 4 per cent were provided.[9]

The grain insurance programme called for a transfer of grain to any developing country in the world when a country's grain production fell more than a given percentage below trend level. Such an insurance programme would permit each developing country to achieve a high degree of stability in its domestic supply of grain and such stability could be achieved at relatively low cost to the donor countries. If the developing countries were willing and able to adopt a modest storage programme of their own, year-to-year variability in grain availability could be held to shortfalls of no more than 3 to 4 per cent. Thus a substantial degree of internal price stability could be achieved at low cost by each developing country.

The selection of the percentage shortfall from trend production that would trigger the transfer of grain should reflect two considerations – the incentive for holding reserves in developing countries, and the effect of the insurance payments on the output behaviour of producers in these countries. If the percentage of the shortfall covered is too low – say 1 or 2 per cent – there would be no economic incentive to hold reserves and the magnitude of the grain transfers would be large enough to significantly reduce the expected return to local producers and thus adversely affect local grain production. By a process of trial and error, I concluded that the most appropriate criterion would be 6 per cent – all production shortfalls in excess of 6 per cent would be met. But the difference in the amount transferred for 1955 to 1973 was not increased significantly when criteria of 5 and 4 per cent were used.

The primary objective of the proposal was to assist developing countries to hold year-to-year variations in grain consumption to reasonable or acceptable levels. In my opinion, this is the most meaningful concept of food security. The proposal would constitute the primary form of food aid provided by the countries that participate in the grain insurance programme. This would not preclude the provision of the specifically targeted uses referred to earlier, such as nutrition programmes for women and children, school lunch programmes, food for work programmes used to create rural infrastructure and to meet emergencies due to destruction of existing supplies by natural disasters, such as earthquakes and floods. The proposal would provide a solution to an important problem confronting many developing countries, namely to largely offset reductions in food supplies so extreme that significant hardship would result. I know of no similarly important objective that has been met by most of the food aid that has been distributed over the past three decades.

The proposal was not put forward as a solution to the long-run objective of increasing per capita food production and consumption in the developing countries. Neither this proposal nor any other form of food aid can make a significant contribution to the expansion of food production. The grain insurance proposal, if put into effect, would not have an important negative effect on the growth of food production and the same cannot be said about the methods of distributing food aid that have prevailed during the history of large-scale food aid.

Table 8.2 estimates the annual payments that would have been made under the insurance programme for 1955 through 1973. All developing countries that produced more than 1 million tons of grain were included. No countries were excluded for political reasons, although North Korea and North Vietnam were excluded because of the absence of published grain production data. China was also excluded due to the questionable accuracy of the then-available data on grain production estimates. The limitation of the analysis to countries that produced more than 1 million tons of grain had little effect on the results.

The average annual payment for the nineteen-year period would have been 4.0 million tons if the insurance premium covered all shortfalls in excess of 6 per cent for each developing country and 5.2 million tons if the insurance criterion had been 4 per cent. With the 6 per cent criterion, the largest payments would have been 14.8 million tons in 1966 and 13.4 million tons in 1973; with the 4 per cent criterion the largest payments would have been 18.1 million and 15.7 million.

Table 8.2   Insurance payments to developing countries for different programmes, 1955–73 (million tons)

Year	6%	5%	4%
1955	2.2	2.4	2.8
1956	1.0	1.2	1.6
1957	4.5	5.8	7.3
1958	3.0	3.6	4.4
1959	2.8	3.1	3.4
1960	3.3	3.7	4.1
1961	2.9	3.2	3.6
1962	0.1	0.2	0.3
1963	2.1	2.4	2.7
1964	1.0	1.1	1.3
1965	8.1	9.3	10.5
1966	14.8	16.3	18.1
1967	2.2	2.5	2.8
1968	2.2	2.3	2.5
1969	0.6	0.9	1.2
1970	1.2	1.5	1.9
1971	3.6	4.4	4.9
1972	7.9	8.7	10.3
1973	13.4	14.5	15.7
TOTAL	76.9	87.1	99.4

The grain insurance proposal requires reasonably accurate data on annual grain production – for the current year and enough prior years to permit the calculation of the trend level of production for the current year.[10] The proposal would not require data on stocks in the recipient country.

At the time the insurance proposal was made there were serious questions concerning the accuracy of the estimates of Chinese grain production. China was not included in the estimates for the insurance proposal because the production data were subject to such great uncertainty. In recent years official estimates of grain production have been made available for 1949 to date. These data reveal the sharp reductions in grain production that occurred in the years following 1958. Analysis of the 1982 Chinese census data reveal that as many as 30 million died during the 1959–61 famine. While there was contemporary evidence of famine conditions at the time, no one outside China imagined such an enormous number of deaths. The food shortages were more the result of inappropriate policies than natural causes.[11]

170   *World Agriculture in Disarray*

But the sources of the shortages are not important for present purposes. A question that is important to the evaluation of the insurance proposal was that the United States alone or in cooperation with other major grain producers would be able to make payments to China during the famine years. If there had been a commitment to supply all shortfalls in grain production in excess of 6 per cent of trend level, could this commitment have been met?

Chinese grain production increased significantly during the 1950s, culminating in production of 200 million tons in 1958. Some of the increase in production was overcoming the negative impacts of years of war and revolution. Thus it is quite difficult to determine what the trend level of production might have been for 1959–61. In evaluating the insurance proposal I have assumed that the trend level of production would have been the average level of grain production for 1954–58 of 188.3 million tons. The insurance proposal would have provided any shortfall in grain production greater than 6 per cent or a shortfall of grain production below 177 million tons.

Starting with 1959, the shortfalls in annual grain production were (tons) 7.0 million, 33.5 million, 29.5 million, 17.0 million and 7.0 million for a total of 94 million. The Chinese started to import grain in 1961 and in that and the subsequent two years imported a net of 16.7 million tons. Consequently the additional imports that would have been required to have supplied the Chinese economy with 177 million tons of grain annually from 1959 through 1963 was 77 million tons. Could this have been supplied by the United States? The answer is in the affirmative. World and United States grain stocks were at high levels in 1960, and efforts were made to reduce these stocks through idling cropland in the United States. During 1961–63 the United States idled an average of 13 million hectares of grain land annually. If there had been no idling or diversion of land during these years and if the average yield on the idled land had been 60 per cent of the actual yields, this land would have produced about 67 million tons of grain. The United States continued to idle land in 1964 and 1965, increasing the annual average of idle land to 16 million hectares. This implies that grain stocks were larger than desired at the end of the 1963 crop year and could have been reduced by an additional 10 million tons, which is what would have been required to meet the total commitment of the insurance programme to China. I would argue that the insurance scheme would have been able to meet this remarkably strong test.

It should be recognized that there are populations in developing countries that rely on food products other than grains for a significant part of their caloric intake. The grain insurance proposal could be adapted to these circumstances. It would be possible to translate manioc or cassava and potato production, for example, into grain equivalents and include such products in the production data. Unfortunately, the production data for such products are less reliable than for grains. In addition, some recognition should be given to the populations, albeit small in size, that depend on livestock products for a major source of calories. The malnutrition that occurred in the Sahel in the mid-1970s was due primarily to the devastation of the livestock herd and not to a reduction in grain production.

If a developing country also maintained an optimal storage reserve programme it could hold consumption variations to a very low level at very modest storage costs. An example was worked out for India for 1968 to 1974. If India had followed an optimal carry-over policy while holding net trade constant during these years the average level of the carry-overs would have been 6.5 million tons in the absence of the insurance programme. With the insurance programme and a 6 per cent criterion, the annual level of reserves would have been 1.5 million tons and with the 4 per cent criterion only 0.5 million tons. Without the insurance programme India would have had 41.5 million ton-years of carry-over; with the 6 per cent storage programme the carry-overs would have been reduced to 12 million ton-years. The savings in interest and storage costs would have been approximately $450 million if the price of grain were $150 per ton. The saving would have required the delivery of 4.3 million tons of grain with a value of $650 million. During the seven-year period with the insurance programme grain consumption would have exceeded consumption without the programme by a little more than 4 million tons, the sum of the insurance payments, and this result needs to be included in any cost-benefit calculation of the insurance proposal.

Table 8.3 presents the optimal carry-over levels for a particular year for three probability levels and for three criteria for the level of insurance payments for selected developing countries and regions. These results assume no use of international trade to offset variations in local supplies. This table supplements the detailed discussion of the insurance programme and optimal storage levels for India presented above. If the results in Table 8.3 are compared with those in Table 8.1, it is evident in most cases that with the insurance programme the optimal reserve levels would have been reduced significantly.

Other studies of the relative contributions of international trade and buffer stocks to the stability of food supplies came to results similar to

Table 8.3   Optimal carry-over levels for selected developing countries and regions with alternative insurance programmes in effect, 1975 (million tons)

Country or region and insurance programme	Probability levels for carry-overs[a]		
	0.5	0.75	0.95
A. 6 per cent			
Burma	0.1	0.3	0.7
India	1.5	3.5	7.5
Indonesia	0.7	1.5	2.9
Pakistan–Bangladesh	0.3	1.5	2.7
Philippines	0.0	0.1	0.3
Thailand	0.6	1.2	2.1
Other Far East[b]	0.3	0.7	1.5
Africa	0.0	1.0	3.0
Far East[b]	2.0	5.0	10.0
Latin America	0.5	2.5	5.5
Near East	0.5	1.5	5.0
All developing regions[b]	2.0	6.0	14.0
B. 5 per cent			
Burma	0.0	0.2	0.7
India	1.0	2.5	7.0
Indonesia	0.5	1.3	2.7
Pakistan–Bangladesh	0.3	1.3	2.5
Philippines	0.0	0.1	0.3
Thailand	0.3	1.0	1.8
Other Far East[b]	0.2	0.6	1.5
Africa	0.0	1.0	3.0
Far East[b]	2.0	5.0	9.0
Latin America	0.5	2.5	5.0
Near East	0.5	1.5	5.0
All developing regions[b]	0.0	6.0	13.5
C. 4 per cent			
Burma	0.0	0.2	0.6
India	0.5	2.5	6.0
Indonesia	0.5	1.1	2.6
Pakistan–Bangladesh	0.2	1.0	2.2
Philippines	0.0	0.0	0.2
Thailand	0.3	0.8	1.8
Other Far East[b]	0.0	0.6	1.3
Africa	0.0	1.0	3.0
Far East[b]	1.0	4.0	8.0
Latin America	0.5	2.0	4.5
Near East	0.0	1.5	4.5
All developing regions[b]	0.0	3.5	12.0

[a]Price elasticity of demand equals −0.1.   [b]Excludes China.

those reported above. David Bigman and Shlomo Reutlinger, in an article in the *American Journal of Agricultural Economics*, analyzed the effectiveness of storage policies with no trade, limited trade and free trade with and without storage policies. They assumed that domestic production was a random variable with a given probability distribution; the orders of magnitudes were similar to those of India. They analyzed the effects of a storage programme with a 6 million tons capacity. Their conclusion: 'A noteworthy characteristic of our results is the strong stabilizing effect of international trade which far exceeds the effect of a sizable buffer stock.'[12]

In the economy with a buffer stock programme the standard deviation of consumption would be 4.8 per cent; if there were free trade and no buffer stocks, the standard deviation would have been 3.5 per cent. These were the results if there were no correlation between the country's production and world production. If the correlation squared were 0.3, the standard deviation of consumption with free trade and no buffer stocks would have been 4.2 per cent; with no trade the existence of production correlation has no effect on the variability of consumption. Put another way, the buffer stock programme with no trade would have resulted in the probability of a consumption shortage greater than 5 million tons (4.5 per cent) or 14.1 per cent or approximately one year out of seven. Under free trade and no buffer stocks the probability of a shortfall greater than 5 million tons would have been only 6.2 per cent. If there were a combination of a storage programme with a 6 million ton capacity and free trade, the probability of a shortfall in consumption of greater than 5 million tons would have been reduced to 3 per cent.

The Bigman–Reutlinger article analyzed the effect of the different approaches to food security on the variability of consumer prices. In its base case variability of domestic production, no trade with the 6 million ton stock, the standard deviation of price was simulated to be $43 per ton compared with an average price of $140 per ton; with free trade and no buffer stocks the standard deviation would have been much lower at $27 per ton. Thus free trade achieves a significantly lower degree of price variability, but does so without the resource costs of operating a storage programme. The authors concluded their study:

> The single most important observation based on our analysis is that for most countries international trade would be a good way of achieving greater stability in the domestic market. ... [O]ur analysis shows that buffer stocks sufficiently large to stabilize supplies can be very costly. ... In this context and in recognition of the potentially strong stabilizing effects of trade, the international

community also should reevaluate the directions of its efforts aimed at ensuring a stable food supply in developing countries.[13]

Barbara Huddleston and Panos Konandreas, of the International Food Policy Research Institute, presented an alternative insurance proposal. In their proposal, whenever the food import bill of a developing country exceeded 130 per cent of trend level, the country would be compensated for the amount of the excess. A second feature of the proposal was that an international grain reserve would be created that would release grain to developing countries when there was a cereal production shortfall greater than 5 per cent below trend *and* when the world wheat price exceeded $200 per ton. The grain reserve was to be accumulated when the wheat price was below $120 per ton. Both prices were in terms of 1977 American dollars. For 1978–82 it was estimated that the expected discounted cost of the scheme in 1977 dollars would have been approximately $3.7 billion.[14]

An important result was the discovery that the cost of the scheme was independent of the size of the grain reserve up to 20 million tons. In other words, the expected cost of the insurance programme was the same whether the reserve was zero or any reserve level up to 20 million tons. This result is consistent with the other studies that emphasize the importance of trade and the minimal role of reserves in assuring world food security.

An innovation in the provision of food security for developing countries was the creation of the food financing facility of the International Monetary Fund (IMF). The facility provides financing to a low-income country when the cost of cereal imports exceeds trend imports for reasons beyond the control of the country and the excess of costs is not offset by export earnings in excess of trend. A food financing facility was established within the IMF's compensatory financing facility (CFF). As originally designed, the CFF provided for credit to offset declines in export earnings. The food financing facility introduces excess import costs as a basis for credit. This was done by counting cereal imports as negative exports and financing is made available when there is a net export shortfall from trend. The borrowing limit under the food or cereal facility was 100 per cent of the quota under the CFF, but the combined borrowing from the two facilities cannot exceed 125 per cent of the quota in the CFF.

There are those who believe that a country should be permitted to finance any excess cereal imports regardless of the state of export earnings. The criteria used recognize, however, that when the excess import costs are due to relatively high prices, export earnings may also be above trend level. In many cases there is a positive correlation among the prices of a country's exports and imports and so high import costs may be offset by an increase in export earnings.

As of the late 1980s only limited use has been made of the financing possible under the cereal import facility. It is not altogether clear why this was the case. A possible explanation was that some developing countries faced with difficulties in paying for cereal imports were successful in obtaining the required food aid. Another possibility is that it may have been easier to obtain financing through the CFF without resort to the special provisions of the cereal import facility.

There is disagreement concerning whether developing countries should have insurance against both price and quantity variations that affect their import bills. The IMF's food financing facility makes financing available against both risks. But there is a quite limited aid component in such financing and the repayment criteria are quite strict. The various insurance proposals include a significant aid component. The Huddleston–Konandreas insurance proposal puts significant emphasis upon the food insecurity arising from price variations. Estimates made by Dr Valdés and Dr Konandreas on the sources of variability of the food import bill for 24 developing countries for 1961–76 revealed that only a quarter of the variability was due to import price variability. For most countries that imported a significant amount of food the interaction between quantity and price was negative, indicating that when volume was high, prices were low and vice versa. While the particular results reflect the high degree of price stability in international markets that existed in the 1960s, it may be noted that the high degree of price instability that existed in the early and mid-1970s has not been repeated during the 1980s.[15]

A further bit of evidence on the need to insure developing countries against price risk may be found in the experience of the net agricultural trade balance during 1973–75, years with sharp increases in international market prices of agricultural products. Developing countries as a group are net exporters of agricultural products. Due to the intercorrelations among the prices of agricultural products, it is not unreasonable to assume that when import bills are high, due to high prices, export receipts are also likely to be high. This is exactly what happened during the three years 1973–75 compared with the prior years. For the 31 developing countries with populations in excess of 7 million the annual average value of the excess of agricultural exports over agricultural imports increased by $4.3 billion between 1969–71 and 1973–75. For the 31 countries the excess of the value of agricultural exports over imports was $11.6 billion for 1973–75.[16]

An analysis for the United Nations Conference on Trade and Development (UNCTAD) by Peter Svedberg of the correlation between cereal prices and an index of primary commodity prices for 1950–83 resulted in an R^2 of 0.45, indicating that a significant part of the price variability for cereal imports was offset by variations in the export prices received by developing countries. It should be noted that the cereal price variable was either the deviation from trend or a moving average and not the absolute price. Almost half of the variation from trend or the moving average in cereals price was related to the price index for primary commodities.[17]

There is some disagreement about what has happened to production variability in the developing countries and the world as a whole. Peter B. R. Hazell, in another study for the International Food Policy Research Institute, has argued that grain production in India was more unstable after than before the Green Revolution. In fact, he concludes that the coefficient of variation for 1967/68–1977/78 was almost 50 per cent greater than during 1954/55–1964/65.[18] The coefficient of variation – the standard deviation as a per cent of the mean – increased from 4.03 to 5.85 from the earlier to the later period. Assuming an average grain output of 100 million tons, a coefficient of variation of 4.03 means that two times out of three grain production would vary between about 92 million and 108 million tons; the larger coefficient means that the output variation two times out of three would vary between 88.3 million and 111.7 million tons.

There is an important caveat that must be noted in interpreting Dr Hazell's results. In choosing his time periods, he left out two years of very low production, namely 1965/66 and 1966/67. These two years preceded the years when there was a significant acreage devoted to the new high-yielding varieties of rice and wheat. Thus they belonged to the pre-Green Revolution period. Peter Svedberg undertook a similar analysis and included these two years in the earlier period and obtained a result opposite to Dr Hazell's. Dr Svedberg's analysis was for a longer period.

Dr Svedberg analyzed variability of Indian grain production for 1954 to 1982, breaking the period at 1969 and 1970. With this distribution of the years, the coefficient of variation for the later period was slightly lower than for the earlier period. For all food production the later period was much more stable – the coefficient of variation declined from 0.22 to 0.14. Dr Svedberg's analysis for a considerable number of developing countries found a small decrease in production variability for all food and a small increase for cereals. The percentage changes – one minus and one plus – were very nearly the same.

Some Additional Comments

Over the past two decades there has been a significant improvement in both world food adequacy and food security in all of the developing areas except Africa. Densely populated and resource-poor Asia has improved its food situation significantly over the period of time while in much of Africa per capita domestic food production has declined and a continent that was a significant exporter of food during the 1960s was a major importer in the 1980s.

As is made clear in the World Bank's *World Development Report 1986*, the deteriorating food situation throughout most African countries was due to the nature of policies governments followed towards agriculture.[19] Through a combination of direct taxes on agriculture, such as export taxes, price controls on food, subsidized food imports and overvalued currencies, the incentives for agricultural production were seriously eroded and agricultural output suffered as a consequence. Added to the adverse effects of governmental policies towards agriculture and food in most African countries, millions of people suffered from civil war, oppression and the use of famine as a military weapon in several countries. The famines that have occurred in Uganda, Ethiopia, Mozambique and Angola were largely due to man's inhumanity to man, not to nature or any inadequacy in the ability of farm people to use the resources at hand effectively if there had been appropriate rewards and peace.

Food inadequacy in developing countries is due primarily to poverty or lack of income and not to unavailability of food supplies. With the continuing development of a world food system, production shortfalls are not a significant factor in causing malnutrition and hunger. True, in some cases production shortfalls are a primary source of income loss and the inability to purchase food. But it is now true that in almost all of the world, governments permitting, food supplies are available to those who have the means to purchase the food. This was not true a half-century or so ago in large parts of Asia, but with the improvements in communication and transport that have occurred in the interim there are few people in the world who cannot have access to food.

T. W. Schultz, the Nobel Prize economist, writing in his *Transforming Traditional Agriculture*, published in 1964, made the case that farmers in the developing countries were poor but efficient. They were not poor because they made inefficient use of their available resources; they were poor because they had few resources.[20] He argued that whenever superior alternatives were made available to the farmers of the developing countries that they would adopt those alternatives. His basic thesis was confirmed by the rapid adoption and spread of the high-yield varieties of rice and wheat, first in Asia and later in other developing countries.[21] In addition, after the mid-1960s there was a substantial expansion of irrigation in the world's two most populous countries, India and China, and in the developing world as a whole. The irrigated areas of India and China together increased from 54 million hectares in 1961–65 to 75 million hectares in 1985.[22] Depending on the circumstances, a hectare of irrigated land yields from two to four times as much as the same land before it was irrigated. Consequently, irrigating a hectare of land is similar to 'finding' one to three additional hectares of cropland. Experience has shown that both the private and public sectors have responded to new opportunities for increasing agricultural production.

The principal contributions that the industrial countries can make to improve food availability, increase food security, and reduce malnutrition in the developing countries lie outside the area of food aid. Only brief note of those contributions is appropriate here. Among the high-priority areas are the support of agricultural research, including improvement of national systems; reducing the barriers to trade in agricultural products and improving access to the markets of the industrial countries for the labour-intensive manufactured products of the developing countries. Fundamentally, what is important is to undertake those activities that will increase the productivity of the resources that exist in the developing countries. Relative to the industrial countries, the developing countries have an excess of agricultural resources and of unskilled and low-skilled workers. Research and relatively open international markets will improve the productivity of the agricultural resources as will freer trade in labour-intensive manufactured products expand the opportunities to provide more and higher-paying jobs for large numbers of workers in the developing countries. It is through these and related changes that real incomes can grow and the major cause of malnutrition – low incomes – can be eliminated.

9 Who Gains from Agricultural Protection?

A previous chapter emphasized the particular problems that confront agriculture when economic growth occurs. Agriculture is a declining industry; when economic growth occurs it provides a declining percentage of total national employment opportunities for mobile resources, especially labour. Since it is necessary under these circumstances to transfer labour continuously out of agriculture to other occupations, the return to farm labour will be less than the return to labour of similar education, skills and capacities engaged in other activities. At least this will be true in any economy in which decisions concerning choice of jobs is left to the individual; individuals do not voluntarily change jobs unless they anticipate a gain from doing so.

With very few exceptions, the available data on farm and non-farm incomes appear to indicate that the return to farm labour is substantially below the earnings of non-farm labour. Such a conclusion appears justified from comparisons of wage rates or of the national income produced per worker in agriculture and in non-agriculture.[1] While we shall return to this topic and subject it to closer examination in a later chapter, for the time being let us assume that the return to labour in agriculture is less than the return to comparable labour employed elsewhere. The evaluation of the price and subsidy policies for agriculture in the industrial country should consider whether these policies are, in fact, capable of significantly reducing any income differential that may exist.

In both political and farm circles it is almost universally assumed that it is obvious that higher farm prices or a subsidy on an input used in farm production will result in higher income to farm labour. After all, net income is the difference between gross income and production expenses; and if gross income is increased by higher output prices or production expenses are reduced by a lower price for an input such as fertilizer, net income must increase. This line of reasoning is based on a common fallacy, namely that of generalizing from the specific.

The seeming plausibility of the conclusion that higher prices will result in higher net farm incomes can be easily illustrated. Assume that you have data for a farm that produces only one product (wheat) and uses land owned by the farm operator, labour provided by the farm operator and members of his family, purchases inputs valued at $20 000 per year, produces 400 tons of wheat and the price is $120 per ton. The gross income would be $48 000 and the net return to land and labour would be $28 000. In the next year the price of wheat is increased to $150 per ton and the gross income increases to $60 000 and the net return to $40 000. Thus a price increase of 25 per cent results in an increase of 42 per cent in net income. The 42 per cent increase in net income would actually be a minimum since additional net income could be earned at the higher output price, if it had been anticipated, by increasing the use of purchased inputs (until their marginal cost equalled the value of their marginal product) and, perhaps, by hiring some additional labour or by inducing a member of the family to work on the farm rather than elsewhere.

The last two adjustments – hiring labour or a family member working on the farm rather than elsewhere – are of the kind that limits the longer-run effectiveness of higher prices as a means of increasing income in agriculture. A part of the problem with the example is the failure to differentiate between the sources of productivity and income of the farm – the land (with associated capital) and the labour of the operator and his family. A part of the increased farm income in the short run would be attributed to an increase in rent and a part would be attributed to a higher return on labour. Let us assume for the moment that nothing can be done to increase the supply of land for this farm or the country as a whole and that the rent on land increases by a minimum of 40 per cent. As long as the price of grain stays at $150 per ton and no new inputs become available, the new higher level of rent would be maintained. Thus, to this extent, it is correct to say that higher output prices would increase farm incomes both immediately and for the long run.

But can the same be said of the return to labour? There would be an immediate increase in the return to the labour of the operator and his family. But most of this increase would be gradually eroded by the incentive to employ more labour in agriculture. Unless the entry into agriculture were limited or controlled, the return to labour would sooner or later return to approximately the same level as it would have been if the price of grain had been $120 instead of $150 per ton. Since almost everywhere in the industrial countries farm employment is declining, the time period involved for the approximate equalization of labour returns for the two different output prices can be quite short, perhaps no longer than five years.

I do not say that the return per worker-year would be identical in the two cases, but only that the difference would be very small. The reason that it would not be identical is that the level of employment in agriculture would be larger with the $150 price than with the $120 price and thus over the period involved the rate of decline of farm employment would be smaller with the higher price than with the lower price. But in the long run this difference in return would become very small, for after the supply of labour has adjusted itself to the higher price, there is nothing in the continued maintenance of the higher price that would reduce the forces leading to a decline in the relative demand for labour in agriculture. Certainly the higher output price will not in any way reduce the necessity of substituting other inputs for labour in agriculture as the real earnings of farm labour increase in line with alternatives elsewhere in the economy.

One assumption is crucial to my conclusion, namely that in the long run the elasticity of supply of labour to agriculture in industrial countries is substantial. If agriculture had to attract additional workers from other lines of work, this might be an unreasonable assumption. But in the industrial countries, agriculture has only to retain some part of the youth who have grown up on farms and who would otherwise leave farms for other work in order to achieve an increase in the farm labour force. The response to the higher grain price need not be an absolute increase in the number of farm workers; it need only be a temporarily slower rate of decline than would have occurred with the lower output price.

As noted in Chapter 4, the farm labour force in the industrial countries declined by 2.5 to 5.0 per cent annually during the 1960s and continued at those rates during the 1970s and 1980s in countries with some 10 per cent of the labour force engaged in agriculture. Thus if the higher output price were to make profitable the employment of 10 per cent more workers than the lower output price, a halt to the outflow of workers would be required for only two to four years.

Before turning to the information on the elasticity of supply of labour to agriculture or, put another way, the mobility of the farm population, a few words should be said about the more or less permanent increase in rent. Is this not an important and desirable consequence, especially if the farm operators own most of the farm land or rent it on very long-term fixed leases? If the long-run result is approximately the same annual return to farm labour, but a significantly higher return to land, would not farm people be better off?

Increases in Land Rent

Land rent is not now a majority component of the net income of agriculture. Colin Clark, the Australian economist, brought together a number of estimates of land rent in Britain and generally such rent constituted a third or less of the net income from agriculture, with net income defined to include the return to hired farm workers.[2] A considerable part of the income defined as rent undoubtedly went to investments in farm structures, such as buildings and fences. Estimates for the United States indicate that during the 1950s rent on land, after eliminating the return to buildings, averaged less than a quarter of the value added by agriculture.[3] Estimates by the author for the 1970s are that rent still accounted for about 25 per cent of the value added in United States agriculture. Part of the rent, as argued later, is due to the effects of government farm programmes on land rents and values. In Japan, which has the highest ratio of labour to farm land of any developed country, the share of land in value added was estimated to be 38 per cent in the early 1960s.[4] Consequently the long-run increase in farm income that would result in an increase in the rate of return to resources rather than primarily to increase the quantity of resources in agriculture would apply to only a quarter to a third of the resources engaged in agriculture.

If the share of the value added in agriculture contributed by land remained constant, land rents would rise by approximately the same percentage as the increase in output prices. In fact, it appears that over time the share of land in either value added or gross output has been falling due to the effective substitution of other inputs for land. Thus a percentage increase in land rents equal to the percentage increase in output prices might represent the upper limit.[5]

There is no doubt that those who own land gain when governments intervene and increase farm output prices. Serious questions, though, can be raised concerning the justification for such an income transfer and the long-run consequences of it. In the abstract there is neither more nor less justification for increases in the return to land than to any other input. But the effects of such transfers on the distribution of income (and of wealth) may well be quite inconsistent with the general views of the desired income distribution accepted in most democratic societies. The income transfer to land would be achieved as a result of higher food prices which would constitute a larger relative charge against low-income families in the economy. Low-income families spend a larger fraction of their income on food than families with average or above-average incomes. Higher food prices are similar to a regressive tax and fall most heavily on those at the lower end of the income distribution. The distribution of the increased rent, in most economies, would go largely to individuals with relatively high incomes since there is a greater degree of concentration in the ownership of farm land than there is in farm income. Even if a country's farm families have lower average incomes than non-farm families, it does not follow that this is true of the families or individuals who own farm land.

It is quite certain that within agriculture the transfer of income resulting from higher output prices goes primarily to higher income families. For one thing, the families of hired farm workers who have the lowest incomes within agriculture gain nothing from the increased rent. The farmers who own smallholdings gain little in absolute terms and in some countries these farmers have incomes of the same order as the hired farm workers. The farm operator who rents part or all of his land gains little, unless he has a long-term lease with a fixed rent in money terms. The primary gainers are the farmers who own their land and have average or larger farms and landlords. If the data on income distribution in the United States are at all representative of the distribution in other industrial countries, the farmers who produce most of farm output (say three-fourths or more) have average family incomes that are above the national average for all families.[6] Thus there are no equity grounds that can be brought to bear to justify the transfer of income from consumers, including low-income consumers, to relatively high-income owners of farm land.

But one needs to look further at the nature and duration of the gains realized by those who own land and wish to continue in farming or to have their children do so. Such families would have both greater wealth and greater income. But there is no reason to believe that the rate of return on investment in land would change; the percentage rise in land value would be the same as the percentage increase in rent. The rise in land values can lead to somewhat smaller farms than would otherwise exist since it may be feasible to pass a given farm on to two sons rather than one, especially if there is the possibility of some enlargement through purchase or rental. This process would result in some reduction in the amount of farm land capital per farm operator and, measured by area, farms would be smaller as a result of the higher land values. Any new land that would be purchased would be at the higher price and there would be no gain to the purchaser due to the higher rent resulting from the higher output price. To put it in a slightly different context, higher land values encourage retaining more resources in agriculture, especially management resources, but also resources of a capital nature that are good substitutes for land.

Higher land values induced by high output prices are of no value whatsoever to the individual who enters agriculture after the adjustment in land values has occurred. Such an individual pays the amount for land that equalizes investment opportunity in land and in other investment alternatives. In fact, such a situation exposes the entrant to considerable risk since what government has given, it can take away – namely the higher output price.

A dramatic indication of the risks of purchasing farm land at high prices occurred in the United States during the 1980s. In nominal terms the value of farm land nearly quadrupled between 1970 and 1981 and almost doubled in real terms. There were many reasons for the sharp rise in land values – low and often negative real interest rates, the increase in net farm incomes during the mid-1970s, expectations about future growth of world demand for food and the confidence that farm programmes would continue to minimize downside risks. Following 1981, however, the prices of farm land fell precipitously in most states and many farm families that had bought farm land during the 1970s were in great financial difficulties and a significant number lost not only the newly-acquired land but all of their land and other assets. The price of the highly productive land in Iowa fell by more than 60 per cent between 1981 and 1987. For the United States as a whole, the nominal price of land fell by a third; the real price declined by 45 per cent. It is clear that for some farm people high land prices became their albatross. Whatever role governmental policy had in increasing land prices in the 1970s benefited those who sold the land, but had adverse effects on those who bought land with borrowed funds.[7]

One of the reasons why it is so difficult to change price policy to achieve prices more in line with import costs or export values is that lower farmland prices would result in huge capital losses. In many countries the loss in land values due to changing from current farm price and subsidy programmes to prices near to world prices would knock an enormous amount off farmland values and in some countries the loss in value could amount to a third or more of present land values.

The example used earlier to illustrate the income effects of higher product prices is a highly simplified one. It assumes that there will be no change in the quantity or value of purchased inputs. Obviously this would not be the case. The previous level of purchased inputs would no longer be the most profitable one; more purchased inputs would be used. The primary effect of the increase in purchased inputs would be to increase the level of output and thus the cost to taxpayers of maintaining the higher price for output. A secondary effect, due to the rise in land prices and rents, would be to add purchased inputs that would substitute for land, since its price would rise much more than the price of labour.

Higher Prices and Returns to Farm Labour

An increase in farm prices, due either to market forces or to governmental action, affects the return to farm labour in a complex manner. The higher prices increase the value of the product produced by labour and in a competitive situation such an increase would be reflected in higher actual or imputed wages paid to labour. The magnitude of the increase in the value of the product that can be attributed to labour depends on the case with which other inputs can be substituted for labour as the price of labour rises, the number of additional workers that will be forthcoming at the higher wage rate or the increase in work done by the existing labour force, and the change in the prices of other inputs that are used in agriculture. If the price of other inputs remain unchanged after the increase in output prices, there will be more substitution of other inputs for labour as its wage rate increases and such substitution will dampen the increase in wage rates. If the prices of other inputs increase as much or more than the wage rate, such substitution against labour will not occur.

Unfortunately for the success of policies that depend on increasing market prices for the achievement of increased returns to farm labour in the industrial countries there is a major class of farm inputs whose prices are little affected by the level of farm output prices. This is true of most inputs purchased from the non-farm sector of the economy, such as fertilizers, tractors, fuel and insecticides, and feeds and feedstuffs imported from abroad, especially when variable import levies are used to stabilize the costs of such items to the domestic purchasers. Thus even if the supply of labour to agriculture were not at all responsive to the change in the wage rate, it is quite likely that the increase in wage rates would be less in percentage terms than the increase in market prices since inputs whose prices had not risen would be substituted for the higher-priced labour.

We know that the quantity of farm labour available to agriculture is a function of the return to that labour in agriculture compared with what reasonably comparable labour receives elsewhere in the relevant economy. Thus part of the effect of higher output prices is to increase employment in farming and thus offset some of the very short-run positive effect of higher output prices on wage rates. Whether or not higher output prices are an effective instrument for increasing the returns to farm labour is a question that policy-makers in the industrial countries have seldom asked, yet it is a question that can be answered by the analytical framework developed by economists. Not only does the analytical framework exist – most of it can be found in one of the appendices to Sir John Hicks' classic work, *The Theory of Wages* – but some reasonable empirical estimates are also available, although, as far as I know, they have been largely, if not entirely, neglected in the determination of farm price and subsidy policies. It is to this work that we shall now turn.

Supply of Labour to Agriculture

There have been a number of empirical studies of the supply of labour to agriculture over the past three decades, especially for the United States. Most of the studies were made during the 1960s, although one study was completed in 1988. The interest in the subject has been greater in the United States than elsewhere and most of the emphasis in this brief review is for the United States.

One of the earliest systematic studies of the supply and demand of farm labour in the United States was completed in the late 1960s by Edward W. Tyrchniewicz and G. Edward Schuh at Purdue University.[8] Micha Gisser, now at the University of New Mexico, also made important contributions to the subject by including the effect of schooling on both the productivity of labour in agriculture and the mobility response to earnings differentials. These studies were based on data available before the early 1960s. Changes in the conditions that affect the supply of labour to agriculture since the early 1960s have probably been to increase the elasticity of supply of labour. Over the past quarter-century, changes have occurred in communication and transport that make it easier to transfer labour into or out of farming either through change of residence or by varying the amount of off-farm work performed. In the United States off-farm income increased from 44 per cent of total income of farm-operator families in 1960 to 55 per cent in 1970 and to 61 per cent in 1980.[9] From 1980 to 1986 off-farm income as a percentage of total income varied from 55 to 60 per cent of the total incomes of farm families.

A recent study by Andrew Barkley, of Kansas State University (see Note 36), utilizing data for the United States for 1940 through the mid-1980s, supports the above presumptions that the elasticity of labour supply to earnings differentials between agriculture and other activities has increased over time.

Dr Tyrchniewicz and Professor Schuh derived estimates of the demand and supply functions for three categories of farm labour, namely hired workers, unpaid family workers and farm operators. The results for operator labour were unsatisfactory and the authors attached no significance to the results. The trend variable tended to explain almost all of the change in operator labour engaged in agriculture and this meant that the analysis added little to our understanding. The results, however, for hired and unpaid family workers met all of the usual statistical and economic criteria and are worthy of our attention.

The study indicated that the supply of hired and unpaid family workers increased with higher farm wage rates and declined with an increase in non-farm income adjusted for unemployment. Both the short-run and long-run elasticities of the quantity of farm labour with respect to non-farm income were negative and greater than unity. The short-run elasticities of supply were − 1.42 for hired labour and − 1.47 for unpaid family workers while the long-run elasticities were − 3.38 for hired labour and − 3.26 for unpaid family workers. Thus, holding farm wage rates constant, an increase of non-farm income per worker of 10 per cent would reduce the supply of farm workers by more than 30 per cent. Of course, as the number of farm workers was reduced, the farm wage rate (or earnings of unpaid family workers) would not remain constant, but would increase and act to reduce, although not eliminate, the decline in the number of farm workers.

An increase in farm wage rates increases the supply of labour to agriculture. This elasticity was approximately 1.5 in the long run. Thus a 10 per cent increase in farm wage rates would increase the quantity of hired and unpaid family labour by about 15 per cent. On balance, the analysis indicates that if both farm wage rates and non-farm earnings increase by 10 per cent, the number of these two categories of workers in agriculture would decline by about 17 per cent. This large decline was presumably due to the difference in the real incomes that can be derived from farm and non-farm employment and the existence of a considerable disequilibrium in the labour market during the period of analysis. If farm wage rates and non-farm earnings were identical, one would expect the elasticities of supply with respect to farm wage rates, on the one hand, and to non-farm earnings, on the other hand, to have the same absolute value. While there is, however, a net transfer of labour out of agriculture, the anticipated earnings are not the same in agriculture and in the non-farm sector.

The analysis also provided an estimate of the effect of real farm prices on the quantity of farm labour demanded if the farm wage rate remains unchanged and given the elasticity of quantity demanded for farm labour with respect to the wage rate. Taken together this information permits one to estimate the change in the return to farm labour *if the supply of labour were held constant.* For the purposes of this illustration, the elasticity of demand for labour with respect to the wage rate is -0.26 and the elasticity of demand for labour with respect to real farm prices is 0.31. The latter elasticity tells us that if real farm prices increased by 10 per cent and if the wage rate remained constant, the amount of labour demanded would increase by 3.1 per cent. If the quantity of labour available is held constant, the price of labour must rise. The increase in the wage rate due to the 10 per cent increase in real farm prices and a fixed supply of labour would be the product of 3.1 per cent and the reciprocal of 0.26, the elasticity of demand for labour with respect to its price.[10] The amount of labour available, under the assumptions made, is 3.1 per cent less than demanded at a constant price of labour. Because of the very low price elasticity of demand for labour in the short run, the wage rate must increase significantly to remove the excess demand. The increase in the price of labour would be 11.9 per cent as indicated in Figure 9.1.

But the substantial increase in the price of labour is due to holding the quantity of labour constant. The same analysis indicates that the short-run elasticity of the supply of labour with respect to the price of labour is 0.65. Thus if the increase in the return to labour remained at 11.9 per cent, the quantity of labour supplied would increase by 7.7 per cent (the product of 11.9 and 0.65). But this would be an impossible

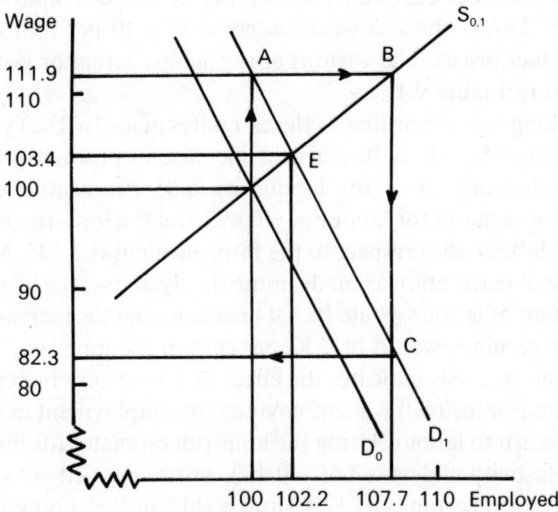

Figure 9.1

A – Demand equilibrium, if supply of labour held constant
B – Supply equilibrium, if wage rate were 111.9
C – Demand equilibrium, if quantity of labour were 107.7
E – Equilibrium of supply and demand with D_1 and $S_{0,1}$
D_0 – Demand curve for labour before output price increase
D_1 – Demand curve for labour after output price increase of 10 per cent
$S_{0,1}$ – Supply curve of labour in both periods

situation. An increase in the quantity of labour of this magnitude
would not be acceptable to employers (even if the employer and worker
were the same individual) without a substantial decline in the return to
or price of labour. In fact, 7.7 per cent more labour would be used
subsequent to the 10 per cent increase in output price only after the 11.9
per cent increase in wage rate had been eliminated and a further decline
in the wage rate of 17.7 per cent had occurred. The 7.7 per cent increase
in labour supplied would result in an increase in the quantity of labour
of 4.6 per cent over and above the amount that would be employed at
the wage rate *before* the increase in output prices. The 4.6 per cent
increase in quantity supplied, given the price elasticity of demand for
labour, would reduce the price of labour by 17.7 per cent (4.4 times the
reciprocal of 0.26, or times 3.846). Obviously the increase in the
quantity of labour supplied would not occur either. After adjustments
in both demand and supply for labour, assuming no shift in the supply
schedule due to a change in non-farm income, the wage rate would

increase by 3.4 per cent and the quantity of labour employed by 2.21 per cent.[11] This is the short-run outcome of a 10 per cent increase in farm product prices. The various adjustments, actual or potential, are illustrated in Figure 9.1.

In the long run, according to the estimates made by Dr Tyrchniewicz and Professor Schuh, a 10 per cent increase in product prices would shift the demand curve for labour by 5.85 per cent; the long-run elasticity of demand for labour is −0.492 and the long-run elasticity of supply of labour with respect to the farm earnings is 1.545. Making the same type of calculation as made immediately above, the increase in the employment of labour would be 4.44 per cent and the increase in wages or labour earnings would be 2.87 per cent in the long run.[12]

The same analysis indicates the effect of a 1 per cent increase in non-farm income adjusted for unemployment on employment in agriculture and the return to labour. Using the long-run estimates for hired labour, with an elasticity of demand of −0.492, a price elasticity of supply with respect to farm earnings of 1.545 and a shift in the supply function of −3.38 for each percentage change in non-farm income, and assuming that the farm labour force would grow about 1 per cent annually because of population growth, the decrease in farm employment would be 0.82 per cent and the increase in return to labour 1.66 per cent.[13] An increase in non-farm earnings of 2 per cent would increase returns to farm labour by 2.8 per cent while reducing employment by 1.4 per cent. Thus in the long run a *one-time* increase of 2 per cent in non-farm earnings would increase the return to farm labour as much as a *one-time* 10 per cent increase in product prices.

During 1929 to 1961, the period used for the study, the wages and earnings of farm labour were substantially below the earnings of comparable labour in the non-farm economy, even after adjustment for differences in labour quality and cost of living, in the United States. Since 1970 the differences in labour earnings have narrowed significantly. Thus it may now be more accurate to assume that if the long-run elasticity of supply of labour with respect to farm earnings is 1.545, the same absolute value would apply to elasticity with respect to non-farm earnings. In other words, a 1 per cent increase in non-farm earnings, the farm labour earnings constant, would have the same absolute effect on the supply of labour to agriculture as a 1 per cent increase in farm labour earnings, holding non-farm income constant, would have. Put another way, all other things constant, a 1 per cent increase in both farm labour earnings and in non-farm income, the supply of labour to agriculture would remain unchanged.

With the assumption that the elasticity of farm labour supply with respect to non-farm income is − 1.545 and the other elasticities are as given above, a 2 per cent increase in non-farm income with constant output prices would increase the earnings of farm labour by 1.52 per cent and reduce farm employment by 0.75 per cent. Under the assumption made here, it would take a one-time increase in non-farm income of about 3.5 per cent to increase the return to farm labour as much as a one-time 10 per cent increase in product prices. The increase in non-farm income has occurred in less than two years during most of the post-Second World War period in the industrial economies.

In a study of the effect of increased schooling on the rate of out-migration of labour from agriculture, Micha Gisser developed a model and certain empirical estimates that are appropriate for understanding the effect of increasing output prices on the return to farm labour as well as of the effect of increasing out-migration on the return to labour. Based on a combined cross-section and time series analysis of state data in the United States, he obtained an elasticity of supply of farm labour with respect to its wage rate of 2.67; this should be interpreted as an estimate of the long-run supply elasticity.[14] This estimate, which is for all farm labour, is higher than that reported above for hired and family labour (approximately 1.5).

The entire model permits estimating the effects of increasing demand for farm products, of shifting the supply function of labour to the left, of controlling acreage and of increasing the level of schooling on the return to farm labour. Some of Professor Gisser's conclusions are relevant to the present discussion. A 5 per cent horizontal shift in the demand for farm output if the elasticity of labour supply is 3, would 'raise farm wages by about 2 per cent, and increase farm employment by about 7 per cent'.[15] A 10 per cent reduction in land use would 'lead to somewhere between 0.5 to 1.3 per cent increase in farm wages and 1.3 to 1.6 per cent increase in farm employment'.[16]

According to Professor Gisser's model, a reduction in the farm labour force of 1 per cent would increase the return to farm labour by about 1.4 per cent if the elasticity of demand for output is − 0.5 and the elasticity of supply of labour is approximately 3.0.

Perhaps the most important result obtained by Professor Gisser relates to the effect of increased schooling on the returns to farm labour. He found that more schooling had two effects on the return to farm labour: (i) an increase in schooling had a positive effect on the productivity of farm labour and (ii) an increase in schooling resulted in an increase in out-migration. A 10 per cent increase in the amount of schooling, as measured by years of schooling, resulted in a 5 per cent increase in the return to farm labour. He found that the marginal cost of an additional year of schooling could be recouped through additional earnings in three to four years.[17] The costs of schooling included both public and private costs, including forgone earnings while in school.

Equally or more important, schooling had a significant effect on the supply of labour in agriculture through influencing the rate of out-migration:[18] 'increasing the level of schooling in rural farm areas 10 per cent will induce a 6–7 per cent farm out-migration and will raise the farm wage rate 5 per cent'. Thus the two effects of increased schooling on the return to farm labour are of major significance – of far greater significance than a 10 per cent increase in farm prices resulting from price-support programmes. According to the estimates made earlier a 10 per cent increase in farm prices would increase the return to farm labour by about 2.9 to 3.4 per cent.

Price Supports, Land Allotments and Returns to Farm Land

The United States has made much use of land allotments and other approaches to limiting land use as a part of its efforts to increase farm prices. Other governments have also used similar devices for particular commodities, although to a lesser degree than the United States.

John Floyd, of the University of Washington, made estimates for the United States of the differential effects on the returns to labour and land of three methods of achieving a 10 per cent increase in farm prices.[19] The three methods were a 10 per cent increase in support prices without control of output, a reduction of acreage sufficient to reduce output enough to increase farm prices by 10 per cent and marketing controls that limited the amount marketed sufficient to increase prices by 10 per cent. Under various reasonable assumptions he found that a 10 per cent increase in output prices would increase the return per unit of land up to eight times as much as the increase in the return to labour. The critical factor in the differential increases in returns is the difference in elasticities of supply of labour and land. The largest difference in the increased returns to land and labour occurred when the elasticity of supply of labour was assumed to be 3; a difference of approximately two times as large an increase in land return as in labour return occurred when the elasticity of supply of labour was assumed to be very low, namely 0.5.

The use of acreage controls as a means of increasing prices significantly reduced the gain to labour and, under some assumptions, the increased price resulted in no increase in the return to labour while the return to land was increased by 10 per cent. If the government were to pay farmers for the land removed from production, as has been the case in the United States, the increase in return to land could be very large.

If the price increase were achieved by output control through limiting the amount marketed, the return to labour would actually decline. The value of the certificates to market output, if tied to land, would increase land values or returns by as much as 60 per cent. The decline in the return to labour would occur because all land would be used in producing the lower level of output since the farmland has no reasonable alternative use; the amount of labour required to produce the smaller output would be reduced and the demand for farm labour would decline.

It is possible to provide empirical tests of the general conclusions reached by Professor Floyd, as well as the conclusions of the earlier analysis that most of the increased returns go to land, by data that are available on the effects of farm programmes in the United States on the return to farmland. Much of the rest of this section is concerned with research on the effect of the tobacco programmes on the value of tobacco allotments. While the tobacco programme in the United States, which has been in continuous operation since 1935, was formally an acreage limitation programme (since producers were given an acreage allotment) in its actual operation it was more accurately described as an output limitation programme (as described by Professor Floyd). In recent years the tobacco programme has invoked an output quota. The acreage allotment was essentially the 'right' to produce tobacco; the amount of land suitable for growing tobacco has always been much greater than the amount actually used for that purpose. The alternative uses for the land provide a much lower return and there has never been any restriction on the use of land removed from tobacco production. In addition, the right to produce tobacco can be transferred from one farmer to another. In the early years this required the actual sale of land, but later (since 1963) the allotments could be rented or transferred to a farmer on an annual basis. One need not be a farmer to own a tobacco allotment. There have been no direct payments to producers under the tobacco programme, by contrast to the practice in the cotton, wheat and feed-grain programmes where most of the income transfers have been through direct payments and not higher market prices.

Various methods have been used to estimate the value of an acre of tobacco allotment, either in terms of its annual rental or its capitalized value. The techniques used include linear programming, residual returns to land derived from estimates of production costs, regression analyses of actual farm sales prices as related to the size of the tobacco allotment and interviews of knowledgeable persons. At a time subsequent to several of the studies a change in the tobacco programme permitted a market test of at least some of the estimates. Since 1963 the programme has permitted farmers to transfer their allotments to another farmer living in the same county; obviously the transfer has been at a price. One study found that in 1963, in two counties that produced flue-cured tobacco, the annual rent for a hectare of tobacco allotment was in excess of $750 per hectare, or about $0.38 per kilogram of tobacco produced. The average price received by farmers for tobacco was about $1.28 per kilogram. Note that what was being paid for was the allotment, not the actual land. The land had to be provided by the farmer who rented the allotment. The market price for cropland suitable for the production of tobacco in 1963 was in the general range of $600–700 per hectare; thus the *annual* rental value of a hectare of tobacco allotment was equal to or greater than the market price of the land on which the tobacco was grown if that land did not have a tobacco allotment. Studies made in 1966 and 1967 indicated that the rents paid for tobacco allotments in North Carolina, the major tobacco-producing state, were about $0.42 per kilogram compared with an average selling price of tobacco of $1.40. The annual rental value was $1000 to $1430 per hectare; these estimates were very close to an estimate derived by subtracting labour costs, other variable costs and land rent (exclusive of the rent of the allotment) from total revenue from a hectare of tobacco.

Regression analyses of the sales value of farms as affected by the size of the tobacco allotments indicate that a hectare of tobacco allotment had a capitalized or market value of $4000 to $7000 per hectare in the late 1950s and early 1960s. This should be compared with the estimated market value of land without acreage allotments of about $600–700 per hectare.[20]

The studies of the effects of the tobacco programme on the returns to land that have been summarized above do not speak directly to the effects of the programme on the return to farm labour. These studies show only that the return to land with an allotment and the market value of the allotment are very large relative to the value of the land actually used to produce the tobacco. One important study has been made of the effects of the tobacco programme on the return to farm labour in the states of North Carolina and Virginia.[21] The author, J. L. Hedrick, estimates that the effect of the tobacco programme was to increase the price received by farmers in 1960 by approximately 20 per cent.

A significant fraction of the tobacco in Virginia and North Carolina is produced under a cropper arrangement where the cropper receives a given fraction of the value of output (50 per cent), pays half of current operating expenses such as seed, fertilizer and insecticides, and provides all of the labour. Over the period in which the tobacco programme has been in effect, the share paid by the cropper to the landlord has not changed. On the surface it would appear that the owner of the land (and the allotment) and the cropper would share equally in the income gains from the higher prices received because of the tobacco programme. In the very short run the equal sharing would occur. But in the longer run one should not expect such equal sharing. Based on our earlier analysis, and the results obtained by Dr Hedrick, the conclusion that in the long run all, or virtually all, of the income gains went to the landlord who owned the land and the tobacco allotment is confirmed. Estimates were made of the hourly return to the labour of the cropper and his family members. These estimated hourly returns were then compared with average wages in manufacturing in the United States and to wages of various occupational groups in the two states.

In 1922–27, which was a period of full employment, the Virginia cropper return was 32 per cent of the national average wage in manufacturing; in 1952–62, 34 per cent. The North Carolina percentages for the same years were 42 and 42. In other words, the increase in hourly returns to croppers was exactly the same as the increase in national average wages in manufacturing. The author recognized that the manufacturing national wage probably was not available to the farm workers in his analysis. The comparisons with occupational groups in Virginia and North Carolina include categories more comparable with the education and skills of the cropper labour. Actually there are difficulties with Virginia since a significant number of the employed workers in Virginia are federal employees. Since the trends in the earnings ratios are the same, reference will only be made to the more comparable data for North Carolina. The first year for which a comparison is available is 1940, while the last year is 1960. While the tobacco programme was in effect before 1940, the estimates of James

Seagraves, now at Rutgers University in New Jersey, indicate that the annual return to a hectare of tobacco allotment was rather modest in that year, namely $75 compared with $1475 in 1960. Thus the comparison of relative earnings in 1940 and in 1960 seems appropriate to reflect any effect the tobacco programme may have had on the long-run earnings of labour used in producing tobacco.

The tabulation indicates the changes in ratio of earnings of cropper labour to earnings of other occupational groups (male workers):

	1940	*1960*
Craftsmen, foreman, kindred	0.51	0.50
Operatives and kindred workers	0.66	0.63
Service workers	0.92	0.78
Labourers, except farm and mine	1.02	1.05

In only one of the four comparisons was there a significant decrease in the relative earnings of cropper labour. The author concluded: 'it was found that neither tenure inflexibilities nor labour immobilities have permitted the control programme to influence earnings of the human factor over the long run ...'. The real returns to the human factor increased by 145 per cent or at an annual rate of 2.6 per cent. It is worthy of note that the return per farm of constant total area, but with a reduction in tobacco area of about a third, increased by 500 per cent in dollars of constant purchasing power over the same period of time.

While the tobacco programme has probably had more effect on the return to land than any of the other farm programmes in the United States, Dr Hedrick's estimates of the decline in return to land used to produce tobacco in 1960 if the programme were abolished are both instructive and discouraging. For both of the states it is estimated that abandoning the programme would reduce rent per unit of land used to produce tobacco in 1960 by 85 per cent.[22] Without the programme the return to land used in producing tobacco would be only 15 per cent of what it was with the programme in effect. The effect on market values of land is obvious and the prospective major reduction in land values is an important political reason for continuing the tobacco programme.

Estimates of the value of allotments for peanuts, cotton and corn have also been made.[23] None of the estimates reach the extremes found for tobacco, but none are so small as to be ignored, either. The market value of a hectare of peanut allotment in North Carolina in the late 1950s was about $1670 and a hectare of cotton allotment in the same area was $1150. A second study of the value of peanut allotment obtained a value of $1400 per hectare. In the mid-1980s the annual rental for a peanut allotment in the south-east of the United States was about $120 per ton. This equalled 20 per cent of the price of quota peanuts and would be approximately $440 per year per hectare. If the value of the allotment were four times the annual rental, the value would be $1760 per hectare. Nominally this value is only a little more than the value in the 1950s. This means the real value of the peanut allotment has declined by approximately 70 per cent. Estimates of the annual value of a hectare of corn allotment ranged from $25 to $50 in Iowa in the early 1960s; the appropriate rate for capitalization into land values was probably 10 per cent.

The conclusion that almost all of the long-run income gains from support prices above equilibrium levels goes to higher returns to land is supported by a considerable number of able economists. Willard Cochrane, who was closely associated with American farm programmes from 1961 to 1964, has put it this way: 'increased farm incomes resulting from increased levels of price support would quickly be capitalized into increased land values.'[24]

Luther Tweeten has stated:[25]

> Land price is an important variable in public policy. Long-term fluctuations in farm income tend to be absorbed by land values. Raising the level of farm income by government programs of the type used from 1955 to 1969 tends to result in capitalization of program benefits into land. ... While land prices on the larger, well-organized farms tend to adjust to farming income, leaving a parity return on resources, it does not necessarily follow that any level of farm income is equally satisfactory to farmers. A reduction in farm income can wipe out equities, raise mortgage foreclosures, and cause other financial hardships, while the market adjusts the land price down to a lower equilibrium level consistent with less farm income.

Earl Heady and Leo Mayer, in a study at Iowa State University, made the same point:[26] 'The second major improvement [in American farm programmes] ... should be modifications to prevent the capitalization of program benefits into real estate values. ... After the resources change hands through the market, the gains of the program are cancelled and the function of public expenditure is mainly to maintain asset values so that the new owner does not suffer a capital loss.'

Since the above was written in the first edition of *World Agriculture in Disarray* there has been considerably more evidence which supports the conclusion that most of the benefits of price supports and the allocation of the rights to produce farm products go to some fixed resource. This fixed resource can be land if control of the land input is the means used to determine who may grow a crop at all or under conditions that will provide major inducements through price supports and deficiency payments to limit the amount of land devoted to the crop. In the United States the benefits of the programmes for grains and cotton have come primarily through the access to high price supports and various payments made to those producers who agree to divert or set aside part of their land. It is the amount of land that a farmer controls that determines the income transfer received. Consequently the programmes have increased the price of farmland. A farmer who buys land includes the anticipated returns from the farm programmes as an element in his bid price. Similarly, a farmer who rents farmland determines the amount of rent that he can pay based on the effect of the programmes on the anticipated return from renting the land. And since the price of land is largely determined by anticipated returns from rent, other factors such as the rate of discount held constant, the increased income from the programmes becomes largely reflected in the price of land.

In 1984 the European Community introduced quotas that limited the amount of milk that could be produced by farmers in each member country. Rather quickly it was decided that if this approach to limiting milk production was to be effective, the quotas had to be assigned to individual producers. Once the quotas were assigned to individual producers the issue arose concerning whether the quotas could be freely bought and sold. Since permitting a market in the quotas would make it immediately apparent how valuable were the quotas, it was decided that the quotas could not be readily transferred. It is certain, based on North American experience, that the value of the quotas will become embedded in the value of farmland since the milk quotas will stay with the land. The European Community's policy will not prevent quotas from being transferred; the policy will simply make it difficult, although not impossible, to determine the value of the quotas – the value of the right to produce milk. A review of the Canadian experience with freely transferable quotas for producing milk and poultry products shows very clearly why the policy-makers in the Community want to conceal from the consumer who is being exploited by the Community's dairy policy.

The need to limit the amount of milk that a farmer produces is clear evidence that the price of milk is higher than need be to induce the amount of output for which there is a market at the established price. If the European Community had permitted the marketing of the quotas, it would have been evident to all how much higher the price of milk is than was needed to obtain the supply to meet Community consumption and the amount that could be exported for a reasonable return.

In an all-too-rare display of political courage, in the late 1970s the Economic Council of Canada commissioned a series of studies on regulation and government intervention in Canadian agriculture. The studies covered most of the governmental interventions in agriculture in Canada, including those for grains, beef, pork, dairy products, poultry, eggs and certain processed vegetables. The regulation of the dairy, poultry and egg industries involves the use of output quotas. In most cases the quotas can be bought and sold, thus permitting a determination of the value that farmers put on the particular quotas.

Richard Barichello estimated, in his study for the Economic Council of Canada, that the regulation of fluid and industrial milk markets in Canada resulted in a transfer of $671 000 000 (Canadian) to milk producers in 1980, the transfer cost to consumers being C$686 000 000 and to taxpayers C$303 000 000.[27] The transfer to producers thus added about C$0.10 per litre of milk and cost consumers and taxpayers approximately C$0.14 per litre. The estimated market value of the milk quotas, as of mid-1978, was C$1 248 000 000. A farmer who wished to expand his dairy herd or to enter dairy production must purchase a quota. In a later paper, Dr Barichello estimated that in British Columbia in 1983 a farmer had to pay C$400 for the right to produce a litre of milk per day. The milk price was about C$42 per 100 litres.[28]

The production of broilers, turkeys and eggs is also regulated by quotas. Broiler output is limited by the allocation of square feet of cage space which has the undesirable side-effect of causing the crowding of the chickens. In February 1980 the quota value per bird ranged from C$4 to C$12.[29] Egg output was limited by the number of laying hens and the market price of the quota range from C$5 to C$32. The ownership of the quotas involves an asset of very substantial value, a value so large that the programmes can hardly be considered as designed for farmers of modest means or wealth. The capital value of the broiler quota per producer was estimated to be C$193 000 and C$123 000 per producer for eggs. There are maximum size limits for the quotas. For the three major producing provinces the capital values of the quotas for the maximum quotas that are assigned range from

C$614 000 to C$713 000 for broilers producers and C$450 000 to C$640 000 for egg producers.[30] These are capital assets that were created by the grant of quotas and paid for primarily by consumers through higher market prices for the products.

Peter Arcus, in another study for the Economic Council of Canada, described the distribution of the benefits of the poultry and egg quotas as follows:[31]

> Taken overall then, market regulation, for those persons who were in the broiler and egg industries prior to and at the time of the commencement of market regulation, has been positive and substantial.
>
> Further, it has been possible for those people who have quit the industry since the commencement of regulation, to take with them the benefits of the regulatory process to that date. . . . From this asset (the sale of the quotas), a generous annual income can be obtained for the balance of that producer's life, and indeed, into the next generation as these assets are transferred.
>
> The benefits of the regulatory system for new producers are quite different. For these producers, who are those who have purchased production facilities and the quota within, say, the last twelve months, the financial benefits are greatly reduced, if in fact they exist at all. For these people, prices are not in fact higher, nor is there any increased income deriving from the regulatory process. . . . For these producers, current prices are probably only sufficient to cover existing cash costs and debt service.
>
> For this category of producers, it is no longer clear that the regulatory mechanism is supporting the maintenance of the family farm. If the family has to come up with an additional several hundred thousand dollars in order to purchase the quota, it is hard to see that this additional financial burden is favourable to new families entering the industry.

The Canadian quota systems are administered by the provinces, with support from the federal government through rigid control of imports, provision for export subsidies and, in the case of milk, a price support for manufactured milk. Because the programmes are provincial the quotas are not transferable among provinces and within provinces there are limits, such as maximum farm quotas and regional transfer restrictions within provinces.[32] Thus even the quota prices presented here are less than what the prices would be if the quotas were freely transferable throughout Canada. Recognizing that quota prices vary from one province to another, Table 9.1 includes data on the quota prices for the province of Ontario for 1984.

Table 9.1   Market value of quotas in Ontario, 1984

Product	Unit price	Family-size unit	Quota cost to enter
Fluid milk	$200/litre/day		
Mfg milk	$0.90/litre/year	40 cows	$180 000
Eggs	$30/hen	25 000 layers	$750 000
Broilers	$10/unit	50 000 birds/cycle	$450 000
Turkeys	$0.70/lb	25 000 birds/yr	$350 000
Tobacco	$2.00/lb	40 acres	$400 000

Source: T. K. Warley, 'Canada's Agricultural and Food Trade Policies: a Synoptic View', in D. Gale Johnson, Kenzo Hemmi and Pierre Lardinois, *Agricultural Policy and Trade: Adjusting Domestic Programs in an International Framework*, Report to the Trilateral Commission No. 29 (New York: New York University Press, 1985).

The leasing of tobacco allotments in the United States continued through the 1970s and into the 1980s. A study of the lease rates for tobacco allotments in North Carolina found that for 1966–69 the average lease rate per kilogram of tobacco quota was 22.9 per cent of the tobacco price the previous year.[33] For 1977–81 the lease rate for a kilogram of quota had increased to 25.6 per cent of the previous year's price. With North Carolina tobacco selling at an average price of $3.20 per kilogram in 1980, and with an average yield of 2400 kilograms per hectare the annual rental value of the quota for a hectare of tobacco was approximately $1950. The annual rental value of the tobacco allotment can be compared with the rent of $100 to $150 per hectare of cropland in North Carolina in the early 1980s.

Data on who actually grows tobacco permitted by the quotas indicates that half or more of the benefits go to individuals other than those actually growing the tobacco. For burley tobacco only 48 per cent of the tobacco is produced by the persons owning the quotas; for flue-cured tobacco only 24 per cent is owned by the actual producer. For these two types of tobacco together only about a third of the quotas are owned by individuals now farming. If the original intent of the legislation had been to increase the incomes of farmers, it is now clear that most of the income benefits go to persons who are not now farmers.

Contrary to most other farm commodity programmes in the United States, the price support aspects of the tobacco programme have involved little direct governmental expenditure. The tobacco programme has transferred a degree of monopoly power to the owners of tobacco allotments or quotas. As often happens to groups that exercise monopoly power over prices, such groups find that their share of the market is declining over time. During 1955–59, the United States accounted for 35 per cent of world tobacco exports; in 1982 the United States share was just 18 per cent. Since the American tobacco price is the world price for tobacco of similar type and quality, the monopoly price encourages output expansion in the rest of the world and a loss of the market for the United States. The United States is probably a low-cost producer of tobacco; this seems indicated by the large percentage of the price of tobacco that farmers are willing to pay to rent a quota. If the quotas were abolished, the supply price of tobacco could well fall by at least a quarter and perhaps by as much as a third. This assumes that the returns to resources actually used in producing tobacco would remain unchanged.

The clearest indication of the distribution of benefits from price supports and output quotas is provided when quotas are transferable from one farmer to another. The quotas may either be transferred on an annual basis or sold outright. In either case, it is evident that the farmers who at any one time have rented a quota, or have purchased one, realize very little benefit from the higher consumer prices. The farmer who increases his output capacity by renting, or by purchasing, a quota is making an input decision similar to the one he makes when he purchases fertilizer, a tractor or more farm land. A difference of degree emerges when quota rights are purchased. Such purchases involve a risky asset – the government programme can be modified at any time. Consequently, evidence from both the United States and Canada indicates that the rate of discount applied to the annual value of the quota is higher than for most other long-term investments made by farmers. Roughly speaking, the discount rate used to value future earnings from quotas is approximately 25 per cent. Thus individuals who have recently purchased a quota do receive a net return from owning the quota, but the net return can be reasonably said to be a return for risk.

A different approach for estimating the effects of government programmes was taken by John Rosine and Peter Helmberger at the

University of Wisconsin. They undertook a statistical analysis of the United States farm sector for 1948–70 that extended the models developed by John Floyd and Micha Gisser for the study of agricultural policy.[34] (The Floyd and Gisser studies are summarized earlier in this chapter.) A labour-supply function was estimated for the period 1929–70; the elasticity of the supply of labour to agriculture with respect to the farm wage rate was estimated to be 2.6, well within the ranges of the estimates made by Dr Tyrchniewicz and Professor Schuh and by Professor Gisser.

The model was used to estimate the effects of the government programmes on the return to farm resources (labour, capital and land) and the employment of labour. Their conclusion with respect to the distributions of the net benefits of farm programmes:

> In recent years benefits to land accounted for about 92 per cent of total benefits. ... The estimates in this study indicate that land diversion programs aimed at lowering commodity surpluses have had the effect of shifting benefits to land in a fairly dramatic fashion. In 1970, for example, 95 per cent of land diversion benefits and 80 per cent of the remaining farm program benefits accrued to landowners.[35]

For 1970 the model estimated that the government farm programmes increased farm wages by no more than 2.3 per cent while increasing land rent by 22 per cent. Farm employment was estimated to have been increased by about 5.5 per cent and farm output by about 2 per cent and output price by a little less than 6 per cent. Their results confirm the conclusion that higher farm output prices and land diversion have little effect on the returns to farm labour while resulting in a substantial increase in the return to land.

Andrew Barkley has estimated supply functions for farm labour in the United States, based on data for 1940–85. The elasticity of supply is in terms of the relative earnings in agriculture to non-farm incomes. He obtained supply functions for all farm labour and for three categories of labour – hired, operator and family workers. The elasticity of supply for all farm labour was 2.65; for hired workers, 6.3; for farm operators, 3.3; and for family workers, 1.5.[36] These elasticity estimates are approximately the same as the one obtained by Professor Gisser and higher than the Tyrchniewicz–Schuh estimates of 1.545 for hired workers and 1.513 for family workers. They did not obtain a statistically significant estimate of the supply elasticity for farm operators. It

seems reasonable to conclude that Dr Barkley's supply elasticities are
higher than some of the estimates derived from earlier data.

Higher Land and Quota Values

Even though high farm output prices or subsidies do not increase the
returns to farm labour or mobile capital in the long run, they are
translated into higher land prices or into values of quotas where such
exist. The higher prices for land or the positive prices of quotas do
translate into higher farm incomes than would prevail in the absence of
protection. Is this result not a positive one? Cannot it be argued that
higher net farm incomes are better than lower net farm incomes, even
when the increased income goes to owners of farmland and quotas
rather than to farm labour and management? In my opinion, it is
difficult to argue that the answer to the two questions can be an
affirmative one. In the next few pages, an effort will be made to show
why policy-makers should not be satisfied with their efforts if the
addition to net farm incomes are due to higher land prices or quota
values. Higher farm incomes from these sources do not ensure that the
incomes of most farm families have been increased as a consequence of
farm price and subsidy policies.

Agricultural policy-makers seldom, if ever, express concern about
the effects of price and output subsidies on the price of land or the value
of quotas, as in the case of Canada poultry and dairy or tobacco and
peanuts in the United States or the implicit value of the dairy quotas in
the European Community. One explanation for this lack of concern
may be the assumption that most current farmers have higher net
incomes as a result of the higher asset values, whether that be because
of higher land prices or higher values for quotas that give a producer
the right to produce a particular product. The effect of such higher
values on net incomes of existing farmers depends on how the farmland
or the quotas are acquired by those farmers. If the land were owned at
the time the higher prices were instituted or were inherited, then the
income of that farm family is enhanced. Similarly, if the quota owner
was one of the original recipients of the quota, the family will have an
income that reflects the return on the quota value. Given the high
values of many of the quotas, the enhancement of the income could be
substantial.

Regrettably, there is little or no evidence that supports this favourable view of the situation as reflecting the situation for the majority of farm families. It is unfortunate that there is not much reliable information on the rapidity with which farmland and quotas change hands. But there is some evidence, especially from Canada. Data for 1976 to 1981 indicate that for commercial or full-time farms, the entry rate was nearly 14 per cent for the five years or about 3 per cent annually. Thus for a period of two decades, well over half of all farm operator families will be new entrants.[37] But even more striking was the fact that for three five-year periods, starting in 1966 and ending in 1981, approximately a third of all land owned by farm operators was transferred to another operator each five-year period. New farm entrants acquired 13 to 20 per cent of all land owned by former operators and continuing farm operators acquired another 12 to 14 per cent of such land.[38] This data set does not reveal if the land were transferred through inheritance or by sale and purchase. It is highly probable, however, that almost all of the acquisitions by existing and expanding farm operators was purchased.

The Canadian data set includes information on the entry rate for farms specializing in livestock and poultry products, including those that have quota schemes where the values of the quotas represent large values per farm (see Table 9.1). For the largest 25 per cent of Canada's farms that produce 74 per cent of gross sales, the average entry rate for 1976–81 was 13.7 per cent. This is for all farm products. The highest entry rate of 25.8 per cent was for poultry. For the large farms in the dairy sector, most of which fall under a quota scheme, the entry rate was 11.9 per cent for 1976–81.[39] In either case, but especially for poultry, over the period of five years a substantial percentage of all farmers must acquire the right to produce a product by acquiring the appropriate quota. Thus many farmers have paid for the income enhancement that the quota schemes make possible. In doing so, they have transferred a large share of all future benefits to prior owners.

In his discussion of the Ehrensaft et al. paper (cited in Note 37), Luther Tweeten said that it shows

that net changes in farm numbers which make the adjustment process appear to be [a] very deliberate and stable mask underlying dynamic and vigorous gross entry and exit pattern especially for smaller farms. Some years back a United States study by Dale Hathaway [at Michigan State University], using social-security data revealed that as many as nine persons entered farming for each ten who left. Other more reliable but still perhaps flawed data indicated a ratio of more nearly two persons entering for each three persons exiting. If people enter and exit mainly because of economic circumstances, the implication is that the farm population would increase sharply indeed under favorable economic circumstance, even if only by reducing exits without increasing entrants.[40]

Later in the same discussion, Professor Tweeten presents some results from an Oklahoma micro-economic data set. The data set showed 'that a relatively small proportion, one-fourth to two-fifths, of the land was obtained through concessional sales or gifts from friends or relatives. Operators of large farms depended less on friends or relatives for a concessional start in farming than did operators of smaller farms.'[41] These data are consistent with the inferences that could be drawn from the Canadian data, namely that many farmers, probably the majority of the larger commercial farmers in North America at any one time, paid the full market price for their land at the time of acquisition. Thus a large fraction of the anticipated future benefits from farm subsidy programmes have been paid for by existing farmers who have little to gain from the continuation of such programmes but a great deal to lose if the programmes are abandoned.

Data on farm transfers for the United States are consistent with the Oklahoma data cited by Professor Tweeten, namely that two-fifths or less of all farm land transfers are based on inheritance or gifts. For 1975–79 less than 30 per cent of all farm transfers were in the category 'Includes inheritances and gifts, administrators' and executors' sales, and miscellaneous or unclassified sales.'[42]

The Canadian and the United States data show that the annual decline of 2 to 3 per cent in the number of farms conceal a very active pattern of entry and exit among farm operators. In some cases new farm operators during a five-year period may account for as much as a quarter of all farm operators at the end of the five-year period. It is reasonable to conclude from the available data that at any given time a majority and perhaps as many as two-thirds of the owners of farmland and quotas in North America have been acquired by purchase. The owners of the land and quotas have, in effect, paid for the land and quotas and do not have higher net family incomes than they would have in the absence of the price and subsidy programmes. Had the land prices been lower and the quotas did not exist, the funds used to pay for the added price of land or the quotas could have been invested elsewhere, or quite likely, farm indebtedness would be lower because of the lower capital requirements required for an economic-sized farm.

Adjustments in the Labour Market

The conclusion stated earlier was that in the long run an increase in output price will have little effect on the value of labour or its wage rate. The primary effect on labour is on the quantity of labour engaged in agriculture. Note that this conclusion does not say that five or any other number of years after the output price has been increased and maintained that wage rates would not be any higher than at the beginning of the period. What is said is that at some not-too-distant date in the future, the wage rate in agriculture would be approximately the same, whether or not the output price had been increased. In an economy with rising real per capita incomes the return to farm labour would increase, as it has historically.

The validity of the conclusion rests on how the supply of labour to agriculture adjusts to changes in conditions in agriculture and in the rest of the economy. It seems reasonable to assume that farm people decide to remain employed in agriculture on the basis of the relationship between their anticipated earnings in agriculture and in alternative employment outside of agriculture. One of the complexities of this decision is that the returns from alternative employment constitutes a moving target, increasing over time in industrial economies, although not necessarily at a uniform rate from year to year. Thus if income opportunities in farming increase quite significantly due to a rise in output prices, this may influence many individuals not to transfer from farming to other occupations. But if the increase is for 'once and for all', as would be the case if the only change were an increase in output prices, it would soon be true that the increase in non-farm wage earnings would re-establish the same differential in earnings that had existed before the increase in farm earnings. How long this process would take would depend, of course, on the increase in farm earnings and the annual rate of increase in non-farm wages.

Figure 9.2 illustrates, hypothetically, the immediate effect of an increase in farm prices on returns to labour in agriculture and how the increase in returns relative to non-farm wages would gradually disappear. In one case (line 3) it is assumed that the farm-labour force remains stable until the previous differential in earnings has been re-established. In the other case (line 4) it is assumed that there is a

continuing decline in the farm-labour force, but at a slower rate than if
the output price had not been increased. But in either case, after a fairly
short time, the earlier differential in earnings is re-established and the
increase in output price has no long-term effect on returns to labour in
agriculture.

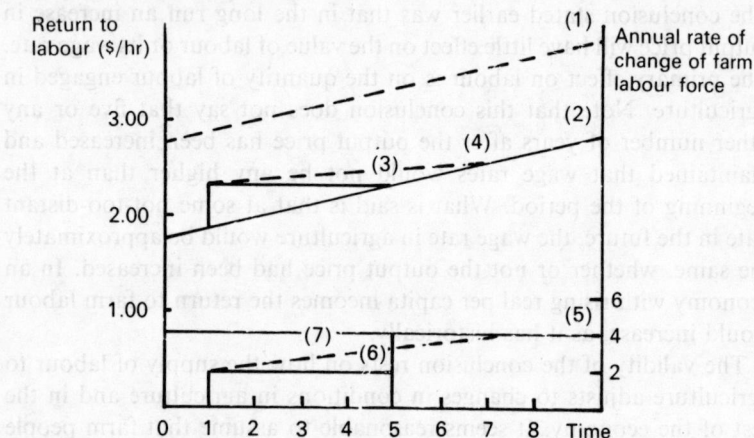

Figure 9.2

Explanation of lines by number:
(1) Non-farm wage rate
(2) Returns to farm labour if wheat price remains at $70 and farm labour force
    decreases by 4 per cent annually (line 5)
(3) Return to farm labour if wheat price is increased to $85 and farm labour
    force remains stable from year 1 to 5
(4) Alternative path of return to farm labour if wheat price is increased to $85
    but farm labour force declines by the pattern indicated in line 7
(5) Farm labour force declines at constant rate of 4 per cent annually
(6) Farm labour force declines at 2 per cent annually for year 1 through year 5
    and then returns to 4 per cent annual rate
(7) Farm labour force decline gradually increases from 2 per cent annually to 4
    per cent in year 7 when income differential returns to level in year '0'

In Figure 9.2 it is assumed that in the long run (year 5 and later) the
increase in output price has no effect on the return to farm labour. This
is not quite correct since farm employment would be slightly greater
with the higher farm prices. According to the earlier analysis based on
the work by Dr Tyrchniewicz and Professor Schuh, the increase in
employment might be 4.5 per cent which would result in increased
return to labour of less than 3 per cent. But this effect is so small that it
would be difficult to indicate on the graph.

If the higher farm output prices were effective in increasing the return to farm labour, it would be reasonable to expect that countries with the higher output prices would have had a slower rate of decline in farm employment over the past two decades. Thus the much higher product prices that have prevailed in Japan and the European Community than in North America and Australia should have been reflected in a slower rate of movement of labour out of agriculture. In other words, if higher product prices were translated into higher returns to farm labour relative to non-farm earnings in the same country, farm employment should be positively influenced compared with a country with relatively low product prices.

But actual experience since the Second World War, or more particularly since 1960, fails to support such a view. As has been argued above, the return to labour in agriculture is a function of the alternative earnings possibilities in the rest of the economy. The point that is now being made is even more damaging to the case for high price supports that impose large costs on consumers and taxpayers. Such costs are ineffective in influencing the level of farm employment or the share of farm employment in the national economy. One argument that is often made for high price supports is that it is socially desirable to maintain a large and viable rural population. Even if one accepts this objective, it does not follow that high output prices are the appropriate way of achieving the end. The end may be better achieved by a policy or policies resulting in wide dispersion of non-farm employment opportunities in rural areas and away from the large cities.

The evidence that high rates of protection or high price supports have not been effective in stemming the reduction in farm employment is provided in Chapter 11, specifically in Tables 11.3 and 11.4. Briefly, what is shown is that countries with the highest rates of protection have generally had higher rates of employment decline than countries with lower rates of protection. For example, the rates of decline in farm employment in the European Community and Japan, which have had relatively high rates of protection, have been higher than in North America and Australia, with low rates of protection.

Obviously it could be argued that if farm prices had been lower in the European Community and Japan that the outflow of labour would have been more rapid than it was during the 1960s and 1970s. This might have been true, but it is not obvious that slowing down the outflow of labour during those two decades would have been a desirable outcome for most of the people who remained in agriculture. It would have meant that the adjustment process was delayed and in the case of the European Community would have been delayed from a period when jobs were plentiful, prior to the mid-1970s, to a time when there were high rates of unemployment, the 1980s. Yet the annual decline in farm employment has continued at a rate of more than 5 per cent in the Community in spite of unemployment levels of 8 to 11 per cent in the 1980s.

A reasonable interpretation of the major point of this section is that the primary determinant of the incomes of farm people is the per capita income generated by the economy in which the farm people live. The per capita income level, combined with macro-economic policies that maintain high levels of employment and a reasonably stable price level, are of far greater significance in determining the return to the human resources possessed by farm people than the price and income policies that impose such enormous costs on taxpayers and consumers.

The basis for the conclusion that the primary determinant of the returns to farm labour and of farm family incomes is the income level of the country in which they live, is that the returns to farm resources is determined by the alternative employments that are available. As shown earlier, agriculture is a sector that declines as a source of employment for labour and, consequently, each year many farm people must seek employment in the non-farm sector. The same is true for capital; agriculture's share of national investment also declines. It is only the return to land or to quotas artificially created that can be influenced by price and subsidy policies.

While more of a debater's point than an analytically sound argument, it may be pointed out that if the level of farm prices was a primary determinant of the incomes of farm families, farm incomes in Portugal in the late 1980s would be higher than in France. As Portugal entered the European Community, she reduced many of her price support levels; her farm prices were generally higher than in France. Thus, if output prices were a primary factor determining the returns to farm labour and capital, then Portuguese farm families should have incomes at least as high as the French. But such is not the case and could not be, since the per capita GNP in France is approximately five times that of Portugal.

A Constant Degree of Protection is Not Enough

Efforts to increase net farm incomes by higher prices have one important disability that is seldom recognized by either economists or farm policy-makers, although farmers appear to be fully aware of it. I refer to the fact that a price increase has a once-and-for-all effect on the returns to farm resources and thus if price increases are to be the major instrument for increasing farm incomes, price increases must occur continuously. The increases are required not just to keep up with changes in the general rate of inflation, but the increases must be real – farm prices must rise relative to all other prices. The farmers who demonstrated in the streets of Brussels in the spring of 1971 were good economists. Given the emphasis in the European Community's farm policy on output prices as the major policy instrument, the farmers were quite right in saying that, unless prices were increased further, the policy would fail to contribute significantly either to the absolute or the relative levels of their income. The farmers were in effect saying to the Community's policy-makers: 'You haven't done anything for us recently.' They were also saying that they had been misled in their expectations. But they were asking for something that the Community's policy-makers could not deliver, namely a more or less constant rate of increase in real output prices.[43]

Alone a constant or fixed rate of protection, no matter how high it is, will not ensure that farm incomes will increase at the same rate as incomes in the rest of the economy or would for long remain at or above non-farm incomes. Even if the differential between farm and non-farm incomes were eliminated by a high enough rate of protection, there can be no assurance that whatever differential there may have been would not re-emerge as non-farm incomes increased. In other words, if farm prices were increased enough to bring farm and non-farm labour earnings for comparable workers into equality in the first year following the increase in prices, further out-migration of labour would be required to maintain that equality. And if the out-migration of labour were reduced by the higher farm earnings, the earlier differential in earnings would gradually return. In the long run, it is the supply of farm labour, and not the demand for the labour, that has the major effect on the return to farm labour. There is no escape from this simple but very important economic relationship.

The income of the European Community's farmer has increased under essentially stable or slowly declining farm prices in recent years and will continue to increase under such circumstances in the future. But the increases that have been achieved are not due to the earlier increases in farm output prices; they have been due to the transfer of workers out of agriculture and, perhaps, to increased production efficiency. In saying that the effect of a price increase on farm incomes is a once-and-for-all effect, it is not meant that all of the income effects occur immediately. But if some time is allowed for farmers to adjust to the higher prices by changing their level of capital investment to the amount that is just marginally profitable at the new level of prices and increase their use of purchased inputs and hired labour to the new level of prices, no further increases in income can be properly attributed to the new level of prices even if such prices are stable in real rather than absolute terms. Further increases in income can occur only as input prices are reduced through lower costs elsewhere in the economy (or government subsidy), through increased efficiency in production,[44] through an increase in skill and capacity of farm people or through a recombination of farm-owned resources in response to higher alternative earnings elsewhere in the economy. The recombination of resources will occur primarily through a reduction in the employment of labour due to out-migration from agriculture due to rising real returns to labour throughout the economy.

Except as the short-run increase in incomes that results from the price increase results in increased efficiency in production or induces greater investments in farm human capital, none of the sources of increased return to farm resources can be attributed to the higher prices. But the increase in efficiency, which would consist largely of more rapid adoption of new and lower priced inputs, would not be an unmixed blessing. In fact, the long-run effects of the innovations that would be induced by the higher returns to farm labour and land would be the introduction of further substitutes for these two factors. Both labour and land-saving inputs would be demanded in greater quantities and research efforts would be undertaken to discover new inputs that would substitute for both labour and land. The efforts of farmers to produce at lower cost would result in a reduction in the demand for labour and land and thus a fall in the return to labour and to land compared with the respective returns if production innovations were not made.

As in the case of higher output prices, a given reduction, either in percentage or absolute terms, in the farm labour force will increase the return to labour once and for all. A further increase in labour return requires an additional reduction in the labour force, not an increase in the rate of reduction, but a further reduction. Thus if a 5 per cent reduction in the labour force increases the return to a unit of labour remaining in agriculture by 5 per cent, this increase would persist if the farm labour force remained constant, other things equal.[45] A further increase in the return to labour would require a further reduction in the size of the labour force just as a further increase in prices would be required to achieve a further increase in the return to labour. Analytically, it can therefore be said that an increase in output prices or a reduction in farm employment have similar effects on the return to labour; each change must be repeated if further increases in the return to labour are to be achieved.

In practical terms, however, the significance of the two instruments is quite different. It is nearly impossible to imagine that real farm prices can be increased at 5 per cent annually for any extended period of time; to do so would require doubling in 14 years.[46] But it is clearly possible that farm employment can be reduced by 50 per cent in fourteen years because this has been approximately what has occurred in Western Europe and North America in that time period. And if farm output prices remain unchanged while the labour force in agriculture is being reduced by 50 per cent, the effect on the return to labour will be approximately the same as if real farm output prices had doubled.

Agriculture in the United States during the 1960s provides an ideal test of the above conclusions. Farm product prices increased by 15 per cent during the decade; the index of prices paid for production items increased by 25 per cent. Real farm prices as measured by the ratio of the index of prices received to the index of prices paid for production items, fell by 8 per cent, although if one adds the government payments to farmers, the adjusted prices received index decreased about 4 per cent. In either case, real farm prices fell somewhat.

According to estimates by the United States Department of Agriculture of changes in the ratio of total output to total input, productivity – as conventionally measured – increased by 15 per cent during the decade. If changes in farm wage rates are used as a proxy for changes in the return to farm labour we may estimate that in absolute dollar terms returns per farm worker in the United States increased by 73 per cent between 1960 and 1970.[47] This compares with an increase in farm product prices of only 15 per cent and a productivity improvement of 15 per cent. Thus only a small part of the increase in returns to farm labour can be attributed to higher output prices.

Most of the increase of 32 per cent in real returns to farm labour was due to changes in the ratio of all other inputs to labour or, put differently, to the increase in the marginal physical product of labour. The increase in the average physical product of labour is due to the increase in farm output of 10 per cent during the decade and a reduction of the farm labour force of 30 to 35 per cent. If it is assumed that the production function has an elasticity of substitution between labour and all other inputs of unity and the production function coefficients did not change over the decade, the increase in the marginal physical product of farm labour between 1960 and 1970 was 75 per cent.[48]

The increase in the estimated marginal physical product of farm labour of 75 per cent, if adjusted for the change in farm prices and the increase in productivity, is a larger increase than implied by the 73 per cent increase in money returns to labour. Given the substantial increase in the importance of purchased inputs, the labour coefficient in the production function probably declined somewhat. But taking all changes together, the increase in returns to labour was close to what our simple model predicted.

It is clear that in the United States during the 1960s adjustments through the labour market were primarily responsible for the substantial increase in money and real returns to farm labour. Neither significant changes in output prices nor total productivity change could have had a significant role. The implication of this conclusion is that the large income transfer from consumers and taxpayers to farmers did very little to improve the earnings of farm workers. If we assume that farm prices, including all direct payments as an addition to prices, have been increased by about 15 per cent by government programmes,[49] the transfers could have resulted in a once-and-for-all increase in the return to farm labour of 15 per cent, at most, and probably nearer to 10 per cent. Accordingly, a continuing annual series of transfers that persisted for well over two decades is required to achieve a one-time increase in returns to farm labour of 10 to 15 per cent, an increase that has been achieved not once, but repeatedly, by labour transfers in a period of three to five years.

There is no doubt that returns to land are higher because of the transfers as well as the total capital investment in reproducible assets. In fact, rough calculations of the increase in the national income produced by agriculture in 1970 compared with 1960 indicate that at least two-thirds of the increase of $6600 million could be attributed to increased return to land and capital.

An analysis of the consequences of large income transfers from consumers and taxpayers to farmers in other industrial countries would duplicate the analysis for the United States. Farm incomes have been increasing in real terms in recent years, but the primary source of the increase has been labour migration and transfer to non-farm jobs while retaining a farm residence and not the enormous income transfers. In fact, the governments of the industrial countries, with only two important exceptions, were not able significantly to increase real farm prices during the 1960s. The two exceptions were Japan and France and only in the former case was a significant increase (30 per cent) realized; largely at the expense of their partners in the European Community, France achieved an increase of about 10 per cent. In both instances, real farm prices decreased after 1970 (see Table 6.9 above). The governmental efforts made in most industrial countries were not successful in increasing real farm prices in the 1960s, with the noted exceptions, and have not been able to resist the long-term declining trend in real farm prices since 1970. During the 1970s the three new entrants to the Community – Denmark, Ireland and the United Kingdom – had higher real farm prices than in 1970, but by the end of the decade prices had returned to or below the 1970 levels.[50] Consequently very large transfers have been and will be required just to maintain a level of real farm prices that decline by 1 or 2 per cent annually. By the end of the 1980s, the labour markets have rather fully adjusted and returns to farm labour are approximately what they would have been in the absence of the farm programmes. The net income transfers that remain go to the owners of land, and to pay for the larger volume of investment in buildings, machinery and equipment, and for larger quantities of current inputs such as fertilizer, insecticides and herbicides.

Concluding Comments

A major degree of agricultural protection contributes little or nothing to the long-run solution of the farm income problem; what is required if protection is to be the primary instrument for increasing or even maintaining the relative income position of farm families is a continuously increasing degree of protection. In other words, high prices alone are meaningless as a long-run farm-income measure; continuously increasing real farm prices must be achieved if real farm incomes are to keep pace with real incomes in the rest of the economy.

The belief that high farm prices are enough has been widely held. While there is increasing acceptance of the view that high farm prices do not represent the solution to the farm-income problem, there is great reluctance in most countries to accept a gradual reduction of the high degrees of protection afforded agriculture in the industrial countries in the early 1990s. Yet the reasons that have prevented high farm prices from providing a solution to the farm-income problem also support the view that a phased and gradual reduction in the level of farm prices in the industrial countries to something approximating world market levels would have little effect on the long-run real and relative income position of farm labour, including the labour of farm operators. This conclusion assumes, I should add, that the industrial countries maintain a high level of employment.

While one can be relatively sanguine about the effects of lowering prices to more reasonable levels upon the return to farm labour, other types of income would be significantly reduced. Farm land values, increasing at a rapid pace in the industrial countries from 1950 to 1980, would be drastically affected. And many of the firms that provide products and services to farmers would be faced with a gradually declining demand rather than an increasing one dependent, at least in part, on the high farm prices that have been maintained.

The migration of labour from agriculture to the rest of the economy is the only long-run solution to the farm-income problem. Migration is also, fortunately, a process that not only improves the relative income position of those who remain in agriculture; it also contributes to the economic welfare of the society as a whole. This important point cannot be left put so badly. With the frustration that besets policy-makers due to the rising costs of farm policies and the apparent failure of high farm prices to provide the answer to the farm income problem, there is also a tendency to reject migration as an adequate solution to the farm problem. Why is it that relative farm incomes have not improved more in recent years given that there has been, in the developed world generally, a high rate of migration out of agriculture? If migration is the answer to the farm-income problem, why isn't the farm-income problem already solved? We shall turn to these and similar questions in Chapter 10.

10 What Difference Does Trade Make?

Trade is important, although those of us who have special interests, as scholars or direct participants in exporting and importing, should not be guilty of over-estimating its importance. Achieving free trade in all products, agricultural as well as non-agricultural, will not bring the millennium; poor countries will not immediately, or even in the longer run, become rich as a result; nor will high-income countries realize major gains in national income that can be used to meet the costs of curing their social ills, such as poverty, urban congestion, crime or pollution. Achieving free trade is only one of a number of policy measures that governments can undertake to improve the efficiency with which their economies function and thus increase the national welfare. In saying this I do not imply that the only component of national welfare is more output – more income. But most of the social and economic problems that beset all countries, rich and poor, can be met more easily from a larger rather than a smaller national output.

While reducing the barriers to international trade is only one of several measures that all countries can consider, this in no way depreciates the importance of moving towards free trade nor the favourable consequences of doing so. It is in fact desirable that achieving free trade would have fairly modest effects on the world's real output of goods and services – its real income – since the rather limited effects of moving to free trade imply that the largely misguided trade restriction policies of most governments have done significant but limited damage to their economies. Damage has been done, but the extent of the damage has been minimized by the very substantial flexibility that seems to exist in all economies. Economies do seem to have the capacity largely to offset a lot of mistakes due either to ignorance or avarice.

While it is true that most of the serious problems of the world would still be with us if there were free trade, or something close to it, it is evident that if benefit-cost analysis were applied to the acts of politicians and their advisers there would be few competitors for those who achieved free trade for the prize that went to the highest benefit-cost ratio. I refer not only to benefits that can be measured in gains in real

217

output. In fact, if we had the proper instruments for measurement, the gains in the value of real output might be only a small part of the total gains from free trade. Nor do I refer to the benefit that may come from the increased discipline of the market that results in increased productive efficiency.

Instead I have in mind primarily two other kinds of important benefits. One is that protection involves substantial income transfers that are often quite inconsistent with any notions of equity to which many societies claim to adhere. The other is that protection has all too often provided an excuse for avoiding or ignoring important social and economic issues. This is especially true of agriculture. Governments have found barriers to trade, either direct ones or indirect ones involving the use of subsidies, to be politically the most acceptable instruments even though the difficulties that are to be overcome do not have their origins in the low farm prices that are to be increased by trade restrictions. Low farm incomes, either in a relative or absolute sense, are the result of many difficulties facing farm people and of these difficulties low farm prices are among the least important.

Costs of Protection – to the Protected

In this section I shall be concerned solely with the costs of protection to the nation imposing the restrictions on trade; the next section will consider the costs borne by the external victims, namely those foreigners who lose the opportunity to sell and to buy. The primary emphasis is on protection that results in an interference with trade. The interference, however, includes measures other than tariffs, quotas or export subsidies. A reduction in imports is no less real or significant if it occurs as a result of expansion of production engendered by deficiency payments rather than from a tariff or quota. Similarly exports can be encouraged by input subsidies or deficiency payments related to output as well as by the direct use of export subsidies. Thus protection is here defined to include techniques that may be used to increase domestic production above the level that would prevail if farmers received the world market prices and nothing more.

The costs of protection may fall into three main categories: (i) the loss in consumer welfare due to the consumption alternatives that consumers forgo because the prices they face do not represent the real cost alternatives; (ii) the excess production cost of domestic production compared with the cost of acquiring the same marginal output through trade; and (iii) the transfer of income from consumers and taxpayers to farmers and, perhaps, to resource owners that supply inputs to farmers. In the literature of international trade, as well as in the study of the economics of welfare, only the first two of these costs are considered to be 'real' costs. And this is a correct approach if the only or primary concern is that of the value of goods and services that a nation loses through the imposition of trade-interfering devices; these are the losses directly associated with a country not taking advantage of the opportunity of obtaining all of its goods and services at the lowest possible cost. In such analyses, and there are so many that there is no point in citing only a few, the transfers of income from consumers and taxpayers are not considered to be a 'real' cost of protection.

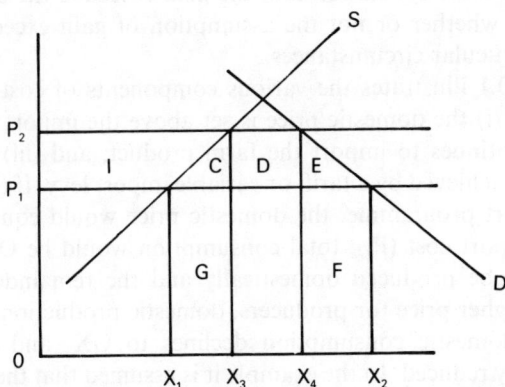

Figure 10.1

In a static analysis, assuming price and wage flexibility in the domestic economy, there are additional costs that the conclusion ignores. There are effects on resource-use due to the collection of taxes related either to income or expenditure; such taxes influence work effort and cause some resources to be reallocated. The disincentive effects of high food prices are similar. As will be noted later, in a world in which wages and prices are relatively inflexible and resources are less than fully mobile, agricultural protection may have significant adverse effects on national income and unemployment.

In addition, I wish to argue that it is both reasonable and necessary to view the income transfers as a cost of protection, although the perspective from which one starts is a different one than that underlying usual and appropriate analyses of the welfare costs of protection.

The perspective that permits, perhaps one should say requires, consideration of income transfers as a cost of protection is that taxpayers and consumers are required to make the income transfers and the income transfers are made for some purpose. Therefore the relationship between the costs of the transfer, on the one hand, and the benefits derived from the purpose or end of the transfer, on the other, is a legitimate focus of inquiry. In arguing that the transfer should be considered as a cost there is not a presumption that there is no gain associated with the cost; the gain can presumably be greater than, equal to or less than the cost involved. In this sense, there would be a net cost if the value of the gains from the transfer, however measured, were less than the cost. Presumably the decision to require the income transfer was based on the conclusion that the gain exceeded the cost. What is involved is whether or not the assumption of gain exceeding cost is valid in particular circumstances.

Figure 10.1 illustrates the various components of cost under these conditions: (i) the domestic price is set above the import cost; (ii) the country continues to import the farm product; and (iii) the support price (P_2) is achieved by a tariff or variable import levy. If there were no price-support programme, the domestic price would equal the world price or import cost (P_1); total consumption would be OX_2 of which OX_1 would be produced domestically and the remainder imported. With the higher price for producers, domestic production increases to OX_3 and domestic consumption declines to OX_4 and imports are substantially reduced. In the example it is assumed that the world price is not affected by the reduction of imports.

The various cost elements referred to above can now be estimated from the labelled areas in Figure 10.1. If the price elasticity of demand for the farm product is less than one, consumers will pay more money for less of the product. The increase in consumer money costs would be $(I + C + D) - F$ of which D represents the funds collected by the treasury from the import tariff or variable levy. Thus the combined money cost of consumers and taxpayers would be $(I + C) - (F)$. If one looks at the costs more analytically, he sees that (I) represents the increase in net income to producers – the presumed increase in rent or the income that farm resource owners would receive in excess of what they would receive if the product price were P_1. The triangle (C) is the additional resource cost due to the increase in output and represents the 'wastage' of resources due to domestic production rather than importation. In other words, C represents the increase in resource costs due to producing X_1X_3 domestically instead of importing the same quantity.

The triangle (E) is the loss in consumers' surplus – the loss incurred by consumers because the opportunity to purchase more of this product is foreclosed by the higher price. Therefore the real costs are C + E while two transfers are involved. One is the transfer from consumers to farmers (I) and from consumers to taxpayers (D) since assuming a constant total governmental expenditure, other taxes may be reduced by (D). Consumers may also consider (C) as a part of the transfer, although it would not be so viewed by the farmer. If the general tax structure is progressive and if the farm commodity is one with low income and price elasticities, the income transfer from consumers to taxpayers is likely to involve a net transfer of income from low-income to high-income citizens.

Figure 10.1 can be used to illustrate the distribution of costs if the difference between P_1 and P_2 is achieved by a deficiency payment rather than by control of imports. The average return to farmers would be the same, namely P_2. The increase in total return to farmers would also be the same as would the components – an income transfer of (I) and an increase in real costs of (C); these two areas would represent the cost of the deficiency payment to taxpayers. The consumers would not suffer either a money cost or a loss of consumer welfare since their consumption would be the quantity OX_2 at the lowest available price, P_1. The resource cost (C) is a real cost of the programme, as conventionally measured, to the economy if it is assumed that the reduction of imports due to the increase in domestic production (X_1X_3) has no adverse effects on the export sector of the economy.

A few words should be said about the two rectangles in Figure 10.1, namely G and F. The first, G, is a component of the increase in the gross income of farmers. It represents a part – the major part – of the cost of increasing output by X_1X_3 and is a measure of what those costs would be if the additional output could have been produced at a marginal cost of P_1, the import price of the product. The fact that G is one of the elements in the increase of the gross income of farmers may be one of the reasons that the effectiveness of increased prices in improving the income position of farmers is generally over-estimated by policy-makers. The increase in returns due to higher farm prices, over what such resources would earn if employed elsewhere, that is due to the expansion of output by X_1X_3 is very small – approximately equal to the value of the triangle C.

The other rectangle, F, represents the value of the reduction in consumption of food when the food is valued at import prices. What is the appropriate economic interpretation of this rectangle? From the standpoint of the economy as a whole it can be said the area represents neither a gain nor a loss since the expenditure represented by the area can be made for other goods and services without a loss of consumers' surplus. The individuals receiving the area (I) would spend their additional income for other goods and services and the loss in consumers' surplus for the economy is already reflected in E. But if one takes the viewpoint of the consumer *qua* consumer, or the viewpoint of all consumers except those who are the recipients of I, F represents a loss. Such consumers are paying more and getting less food and less of all consumer goods and services. The last sentence is correct only if the price elasticity is greater than unity; F represents a loss to consumers *qua* consumers, although part of F could be offset by the reduction in total expenditure for food.[1]

Taken together, F and G represent the reduction in the value of imports of the commodity if it is assumed that the elasticity of supply of imports to the country is perfectly elastic.

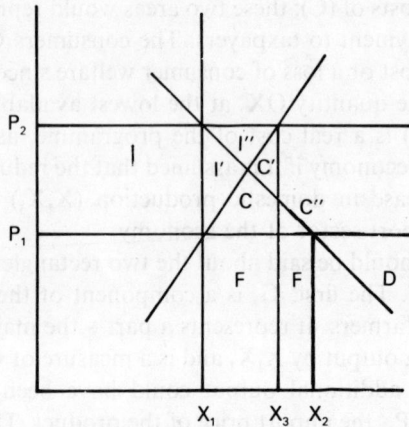

Figure 10.2

Figure 10.2 is similar to Figure 10.1 except that it depicts a situation in which the country would import if the farm price were the world price (P_1) and would export, with a subsidy, if the domestic price were P_2. It is assumed that the higher farm price would be achieved by import controls and export subsidies. In the example depicted in Figure 10.2, there would be no income realized from a variable levy or other form of import duty – any imports that came in and on which a levy were collected would be offset by an equal export subsidy on an equal volume. In the figure, it is assumed that the price elasticity of demand has an absolute value greater than the price elasticity of supply. Thus increasing the domestic price from P_1 to P_2 reduces consumption by a greater amount than production is increased. The income transfer to farmers is $(I + I' + I'')$. The real resource cost due to expanding high-cost domestic production is $(C + C')$. The increase in consumer expenditures is $(I - F)$, but since the volume consumed has been reduced, the loss in consumers' surplus is $(I' + C + C'')$. The cost of the export subsidy is equal to the difference between the domestic price (P_2) and the world price (P_1) multiplied by the amount exported (X_1X_3). As far as this economy is concerned, the part of increased resource costs and the part of consumers' surplus that overlap $(C + C')$ should be counted twice. The loss to consumers would exist regardless of where the domestic supply S_d intersects the world price line.

In Figure 10.1 the rectangles $(F + G)$ also represent the savings in foreign exchange achieved through reducing imports. If the country has an appropriate exchange rate, it also represents the loss of foreign exchange earnings suffered by the export sector of the economy. When a country has an over-valued currency, however, the rectangles $(F + G)$ are often assigned a substantial positive value, in fact a value approximately equal to the number of currency units involved.

The examples depicted in the two figures indicate that the costs represented by the resources wasted and the loss on consumers' surplus are substantially smaller than the income transfer imposed on consumers. This is not just an artifact of the particular examples, but appears to be generally true. The reason for the much greater magnitude of the income transfer is that the income transfer is the product of the tariff and the quantity consumed after the tariff is imposed, while the excess resource cost $(C + C')$ is a part of the transfer as seen by the consumer and the loss in consumers' surplus is (approximately) one-half of $(P_2 - P_1)$ multiplied by the decline in quantity consumed due to the increase in price.

The above approach to the comparison of the income transfer imposed on consumers and the real income forgone $(C + D)$ may be criticized because of the apparent double counting of (C). (C) is a real cost since it measures the excess production cost but in the framework accepted here this is one of the outcomes paid for by the excess money cost imposed upon the consumer. In one sense it is irrelevant to the consumer whether the increased money handed over to the producer goes for additional real costs or for additional rents. In fact, if the consumer is convinced that farmers 'deserve' higher incomes, the consumer would be angered by the fact that part of his gratuity is wasted on additional costs that benefit no one. If the consumer wants his income transfer to result in a benefit to a fellow citizen he would prefer a policy measure that held output at OX_1 and transferred the amount $(I + C)$ to the farmers. This would make farmers better off and consumers no worse off.

Measuring the Welfare Costs

How large are the losses due to protectionism? Empirical estimates have been made of loss in real income due to trade restrictions based on partial equilibrium analyses. Arnold C. Harberger, of the University of Chicago, estimated that during the 1950s the various trade restrictions in Chile restricted trade equivalent to that of a tariff of 50 per cent. Assuming that trade would double if trade restrictions were removed, he estimated that the welfare gain would be 'no more than $2\frac{1}{2}$ per cent of the national income'. Harry G. Johnson, when at the University of Manchester, made an estimate of the gains to Britain if there were free trade with the rest of Western Europe, based on projections of the value of trade in 1970. His conclusion was that the gain to Britain would be a maximum of 1 per cent of the national income of the United Kingdom.[2] A study of the short-run effects of lowering import duties on industrial products in West Germany in the 1950s concluded that when duties were lowered by half or by about 10 percentage points the gain amounted to 0.18 per cent of the national income.[3] The period of adjustment was short (about two years) and the demand curve for all industrial products was assumed to have zero price elasticity, although since the increase in imports was based on actual change in imports after the tariff reductions the assumption with respect to demand was quite unimportant in affecting the estimated gain.

An excellent study directly related to agricultural trade was prepared by T. E. Josling, entitled *Agriculture and Britain's Trade Policy Dilemma*, for the Trade Policy Research Centre in London in 1970. The study was designed to estimate the effects of British entry into the European Community. He made four estimates of the various costs of British agricultural and trade policy: (i) The out-going system of deficiency payments; (ii) the substitution of variable import levies for the deficiency payments; (iii) the variable import-levy system with Britain inside the Community, but with British prices; and (iv) the variable import-levy system with Britain inside the Community, but with Common Market prices for farm products.[4] His estimates of various costs and transfers are given in Table 10.1. The time period for the estimates is not given, but is for the late 1960s. As background, consumption of farm food products was £3050 million of which £1500 million was imported. The existing deficiency-payment scheme increased average returns to producers by 10 per cent. Joining the Community would increase market prices by 25 per cent and produce average returns over the current level, including the deficiency payments, by about 15 per cent. Under the deficiency-payment system, payments were £150 million and domestic gross farm receipts were £1700 million. The higher producer returns under the deficiency-payment system were estimated at £212 million of which £65 million went for extra resources leaving a net additional return of £147 million (see first column of Table 10.1).

Further assumptions based on available estimates of demand and supply elasticities were made. With respect to supply, it was estimated that with a supply elasticity of 0.4 for domestic farm production, the deficiency-payment system increased farm output by 4 per cent; the European Community prices would increase output by an additional 6 per cent, or 10 per cent above domestic supply at world prices. The United Kingdom price elasticity of demand was estimated to be -0.16 so that current United Kingdom producer prices achieved by a variable import-levy system that would increase consumer prices by 10 per cent would reduce consumption by 1.6 per cent; raising prices to the Community level would reduce consumption by an additional 2.4 per cent.

We may now turn to Professor Josling's estimates as given in Table 10.1. The last row of the table gives the estimates of the resource cost for the first and second policies. The loss in real income from the deficiency-payment system was estimated at £3 million, which was 0.1 per cent of the total British consumption of food or 0.2 per cent of domestic gross farm receipts or only about 2 per cent of the net additional returns to British farmers (row 3, column 1). Thus the resource cost of the transfer involved in the deficiency-payment system was very small. A change to the variable import-levy system would shift the costs from the treasury to consumers; in fact, the treasury would come out ahead, which may explain why tariffs and variable import levies are more popular with governments than deficiency payments. The additional real cost of the variable import-levy system compared with the deficiency-payment system is very small – only £2 million or a

Table 10.1   Economic costs and returns of various British agricultural policies relative to free market conditions

	Deficiency-payment system with UK outside EC £m	Variable import-levy system with UK outside EC £m	Variable import-levy system with UK inside EC but UK prices £m	Variable import-levy system with UK inside EC and EC (high) prices (£m)
Extra producer gross returns	212	212	212	560
Cost of extra resources	65	65	65	174
Net additional return to British producer	147	147	147	386
Net consumer food expenditure	–	246	246	605
Loss in consumer valuation	–	51	51	137
Loss in consumer welfare	–	297	297	742
Internal transfer from consumers	–	295	150	405
Net loss in consumer welfare	–	2	147	337
Gross internal transfer to producer	150	150	150	405
Net producer returns	147	147	147	386
Cost of transfer	3	3	3	19
Net cost of policy to Britain	3	5	150	356
Net real cost of policy	3	5	5	34

Source: T. E. Josling, *Agriculture and Britain's Trade Policy Dilemma,* Thames Essay No. 2 (London: Trade Policy Research Centre, 1970), p. 24.

total of £5 million. The loss in real income of the variable import-levy system would be less than 4 per cent of the net additional returns received by the producer.

The last rows of Table 10.1 reflect the resource cost of these two policies in the same sense as it does for the first two policies. If the United Kingdom did not have to transfer the variable import-levy receipts to the European Community the loss in real income to the United Kingdom under the variable import-levy system with British prices and membership in the Community would remain at £5 million.

What is involved is a *transfer* of £145 million from the United Kingdom to the other members of the Community. As Professor Josling indicated, this is a cost of Common Market membership for the United Kingdom, but it is cost in the same sense as a transfer from the British Treasury or consumers to British farmers is a cost. One can readily understand, however, why a British citizen would view the two costs rather differently.

The last row of Table 10.1, which I derived from Professor Josling's estimates, shows the sum of the excess resource cost and the loss of consumers' surplus. These costs are what are normally referred to as the real costs of protection. The next to the last row in the table indicated the net cost of the various programmes to Britain and this row includes both the real costs and, when applicable, transfers that would be made to the European Community. If the British were members of a Community that adopted the then-prevailing British prices, the transfer would be £145 million; if the United Kingdom were a member of the Common Market with the late 1960s levels of Community farm prices the transfer to the other members of this Community would be £322 million.

The resource or real costs (excluding the transfer to the European Community) due to Common Market membership with Common Market prices was much higher absolutely than for either the deficiency-payment scheme or a variable import-levy scheme with British prices. In fact, the real cost becomes rather large at £34 million. The increase in prices from 10 per cent in excess of world prices to 25 per cent in excess is responsible for the increase in real cost from £5 million to £34 million. With Common Market prices the British producer would realize an increase in income of £386 million and the resource cost would be about 9 per cent of the income transfer. In one sense it might appear that an efficient means had been found for increasing farm income, since the apparent increase in income is eleven times the real cost. The consumer of food, however, might take a different viewpoint since his cost was £742 million. Even if you subtract the transfer to the Community, the cost to the consumer was £420 million, which is greater than the increase in return to farm resources. And so it must be greater by the amount of the real resource costs. As is sometimes said, there is no such thing as a free lunch.

Given the general structure of Professor Josling's example, the resulting relationship between the magnitude of the transfer and the real costs would be moderately affected by significant variations in the elasticities of supply and demand. If the elasticity of domestically produced food were unity instead of 0.4, the excess resource cost with British price increases from £3 million to £7.5 million and under Common Market prices from £19 million to £47.5 million. The largest of the estimates of excess resource costs, however, is still less than 12 per cent of the gross transfer to producers and only about 7 per cent of the total cost to consumers. The upper limit of the price elasticity of demand for food products in the United Kingdom or other high-income countries can hardly be more than double the elasticity used (-0.16) or about -0.3. If the larger price elasticity of demand were used, this would double the value of the loss in consumers' surplus and it would still be relatively small for either British or Common Market prices.[5]

The analysis presented up to this point is both static and partial. This was true of the previous section of this chapter and the estimates of welfare costs summarized above. The effects of agricultural protection were solely in terms of outcomes within the agricultural and food sector and the consequences on other parts of the economy have been alluded to but not measured. In recent years there have been several general equilibrium studies of the effect of agricultural protection that indicate that the losses in welfare as measured by gross national product and employment are far higher than implied by static and partial analyses.

Several general equilibrium studies were organized by the Centre for International Economics (CIE) in Canberra, Australia, under the general direction of Andy Stoeckel, its director. Studies of the effects of agricultural protection in terms of losses of national income and unemployment were completed for the European Community, Japan, the United States and developing countries as a whole, as well as Germany and Korea.

What partial and individual sector analysis ignores is that protecting one sector taxes another. In an important paper for the Trade Policy Research Centre in London, Kenneth W. Clements and Larry Sjaastad have shown how import barriers act as an export tax.[6] Consequently, to understand the full effects of import protection one must consider the effects of such protection on the export sector and, in most cases, on the non-traded sector, if that sector depends on imported products or competes with the import-protected sector for resources. It has long been recognized that when imports are restricted, exports are also reduced. What is new is that by the use of general equilibrium analysis it is possible to estimate the probable effects of the import restrictions on the entire economy rather than only the sector that is directly affected.

What do the CIE general equilibrium studies show? They show real welfare costs many times as large as indicated by the partial equilibrium studies. Juergen B. Donges and his associates at the Institut für Weltwirtschaft in Kiel estimated that if there were worldwide liberalization of agriculture, the gains to West Germany would be very large, given that agriculture produces just 2 per cent of the country's gross domestic product. Agricultural liberalization was projected to increase gross national product by 3.3 per cent and real income by 2.5 per cent. The loss of employment due to agricultural protection was estimated at 4 per cent or, as of 1987, 850 000 jobs. The reduction in the economy-wide unemployment rate could be from 9 per cent to 5 per cent as of 1987.[7]

The CIE study for the European Community as a whole projected that agricultural protection had caused a loss of 2 to 4 million jobs and liberalization would increase manufacturing output by more than 1 per cent.[8]

It is not surprising, given the high levels of protection of agriculture in Japan and Korea, that the CIE studies showed the costs of agricultural protection there to be very large. For Japan agricultural liberalization would increase the average real wage per worker by 2.5 per cent. The costs of agricultural protection in Korea are greater in a relative sense since agriculture accounts for a much larger share of gross domestic product than in Japan and the level of agricultural protection in Korea is of the same order as in Japan. Due primarily to the fall in domestic price, real wages could increase by about 6 per cent. In both countries, land prices would decline sharply, nearly 70 per cent in Japan and almost 45 per cent in Korea.[9]

There were three studies in the CIE programme of the gains that would be realized from agricultural liberalization in the United States. The studies did not use the same assumptions and thus their results cannot be directly compared. The loss in gross domestic product due to protection of agriculture is estimated in two of the studies at somewhat more than 0.3 per cent of GDP. This may not seem large until it is remembered that agriculture produces only 2 per cent of GDP. The studies indicated that liberalization of agriculture would have significant effects on the trade and budget deficits, reducing each by about a quarter. In the United States agricultural protection has acted, at least prior to 1986, to reduce both agricultural and non-agricultural exports. Thus liberalization would act to increase both.[10]

A model in the CIE programme that estimated the effects of agricultural liberalization by the industrial countries on the developing countries showed much larger gains than any of the partial equilibrium estimates.[11] Assuming that industrial country liberalization increased international market prices by 10 per cent, the net gain in terms of national income for the developing countries would be $26 billion (1988). All groups of developing countries would gain except the oil exporters. The income gain would be somewhat more than 5 per cent of gross domestic product, primarily due to the increase in international market prices and the gains in economic efficiency that would result from increased trade.

Obviously the CIE studies were based on certain critical assumptions. For Germany and the European Community a very critical assumption is that of rigid wages. The loss in employment and some part, although far from all, of the income losses from agricultural protection are due to that assumption. But the assumption has considerable empirical validity and criticism of the results requires showing that the assumption is invalid. The fact that several studies done by different groups of researchers arrive at much larger negative effects of agricultural protection than had been derived from partial equilibrium studies requires that we revise the general view that the welfare or real income losses from protection are so small that they need to be given little weight. The questions raised by the new studies make it incumbent on policy-makers to give serious attention to reconsidering the potential gains and losses from agricultural protection. The potential losses in income and employment revealed by the recent studies are large and should no longer be ignored in discussions of agricultural policies.

Costs of Protection – to the Excluded

The previous section viewed the cost of protection imposed on the country that restricts trade in one sector of its economy, such as agriculture. In the analysis it was assumed that trade restrictions did not change the terms of trade in favour of that country. If that assumption is maintained, the analysis applies equally to the costs that would be imposed on countries that have lost part of their opportunity to export as a result of protection imposed by another. Assume that all exporters impose an export tax on products that are subject to trade restrictions in importing countries, with the size of the export tax set to maintain world prices at the level that would prevail with free trade. In this way the terms of trade would not be affected by the trade restrictions.

If the usual assumptions are made about elasticities of supply and demand, an exporting country would suffer a loss of exports and the internal prices of export products would fall relative to the prices of both domestic and imported goods. Output of goods formerly imported will increase in response to their higher relative prices, while the output of the surplus product will fall in response to its lower price. There will be both excess resource costs and consumers' surplus losses compared with the free trade situation. The relative prices that would prevail in the domestic market would not reflect the real opportunity costs of obtaining imported goods through exportation.

The primary difference between the two cases is the source of the income transfers. In the exporting countries the transfer will be from the producers of the exported product to the consumers of that product who will not only receive some gain in consumers' surplus due to increased consumption but will also be the recipients of a substantial saving in expenditure on their previous level of consumption. The consumers will lose some or all of the gain in consumers' surplus on the exported product due to the reduced availability of imported products, but this statement probably would not be true of consumers other than those who were also producers of the exported product. If the export tax is used in the manner described above, the producers will also be making a transfer to other taxpayers.

But the conclusion reached earlier will hold, namely that the income transfer would be much larger than the real costs of the restricted opportunity to export so long as some exports continue. Thus when industrial countries restrict trade in agricultural products they are not only imposing income transfers from consumers to producers in their own countries. They are also imposing income transfers from producers to consumers (and to some degree to producers of imported products) in other countries. And if the exported good is an agricultural product, it is highly probable that a significant part of the income transfer would be from low-income farm families to higher-income urban families if the country involved is a developing one.

While accepting the conclusion that the real losses due to restrictions on the opportunity to export are modest compared with the income transfers and with the national income of the exporting country, certain other costs should be recognized if a developing country is involved. It is highly improbable that any single developing country, or developing countries as a group, can prevent the decline in their terms of trade. It is theoretically possible to do so; however, experience indicates the virtual practical impossibility of doing so. If it were easy to prevent such declines in the terms of trade, we would see many more commodity agreements entered into by developing countries. It is evident that for sugar producers that are outside any of the preferential arrangements the terms of trade have been changed in an adverse direction and yet the sugar producers have been unable to modify the situation. So it is reasonable to expect that protection of agricultural producers in the industrial countries will result in transfers from the developing to the industrial countries for those farm products produced in both types of economies. For a limited number of farm products the transfers could be and are substantial.

Another real cost imposed on developing countries by trade restrictions would arise if the costs of borrowing are substantially higher for developing than for industrial countries. Thus the loss of the opportunity to earn foreign exchange may impose substantially higher costs on the developing than the industrial countries for each dollar of foreign exchange that is lost. When a developing country is dependent on the importation of capital goods and services, a loss of export opportunities requires a reduction in the purchase of such goods and services or an increase in foreign borrowing. If the rate of interest is substantially higher than that paid by the industrial countries, the earlier analysis may have seriously underestimated the real costs of trade restrictions.

A further substantial cost is that the loss of export opportunities would enhance the popularity of a policy of industrialization based on import substitution.[12] Such policies impose further real losses in national income. While it could be argued that developing countries embark upon industrialization based on import-substitution of their own volition and that adoption of the policy should not be blamed on trade restrictions imposed by the industrial countries, the point can hardly be made in good grace by industrial countries that protect their agriculture to the extent they do. It may also be noted that such inefficient industrialization involves further additional income transfers from farm to urban areas. Most of the import-substitution activities are located in urban areas and most of the loss in export opportunities still affects rural areas in developing countries; taken together the income transfers from rural to urban areas may reach large magnitudes.

The lower prices of agricultural products slow down the adoption of new inputs and the modernization of agriculture in the developing countries. This cost may well be substantial in real terms over the long run. If the import-substitution policy is extended to the industries that produce the new farm inputs, the impact of trade restrictions will be significantly enlarged.

It would be erroneous to assume that the only real costs of trade restrictions on the countries that lose export opportunities are the excess production costs and loss of consumers' surplus as these are usually measured. The costs delineated above may well be substantially greater than the total of the excess production costs and loss of consumers' surplus, but as far as I know they have not been measured.

Benefits of the Transfers

Since I doubt if anyone is willing to argue that the transfers occurring in the developing or other exporting countries have a net social advantage, the benefits of the transfers will be considered only for the countries engaging in the protection. As argued above, the largest component of the costs to consumers and taxpayers in the industrial countries due to protection of agriculture is the income transfer to producers of agricultural products. Can it be said that net farm income would be increased by the area I in Figure 10.1? If net farm income is defined to include the income going to the owners of all agricultural resources and if the time period under consideration is the one appropriate to the particular supply function for agriculture, the answer is in the affirmative. Thus the analysis seems to imply that if the tariff or import-levy revenue were used to reduce other taxes, the consumer plus taxpayer would find that a large fraction of the transfer would go to increase the incomes of farm resource owners, including labour. But more probing indicates that such an impression would be largely mistaken.

The first consideration would be the distribution of the gains to the various categories of resource owners. As argued in Chapter 9, the greatest proportionate gains in resource prices are realized by the resources with the lowest price elasticities of supply. In the case of agriculture, the resource with the lowest price elasticity of supply is land. Under reasonable assumptions a 20 per cent output price increase could result in at least a 30 to 40 per cent increase in the current return (rent) to land. The increase in the return to labour would be much smaller, even in the short run, and almost nominal in the long run if the elasticity of supply is of the order of magnitude indicated in Chapter 9.

For reproducible capital (farm machinery, buildings) most of the increase in return would soon be required to recoup the return on additional investment. In other words, there is little likelihood that the rate of return to such investment would increase except in the very short run.

Thus the transfer, as financed by consumers and taxpayers, will go primarily to increased return to land and to pay the competitive return on additional reproducible capital. Some of the increase in gross returns will go to pay additional workers that will be induced to remain in agriculture as a result of the slightly elevated return to farm labour. In the models of the labour market presented in Chapter 9 the percentage increase in farm employment due to higher output prices might be two to three times as great as the increase in the return to labour. The pay for the additional workers, however, except that part which is due to the higher return to labour, is not a part of the income transfer since such pay or return is a part of expenditure required to pay for the resources used to produce the additional output. But the part of the total income transfer that goes to labour will be very small.

If one accepts the long-run model presented in Chapter 9, based on the supply and demand functions for labour derived by Edward Schuh and Edward Tyrchniewicz, and adds the assumption that the long-run elasticity of farm output is unity, a 10 per cent increase in output prices would have the income effects shown in the table:[13]

Gross farm income + 21 per cent	
Distributed as follows:	
Payment for additional resources, excluding	
excess resource costs	47.6 per cent
Excess resource costs	2.4
Return to labour previously employed	4.8
Return to land and capital (residual)	45.2
TOTAL	100.0 per cent

The calculations indicate that the increased return to labour previously employed would amount to only 4.8 per cent of the total increase in gross farm income. Even if one considers only the increase in income that went to the resources previously employed in agriculture, less than a tenth of that amount would accrue to the previously employed farm labour. Because of the assumption of unit elasticity of supply, exactly half of the increase in gross farm income is income transfer and exactly half goes for additional resources to produce an increase of 10 per cent in output and to pay the excess resource costs, which are a minor part of the total.

If the primary objective of the income transfer from consumers and taxpayers is to increase the return to farm labour, it is obvious that an equal increase in farm labour returns could be achieved by direct grants to labour at a very much lower cost.

Obviously the income of owners of farmland and capital would be increased and by a substantial margin. Is this an achievement that is worth taxing all consumers of food for, if the transfer is made through higher food prices? In most industrial countries it would mean net transfers from many low-income consumers to many high-income resource owners.

In an important but largely ignored study, T. E. Josling and Donna Hamway estimated, for the Trade Policy Research Centre in London, the income-distribution effects of the European Community's variable levy system if the United Kingdom had been a member of the European Community in 1969.[14] The comparison was with the producer and consumer prices that would have prevailed under free trade. The study was a short-run analysis in the sense that it did not take into account changes in factor supplies in response to the different output prices. The effect of higher consumer prices on consumption was reflected in the estimates.

Table 10.2 presents estimates of the transfer between and within income groups based on the actual farm sizes and income distribution that existed in the late 1960s. The first row indicates the transfer to farmers by income group. Since the transfer is net of the increase in costs imposed on consumers, it is worthy of note that the lowest income group of farm families were projected to have had their real income lowered by the United Kingdom's accession to the European Community and institutions of the Community's common agricultural policy.

The second row represents the effect of the additional costs of higher food prices that would result from the CAP. Thus the negative sign reflects the transfers from all consumers, other than farmers. Not all of the transfers goes to United Kingdom farmers. Since the United Kingdom was a net food importer, some of the transfer would go to Brussels, as in fact did occur. The last row indicates the net transfers by income groups. The median family income was in the £1301 to £1850 group. It is of interest to compare net transfers between the lowest four income groups and the five highest income groups. The income transfer to the lowest income farm families was estimated at £77 million

Table 10.2 Net transfer among income groups for the United Kingdom, under the European Community's price policy compared with free trade, c. 1969

Range of income (£) £ per year[a]	<500	501–1,100	1,101–1,300	1,301–1,850	1,851–2,350	2,351–2,800	2,801–3,400	3,401–5,000	5,001+
Farm households (£ million)	−9.9	24.4	21.1	41.4	71.1	26.5	63.2	64.6	140.8
Other households (£ million)	−47.6	−200.5	−100.1	−233.2	−67.2	−13.0	2.4	3.3	20.2
Net transfer (£ million)	−57.5	−175.8	−79.0	−191.9	4.0	13.5	60.8	61.2	120.61

[a]The median level of household income was approximately £1850.

Source: T. E. Josling and Donna Hamway, 'Distribution of Costs and Benefits of Farm Policy', in Josling, Brian Davey, Alister McFarquhar, A. C. Hannah and Hamway, *Burdens and Benefits of Farm Support Policies*, Agricultural Trade Paper No. 1 (London: Trade Policy Research Centre, 1972), p. 79.

compared with £366 million for the five higher income groups. The low-income farm groups would pay £581 million more for their food under the CAP prices than under free trade while the highest five income groups faced higher costs of just £106 million.

If one combines the two groups (farmers and consumers) by income levels, the lowest four income groups suffered an income loss of £504 million while the remaining and higher income groups had a net gain of £260 million. Under the assumptions, the net transfer to Brussels was £244 million. But even if that amount had been transferred to farmers within the United Kingdom, and all of it had gone to the lowest four farm-income groups, there would still have been a net transfer from low-income families to high-income families. The estimates confirm the conclusion that there is a net income transfer from low-income consumers to high-income farmers. And the transfer is not simply a minor nuisance; for low-income households the additional cost exceeded 4 per cent of their income.

The farm price and income programmes in the United States since the early 1970s have functioned primarily through governmental expenditures, including direct payments, rather than by measures that held domestic prices above border prices. True, there were exceptions, particularly dairy, sugar, peanuts and beef. But the only quantitatively important exception has been dairy. It is reasonable to assume that at least 80 per cent of the income transfer that is realized by farmers is in the form of direct payments. This statement ignores any effect the United States supply management programmes may have on world market prices since such effects are not included in the usual measures of protection. Such effects are not included in the measures of producer subsidy equivalents since no difference between domestic and border prices emerges. The point to which this discussion is leading is that a reasonable approximation can be made of the distribution of the farm programme benefits by considering the distribution of direct payments. It is that discussion to which we now turn.

Earlier in this chapter the long-run model of the relationship between output prices and the returns to farm resources was used to estimate the effects of a 10 per cent increase in output prices which would be distributed within agriculture between labour, land and capital. For this model it makes no difference whether the increase in return per unit of output is due to higher market prices or to deficiency payments determined primarily by output. This model predicts that approximately 90 per cent of the increase in net returns to farm resources would go to land and capital and only 10 per cent to labour. In the first edition of this book these results were used to derive the estimate that the largest one-sixth of the United States farms received half of the total net benefits of the farm price and income support programmes in 1966. It was noted that these farm operator families had net incomes in excess of $21 000 or about double the national average family incomes.

In the United States efforts have been made to limit the maximum size of payments going to a farm or an individual. These efforts have been the only response the political process has made to the fact that most of the benefits of the farm programmes go to a relatively small number of high-income farm families. Have maximum payments been effective in changing the distribution of farm programme benefits? The evidence is very clear that the effectiveness has been nil. Nor have any other changes, deliberate or inadvertent, in the nature of the farm programmes had the effect of reducing the share of the benefits going to the largest farms. Table 10.3 includes data for 1985 that substantiates this conclusion.

Table 10.3 Average value of net farm-operator assets, farm-family incomes from farming and from all sources and government payments by value of farm sales in the United States, 1985

Value of sales (000s)	Average value of net farm-operator assets (000s)	Average farm income from farming (000s)	Average farm-family incomes from all sources (000s)	Average government payments (per farm)	Percentage of farms	Percentage of total farm-operator assets[a]
500+	2 600	640.0	655.5	37 499	1.2	14.6
250–499	1 208	99.7	111.1	21 783	2.9	14.5
100–249	611	36.7	47.2	12 845	9.7	23.5
40–99	360	6.6	17.4	5 193	14.2	19.7
20–39	225	−0.1	14.2	2 040	10.1	8.2
10–19	165	−2.0	16.9	678	10.7	6.3
5–9	115	−1.2	20.3	233	11.8	4.7
<5	61	−4.2	18.4	447	39.4	8.4
Average		13.9	31.8	3 387		

[a]Excludes value of dwellings and other assets and liabilities associated with the operator household – an estimate of assets used for farm production.
Source: *Economic Indicators of the Farm Sector: National Financial Summary, 1985* (Washington: United States Department of Agriculture, 1986), pp. 46–51 and 80.

The table includes a variety of information about the distribution of farm assets, net incomes from farming and net incomes from all sources for farm-operator families, government payments per farm and the percentage of farms and total productive assets per farm by farms classified by value of sales. In 1985 direct government payments totalled $7.7 billion, somewhat lower than the previous two years but much higher than in 1981 and 1982. Net farm income, including government payments, was $31.6 billion.

The largest 13.8 per cent of the farms (sales in excess of $100 000) received 68.7 per cent of the direct government payments. Farm families on these large farms had net family incomes from all sources of $116 000 and received nearly $13 000 in direct payment. The largest farms (with sales in excess of $500 000) received direct payments that exceeded the average family income in the United States of $29 066 in 1985. The families in the three largest sales groups have far more assets than the average urban family with the net assets ranging from $611 000 to $2 600 000.

The last column of Table 10.3 gives the distribution of productive farm assets by farms classified by the value of sales. The largest three groups of farms have 52.6 per cent of the total assets; the percentage of the assets owned by the largest 16.2 per cent of the farms (to be comparable to the comparisons made for 1966) is no less than 56 per cent. Thus if 90 per cent of the net benefits accrue to land and capital, the largest one-sixth of the farms receive 50 per cent of the net benefits. This is the same estimate as was derived for 1966.

Based on the distribution of direct payments, the benefits were more unequally distributed in 1985 than in 1966. In 1966 the sixth of the farms with the largest sales received 50 per cent of the direct payments compared with slightly more than 70 per cent in 1985.[15]

Both approaches for estimating the distribution of the benefits of farm programmes agree that a relatively small percentage of the farms receive at least half of the total benefits that accrue to farmers. Based on the distribution of direct payments, benefits were more unequally distributed in 1985 than in 1966. Based on the distribution of farm assets, there was no change in the estimated share of net benefits going to the largest sixth of the farms.

In recent years the press in the European Community and the United States frequently noted that the governmental costs of farm pro-grammes in some years exceeded $20 billion. Such statements were factually correct. All too often, though, it is assumed that the farmers in the Community and the United States actually received such large amounts in terms of increased income. It is worth taking a little space to review the total governmental expenditures for the United States and the Community. Data are presented for 1985, the most recent data available at the time of writing.

As noted earlier, in the United States direct payments to farmers in 1985 totalled $7.7 billion. Of this amount $1253 million were diversion payments – payments to induce farmers to keep part of their land out of cultivation. Payments for storage costs were $760 million. Deficiency payments, representing the difference between the target prices and the price support levels, amounted to $5.7 billion. Thus the total cost of $21.6 billion in 1985 was far in excess of what was received by farmers. The cost of operating the programmes, primarily commodity loans and purchases to maintain the support prices amounted to $11.8 billion. In addition, purchases of dairy products cost $2.0 billion.

Perhaps the data for a single year are atypical. For 1981–85 the total governmental cost was $62.9 billion. Deficiency payments, including the payment-in-kind commodities distributed in 1983 and /1984, totalled $21.86 billion. Diversion payments were $3.8 billion and disaster payments came to $1.6 billion. Storage costs came to $22.3 billion or slightly more than the deficiency payments. Dairy purchases had a net cost of $11.1 billion. For the five-year period a somewhat higher percentage of the total governmental costs were paid to the farmers than for the 1985 year.[16] To receive the deficiency and diversion payments farmers diverted an annual average of 12 million hectares of cropland.

The data on the governmental costs of the European Community and United States farm programmes make it evident that a large fraction of the expenditures are for costs that do not directly benefit the farmers. Storage costs, including the interest costs of holding stocks, account for a significant part of the total expenditures. Owners of storage space are clearly important beneficiaries of the price-support programmes under discussion. There is an unknown number of bureaucrats who carry out the programmes and receive compensation for their activities, even if their social product is nil or negative.

These data clearly suggest that there must be ways of transferring money to farmers at a much lower cost than the methods used currently. But there are other interests being served by these programmes. Reference has been made to storage costs. Those who supply inputs to agriculture or market and process farm products have an interest in maintaining a high level of farm production. Efforts to decouple payments from current farm production decisions are resisted by input and marketing firms in the United States.

Free Trade and Increase in Exports by Developing Countries

In 1964 I wrote the following:

> The protection given agriculture in the industrial countries restricts exports from the less developed countries in one or both of two ways – increasing output and reducing consumption. Only in the United Kingdom have the consumption effects been largely eliminated through use of deficiency payments. If the increase in prices received by producers averages 20 to 25 per cent and if the increase in prices paid by consumers averages 15 to 20 per cent, even very low elasticities of supply and demand will result in substantial contraction in the demand for exports of less developed regions. If supply elasticities are as low as 0.15 and demand elasticities 0.2, the effect on the value of agricultural imports of the industrial countries would be as much as $3500 million to $4500 million. Some of the increased import demand would be met by developed countries such as Canada and Australia. But if the increase in developing-country exports were to be only half that indicated or about $2000 million, the importance is very great when compared with total developing-country exports of agricultural products of approximately $12 000 million.[17]

In the original edition of this book, I assumed a substantially higher elasticity of supply of farm products in the industrial countries. Based on Chapter 6, the elasticity of supply of at least 0.5 was assumed. This change in assumption increased the estimated increase in imports of farm products of the industrial countries to perhaps $8000 million in 1970 prices. It was assumed that the developing countries would realize only half of the increase in exports. Almost certainly the United States would obtain a higher fraction of the increase in exports than I had assumed in 1964 and the same would undoubtedly be true of Australia and perhaps also of Canada. Such was the case and the developed countries had a larger share of world agricultural exports in 1980 than in the 1960s.

The rough estimates of the potential gain in export revenue of the developing countries referred to above failed to take into account the numerous interventions that would affect their response to any reduction in barriers to agricultural imports by the industrial market economies. If a country had price supports that held domestic prices above world market levels, then trade liberalization might not result in any increase in exports since the domestic producer price might well remain above the border price. This would have been true even if the domestic price in excess of the border price were an offset to an over-valued currency. But unless the over-valuation were corrected and domestic prices adjusted, developing country exports would not be increased unless export subsidies were used.

Few developing countries have export subsidies for farm products. In fact, the imposition of export taxes is reasonably common. The export taxes reduce domestic prices below world market prices. Thus reduction of trade barriers by the industrial market economies could result in more exports and an increase in domestic prices in the developing economies or an increase in export taxes that would keep domestic prices stable and prevent any increase in exports.

As the World Bank's *World Development Report 1986*[18] makes clear, developing countries, especially the low-income and middle-income countries, are more likely to depress domestic producer prices below world market levels than to raise them above such levels.

It needs to be recognized that not all of the agricultural exports from the developing countries are subject to significant degrees of protection in the industrial countries. Lint cotton, jute, sisal and natural rubber are subjected to few trade barriers. Trade barriers for oilseeds and their products, other than preferential arrangements, are not nearly as severe as those on grains. In fact, the European Community's pattern of trade interventions, with variable levies on feed-grains and nil duties on the importation of oilseeds, has resulted in an increase in world exports of oilseeds. The situation with respect to bananas, coffee, tea and cocoa beans is mixed with a number of countries permitting free or nearly free entry, while other countries have high tariffs or internal taxes or impose quotas. It appears that approximately half of the agricultural exports of developing countries to the industrial countries were not subject to major restraints due to the desire to protect domestic production.

In their study for the International Food Policy Research Institute in Washington, discussed in Chapter 7, Joachim Zietz and Alberto Valdés undertook systematic studies of the effects of significant liberalization of agricultural trade by the OECD countries.[19] In a paper published in 1987, Dr Valdés summarized the estimates of the effects of a 50 per cent reduction in OECD protection for all agricultural products exported by the developing countries. The levels of protection that were used as a base were those for 1975–77 and the results were recalculated in 1985 dollars. It should be noted that levels of protection in 1975–77 were generally lower than those prevailing in the mid-1980s. They projected that agricultural exports from all developing countries would increase by $5.9 billion or by approximately 11 per cent. Half of the increase in exports was projected to be in sugar and meats, primarily beef. Another analysis, also reported by Dr Valdés, indicated that the estimates of export increases for sugar, beef, wheat and maize, assuming that all barriers to trade were removed by the industrial countries, changes in world market prices were taken into account and assuming 1979–81 levels of protection, were for a total of $9 to $12 billion (1980 dollars) or $11 to $14 billion (1985 dollars).

A study by Rodney Tyers and Kym Anderson, based on 1980–82 protection levels, gave estimates of the increased volume of exports by the developing countries very close to those derived by Dr Zietz and Dr Valdés.[20] The increase in developing-country exports as a result of trade liberalization are estimated to range from 10 to somewhat more than 20 per cent. But not all developing countries would share in the benefits from trade liberalization. There has been a dramatic change in the many developing countries' balance of trade in agricultural products from the 1960s to the 1980s. In the 1960s the developing market economies had a net surplus of $7.8 billion. This surplus had declined to $5.6 billion in 1983–85. Several developing countries shifted from being net exporters to become net importers. Since one of the effects of trade liberalization in agricultural products would be to increase world market prices, it has been argued that low-income developing countries that are significant net importers of agricultural products would face higher import bills. This is an impression that has been left by some of the trade models that emphasized primarily temperate-zone products. But the Zeitz–Valdés study of 99 commodities, including numerous tropical products of interest to developing countries, indicated that with even the relatively low levels of protection in industrial market economies in 1975–77, the increase in export revenue of $5.9 billion was more than four times the increase in import costs of $1.4 billion that would result from increased international prices.

This is not to say that there are no countries that would lose from agricultural trade liberalization. Some developing countries are beneficiaries of preference systems. If there were liberalization of trade in sugar, most of the countries that have preferential access to the European Community's sugar market would lose since the Community sugar price is higher than the world price would be under free trade in sugar.[21] Similarly when the United States was a significant net importer of sugar (about 4 million tons) and the domestic price was two or more times the world market price, developing countries that had quotas for the United States market favoured the continuation of the sugar programme. The short-run benefits seemed obvious; what was missed was that in the long run United States sugar imports would be nil. Such became the case in the late 1980s.

Benefits of Free Trade

I have attempted to develop several different approaches to the answer to the title of this chapter: 'What Difference Does Trade Make?' It is fairly clear that at least in the short run the losses in national income or welfare that result from restrictions of trade are a small fraction of national output. The income transfers that are made from consumers to farmers and taxpayers, or from consumers and taxpayers to farmers, are many times as large as the probable real costs of protection in the industrial countries. Similarly it is probable that the transfers that occur in developing countries because of the loss of export opportunities are significantly greater than the real costs.

It was also argued that the total costs of the loss of export opportunities to the developing countries may be substantially larger than the value of the excess production costs of expanding the production of imported goods plus the loss of consumers' surplus. Difficulties and costs in borrowing to acquire foreign exchange for investment purposes, the loss of income due to deterioration of the terms of trade, the impetus given to a policy of industrialization based on import substitution; and the long-run effects of lower farm products on the modernization of agriculture probably would result in losses in real national income over time that would be substantially larger than the conventionally measured welfare losses resulting from trade restrictions. And of these four potential sources of loss, the loss of real income due to the deterioration of the terms of trade might well be the least important, since long-run supply adjustments appear to redress gradually the deterioration in the terms of trade for farm products.

It was concluded that the long-run increases in farm incomes achieved by protection were relatively small compared with the magnitude of the income transfers. The real income gains to farm labour are quite rapidly overtaken by the normal out-migration of labour from agriculture. In any case, the percentage increase in returns to farm labour that can be achieved by higher farm prices is quite small compared with the actual increases in real returns that occur as a result of economic growth. The real income transfers that do occur in agriculture are primarily the increased returns to farm land and, so far as I know, no one has been able to attribute a large social benefit to such a transfer. If the discussion of the distribution of gains from protection presented earlier is approximately correct, it implies that, as protection is maintained over a fairly long period, the real costs increase relative to the magnitude of the income transfers.

The income transfers associated with protection of agriculture in the industrial countries appear to go on more or less indefinitely, largely without analysis of what groups are adversely affected or of what net social gains, if any, are achieved. It would appear that, after such protection has been maintained for a period of time, the main argument for continuation is that the substantial losses would be imposed on resource owners in the protected sector. In the case of agricultural protection, there would be large losses in the capital value of land and other relatively long-life assets; and the readjustment in the labour supply would be painful and serious. It is difficult for governments who have misled a significant and vocal fraction of their citizens to admit that the policies they have been following have been of relatively modest benefit, that most of the net benefits go to relatively high-income groups and that the continuation of the present high transfer costs, or even higher costs, is necessary merely to maintain the status quo with respect to real product prices.

What are the economic benefits from the income transfers to the owners of farm land and capital when so little of the transfer goes to labour? The major short-run benefit is to prevent declines in the value of farm land. This was true during the 1970s and remains true today even though in both the United States and the European Community there have been substantial declines in the value of farm land since the peaks reached in the late 1970s or early 1980s.

Even with the very large public expenditures on farm programmes in the United States, the value of all farm land has declined from $843 billion in early 1981 to $550 billion in early 1987, a decline in nominal dollars of 35 per cent. As noted in Chapter 11, the farm price and income programmes of the United States and the European Community have not been capable of stabilizing either farm incomes or land values. Changes in macro-economic variables, such as interest rates and inflation rates, have been far more powerful in their effects than explicit farm policies.

Perhaps the major cost of protection is that it all too often precludes consideration and implementation of more effective means of achieving desired goals. Where farm incomes are low, the primary reasons are limited resources rather than the level of prices or the availability of non-farm jobs. In almost all societies the education of farm people has been woefully neglected. If there is any lesson that the developing countries should learn from the experience of the industrial countries it is that enormous social and economic costs can and do result from discrimination against farm and other rural people in the provision of educational opportunities.

Interferences with international trade result in large income transfers, both in the countries engaging in the protection and in other countries that lose export opportunities. At least as far as agriculture is concerned, the transfers do not achieve significant social or economic benefits. But unfortunately the transfer process is such a subtle one when it is achieved through higher farm and consumer prices that there is seldom any effort made to relate the sacrifices imposed on consumers to the modest benefits that eventually accrue to the farm population. And nowhere in the political process of the world does there appear to be any mechanism for considering the loss of welfare that import restrictions impose on agricultural producers in the developing countries, either directly or through the long-run effects on economic growth in such countries. Since there is so little concern, however, about the relative benefits and costs of income transfers within the industrial countries, it is perhaps not surprising that there is little or no concern about the effects on those who are a long distance away.

11 Limited Achievement of Farm Policy Objectives

The domestic farm-support policies of the industrial countries impose enormous costs on consumers and taxpayers and such costs, if present policies are continued, will not decline from the levels of the early and mid-1980s. The trade restrictions that governments consider to be essential for these policies have been, are and will continue to be important sources of tension among trading countries. Unless there is a significant degree of liberalization of agricultural trade in the Uruguay Round of multilateral trade negotiations, which got under way in Geneva under the auspices of the GATT in 1987, there is danger that the multilateral trading system as it has evolved since the Second World War will suffer irreparable damage. It has been demonstrated that high farm prices alone are not enough to provide politically acceptable incomes to farm families. So long as the major reliance is placed on protection and high prices, the pressure is for still more protection and still higher prices. Experience since 1960 has shown that governments can provide higher real prices for farm products for only a limited period of time and, at best, governments can temper the downward trend in real prices paid to farmers.

It is also recognized that high or higher farm prices have little to offer the vast majority of farmers in any industrial country. Farms that have relatively little to sell receive little increase in income from higher prices; if their incomes were too low by some social or political standard prior to an output price increase, their incomes will be too low after any price increase that is politically possible. In almost all of the industrial countries, a small minority of the farms are responsible for two-thirds to three-quarters of all farm sales. A small minority means a sixth or at most a fifth of all farmers. Thus if there is a concern about income disparities in the countryside, agricultural protection does not offer even a theoretical solution to the elimination of such disparities. As noted below, actual experience with protection over recent decades is consistent with the theoretical expectation.

Current farm-support policies have contributed to the maintenance of excess productive capacity in agriculture in the industrial countries. The resources engaged in agriculture are capable of producing more than can be disposed of at prices that would provide acceptable remuneration for those resources. As a result governments adopt policies and programmes designed to manage the actual or potential output from the excess resources. On the one hand, governments have adopted protectionist measures, such as export subsidies and import barriers, including quantitative restrictions or variable import levies, that have the result of imposing the consequences of their excess production on international markets. As a result, throughout the 1980s the international market prices for farm products have been seriously depressed, in some cases by as much as 50 per cent and for temperate-zone products an average of perhaps 20 per cent.[1] Some governments have engaged in supply management in an effort to prevent the excess capacity that protection has generated from being translated into excess output for which there is no market at existing domestic prices. What is evident from the experiences of the United States, Japan and Canada who have had supply-management programmes for considerable periods of time, these programmes do not eliminate the excess capacity or the excess resources that are responsible for the excess capacity. Consequently the supply-management programmes have become permanent components of farm programmes and not measures to eliminate a temporary surplus of a farm product. With high support prices or subsidies there is no such thing as a temporary surplus.

What we have seen since 1970 is that agricultural protection has caused a number of industrial countries to adopt supply-management programmes for the same reasons that the United States did so three decades earlier. This development was foreseen in 1970 by Albert Simantov, then Director of Agriculture at the OECD. He suggested that there were two alternative approaches for avoiding surpluses and ensuring that farmers receive an adequate income from farming:[2]

> *The first alternative* consists of (a) letting prices fulfill their role in equating supply and demand without any other major form of government intervention, and (b) granting payments to farmers, preferably payments which are not directly linked to production.
>
> *The second alternative* consists of (a) maintaining farm prices at levels higher than those which would normally equate result from the confrontation of supply and demand, and even in increasing these prices under certain circumstances, and (b) applying production and/or marketing limitations of one sort or another.

Mr Simantov then made a highly accurate forecast: 'What appears more likely is that governments may adopt a *combination of these two alternatives*. It is the most realistic hypothesis at present. This may consist of moderate pressure on prices combined with voluntary or semi-voluntary removal of excess production capacity.' Remembering that this prediction was made in 1970, one notes that Canada, Japan and the European Community have since then followed the paths that he indicated. He was saying, in effect, that most industrial countries would follow a path that was similar in important respects to that followed in the United States during the 1960s and since.

Mr Simantov failed to recognize what is now very clear, namely that while supply management has the ability to limit production to some degree, it does not actually remove the excess capacity. Thus supply management is like grabbing a bear by the tail: you can't let go. As the United States and Canadian experiences have shown, since these two countries have had the longest experience with supply management, barring a radical reform of farm policies, there is no turning back – supply management becomes a permanent component of farm programmes. Mr Simantov deserves credit for one of the earliest endorsements of decoupled payments – 'payments which are not directly linked to production'. Unfortunately little progress has been made in that direction, either.

Given the obvious failures of the United States farm programmes to achieve their objectives, it is quite dismaying that other countries have adopted similar measures over the past two decades, albeit with certain modifications, but broadly the same. The United States farm programmes have imposed large costs on taxpayers and consumers yet only a tiny fraction of the income transfer has gone to low-income farmers. There is little or no evidence that returns to labour used on efficient farms have been increased and a great deal of evidence that almost all of the increased net income accruing to agriculture has been capitalized into the value of land or has been required for competitive returns on the additional capital investment induced by higher prices or programme payments. Is this a reasonable path for others to follow? I would think not, yet it appears to have been followed nevertheless.

Farm-policy Objectives Lack Specificity

It is not easy to determine if farm price and income policies have achieved their objectives. The primary reason for this difficulty is that the policy objectives are seldom if ever stated with sufficient preciseness so that it can be determined if they have been achieved or not. Over the years the OECD surveys of farm income and support policies have attempted to delineate as clearly as possible the objectives sought by the policies. There has seldom been any success in doing so. Perhaps the most precise policy objectives existed when the United States had parity as an objective – first price parity and subsequently income parity. Each has been abandoned, price parity because it was not achievable and income parity because it was difficult to measure and, too, because it was quite clear that the minority of farmers who received most of the benefits from the programmes had incomes that met any reasonable concept of parity income. The 1981 agricultural act described the objectives as 'to provide price and income protection for farmers, assure customers an abundance of food and fiber at reasonable prices, continue food assistance to low-income households and for other purposes'. It is not possible to determine empirically if these objectives have been met.

In my opinion, the most precisely stated farm policy objectives are the ones specified in the Treaty of Rome. As later amplified in Article 31 of the Treaty, the objectives of the CAP were to be:

(a) to increase agricultural productivity by promoting technical progress and by ensuring the rational development of agricultural production and the optimum utilization of the factors of production, in particular labour;
(b) thus to ensure a fair standard of living for the agricultural community, in particular by increasing the individual earnings of persons engaged in agriculture;
(c) to stabilize markets;
(d) to assure the availability of supplies; and
(e) to ensure that supplies reach consumers at reasonable prices.

At the Stresa Conference the objectives were amplified: 'the structures of European agriculture were to be reformed to become more competitive, without any threat to family farms . . .'.[3]

While the objectives of the CAP appear to be models of clarity and precision compared with the objectives of the United States Agriculture and Food Act of 1981, it is impossible for either friend or foe to determine with reasonable preciseness if the objectives of CAP have been met. For example, can one conclude that agricultural productivity has been improved as a consequence of the CAP and related efforts?

There can be no doubt that crop output per hectare increased at a rapid pace after the mid-1960s. Nor is there any doubt that gross farm output per worker has also increased. But these are not the same as increasing productivity as defined by changes in output per unit of input.

As an objective observer, one can ask why it is that policy-makers are not more often diligent in requiring studies and analyses that would assist them in determining the effectiveness of their programmes when the available information is inadequate. With the possible exception of Australia with her Industries Assistance Commission and the recent experience in the United States, when its Economic Research Service in the Department of Agriculture undertook numerous studies to show the ineffectiveness of the United States high price supports as part of an effort to prove the desirability of making American farm policy more market-oriented, governments have shown remarkably little interest in organizing the studies required to determine the effects of their policies and programmes. Agricultural policies are not exceptional in this regard.

In fact, the Commission of the European Community has been more self-consciously concerned about the degree to which the policies it has promulgated have achieved their objectives than has been the case in Japan, Canada or the United States. There have been several efforts to reform the CAP, starting with the Mansholt Plan, not solely because of the high costs of the CAP but because of its limitations in achieving its objectives. Self-critiques of the CAP may be found in many places in addition to the various efforts at policy reform. These include most of the annual reports on *The Agricultural Situation in the Community*, as well as some of the descriptions of the CAP intended for a popular audience.

Examples of critical evaluations can be found in *The Agricultural Policy of the European Community*, first published in 1976 and revised in 1979. In a section that addressed 'Have the objectives of the Treaty of Rome been achieved?', a sub-section was entitled 'Productivity, standard of living, market stability: patchy results'. It is noted that the share of agriculture in GDP had declined between 1968 and 1976 (from 6.4 per cent to 4.8 per cent) and similarly for the population engaged in agriculture (from 12.8 per cent in 1967 to 8.0 per cent in 1976). The latter development was apparently considered to be a failure of the CAP: 'As a result some country areas are becoming depopulated . . ., whereas towns are becoming overcrowded.'[4] It was then noted that the decline in agricultural population had been accompanied by 'a remarkable jump in the productivity of farm labour (GDP per person employed)'. Furthermore, consistent with the data presented for the industrial economies in Chapter 4 above, the comparison of annual growth rates of labour productivity showed that in agriculture the rate was approximately twice that in the rest of the economy. But it was then lamented that there was still a large productivity gap between agriculture and the rest of the economy – 'only 4.0% of the GDP is accounted for by 8.4% of the active population engaged in agriculture'.[5]

This discussion was then followed by a rather gloomy evaluation and prognosis. After noting that productivity growth must be maintained, 'This implies increasingly rapid technical progress against the proper social and structural background, representing a good deal more than *the mere price and market policy which has failed to solve the problems of agriculture by itself*. It is clear that the disparities in agricultural incomes have not disappeared but have grown more marked in every respect: between Member States, between regions (incomes in some Community regions are five times higher than in others), between farms of the same size in the same Member State (incomes on mixed farms are half those in cattle farming) and even between farms of different sizes but of the same type (those of over 50 hectares have incomes twice as large as those between 10 and 20 hectares).'

The conclusion concerning the regional income disparities was noted in the 1980 report on the *Agricultural Situation in the European Community*, but with an added point: 'During the period from 1964/65 to 1976/77, regional disparities in agricultural income (as measured by gross value-added per agricultural worker) increased in the Community. The ratio between the regions with the highest agricultural incomes and those with the lowest rose from 5:1 to 6:1.'[6]

While the candour with respect to some of the unfavourable outcomes is to be commended, there can be nothing but criticism for the poor analysis used to support either the criticisms or the plaudits. It is one of the oddities of democratic societies that they are willing to spend billions of dollars or European currency units (ECUs) on a programme and virtually nothing on systematic and analytically sound studies to determine the effects of the programmes. As implied by an earlier comment, the European Community is in no way unique in this.

In 1987/88 the Commission of the European Community broke with its tradition and funded an important and highly competent study, as described in *Disharmonies in EC and US Agricultural Policy Measures*.[7] The project leader was Ulrich Koester, of the University of Kiel, and members of the team were drawn from agricultural economists in both the European Community and the United States. The study group produced an excellent document that projected the effects of various price-harmonization measures in the European Community and the United States on international market prices and domestic prices, farm incomes, production, consumption and trade. The price-harmonization measures did not represent what the outcomes would have been under free trade but nonetheless would require a substantial reduction in protection. The projected decline in the level of nominal protection, starting from the 1986 level, was from 66 to 25 per cent for the Community and from 31 to 13 per cent for the United States for the options set for cereals, oilseeds, sugar, dairy and livestock prices. It is clear that the reductions in protection that were envisaged were substantial and would have important effects on international trade.

Income Differences

Inadequate analysis results in some critical evaluations of the CAP that may not be warranted. The comparison of the percentage of GDP produced by agriculture and the percentage of the population engaged in agriculture is a very poor measure of either labour productivity or overall productivity. Such a comparison assumes that the agricultural and non-agricultural labour forces have the same capabilities – would have the same marginal product if placed in similar circumstances. It also assumes that the measurements of the two labour forces are equally accurate. Neither assumption is correct. Yet no effort was made to determine how large these effects might be and what influence they might have on the comparisons. Generally speaking, the farm labour force is older and less well-educated than the non-farm labour force. On both counts, farm labour would be less productive than the non-farm labour force. There may also be differences in the way income is measured and the purchasing power of income in the two sectors. The lower incomes are, the greater is the inaccuracy involved in comparing rural and urban incomes.

The measurement of regional income disparities by a comparison of gross value added per worker should receive a failing grade. It grossly exaggerates the degree of disparity, although there is no doubt that disparity exists. But it is a disparity that high output prices or rural structural policies as pursued in the European Community can do almost nothing to correct. The regional income differences for farm people reflect regional differences in the general levels of income. The

1980 report on the agricultural situation in the European Community recognized this by following the discussion of disparities: 'Generally speaking, the regions with above-average level of agricultural income are to be found in a favourable general economic context; the converse is true of regions with a low level of agricultural incomes.'[8] It is intellectually irresponsible to use gross value added per worker to measure inequality of agricultural income per worker, even if one ignores the inappropriateness of using only agricultural income to measure income inequality in rural areas today in industrial countries. One only needs to compare the relationship between gross value added and net agricultural income per worker by the general level of agricultural income. One finds what one should expect, namely that gross value added in high-income agricultural areas has a much larger ratio to net agricultural income than in low-income agricultural areas. Data on net agricultural income are not available by regions but some information can be gained by comparing these values for the high-income agricultural areas of the northern European Community countries to those in the lower income countries, such as Greece. In some northern countries (Denmark and Germany, for example) gross value added is more than double net agricultural income while in Greece net agricultural income is about 85 per cent of gross value added. The difference between gross value and net value added is not income to farm people – it consists of depreciation and interest paid. If the ratio of the gross values added were 5 to 1, the ratio of net agricultural incomes would be about 3 to 1. To give a specific example, in 1985 the gross value added per worker in Denmark was 4.1 times that in Greece, while the net agricultural income per worker was just 2.0 times.[9]

Further, measuring income disparities solely on the basis of farm income and to cite such disparities as evidence of failure of agricultural policies and to do so without determining the amounts of non-farm incomes earned by farm families is certain to mislead. With existing approaches it is impossible to obtain an accurate measure of the labour input from part-time farm households. To emphasize this point, is it reasonable to believe that the net agricultural income per full-time farm worker in Germany in 1985 was less than half of what was realized in Belgium and the same as in Spain and less than a fifth more than in Greece?[10] Yet this is the result if you divide the national estimates of net agricultural income by the number of annual work units. The annual work units presumably are a measure of full-time work but the actual data seem not to be equally reliable for all countries. What should be measured is the farm plus off-farm income of farm families. It is certain that the regional variations in this income concept would be much less than that in gross value added or net agricultural income per farm worker. Even if it were possible to measure accurately the labour input on part-time farms, it is not obvious that this would be the correct approach. It would assume that part-time farmers attempt to achieve the same average product of labour as full-time farmers. Many part-time farmers may view their farming operations as something approaching a hobby and a source of pleasure and recreation rather than as a means of earning income.

A survey of outside gainful activities of farm families undertaken for the Commission of the European Community makes it clear that there is a paucity of information on off-farm activities and incomes derived therefrom.[11] But where data are available there can be little doubt of the importance of off-farm incomes for farm families. It was estimated that in 1981 in France 42 per cent of the total incomes of farm families came from off-farm sources. It was also noted that the data by regions in 1979 showed a wide variation in the relative importance of off-farm income relative to agricultural or farm income – from a low of 18.5 per cent to a high of 121 per cent. It should come as no surprise that the relative importance of off-farm income is the greatest in regions with low measured gross value added per farm worker.

The data for West Germany indicated that in 1982/83 off-farm income of all farm operator families equalled 72 per cent of income from agriculture while in 1983/84 off-farm income was 90 per cent of the agricultural income or the two sources of income were about equal. Another striking result of the data was that there was little difference in family incomes among full-time farmers, part-time with main income from farming and part-time supplementary income farms. There is a number of studies of part-time farming in Italy, but differences among them are substantial. One study indicates that non-farm income amounted to at least 60 per cent and perhaps as much as 70 per cent of the total incomes of all farm-operator families.

Clearly the failure to include all sources of income for farm families makes any conclusion about income disparities suspect and subject to misinterpretation. The failure to give appropriate emphasis to off-farm income in the various income discussions in the Commission reflects, I fear, the view held by policy-makers in the European Community that their primary concern is agriculture or farming and not farm people. This view, unfortunately, is not unique to the Community; almost everywhere national agricultural policies are designed for particular commodities and the process of producing those commodities and not for farm people. Nowhere that I know of is there a policy designed to benefit part-time farm families, either in their farming operations or in their off-farm earning activities.

Policy Objectives

Have the farm policies of the industrial market economies achieved their objectives? As a long-time observer of agricultural policies of the industrial countries, I believe the priority objectives are the following:

Food security
Adequate levels of farm-family incomes
Stability of prices for producers and consumers
Maintaining a large and viable rural sector
Reducing costs of adjustment caused by economic growth
Stability of farm incomes

These objectives are not more precise than those included in the Treaty of Rome. I believe, however, that each has measurable implications and programmes and policies can be analyzed in terms of their accomplishments with respect to them. The discussion, except as noted, is intended to apply to the agricultural policies of the industrial countries as a generic group since there is a great deal of similarity among both policy approaches and objectives.

Food Security

Food security is an appropriate objective of national policy. Policy-makers who follow policies that endanger national food security should be condemned. This seems so self-evident that one can assume that policy-makers do not knowingly pursue such policies unless a much higher-priority objective is being sought. The policy issue is not food security as an objective but how it is to be achieved. In many countries, food self-sufficiency and food security are considered to be synonymous. As can be readily demonstrated, the two are not the same; food self-sufficiency does not assure food security. As noted later, the history of the last half-century shows conclusively that even in industrial countries food self-sufficiency and food security are far from the same.

Food security has been an important objective of agricultural policies of most European and Asian countries for the past century or more. In the past, as now, it was pursued primarily through trade policies, namely by controlling or influencing imports and exports and by providing incentives for increasing domestic agricultural production. Wars and threats of wars, embargoes and blockades constituted serious threats to the food supplies of many countries. It was quite natural that countries should find ways of seeking 'safe and secure' food supplies by encouraging domestic production of important staple food products such as cereals and, at later times, as dietary habits changed, sugar, fats and oils and meats.

No more than a century ago, being self-sufficient in the production of the major sources of calories provided a substantial degree of food security, barring actual invasion and occupation by foreign troops. There is little evidence that there has been any new and systematic thinking about what is required for a secure food supply today and in the future, given the enormous changes that have affected both agriculture and the new threats not just to national security but to survival that have occurred during the past half-century. Although food security is a national objective that merits our acceptance, it is clearly reasonable to ask whether the means used to secure it are capable of meeting that objective or whether other policies would provide the same or greater degree of food security with lower cost to the country and with fewer adverse consequences to the international markets for agricultural products.

Food security, in today's world, is sought by means that are generally inconsistent with the rules governing international commerce that are intended to prevent the use of quantitative restrictions on imports and exports that destabilize international market prices. Instead it seems to be an accepted mode of behaviour for countries to manipulate their imports and/or exports of farm products in an effort to stabilize domestic supplies and prices. In so doing, of course, the supplies available to others are destabilized and may be seriously threatened. Thus it is perhaps not too surprising that when major exporters either impose embargoes on exports or follow price policies that assure domestic consumers favoured access to domestic production, that importing countries should turn to domestic solutions to the problem of food security. In effect, both exporting and importing countries have been guilty of attempting to assure food supplies for their own citizens without concern for the effect that their actions may have on other and frequently much poorer people.

It is essential that there be a careful appraisal of what constitutes food security in today's world. Is it self-sufficiency in food production or even creating a production surplus that is exported? The answer would be in the affirmative only if a country were also self-sufficient or largely so in the sources of the inputs used in agricultural production. Modern agriculture utilizes large amounts of energy in the form of fuel to run motors, to manufacture fertilizer, insecticides and herbicides and to process, transport and store food products. Unless a country has security of supply of energy or the farm inputs produced with it, food self-sufficiency under normal conditions provides for very limited food security. If, in addition, the country imports significant percentages of its livestock feed, its vulnerability is increased in the case of an international crisis leading to military conflicts.

An evaluation of self-sufficiency as the means of achieving food security must take into account the hazards that may affect a country's food security. The hazards that affect food security are generally of two sorts – those due to the actions of countries and those due to nature. One set of hazards is due to national measures that limit access to the available supplies of world food. Extreme and spectacular examples are the use of embargoes, such as the soyabean embargo imposed by the United States in 1973 or the various grain embargoes that the United States imposed on the Soviet Union during the 1970s and in 1980. A less spectacular example includes programmes that assure domestic consumers preferred access to a country's supplies through a price below world market levels such as was done in Australia and Canada in the early 1970s. A third example occurs when a high-income country or a group of countries assure their consumers that they will have a supply of food equal to their demand at fixed prices regardless of variations in their own production or in world food supplies. Price policies in Japan and the European Community function in this way for several important food products, as does the United States sugar programme. If such a commitment is met by varying imports or exports to offset the variability of domestic supply and demand, food insecurity is increased for the rest of the world.

A second major hazard is one that is seldom discussed, at least as it relates to the food supply. This is the possibility of a major war affecting two or more continents and perhaps culminating in a nuclear war. From what we are now told by the experts concerning the effects of a nuclear war, the food security options are very limited. Food self-sufficiency does not appear to be one of them. Such a war is likely to be relatively brief and would result in enormous damage to the infrastructure that is required by modern agriculture as well as by most other aspects of life. If food could not be imported during or following such a

conflagration, neither could energy. Thus self-sufficiency in food production based on imported energy would make the food supply nearly
as vulnerable as dependence on food imports.

The hazard to food security that is given most emphasis in policy
discussions is one that is of relatively little importance for the world as
a whole, namely annual variations in global food output due to climatic
conditions. Since the Second World War world food production has
been very stable around a rising trend. True, there are substantial
variations in regional or national food output, but unfavourable
growing conditions in one area are generally offset by favourable
growing conditions elsewhere. If there were few barriers to international trade in food, national food insecurity would be largely
eliminated. It is more than a little ironic that the most important cause
of international market instability is the national policies of achieving
domestic price stability and food security by managing imports and
exports.

There are alternative approaches for food security. Against the first
type of hazard, namely instability of prices and supplies resulting from
national policies, there are two main lines of approach. One is through
negotiations in which the importing countries make it a condition for
their reducing their protection levels that the major exporters agree to
forgo their policies that give domestic consumers first access to
domestic supplies and/or protect their consumers from variations in
world supply and demand, even when some of those variations arise in
their own country. If there is significant progress in the Uruguay
Round negotiations in reducing agricultural trade barriers, substantial
progress will have been made towards improving food security for
countries dependent on imports. Further, a strong position should be
taken in the GATT against embargoes – there is now a weak admoni-
tion against them – with severe penalties to be imposed if embargoes
are used except in case of actual military hostilities. The penalty could
be as punishing as the withdrawal of most-favoured-nation status for
the country imposing the embargo. This is perhaps extreme but a
strong penalty seems both justified and necessary.

As is true of so many actions taken in agricultural markets that fail
to achieve their objectives, a major study of the various embargoes
imposed on agricultural products by the United States found that the
embargoes did not achieve their stated objectives.[12] The results of the
study did not support the view commonly held by farmers in the United
States that the embargoes did substantial harm to them. It was not
possible to measure the effect of the embargoes, even when ineffective

in limiting access to United States supplies, in giving support to political efforts in importing countries to increase protection levels for agriculture. If the number of references made to the soyabean embargo by officials of the Ministry of Agriculture, Forestry and Fisheries of Japan were indicative of the policy responses, the responses would have been great indeed. But the embargo appears to have been used primarily to maintain political support for existing protection rather than for generating increased protection.

Storage represents the most reliable means to achieve some degree of food security in case of armed conflict. Storage should be considered for both imported agricultural inputs and food products. Storage is costly, although not nearly as costly as maintaining domestic production when it costs two or more times international market prices. It is quite feasible to store more than half a year's consumption needs for cereals, sugar and vegetable oils – the sources of a large share of the calories consumed in industrial market economies. A substantial element of food security in a conventional war exists in the stocks of meat animals that exist at any moment of time.

It is hard to understand the basis for the high degree of confidence with which policy-makers hold the view that food security is enhanced by food self-sufficiency. Both Japan and Germany were nearly self-sufficient in food supplies prior to the Second World War. Yet near the end of the war, and in the years following it, Japan was faced with near-famine conditions which would have become a serious famine without the assistance of the victor in the first few years after the war.[13] Germany also faced serious food shortages by the end of the war and could well have faced famine without the assistance of her former enemies.

Countries that pursue food self-sufficiency to achieve food security have incurred large costs in terms of reduced national income and in creating and sustaining tensions in the international trading system. But self-sufficiency does not ensure food security against the significant hazard, namely widespread military conflict. The only real assurances of food security are a liberal trading system for agricultural products and peace. Peace is the necessary condition.

Adequate Levels of Farm Family Incomes

I have interpreted the major income objective of agricultural protection to be to increase the level of farm family incomes rather than to increase the agricultural income of farm families. There are a number of reasons for this modification of the way the objective is often stated. One is the large and growing importance of non-agricultural or off-farm income in the incomes of farm families. In several of the industrial economies farm families receive nearly half or more of their incomes from off-farm sources. This situation prevails in West Germany, Italy, the United States, Japan and Canada.[14]

It can be argued that the importance of off-farm income in the income of farm families is really irrelevant to the issue of the adequacy of the incomes of the full-time farmers. This argument assumes that the agricultural policies are designed to assist full-time farmers, and the incomes of the part-time farmers are thus irrelevant. In a real sense this is true. But once you accept this approach then the income and employment data should be only for the full-time farmers or for those farmers that produce and sell some large percentage, such as 70 per cent, of all farm products. Data on the farms that are both full-time and produce a large fraction of all farm output are available only for a few countries. In most countries that emphasize agriculture and not farm people in the discussions of the effectiveness of farm programmes, income data for the full-time farm operators are not generally available. Table 10.3 gives data on the farm-operators' income by farm value of farm sales for the United States. The three largest sales groups accounted for 74 per cent of all farm sales in 1985 and had average net family incomes from all sources of $116 000. These are primarily full-time farm operators, with more than 85 per cent of their income coming from farm operations.

It could be argued that the data on net incomes of farm-operator families are biased by the small number of very large farms – the 1.1 per cent of farms with sales in excess of $500 000. These farms do generate large incomes. If, however, the income data are for the approximately 12.5 per cent of the farms with sales of $100 000 to $499 999, net incomes averaged $71 000 with more than 80 per cent from farming. In 1987 the average family incomes of this group of farm operators had increased to $85 000.

It is obvious from the data in Table 10.3 that the commercial farm operators that depend primarily on farming for their income have relatively high incomes. True, policy-makers would attribute part of these incomes to price supports and subsidies, although it is arguable that in the absence of such programmes in the long run the family incomes of the farmers that produced 70 per cent or more of national agricultural output would be approximately what such incomes are with the programmes.[15] Such farms are operated by highly competent entrepreneurs who would not long accept lower returns for the use of resources in agriculture than they could obtain elsewhere in the economy. If such farms had lower incomes, it would be due to the decline in the value of assets, such as land and buildings, that have few alternative uses outside agriculture. While the rate of return on such assets would be the same with or without the programmes, with the lower output prices the value of the assets would be less, and thus some decline in total income would occur.

The concentration of agricultural production in a relatively small percentage of large farms in North America is greater than in Japan and in Western Europe. But even in Japan in 1984, 30 per cent of the farms produced 70 per cent of farm output.[16] This includes all the full-time farms and all part-time farms where the farm income exceeds the off-farm income. But the average incomes of the full-time farm families from all sources are not higher than non-farm incomes, while for both groups of part-time farm families average incomes are above the average for non-farm families. In fact, the lowest-income farm families in Japan are the full-time farmers and their incomes are significantly below the average for non-farm households.[17] According to Yujiro Hayami full-time farms are being operated increasingly by individuals who have been part-time farmers, but become full-time farmers when they retire from their non-farm jobs. Consequently many full-time farms are retirement farms. As Professor Hayami states: 'the numbers of full-time households holding no members below 65 years of age increased sharply in recent years, from 196 000 in absolute numbers (or 32 per cent of the total number of full-time farms) in 1980 to 237 000 or 38 per cent [in 1985]'.[18] To put these percentages in perspective, in 1980 only 9 per cent of the Japanese population was 65 years or older. Consequently, it is evident that the percentage of full-time farm-operator households with all members 65 years and older had to be several times as large as the percentage of the members of the national labour force who were in this age group. This characteristic of the full-time farms is almost certainly the reason why the part-time farms with main income from farming accounting for the same percentage of all farms as the full-time farms (each 15 per cent) produced 40 per cent of all farm output while the full-time farms produced just 29 per cent.[19]

In Japan and in other countries where many farms, including many full-time farms, are operated by the retired or semi-retired, current farm price-support and subsidy programmes contribute to their family incomes. They do so by maintaining farm land values at higher levels than would otherwise prevail and most families in this situation own their farms. Thus these families gain from the higher return to land. They also gain, relative to younger farmers, because if the price supports were removed they would be less likely to find alternative uses for their labour, assuming that they even made an effort to do so. In other words, the older farmers receive substantial rents from high price supports because their resources generally lack profitable alternative uses while the younger farmers, if given time to adjust, can find alternative uses for their labour and capital either in agriculture or outside. It is rather odd that the primary beneficiaries of agricultural protection are the owners of land and the older members of the farm labour force. Providing the older farmers with an acceptable return for their labour has the disadvantage that doing so delays the structural adjustment that would occur if such farmers actually ceased farming. While eventually the land will be made available to younger farmers to expand their farm size, it would assist the necessary adjustments if the process were not delayed by agricultural policies.

The analytical model that explains why price-support and subsidy programmes will not have any long-run effect on the return to farm labour and capital was presented in Chapter 9. This model explains the phenomena noted by the Commission of the European Community in its annual reports on the agricultural situation, namely that real net value added per person employed in agriculture had not increased since 1975. Between 1975 and 1985 farm-gate prices relative to purchased input prices fell very modestly, perhaps by 7 per cent, while real net value added in agriculture declined by approximately 20 per cent.[20] The decline in measured employment was parallel to the decline in real net value added, so that the real net value added per worker was approximately constant for the Community of Ten. Factor productivity, as measured by the ratio of total output to total inputs, probably increased by nearly 2 per cent annually, although the Commission appears not to have access to such a measure. Consequently with productivity change occurring at a higher absolute rate than the decline in real farm prices, if the level and change in farm prices were a major determinant for net farm incomes, real value added per worker should have increased in the years following 1975. But this did not occur. On the basis of available data, it is not obvious what did happen. It is highly probable that the quality of the farm labour force declined due to increased average age and that the importance of off-farm incomes grew during the period. Again, it is quite clear that the absence of data on the incomes from all sources for farm families makes it impossible to know what is happening to the economic welfare of farm families in the

Community. But it is reasonable to assume that adjustments in the supply of mobile factors has been the major factor that has dominated the changes that have occurred in value added and farm employment.

If the measure of the effectiveness of the CAP is the value added per farm worker, taxpayers in the European Community could clearly question the effectiveness of the CAP in achieving its farm-income goals. In 1971, in terms of 1980 prices, the European Agricultural Guidance and Guarantee Fund (FEOGA) guaranteed expenditures were 3.4 billion ECUs; this had increased to 7.4 billion in 1975, to 11.7 billion in 1980 and to 15.4 billion in 1986.[21] This large increase in expenditures, which does not include expenditures by national governments of approximately the same amount nor the increase in costs borne by consumers, was sufficient only to maintain value added per worker at a roughly constant level while real incomes were increasing in the rest of the economy.

The large and increasing governmental expenditures and consumer costs were sufficient to prevent any significant decline in real prices received by farmers between 1970 and 1987, if the deflator used is the prices paid for the means of production. The Commission of the European Community uses three different deflators, often without bothering to state which deflator is being used. The other two deflators – the consumer price index and the implicit price deflator for the gross domestic product – indicate a significant decline in real prices received. If the consumer price index is used, real farm prices declined by 25 per cent between 1975 and 1986 instead of the 3.5 per cent decline indicated by using the prices paid for the means of production as the deflator. Depending on the deflator used, it can be said that the large costs of the CAP prevented any significant decline in real farm prices or that, in spite of the CAP, real farm prices declined by a quarter.

These data provide a discouraging picture of the effectiveness of the CAP in increasing the returns to mobile resources engaged in farming. The increase in the value of farm output between 1975 and 1986 of about 15 per cent was more than absorbed by increased costs to the farmer – intermediate consumption increased at the same rate as output and depreciation at a faster rate than output, as agriculture became more capital-intensive. The significant increases in governmental expenditures on the CAP and the increase in farm production were insufficient to prevent a decline in real net value added in agriculture and it was only because of a 20 per cent decline in farm employment that real net value added per farm worker remained constant over the period.

This recitation of the very high cost of the CAP compared with its minimal achievements in increasing per-worker income from agriculture is not intended to imply that other countries, such as the United States, had farm programmes that were any more successful. Governmental expenditures for farm price-support and income-support programmes also increased sharply between 1971 and the late 1980s. In 1971 such expenditures were $6.4 billion, in 1975 $1.0 billion, in 1980 $3.2 billion, but then they increased rapidly to $15.9 billion in 1985, $22.6 billion in 1986 and then declined to $19.1 billion in 1987 and to $14.7 billion in 1988. Deflated or real prices received by farmers, including direct government payments, declined by 18 per cent during the 1970s and an additional 12 per cent between 1980 and 1987 for a total decline of 28 per cent. The deflator used was prices paid for production items, although in the United States the difference between the prices-paid index and either the GDP deflator or the consumer price index between 1971 and 1986 is at most 6 per cent and thus much smaller than the differences in the European Community.

If one uses a measure of labour input in the United States somewhat comparable with the 'annual work unit' used in the European Community, value added per worker fell by about 10 per cent during the 1970s and then increased in the mid-1980s so that by 1986 it was somewhat more than 10 per cent higher than in 1970. If this were all that happened to the returns to farm-operator families over this period of time, then one could seriously question the effectiveness of the large expenditures that were incurred. The increase in value added per unit of work is probably more than can be credited to the programmes since real value added in agriculture declined by more than 15 per cent between 1970 and 1986. The increase in value added per unit of work was due to the decline in labour of 29 per cent, an adjustment for which the farm programmes deserve little or no credit.[22]

Stable Prices for Consumers

Policy-makers often claim that stable prices are beneficial for consumers. The socialist countries have given great emphasis, often at great cost, to maintaining stable prices for many consumption items. In the Soviet Union, for example, prices for energy and housing have remained unchanged for more than five decades while the prices of bread, meat and other major food items have been unchanged for more than a quarter-century. Since these prices have been held constant in nominal terms and there has been some degree of inflation, very large subsidies have been required to maintain them. But governments other than those in the socialist countries emphasize the importance of stable prices for consumers and often undertake extensive intervention in markets to achieve such stability. In the European Community and Japan, for example, stable prices and assured supply at those prices is the primary benefit that consumers obtain for their acceptance of the price supports and subsidies for farmers.

Why are stable prices considered to be beneficial for consumers? It is sometimes argued that consumers find it difficult to respond to prices that vary significantly from one period of time to another. But what is not ever addressed is whether consumers' interests are best served by stability of prices of individual commodities or by stability of prices generally. In OECD countries stable consumer prices for individual food products are always associated with higher prices than would prevail in the absence of the farm price and subsidy policies that make the stable prices possible. It can be argued that consumers would be better off if price stability were defined more broadly to refer to the stability of an overall price index, such as the consumer price index or the wholesale price index.

The argument that consumers benefit from or prefer stable prices assumes that price stability can be achieved at no cost. Even if stable consumer prices were achieved without enhancing the return to farmers, food prices would be increased due to the costs of the interventions required to provide stable prices. These costs are well-known – the costs of storage, the costs of trade interventions that are required or the losses due to the destruction of excessive supplies of perishable products that cannot be sold at the stable consumer price.

It is important to distinguish between the two aspects of stable prices – stability and level. Even if it were true that consumers gained from stable prices when the level reflected the long-run equilibrium prices, it does not follow that consumers gain when stable prices are above the level indicated. Furthermore, stable prices for consumers in one country may be bought at the cost of greater instability for consumers and producers in other countries. When stable prices are achieved by varying imports and exports, consumers and producers do not react to changing world conditions of demand and supply since the prices they face are not permitted to change. Thus all the variations in such conditions are imposed on others, including those that arise in the country that stabilizes prices.

But it is not obvious that all consumers gain from stable prices. If consumers support stable prices, it is probably the middle and higher income consumers who do so. In a classic article in the *Quarterly Journal of Economics* published almost half a century ago, Frederick Waugh showed that many consumers, especially low-income consumers, gain from unstable prices so long as the mean of the price distribution does not change.[23] Assume that you are a low-income consumer and that your preferences are such that you do not consume any of a given product, say strawberries, at the stable price of $1 per box. Assume that without government intervention that the price of strawberries was equally likely to be $0.50, $1.00 or $1.50. Your preferences are such that you would be willing to pay $0.60 for a box of strawberries and thus if you pay $0.50 you have a consumer's surplus of $0.10 per box. You are not adversely affected when strawberries go to one or the other of the higher prices since you won't buy any at either price. Waugh's argument was somewhat more sophisticated than this, but the example gives the gist of it. Assuming that the average level of consumer prices is the same with either stable or varying prices, the consumer who has the time and/or the inclination to devote time to shopping will gain from prices that vary from time to time while the consumer who does not wish to devote time to shopping or 'finding bargains' could lose from variable prices. It is quite likely that the first group will include individuals with low incomes who place less value on their time while the second group are those with higher incomes and greater emphasis on the value of their time. Stable prices, I conclude, benefit higher-income consumers at the cost of lower-income consumers. Such an outcome is not all that uncommon in societies, whether they be democratic or not.

Stable Prices for Producers

By any reasonable measure the price policies followed by the United States, Canada, the European Community and Japan have reduced the variability of farm prices compared with the variability before the price policies were adopted. Stable producer prices presumably have two advantages: (i) stable prices make it easier for farmers to allocate their resources in a manner that is optimal for them and (ii) stable prices are desirable because of their contribution to stability of farm incomes. Leaving aside for the moment that it is the certainty or reliability of price expectations rather than the stability of prices that reduces mistakes in resource allocation, stable prices have been desired because it was believed that by stabilizing prices farmers could be insulated to some significant degree from the effects of wide fluctuations of prices on incomes. The price fluctuations arose from variations in production (supply) and demand and were potentially quite large due to the short-run low price elasticities of both supply and demand. This was particularly a problem when the domestic market was isolated from international markets. But opening up the domestic market has generally not been considered an appropriate response to price instability because of the view that international market prices are abnormally variable.

While stable prices may assist the individual farmer to maximize his income from his available resources by allocating them to his best advantage, if the stable prices are established without regard to the alternatives for obtaining the same products at lower cost, then there will be overall inefficiency in the use of the resources. If, as is the general case in industrial countries, farm prices are above their equilibrium values, resources will be inefficiently utilized in agriculture and the welfare of the economy would be increased if fewer resources were devoted to agriculture. In fact price stability and certainty may increase the resource waste when the prices themselves are inappropriate. Efficient resource use on the individual farm results in efficient use for the economy only when the 'prices are right'.

Price stability is desired primarily because it is assumed to provide for income stability. But what concept of income is it relevant to stabilize? It seems to me that gross value added, which is gross sales minus current purchased inputs, is not an appropriate concept. Much of gross value added is not income to either farm-operator families or employed farm workers – in some instances half or less of gross value added is retained as net income. Net value added, which is gross value added minus depreciation plus adjustments for certain taxes and subsidies, is less objectionable but even so, it includes payments to non-farm recipients in the form of interest and rent. The most reasonable measures of income to use in determining whether relatively stable output prices result in farm income stability, are the net income of farm operators from farming and that net income plus wages paid to employees. Since the decisions are made by the farm operators, I have chosen to emphasize the net agricultural income of farm-operator families.

Data on year-to-year changes in net agricultural income from farming are given in Table 11.1 for the United States, Denmark, France, Germany and the United Kingdom. If farm-gate prices are deflated by the prices of production items the largest year-to-year variations in prices received for 1973 through 1986 were 8 per cent for

Germany, 18 per cent for France, 14 per cent for the Netherlands and 17 per cent for Denmark. This was for the change from 1973 to 1974. The next largest price change was no greater than 8 per cent.

Table 11.1   Year-to-year changes in real net farm-operator income in the United States, Denmark, France, Germany and the United Kingdom, 1974 to 1986[a] (per cent)

Year[b]	United States	Denmark	France	Germany	United Kingdom
1974	− 27	− 16	− 15	− 18	− 24
1975	− 15	− 41	− 13	20	0
1976	− 26	− 6	− 1	5	11
1977	− 8	22	− 2	− 5	− 12
1978	18	− 1	1	− 6	− 11
1979	0	− 78	0	− 17	− 22
1980	− 47	− 89	− 19	− 22	6
1981	52	754	− 4	8	12
1982	− 21	196	28	30	6
1983	− 45	− 46	− 13	− 34	10
1984	142	154	− 7	27	42
1985	− 2	− 14	− 8	− 22	− 48
1986	13	− 10	0	17	17

[a]Net income of farm-operator families from farming due to production for the calendar year with net incomes in current national prices deflated by gross national or domestic product price deflators.
[b]The year indicated is the second year of a comparison. For example, the 1974 row shows the change in real incomes from 1973 to 1974. The percentage change is calculated as the ratio of one year's income to the prior year's income minus one and multiplied by 100 to transform into percentages.
Sources: *Economic Indicators of the Farm Sector: National Financial Summary, 1985* (Washington: United States Department of Agriculture, 1986), pp. 14 and 24; *Agricultural Incomes in the European Community in 1985 and Since 1973* (Luxembourg: Statistical Office of the European Community, 1986); and *Green Europe Newsflash*, Commission of the European Community, Brussels, April 1986.

The year-to-year changes in the net income of farm-operator families from farming have been substantially greater than the annual variations in prices received by farmers. The most unstable pattern of net farm incomes occurred in Denmark with a combined decline in 1979 and 1980 of 98 per cent with a combined increase for the next two years of nearly 1500 per cent followed by a decline of 46 per cent and a subsequent increase of 154 per cent. The Denmark pattern is clearly extreme, yet it may be noted that in four years (1977 to 1980) the decline of net farm-operator income in Germany was 42 per cent, while in one year less the decline for the United Kingdom was 39 per cent.

The variability of net farm-operator income in the United States was larger than in any of the European Community members except for Denmark. In two years (1980 and 1983) adverse weather was a factor in the United States. But in the majority of the year-to-year comparisons the major factor responsible for the income variations were the consequence of macro-economic variables, especially interest rates. But whatever were the factors responsible for the large variability in net farm incomes, it is obvious that price policies were ineffective in achieving the objective of providing income stability for farm operators.

Another indication that the price policies of the European Community and the United States have not achieved a substantial degree of economic stability for farmers is given by the year-to-year changes in the prices of farm land. Table 11.2 provides such data for the United States, two large agricultural regions, and for five Community countries. Land price variations were substantial, including several instances of declines for periods of four to six years – the United States, France, the Netherlands, Denmark and, more moderately, Germany. Land prices are influenced by expectations concerning land returns and interest rates. In the early 1980s expectations turned pessimistic while both nominal and real interest rates increased. Consequently land prices declined significantly. During the 1970s expectations were optimistic and real interest rates were low and in some cases negative. As a consequence, real land prices increased, especially from 1972 on. The large increase in real land prices in the United Kingdom during 1973 apparently reflected the expectations of the income effects of joining the Community as well as optimistic views concerning future developments in world food demand and supply.

Given a little thought, it should be obvious that stability of output prices, even in real terms, is not sufficient to provide for net farm income stability. Due to the importance of borrowed funds, changes in interest rates can have significant impacts on net income. In the United States expenditures on interest increased from $8.5 billion in 1977 to $21.8 billion in 1982; net farm operator income in 1982 was $17.1 billion. The increase in debt and in interest rates were approximately of equal importance in growth of the total cost of borrowed funds. Further, when national output varies due to natural factors, stable prices eliminate the usual market response to a change in supply. The

Table 11.2   Year-to-year changes in real farmland prices, 1971–86[a] (per cent)

	United States	Corn Belt	Northern Plains	United Kingdom[b]	France	Nether-lands	Denmark	Germany[c]
1971	−2	−4	−4	−12				−3
1972	2	1	1	6	4			10
1973	5	5	5	87	5			7
1974	12	16	17	18	4	13		15
1975	2	4	10	−35	−	34	6	−3
1976	6	15	10	−23	3	−8	8	5
1977	9	23	7	7	2	40	3	14
1978	2	2	−4	30	1	30	−11	11
1979	8	5	7	8	5	−1	−5	14
1980	7	7	8	10	−12	−13	−14	13
1981	1	−1	1	−12	−9	−28	−25	5
1982	−6	−14	−4	−	−11	−17	−21	−10
1983	−8	−17	−7	5	−10	11	−5	−1
1984	−5	−8	−9	−8	−8	31	5	−1
1985	−16	−27	−24	−10	−6	7	16	−6
1986	−15	−17	−18	−17	−7	6	13	−8

Note   A dash denotes a change of less than 1 per cent. A blank means data not available. The percentage changes are for the year ending – thus the 1971 figures are for changes from 1970 to 1971.
[a]Prices in national currencies deflated by gross domestic product implicit price deflator.
[b]England and Wales from 1971–77; England from 1978.
[c]Data prior to 1974 not comparable with 1975 and later.
Sources: *Agricultural Outlook*, United States Department of Agriculture, Washington, June 1986; *Agricultural Statistics, 1980* (Washington: United States Department of Agriculture, 1981); and *The Agricultural Situation in the Community*, Commission of the European Community, Brussels, various reports.

experience of corn producers in the United States in 1988 illustrates this point. The target price for corn was $115 per ton. Corn production in 1988 was about 40 per cent below the previous year and the market price of corn increased by about 70 per cent or somewhat more than $40 per ton. But the deficiency payment for the 1987 corn crop was $43 per ton. In the absence of special drought-relief payments, the corn farmer gained nothing from the price increase since it was almost exactly offset by the decline in deficiency payments. There was no price offset to the decline in production.

But the result was not due to the particular characteristics of the United States price-support programme. Exactly the same result occurs when the market price is stabilized, as it is by the CAP, and national farm output falls. The reduction in output is offset quite directly either by increased imports or decreased exports in order to maintain a constant market price. Thus gross income declines by the same percentage as the decline in output. But since production costs that are insensitive to the output decline are from 50 to 70 per cent of expected gross income, a 10 per cent decline in output could result in a decline in net income of a third. Similarly an increase in output of the same percentage with stable output prices can increase net farm operator income by a third. In other words, it should be obvious that it takes more than stable or certain output prices to achieve economic stability for agriculture. Further, it is difficult to know what degree of stability of income is most advantageous for the continued dominance of family farms in the agricultures of North America and Western Europe. There is some admittedly inconclusive evidence that family farms are more able effectively to deal with uncertainty and instability than are larger-than-family farms that depend upon hired managers and employ significant numbers of hired workers. This issue is relevant to the next section of this chapter dealing with the objective of maintaining a large and viable rural sector.

Maintaining a Large and Viable Rural Sector

There are several reasons why societies may desire a large and viable rural sector. There is a widespread view that there is something preferable about living and working in the countryside. There has been a stream of thought that maintained that urban or city living was clearly inferior to living in rural areas. Crime, decadence, family and personal instability and lack of community have been associated with cities while farm life has been idealized. Admittedly, most cultural and scientific achievements have been created in an urban environment. But the important point is that there is sufficient idealization of rural life to make its maintenance an acceptable political goal, especially for those who do not now or never have milked a cow in a draughty barn when the outside temperature was − 15 degrees Celsius. There has been an association of viable rural communities with the existence of family farms. Without assistance, it is argued, family farms will not long survive in competition with large and corporate-like farms.

If farm-support programmes were an important factor in maintaining rural communities, the effect would be evident in both the level and rate of change in farm employment. As is evident from the data in Chapters 4 and 5 agricultural protection has not been able to maintain the absolute level of farm employment in any industrial country against the adjustments that are associated with economic growth. But there should never have been a realistic expectation that agricultural protection could have prevented a decline in the relative and absolute levels of farm employment as economic growth occurs. If the programmes, however, have had any effect in enhancing the viability of rural sectors, they should have had the effect of having a measurable effect upon the rate of decline in farm employment and in the relative importance of agriculture in the economy.

There is no simple measure that is fully adequate for determining whether high levels of protection have a significant effect on strengthening rural communities. Presumably if we had a general equilibrium model of the economy that was sufficiently sophisticated to reflect the effects of three or more decades of agricultural protection on agricultural investment, productivity and labour employment, we could determine what changes had occurred. This is a much more complex undertaking than the general equilibrium models that project the effects of eliminating protection, starting from where the economies stood as of the early and mid-1980s. These models, which were briefly discussed in Chapter 10, project substantial declines in farm employment with the elimination of protection in Japan, Germany, Korea and the European Community generally. But it is not possible to start from where we are to determine what agricultural employment would have been and what rural communities would look like in, say, 1995 if there had been much lower levels of protection since the Second World War.

While this is not definitive, we can compare what has happened to agricultural employment in countries with significantly different levels of protection for the past three decades. Table 11.3 provides a rough comparison of protection levels at three dates, starting with the 1950s and ending with 1979–81. The data come from different sources and the absolute levels of protection may not be strictly comparable from period to period, but the relative rankings should be reasonably comparable. The measure used is rate of nominal protection, although an effort is made to include direct payments where these are important, especially in the United States. Table 11.4 gives data on the annual rates of change, in per cent, of farm employment. The countries are arranged in the approximate order of their protection levels during 1979–81, although within the European Community the countries are ranked by their level of protection in the mid-1950s.

Table 11.3   Estimated levels of nominal protection, 1956, 1965–67 and 1979–81 (per cent)

	1956	1965–67	1979–81
Australia			5
New Zealand			18
United States	2[a]	8[b]	19
Canada			31
Austria			75
European Community	16[d]	52[d]	75[c]
Denmark	3	5	
Ireland	4	3	
Netherlands	5	37	
Belgium	5	54	
Italy	16	64	
France	18	47	
West Germany	22	54	
United Kingdom	32	28	
Sweden	27	54	128[e]
Japan	42	76	146

[a] 1955.
[b] 1965–69.
[c] Protection level is for the Nordic countries, which includes Norway, Finland, Sweden and Switzerland.
[d] European Community of Six.
[e] European Community of Ten.
Sources: Gavin McCrone, *The Economics of Subsidizing Agriculture* (London: Allen & Unwin, 1962), p. 51; Richard W. Howarth, *Agricultural Support in Western Europe* (London: Institute of Economic Affairs, 1971), p. 29; and Eric Saxon and Kym Anderson, *Japanese Agricultural Protection in Historical Perspective*, Pacific Economic Paper No. 92 (Canberra: Australian National University, 1982), p. 29. The McCrone and Howarth estimates have been adjusted to measure protection in terms of international prices instead of domestic prices.
Masayoshi Honma and Yujiro Hayami, 'Structure of Agricultural Protection in Industrial Countries', in Kym Anderson and Hayami, *The Political Economy of Agricultural Protection* (London: Allen & Unwin, 1986); and *National Policies and Agricultural Trade* (Paris: OECD, 1987), p. 117. The PSEs for 1979–81 have been converted to nominal protection coefficients by dividing the PSE by 100-PSE and subtracting 100 from the result for each country.

If there were an effect of the level of protection on the rate of decline in farm employment, it is not evident from Table 11.4. The countries in the top part of the table have had lower rates of decline in farm employment since 1960 than those in the bottom part. For 1956–60, when protection rates were more similar than were the later ones, the

Table 11.4   Annual rates of change in farm employment, 1956 to 1986 by periods (per cent)

	1956–60	1961–70	1971–80	1981–86
Australia	—[a]	−0.4	−0.6	0.3
New Zealand	−	−0.4	0.6	1.2[c]
United States	−3.2	−4.4	−0.1	−0.9
Canada	−3.6	−2.7	−0.4	0.2
Austria	−	−4.8	−4.0	−2.2
European Community (9)	−3.2	−4.6	−3.4	−2.8
Denmark	−2.1	−3.2	−4.1	−2.1
Ireland	−2.5	−3.2	−3.0	−3.6
Netherlands	−2.7	−3.4	−1.6	0.1
Belgium	−3.7	−5.0	−4.3	−1.4
Italy	−3.8	−5.2	−2.9	−4.3
France	−3.6	−4.1	−3.9	−3.1
West Germany	−3.3	−4.6	−4.4	−1.1
United Kingdom	−1.7	−3.6	−2.0	−1.3
Sweden	−	−5.8	−2.8	−2.5[d]
Norway	−2.5	−3.6	−2.5	−0.9
Finland	−	−4.5	−4.1	−2.7
Switzerland	−4.6[b]	−3.7	−2.0	−0.9
Japan	−2.8	−4.5	−4.2	−3.2

Note   Data for 1956–60 are less accurate than for the later periods.
[a]A dash denotes not available from the same source as the other countries.
[b]1951 to 1960.
[c]1981 to 1985.
[d]Estimated by the author.
Sources: *Labour Force Statistics*, OECD, Paris, for 1954–64, 1957–67, 1964–84 and 1966–86.

rates of decline showed only small differences. A regression analysis was not undertaken because it was not obvious which variable was the exogenous one; the possibility cannot be ruled out that countries with high potential rates of decline of farm employment were the ones that either had or moved to high rates of protection. This undoubtedly explains, at least in part, the high rates of protection in Japan. Masayoshi Honma and Professor Hayami found in their analysis of protection levels that countries in which agriculture's comparative advantage had declined or was declining were the ones with the highest levels of protection.[24] In other words, in the countries in which resources would be drawn to other sectors of the economy from agriculture because productivity was increasing more rapidly elsewhere in the economy adopted increasing and higher protection levels.

Whether the level of protection is exogenous or endogenous, it is quite clear that relatively high rates of protection were not sufficient to cause rates of decline of farm employment that were below those of countries with lower rates of protection. For reasons indicated, the comparison of the two rates does not lead to a conclusive answer with respect to the relationships between levels of protection and the rates of employment decline in agriculture. But if we compare the rates of decline during the 1980s with the earlier periods, it can be inferred that conditions in the non-farm sector of the economy have an effect on the variable.

But it is a far stretch from concluding that significant reductions in farm employment, such as have been realized in North America and Western Europe in the past three decades, means the decline of rural communities. If the expectation that rural communities could not survive after agricultural employment reached some unspecified minimum level had been valid, in most industrial countries rural communities would have already lost their vitality. In several countries, agricultural employment has fallen to less than 3 per cent of total employment in the mid-1980s – Belgium, the United Kingdom and the United States – and in others to less than 5 per cent – Germany, the Netherlands and Canada in 1985. In France and Sweden the percentage of total employment in agriculture was 7 per cent.[25] What has happened to rural communities as employment on farms has been reduced to such low levels? The evidence seems very clear – rural communities appear to have held their own in terms of absolute population as agricultural employment has declined. In the United States the rural population was 54 million in 1950; it held at approximately that level until 1970 and during the 1970s it increased to 59.5 million. True, the rural population declined as a percentage of total population – from 36 per cent in 1950 to 26.5 per cent in 1970 and then remained at that percentage in 1980.[26]

The Canadian experience was very similar to that in the United States. The absolute population of rural communities was slightly higher in 1981 than in 1961 or subsequent census years. The rural population as a percentage of total population declined during the 1960s, but increased during the 1970s and ended at a little more than 24 per cent, down from 30 per cent in 1961. The absolute decline in the rural population of Japan was halted in the 1970s at 24 per cent of the total population. France's experience was similar to that of the three countries already discussed. The population of rural communities declined from 1962 to 1968, losing 2 million and declining from 37 per cent to 30 per cent of the total. But there was little decline between 1968 and 1982 – less than 3 per cent. In 1982 the rural population amounted to 27 per cent of the national population, surprisingly close to the other three countries.

Available data on employment in rural communities are not very plentiful. But for the industrial countries for which the United Nations *Demographic Yearbook* provides such data, it is obvious that the picture of rural communities as consisting primarily of farm people and workers is wide of the mark. In Canada, France, Japan and the United States for the latest period for which data are available, farm employment as a percentage of total rural employment varies from a low of 11 per cent in the United States to a high of 26 per cent in Japan.

Between 1940 and 1970 agricultural employment in the United States declined from 8.0 million to 3.0 million while total employment in rural areas increased from 17.5 million to 18.7 million. Consequently the growth of non-farm employment replaced every farm job that was lost plus a few more. In the period 1975–82 farm employment in France declined by 300 000 while total employment increased by 307 000. Thus twice as many non-farm jobs were created as farm jobs were lost.

Some of the increase in non-farm jobs in rural communities result from increased services to agriculture. While agriculture's share of national output has declined in the industrial countries, total farm production has continued to grow at about 2 per cent per year. This growth, combined with a decline in farm employment, means that more purchased inputs and services are required. Many of these inputs require local businesses to supply them. It is highly probable, though, that most of the increase in non-farm employment in rural communities has little to do with agriculture, but has located in rural areas because of what those areas have to offer. In France, for example, in 1982 male employment in manufacturing in rural areas was almost the same as in agriculture, while female employment in manufacturing was more than 80 per cent of the farm employment.

Reducing Costs of Adjustment

There can be no doubt that economic growth requires significant and rapid adjustment on the part of farm people and of agriculture. This has been well documented in Chapter 4 and in the previous section of this chapter. The required rate of adjustment of farm people and farming since the Second World War has been very rapid in the industrial countries. Because of the positive rate of population growth that prevailed in the 1940s through the 1960s in most of the countries and the rather higher birth rates in farm than urban areas, a 3 per cent per annum decline in farm employment meant that approximately 4 per cent of the potential labour force had to transfer from farm to non-farm jobs each year. The potential labour force includes those actually employed at the beginning of the year plus the new entrants that entered minus those who retired or died. A transfer of 4 per cent of the potential labour force every year for two or more decades imposes significant social and economic costs on farm people. Imagine the uproar that would occur in cities if every year 4 per cent of the work force found their jobs abolished. Yet such has been the fate of farm people even with the high rates of protection that have prevailed in many industrial countries.

I believe that a plausible case can be made for governmental intervention to reduce the costs of agricultural adjustment associated with economic growth. Agriculture is a declining industry and the rate at which it needs to decline is a function of the rate of economic growth in the economy as a whole. When agricultural employment accounts for a significant fraction of national employment, say a quarter or more, the adjustments can be and in many cases have been painful ones. The transfer of workers from farm to non-farm employment may occur only on the basis of a very large difference in labour earnings. When farm employment is a large percentage of total employment, many farm workers have less education and fewer valued work skills than their urban counterparts. Consequently, under these circumstances, it is possible to make a strong case for governmental intervention to ease the costs of adjustment.

Unfortunately agricultural protection does little more than attempt, largely unsuccessfully, to slow down the inevitable adjustment that is required if farm people are to share fully in the fruits of economic growth. The farm programmes associated with protection have seldom, if ever, recognized the need to assist farm people to adjust as required by economic growth. When agricultural employment accounts for a significant part of the total, governments have made little effort to assure that farm people can acquire the same level of human capital that is available to urban residents. Nor have governments given emphasis to employment services that had the objective of helping farm people find non-farm jobs. Nor have resources been spent to assist farm people to move to urban areas. In other words, the farm policies of industrial countries have emphasized product markets and, except for credit, have generally ignored the factor markets, especially the labour market. As I have argued, persuasively I hope, it is through the functioning of the labour market that the labour earnings of farm people are brought up to the earnings levels of non-farm workers and are kept in rough equality over time.

The ill-fated Mansholt Plan for the agriculture of the European Community included a major emphasis on assisting agriculture to adjust to changing conditions. Assistance was to be provided so that 5 million people could leave agriculture between 1970 and 1980 and do so with profit and dignity.[27] In addition, the plan called for farm enlargement to achieve efficient-sized farm units and for a reduction in the amount of land devoted to agriculture. But this far-sighted plan was criticized with such venom that it failed to generate the support required for its adoption.[28] Why an objective of a reduction in farm employment of 5 million in the decade of the 1970s was considered to be a subject of such derision and condemnation is hard to understand, since the reduction of farm employment during the 1960s in the Community of Six was 5.8 million, admittedly from a larger base level of employment. The actual reduction in employment during the 1970s was 2.8 million and would have been larger had the economies continued to grow at the same rate in the 1970s as during the 1960s.

In the economies with less than 7 per cent of their labour force engaged in agriculture, most of the adjustments required of labour due to economic growth have already occurred. This is not the case, of course, of the economies of southern Europe in which a quarter or more of the labour force is in agriculture as of the late 1980s. Even in industrial economies with a small minority of its workers in agriculture, however, reducing the level of protection can require significant adjustments of farm people and in agriculture. But these adjustments impinge on all resources now engaged in farming and are not primarily at the cost of labour. In devising programmes that would minimize the adverse impacts of making agricultural-support programmes more market-oriented, it is necessary to take into account the significant decline in land values and its effect upon the financial structure of agriculture. As has been argued in Chapter 7, there are significant excess resources in the agricultures of North America, Western Europe and Japan. It should be the function of agricultural policies to assist in removing these excess resources with a minimum of adverse consequences for persons now engaged in farming. This and related issues will be the subject of Chapter 12.

12 New Directions for Agricultural Policy in the Industrial Countries

Previous chapters, especially Chapters 9 and 11, have emphasized that the price-support and subsidy policies of the industrial countries have approached the farm income problem from the wrong end, so to speak. These policies attempt to improve the incomes of farm people by increasing demand for farm products and thus the demand for farm inputs. The critically important element determining the incomes of farm people and the returns on their resources are the conditions of factor supply. Over a period of years, supply conditions dominate demand conditions in determining the returns to farm resources. Demand conditions can have some influence over the quantities of resources engaged in agriculture, but, except for land, have no significant long-run effect on resource returns.

The existence of excess resources in agriculture is proof of the effect that demand has on the amounts of resources used in agriculture. But the benefits to farm people of having more resources employed in agriculture than could be sustained in the absence of protection are found solely in the return to land and/or in the value of a production quota. The cost to farm people is the insecurity that is generated by the excess resources held in agriculture by protection. What the political process gives, it can take away.

There is a presumption among policy-makers and representatives of farm groups in the industrial countries that the incomes of farm families are lower than those of non-farm families. As noted in Chapter 11 it is not possible to make a meaningful comparison between the incomes of farmers and non-farmers by comparing the incomes from agriculture of farm families with the total incomes of non-farm families. At a minimum, we must know the farm family incomes from all sources. Even that information is not adequate for meaningful comparisons because the characteristics of farm family members with respect to such relevant factors as age and education may be quite different than that of the comparison group. Age and education are relevant because they influence earnings or income.

Causes of Low Farm Incomes

Why are farm incomes low, if such is the case? There are two primary reasons that could explain it. One is that the rate of return to farm resources is less than in the non-farm sector. This would mean that capital invested in farmland or machines earned less than capital invested in land or machines earned in the non-farm sector or that the real earnings of workers of the same age, education, sex and health differ between those engaged in agriculture or in non-farm activities.

The other reason for low farm incomes could be that farm people have a smaller total of human and non-human resources than do non-farm families. Consequently even if the resources they own receive the same return as elsewhere in the economy, the incomes of farm families will be below that of non-farm families. Agricultural protection does not contribute significantly to increasing the human resources of farm families, although the value of owned land can be increased. An increase in land values, however, is of no benefit to farmers who rent their land, for the rise in land values is a consequence of either actual or anticipated rent increases, nor for farmers who acquire farmland by purchase after protection has been increased.

Lack of Resources

Where there are low incomes of farm families it is generally due to their possession of a smaller total stock of human and non-human resources. This is the primary source of any income discrepancy. It is primarily limited human resources that are responsible for the lower level of incomes. On the average, in the industrial countries farm families have more non-human capital than the average non-farm family, although the distribution of such capital among farm families is highly unequal, as it is among non-farm families. Hired farm workers have little non-human capital and the same is true of many of the farm families operating small farms.

The primary reason for the limited human resources in agriculture has been the difference in the educational attainment of farm and non-farm workers. In most industrial countries this difference has been eliminated, or nearly so, for new entrants to the labour force, but the negative effects will linger on for many years because many farm operators and workers received their education 20 to 40 years ago. For example, in the United States by 1970 the median number of years of

schooling for males 25 to 44 years of age living on farms was 12.1 years
compared with 12.5 years for all such persons in the United States. But
for males 45 years and older the median years completed by farm
residents in 1970 was only 8.6 years compared with 10.7 for the entire
population.

Differences in the amount and quality of education available to farm
and non-farm youth have been substantial in the industrial countries
until the last one or two decades. The differences in the amount and
quality of education in the past has been very great. The situation in
France in the mid-1950s may well have been typical of industrial
countries when farm workers accounted for approximately a quarter of
all workers. In 1954 male farm workers constituted 26.5 per cent of the
total male working population. Of the total number of males 14 years
and older, farmers accounted for only 17 per cent of those who had
successfully passed the primary school certificate or exam, only 2 per
cent of the males with university degrees and only 3 per cent of males
who had technological diplomas.[1]

The authors of *Production and Uses of Selected Farm Products in
France* commented as follows:[2] 'Though there has been progress, high
school and university attendance by farm children is still very low. One
of the main reasons for the lag is the inadequacy of elementary schools
in rural areas. In some 10,000 elementary schools, a single school
master can still be found teaching. . . . No wonder that less than half of
the farmers' children got through their CEP (primary school certificate)
in 1960.' The authors noted that as of the time – the early 1960s –
progress was being made in closing the single-teacher schools and in
increasing the number of farm children that were being educated in
nearby towns. But the important point is that a significant part of any
differential between farm and non-farm incomes that existed during the
1960s and 1970s and even the 1980s was a result of decisions unrelated
to agricultural policy and created a situation that agricultural protection could do little or nothing to alleviate. Yet this fact was never
recognized in the CAP or French agricultural policy, just as it was not
recognized in the United States or any other industrial economy.

For the average individual, be he farmer or not, by far the most
important resource that he or she owns is his or her mental and labour
capacities. This is a fact that is entirely neglected in agricultural policy.
Approximately two-thirds of the net income received by farm-operator
families is a return to labour and management.[3] Governments have
policies to improve farm land, to create farm land, to subsidize new
buildings, to provide low-cost credit to buy land or to encourage

farmers to buy new and improved machines. But few governments view the education of youth in farm areas as an aspect of farm policy. Some attention is given to vocational education for *agricultural* employment and this should not be neglected even though in recent decades as many as three-fourths of all farm youth have taken non-farm jobs on completing their schooling or very soon thereafter. At a given time, a significant part of the income differential between farm and non-farm families that is of concern to policy-makers is the result of neglect of rural education one to four decades earlier. Little can be done about past errors, but much more could be done than is now apparent in the lower-income industrial countries to prevent the same conclusion from applying to them in the early decades of the next century.

Modern agriculture is highly complex and dynamic. Theodore Schultz has argued that one of the important values of education is that it improves an individual's capacity to deal with disequilibrium or unanticipated change. Finis Welch, of the University of California at Los Angeles, found that the returns to higher education – college or university level – were of the same order of magnitude in agriculture as in the rest of the economy. Professor Welch found that the average income of a college graduate engaged in farming was 1.62 times that of a high-school graduate also engaged in farming. For the nation as a whole the ratio was 1.51.[4] The increasing complexity of agriculture and the continuing rapid change which it is undergoing may well increase the relative return to higher education in the years ahead.

Income Differentials and Migration

In the original edition of this book it was noted that there was a rather firmly-held view that migration off farms had been very rapid during the 1950s and 1960s and yet the income differential between farm and non-farm families had remained approximately unchanged.[5] Quotations to this effect were taken from the writings of three reasonably prominent agricultural economists – Albert Simantov, Dale Hathaway and the present writer. Each of us expressed both our surprise and concern at what appeared to be a remarkably high rate of out-migration from agriculture and the little apparent increase in farm relative to non-farm labour earnings. Based on my personal experience with agricultural policy-makers in the United States, the seeming failure of out-migration to improve farm labour earnings was used to support farm programmes that functioned by increasing the demand for and the prices of farm products. It was generally ignored that the high price support and supply management policies were being pursued at the same time out-migration was proceeding at a rapid pace and thus if one arrived at conclusions on the basis of the crude empirical observations with no underlying analytical framework, it would have to be concluded that the policies were no more effective than out-migration in improving farm labour incomes. If out-migration failed to equalize earnings, then the price-support policies failed as well.

We have data for the United States that show very clearly that the earnings differential between farm and non-farm families narrowed significantly from the 1950s through the 1970s. Similar data are available for Japan. One set is presented in Table 12.1 and the other in Table 12.2. The pattern of increase in the ratio of the incomes of farm families to those of non-farm families were remarkably similar, given the significant differences in agricultural policies.

Both of these income comparisons include the income of farm families from all current sources. Neither includes changes in the value of capital assets, such as the value of land. But both series clearly indicate that farm family incomes from all sources have increased relative to non-farm family incomes since the 1950s. Thus the pessimism expressed in the 1950s and 1960s was unwarranted; we simply didn't understand all that was occurring.

The data for Japan in Table 12.2 make it clear that the use of data on relative GNP per worker in agriculture and in the rest of the economy can be very misleading if interpreted to imply anything about the relative income positions of farm families. Compare the following data on GDP per worker as a percentage of the same figure for the rest of the economy: 1960, 37; 1970, 31; 1975, 40; 1980, 34; and 1985, 34. If such data meant anything in the first place, how can one reconcile them with the information in Table 12.2 that indicates an increase in the ratio of farm to non-farm per capita incomes of 68 per cent in 1960 to 91 per cent in 1970 and in excess of 100 per cent for 1980 and later years? The answer is simple. You can't reconcile them and the reason is primarily the lack of comparability in measurement of labour input in the two sectors.

Further data derived from the household surveys in Japan are worthy of note. From these data it is possible to estimate the annual income of workers in farm families who are engaged in farming and those who are primarily in non-farm activities. If all the farm income on their farm is attributed to workers who are engaged only in

Table 12.1 Comparisons of incomes of farm and non-farm families in the United States, selected years 1955 to 1986

Year	Per capita personal income of farm population			Per capita disposable personal income[a]		Farm as percentage of non-farm per capita disposable income
	Farm sources	Non-farm sources	All sources	Farm population	Non-farm population	PER CENT
			DOLLARS			
1955	590	325	915	810	1775	45.6
1960	711	463	1174	1026	2034	50.4
1965	968	860	1828	1606	2505	64.1
1970	1333	1495	2828	2421	3439	70.4
1975	2994	2611	5605	4854	5083	95.5
1980	2950	4717	7667	6471	8074	80.1

AVERAGE INCOMES

Year	Farm-operator households	US households	Farm as percentage of US average
1970	9 472	10 001	95
1975	15 694	13 779	114
1980	18 434	21 063	88
1985	29 436	29 066	101
1986	34 246	30 759	111

[a]Disposable income is income after the deduction of taxes. Represents income from all sources.
Sources: *Economic Indicators of the Farm Sector: National Financial Summary, 1983* (Washington: United States Department of Agriculture, 1984); and *Economic Indicators of the Farm Sector: Farm Sector Review, 1986* (Washington: United States Department of Agriculture, 1988).

Table 12.2   Comparisons of incomes of farm households and urban workers in Japan, selected years 1955 to 1985

Year	Farm household income (000 yen)				Urban worker household income (000 yen)		Relative income (%)	
	Per household							
	Farm	Off-farm[a]	Total (A)	Per capita (B)	Per household (C)	Per capita (D)	Per household (A/C)	Per capita (B/D)
1955	256	102	358	57	350	74	102	77
1960	225	224	449	78	502	115	89	68
1965	365	470	835	157	797	194	105	81
1970	508	1084	1592	326	1390	358	115	91
1975	1146	2815	3961	867	2897	760	137	114
1980	952	4651	5603	1273	4254	1111	132	115
1985	1065	5860	6926	1596	5388	1422	128	112
1985								
Full-time	2520	1969	4489	1207	5388	1422	83	85
Part-time I	4124	3275	7399	1465	5388	1422	137	103
Part-time II	495	6971	7466	1682	5388	1422	139	118

[a]Off-farm income includes private grants and government transfer payments.
Source: Yujiro Hayami, *Japanese Agriculture Under Siege* (London: Macmillan, 1988), pp. 92–3.

own-farming, and if the non-farm income is attributed to individuals who are engaged in farming but have some non-farm employment plus those who only have non-farm employment, the data for 1983 are as follows. The agricultural income per farm worker was 770 000 yen and the wages and salary per worker was 1 970 000 yen. The income per farm worker, as defined, was just 39 per cent of the income of workers in farm families from non-farm sources, primarily wages and salaries. In the majority of cases, these workers come from the same families. In the original edition of this book a similar comparison was presented for 1967.[6] At that time the annual earnings of individuals engaged primarily in agriculture was 68 per cent of the annual earnings from non-farm work.

The shift in the relative earnings between 1967 and 1983 is consistent with the shift in labour allocation by workers in farm households in Japan. In 1967, only 35 per cent of the working members of farm households were engaged in non-farm occupations; by 1983 this percentage had increased to 59.

Why do such seeming differences in earnings exist? Some of the difference reflects the greater number of hours worked per year in the non-farm than in the farm jobs. But much of the difference in productivity and earnings of the two groups of workers results from differences in age, education and sex. In 1985, 61 per cent of the farm work force was female and 44 per cent were 60 years old or over.[7] In his important book, *Japanese Agriculture Under Siege*, Yujiro Hayami notes that since the mid-1970s there has been a significant flow of males from non-agricultural jobs back to farming. This flow, however, consists primarily of persons who had shifted from farm to non-farm work as younger men and are now retiring from their non-farm jobs.[8] For these individuals the opportunity cost of their labour is very low. While no detailed comparison has been made between the farm and non-farm labour forces, it is obvious that the distribution of characteristics of the farm labour force has a much lower expected mean level of earnings than that of the non-farm labour force.[9]

Have migration and job mobility in Japan failed approximately to equalize earnings in farming and in the rest of the economy for reasonably comparable labour? If one looked only at the relative labour productivity measures derived from national accounts and labour force data, one would conclude that the farm to non-farm income differential remains despite large labour transfers, either through migration or taking off-farm work. But how then does one reconcile the equal or greater incomes of farm households than of

urban households? One cannot do so without accepting the view that
there are enormous measurement errors in the estimates of the farm
labour force and that the significant characteristics that influence the
productivities of the farm and non-farm labour forces differ in a major
way.

The income position of farm families relative to non-farm families in
the United States showed large improvement from the mid-1950s
through the 1970s. The data in Table 12.1 indicate that during 1955–59
the per capita disposable income of the farm population was only 50
per cent of the per capita disposable income of the non-farm population; this ratio increased to 59 per cent for 1960–64 and 71 per cent for
1965–69. For the last half of the 1970s the per capita disposable income
of the farm population was 92 per cent of the non-farm. There was a
decline in the ratio to 80 per cent from 1980 to 1983 due to high interest
costs and adverse weather in 1983. Unfortunately the United States
Department of Agriculture discontinued this series in 1983. From 1983
to 1987 the net income of farm families from all sources increased by 65
per cent while national income per capita increased by less than 30 per
cent. Consequently by 1987 per capita disposable income of farm
families must have approached or exceeded the level for non-farm
families. Admittedly, a significant part of the incomes of farm families
in the mid-1980s was due to large government payments. In 1987 the
incomes from off-farm sources exceeded net farm-operator incomes.[10]

The substantial improvement in the relative income position of farm
families and the large increase in real per capita incomes since the late
1950s represented significant achievements.[11] In my opinion, the most
important development of the more than a quarter-century was the
improvement in the incomes of farm families on small farms. In 1960,
62 per cent of all farms had sales of less than $5000; these farms had
total family incomes that were just 37 per cent of farms with sales of
$20 000 to $39 999. If the comparison is with farms with sales of
$10 000 to $19 999, the small farms had 57 per cent as large a total
income. In 1986, 63 per cent of all farms had sales of less than $10 000;
these families had total family incomes that were 85 per cent of families
on farms with sales of $40 000 to $99 999. It is striking to note that farm
operator families on farms with sales of less than $10 000 in 1986 had
family incomes that were 43 per cent of those realized by farms with
sales of $100 000 to $249 999. Only 4.3 per cent of all farms had sales in
excess of $250 000.[12] The farms in the $100 000-249 999 sales groups
had net assets per farm of $1.1 million in 1986 compared with about
$100 000 on the small farms.

Mobility and Migration

In Chapter 10 of the original edition of this book a considerable number of studies of migration were summarized. This material is not repeated here except for a very brief summary of the major points. There have been relatively few studies of the rural to urban migration process in the United States since the early 1970s.

The studies supported several important conclusions. One was that the higher a migrant's income had been on the farm, the higher the income in urban areas. This is what one would expect if the labour markets are functioning reasonably well. The studies indicate that the income gain realized by migrants was larger for those who move to large than to small cities. A third result was that income gains from rural to urban migration were nil during the first few years, but were substantial after five years.

The gains from migration from farm to urban areas were compared with the gains from additional education. It was found that the estimated annual gains from migration were somewhat smaller than the gains from the increase in income of two years of schooling.

But the major point of the migration studies that were summarized was that the small size of the gains from migration indicated that individuals with equal capacities or characteristics that affected labour productivity were earning approximately as much on farms as they could earn in urban areas. Put another way, the migration studies are consistent with the assumption that earnings differentials between farm and non-farm workers are due to differential characteristics, such as age and education, that affect adversely the productivity of individuals in the farm labour force. If this is true, as I believe the evidence indicates, protection is not the answer for eliminating the earnings differential. The answer to the elimination of the earnings differential, where it exists, is to modify the capabilities of those individuals who are now in agriculture, where possible, and to do all that is reasonable to ensure that young farm people who will be the farmers of tomorrow do not suffer the same disabilities that were the fate of the grandparents and parents.

Obviously, some characteristics such as age cannot be changed. If there is serious poverty or deprivation due to age factors, either because of the effect of age on productivity in agriculture or the great handicap of older persons in shifting to non-farm jobs, this should far better be met by direct payments related to age rather than by an increase in output prices.

It seems obvious from what we know about relative income levels of farm and non-farm families in the higher income industrial countries that the differences in age, in education levels and in the sex composition of the farm and non-farm labour forces, and the continuing need for significant rates of migration combined with the universally growing importance of non-farm income for farm families, that the hypothesis that mobility and migration have eliminated most of the differences in returns to comparable labour in agriculture and the rest of the economy is worthy of intensive and careful investigation. To the best of my knowledge, such an investigation has not been undertaken in the European Community or, if such studies exist, the Commission appears not to have taken notice of them.

If the hypothesis is valid, and I believe that it is, the current emphasis on high farm output prices is completely inappropriate. Much more could be done with the same transfers to help those who are poor because they have few resources. Where it exists, prompt action should be taken to eliminate discrimination in education and other human services that have so long been the burden of farm people.

A Digression on the European Community of Twelve

The European Community, as it is constituted at the time of writing, includes eight high-income countries with but 3 to 10 per cent of the population engaged in farming and four middle-income industrial countries with from 11 to 22 per cent of employment in agriculture. Because some 40 per cent of the Community's farm employment is in the lower-income countries, any comparison of the average incomes of farm and non-farm people, even if farm family incomes are properly measured to include income from non-farm sources, will show farm incomes to average significantly below non-farm incomes in the Community. This would be the case even if in each of the twelve countries farm and non-farm family incomes were equal.

As reported on numerous occasions in the annual report of the Commission of the European Community on the agricultural situation, the common agricultural policy failed to reduce regional inequalities in incomes within the Community of Six or the Community of Nine. Thus there can be no expectation that a continuation of existing policies of protection will be effective in reducing such inequalities within the Community of Twelve. Yet discussions with Community officials and with agricultural officials in member governments generally bring forth the comparison in numbers between the 10 million farm workers in the Community and the 3.2 million in the United States as an argument why, for social as well as economic reasons, the CAP cannot be abandoned. In particular, it is argued by such officials that the United States objective of eliminating all subsidies that influence farm production and trade is simply not possible for the Community because there are so many farmers and many of them are quite poor. The assumption is clearly that output prices well above international market prices are required to achieve the income objectives of farm policy and maintain viable rural communities. This assumption, accepted as a conclusion, is a blind act of faith wholly unjustified by the experience of the CAP over more than two decades and by the Commission's own conclusion that farm incomes are determined primarily by the general economic setting within which rural communities are located.

The enlargement of the European Community by the addition of the Mediterranean countries complicates CAP. It does so in a number of ways. One has already been mentioned, namely that the addition of 2.5 million relatively low-income farm families provides a pseudo-justification for continuation of a policy of high prices. In addition, the increase in the number of participants in the political process makes arriving at decisions more difficult. Finally, if resources of the Community were devoted to reducing the differentials between earnings of farm and urban workers, it would mean a major shift in resources away from the agricultures of the northern to the southern countries. Such a shift in the allocation of the Community's financial resources will be very difficult to achieve. As has been emphasized repeatedly throughout this book reducing regional disparities in farm family incomes requires taking measures that affect the conditions of factor supply, especially for labour. To do so requires increasing the human capital possessed by farm workers to the same level as urban workers and to achieve consistent growth of non-farm employment opportunities to provide farm workers with desirable and available alternatives to farm employment. These kinds of reallocation of efforts and resources will not be easy to achieve. Such a shift is not impossible, but to achieve it will require strong and enlightened leadership.

An Agricultural Policy for Industrial Countries

The basic framework for the reform of agricultural policy in the industrial countries involves three major elements. One is to make the programmes more market-oriented. A second is to emphasize measures that affect the supply conditions for farmer-owned resources, especially labour. The third is to provide for a believable and realistic transition programme for going from the current levels of protection to the long-run objective of low or modest levels of protection.

The transition programme is required primarily to cushion the loss in asset values that will result from reducing levels of protection. Reducing protection levels will have a temporary negative effect on farm labour earnings, but that effect will be relatively small compared with the loss in farm land values. The short-run loss in labour earnings, however, should receive some recognition in the transition programme.

For high-income countries, such as Japan, the United States, the Netherlands, Denmark, the United Kingdom, Germany, Belgium and France, the primary emphasis should be on a transition programme that will protect farmers from financial distress due to the loss in land values. Except in a few regions within the named countries, there is only a limited need to improve rural education and the rural infrastructure to increase the human capital possessed by farm people and to minimize the costs of migration.

But for the lower-income industrial countries, such as those in southern Europe, and the upper-income developing countries that are emerging as industrial countries that will soon have no more than 25 per cent of their labour force in agriculture, such as South Korea, there was in the late 1980s a significant bias against rural areas in the provision of education, health and cultural services and, too, in other aspects of the rural infrastructure. In such countries major emphasis needs to be given to eliminating what is clearly an urban bias in terms of investment in people and in creating other conditions conducive to the creation of non-farm jobs in rural areas.

A basic objective of the agricultural programmes for the 1990s for the industrial countries is to eliminate the excess resources engaged in agriculture by transferring them to more socially productive uses elsewhere in the economy. As argued earlier, in the late 1980s there were substantial excess resources in agriculture in the industrial market economies. While no exact measurement of the degree of excess resources is possible on the basis of existing studies, it is reasonable to conclude that the minimum is not less than 10 per cent. This is based on the Dvoskin estimate of 8 per cent for the United States and personal estimates of the effects of protection on resources devoted to agriculture in Japan and Western Europe.

It is easy to misinterpret the implications of a 10 per cent excess of resources. One misinterpretation is that to remove this excess would require very large reductions in farm labour and capital, for all of the land resources would remain in agriculture, given that very little of the land has a suitable alternative use. The error in this analysis is in failing to recognize that very nearly half of all farm inputs are purchased inputs and a further fraction consists of machinery and other purchased capital items. The phrase 'all farm inputs' is used to include all intermediate inputs as well as land, labour and capital. One of the consequences of protection has been to encourage the increased use of intermediate inputs as well as the addition of capital items. It is probably true that high levels of agricultural protection have resulted in a more rapid rate of technological change or productivity improvement than otherwise would have occurred.

Another possible misinterpretation is that agricultural output in the industrial market economies would decline by 10 per cent. The reduction in output would be somewhat smaller than this because of two factors: (i) Certain resources are now not being efficiently utilized, such as crop land in the United States and Japan or the capacity to produce dairy products in the European Community. (ii) The high output prices have encouraged resource combinations, given the relative fixity of the price of land, that have resulted in reducing the marginal productivity of variable inputs compared with what the marginal productivity of the last unit that would have been applied at lower output prices. As the quantities of these variable inputs are reduced in response to lower output prices, the reduction in output would be rather less than implied by the relative importance of that input in production at the higher prices.

One possible objection to the elimination of excess resources in the agricultures of the industrial countries is that any reduction in world food supplies is inappropriate in a world in which there are hungry people. Two responses to this objection are relevant. The first is that while output would fall in the industrial countries, the increase in world market prices would call forth added output in the developing countries if these countries permit the higher prices to be reflected in their domestic markets. The second is that while the industrial market economies are important producers of agricultural products, these economies produce only a third of the world's cereals, a sixth of root crops, a third of the sugar (in spite of high rates of subsidization), two-fifths of the meat and about half of the milk.[13] Thus even if agricultural production in the industrial market economies declined by as much as 10 per cent, which is most unlikely, world agricultural production would fall by no more than about 4 per cent. With some offset from increased production in the developing countries and with the realization of some of the potential for increased agricultural production in the Soviet Union due to economic reform, the reduction in world food production would be less than two year's output growth.

Another point is that the removal of excess resources from the industrial market economies will occur gradually over time. It took the United States approximately fifteen years to largely eliminate its excess agricultural resources, starting in the mid-1950s. It is unlikely that a major reduction in agricultural protection could be achieved in less than a decade. Consequently there would be adequate time for adjustment in world food production if world market prices were to increase more than projected by the available models. If such an outcome occurred, then if market forces are permitted to function in the industrial market and developing market economies, there would not be a need to transfer as many resources out of agriculture in the industrial economies. This is an outcome that should be welcomed, not feared. It would mean that world agriculture had not been pushed as far from long-run equilibrium as seems to have been the case in the late 1980s.

Two major factors resulted in the unusually low world market prices in 1986–87. One was the policy shift made by the United States. After maintaining price supports for grains and cotton from 1981 through 1985 that put a floor under world market prices and made the United States a residual supplier with a declining share of world exports and left it with large stocks, the decision was made to lower price supports, to aggressively seek to reduce stocks and to regain world market share. The effect was a sharp decline in world market prices. In 1987, United States export prices of wheat and maize were at least a third below the long-term trend in these prices, although there was a significant recovery in 1988 due to the small United States crop.[14] The long-term trend was measured from the mid-1920s to the mid-1980s.

The other factor was the continuing impact of the debt difficulties of the developing market economies and the failure of their imports of agricultural products to return to the levels of the early 1980s. In 1986 the value of Latin American agricultural imports was 30 per cent below the 1979–81 average.[15] Hopefully, by the mid-1990s there will be some resolution of the LDC debt problems with a consequent positive effect upon the volume and value of imports of agricultural products. If so, such recovery would go some distance in bringing international market prices back to the long-term trend levels.

The agricultural policy for the 1990s should give emphasis to the conditions of rural life. The agricultural policies of the industrial countries have emphasized the demand for farm products and the availability of inputs, including the amount and terms for credit. Structural policies have emphasized modifying farm structures to permit farm enlargement and reorganization that was intended to increase productivity, but only secondarily to assist rural people and communities to adjust to changing conditions. In large part, the agricultural programmes of the industrial countries are designed to make their farms more productive, while recognizing that the increased potential or actual output is inconsistent with the price objectives that have been accepted. Thus a considerable part of the machinery of farm programmes has been concerned with how to manage the excess supply generated by increased productivity and the additional inputs attracted by high output prices.

Stated briefly the following are the major components of an appropriate agricultural policy for industrial countries:

1. Provide rural farm youth with the same access to education as is available in urban areas; this implies improving the quality of primary and secondary schools and providing access to institutions of higher education on terms as favourable as such access is available to urban youth.

2. A systematic programme to facilitate the transfer of labour from agriculture to non-farm employment through both off-farm work for those who have the possibility of combining farm and non-farm employment and through migration or change of residence; this programme should include an information network about jobs and employment conditions, retraining farm workers and assisting in meeting the costs of migration. Emphasis should be given to creating a rural infrastructure (roads, electricity, shopping, cultural facilities) that would make rural areas attractive for industrial and service employment.

3. A programme for consistent and gradual reduction of price supports and subsidies that affect output to levels that approach the prices that would prevail under a liberal world trading regime in agriculture. It is probably more important that the schedule of

the move towards market orientation be an assured one than that the schedule be carried out in a specific period of time. It would not be unreasonable for the process to take a decade or even longer as long as that there were general agreement that the agreed reduction was to be achieved.

4. A system of payments that are unrelated to current and prospective agricultural output but designed to accomplish two objectives: (i) to cushion the decline in asset values due to the reduction of price supports and subsidies and (ii) to maintain the incomes of low-income farm families who would suffer an income loss from the lower prices and who because of age, physical disability or lack of education could not anticipate an improvement in income through migration or acceptance of a non-farm job if such were available.

Admittedly the four components are very general in nature and would require adaptation for particular countries. But the important feature of the proposed programme is that it is designed to assist the adjustment process that economic growth requires of agriculture. The farm programmes of nearly all industrial countries are not designed to assist farmers to adjust, but rather attempt to resist the adjustments that are required and which will eventually materialize in any case. In effect, current policies represent an effort to slow the transfer of labour out of agriculture, while the framework proposed above puts primary emphasis on assisting the transfer process so that it will occur with minimal cost for those who do transfer out of agriculture. It can be demonstrated that agricultural protection does more than slow the adjustment process. By attracting additional resources in the form of current inputs and machinery and by encouraging technological change, protection adds to the excess capacity of agriculture and makes the long-run reduction of labour even larger than it would have been in the absence of protection. It is important that the earnings differential that induces individuals to transfer out of agriculture be made as small as possible, not so much for the benefit of those who make the transfer but for the benefit of those who remain in agriculture. It is the reduction of the farm labour force by transfers to other sectors that can increase the returns to farm labour to nearly the same level as comparable labour earns elsewhere in the economy. Agricultural protection cannot guarantee this outcome.

Even during priods of slack non-farm employment, the percentage of the labour force engaged in agriculture in the high-income industrial

countries is small enough that increasing the rate of transfer out of
agriculture due to lower output prices and the narrowing of current
earnings differentials, where such exist, for comparable farm and non-
farm workers should not impose significant strains on the non-farm
labour market. According to a number of general equilibrium studies,
if agricultural liberalization is accompanied by liberalization of the
non-farm economy, there will be a significant increase in aggregate
employment all of which will be in the non-farm economy. This is
clearly the result obtained in a study undertaken at the request of the
Commission of the European Community on the effect of the elimination of barriers within the Community – the creation of a single market
by 1992. The study projects an increase in employment of 2 million to 5
million. The increase in employment that is projected to occur would
reduce the unemployment rate of 11.8 per cent that prevailed in the
Community as of 1986 by as much as half.[16] Consequently, according
to the Commission's own study, general economic liberalization would
serve to minimize the costs of agriculture's adjustment to reduced levels
of protection.

The objective of approximately equalizing the incomes of farm and
non-farm people will not be achieved until farm youth have access to
the same amount and quality of education as non-farm youth. Unless
this equality is obtained, it will always be true that the returns to farm
labour will lag behind the rest of the economy. For the indefinite future,
in the industrial countries the majority of farm youth will find it to their
advantage to seek and find non-farm employment. The argument that
the returns to education are lower in rural than urban areas may never
have been valid and it certainly is not valid today or for the foreseeable
future. With the changes that have occurred as agriculture has been
modernized, education is at least as productive for farm workers and
managers as elsewhere in the economy. The day when a strong back
and a willingness to work were all that was required to be a good
farmer is gone. Farming in the industrial countries is now a highly
complex undertaking and rewards advanced education and first-rate
managerial talents. Spending more on the education of an urban than a
rural youth can be justified neither on the grounds of equity nor
efficiency. All that is required to achieve such equality in the provision
of education is to transfer some of the benefits that now go to a
minority of large and well-to-do farmers to the rural education budget.
budget.

The third component of an agricultural policy is a definite commitment and schedule for reducing the level of protection through lower

support prices and subsidies. There is no presumption that the end objective is the complete elimination of protection. But for all of the industrial economies, except New Zealand and Australia, levels of agricultural protection in the late 1980s were so high as to be unsustainable for the long run without resort to stricter and more pervasive supply management programmes and increasing intrusions on farmers' management decisions. In the next chapter the advantages of minimizing levels of protection in order to gain and retain the advantages of the multilateral trading system will be emphasized. But here the emphasis is on what a country might do unilaterally to reform its agricultural policies. And if there is not a general and multilateral reduction in protection, it may be in the interest of an individual country to retain some barriers to imports and subsidies for exports, for world market prices would be below what their levels would be under free trade. Almost all of the industrial countries, however, now have far higher levels of protection than can be justified on the grounds that world market prices are below what their free trade levels would be.

The fourth component of the agricultural policy is the transition programme that should be designed as a complement to the gradual reduction in the levels of protection. The primary objective of the transition programme would be to minimize the losses to resource owners that would result from reducing levels of protection. The largest losses would occur to the owners of farmland and quotas where production quotas are not tied to a farm unit because most of the benefits of protection have gone to land and quota owners. Unfortunately, many current owners of land and quotas have paid a price for their land and quotas that reflected most or all of the anticipated gains from the farm price programmes. If the existing owners of land and quotas were the ones who had benefited from the protection, it would not be unreasonable to ignore any claims they might have for compensation for their losses. But as shown in Chapter 9 such is not the case. The current owners of these assets have acquired their ownership at widely varying times and have different potential losses compared with their acquisition costs.

The transition programme is desirable on political as well as equity grounds. The political influence of farm organizations and of those whose incomes depends on financing, buying and selling to farmers is sufficiently strong in all of the industrial countries to prevent significant reductions in protection unless the resulting losses can be cushioned if not entirely compensated. One needs to be realistic on this point. The existing levels of protection exist because democratic governments have decided to have those levels and these decisions have been in response to political pressures and incentives. There is a possibility of reform of agricultural policies as we enter the 1990s because there is a general worldwide economic liberalization occurring. It is not only that there is general agreement that governmental intervention in agriculture has gone too far but similar views are held with respect to the entire economy as well. The effort to fulfil the objectives of the Treaty of Rome by 1992 is based as much on the need to reduce governmental interventions as on the desirability of achieving a unified Europe.

The interest in liberal reform of economic systems is evident on many sides. These include the deregulation of many industries that had long been subject to highly intrusive governmental regulation, the rapid integration of capital markets among the industrial countries made possible by deregulation, the remarkable economic reforms in China that have had such success for 800 million rural Chinese and which included the abolition of the communes and reinstituting something quite comparable to family farms, the efforts in the Soviet Union and Eastern Europe to replace stagnant centrally-planned economies and the striking efforts of a Labour government in New Zealand to reform its economy by introducing free trade. It is evident that it will be easier to carry out agricultural reform as a part of general reforms that will make economies more productive and more flexible.

The payments associated with the transition programme should have minimal effect on current production decisions. In other words, to use a current buzz-word, the payments should be decoupled. This concept is not new. One can find references to it in writings published in the 1940s.[17] Even though not new, it is an important concept. One of the inconsistent aspects of the farm price programmes of the industrial countries is that even when it is recognized that agricultural output is larger than desired, governments continue to provide payments and subsidies to farmers in a form that encourages them to produce even more. Eventually, when the treasury burden of the unwanted output becomes too great, farmers are either coerced or bribed to submit to supply management programmes to reduce output. This inconsistency in the farm price and income programmes is a consequence of the incorrect premise that has guided them, namely that the incomes of farm families can be increased by increasing the demand for farm products. These programmes have failed to recognize that the return to labour or capital is a function of both supply and demand and that if the demand is very elastic, as it is for labour and capital in the intermediate run, demand may influence the level of employment but with minimal effect on the wage.

Consequently, if the transition programme is to assist the adjustment process while minimizing the losses that occur, the payments must be decoupled. The idea is a simple one. The payments should not be related to current output decisions. Decoupling can be assured in a variety of ways. One way would be to relate the payments to past levels of output with the payments to continue without regard to current and future production. Another way would be to relate the payments to past levels of resource uses – payments per hectare of land and to each individual who worked on farms in some past year. The payments to resources would be based on projections of losses due to the reduction of protection. In the case of land, the payment might be equal to the anticipated loss in the rental value of land, with the payment to be made annually for a specified number of years, such as a decade. In the case of workers, the payments would be related to the potential losses of income over the period of time that would be required for them to adjust to the lower level of prices and for the return to farm labour to return to its previous relationship to non-farm earnings. Such payments would need to be differentiated by the characteristics of the recipients with respect to age, education and health. For young and well-educated farmers payments would be smaller and required for a shorter period of time than for a farmer of 55 with minimal levels of education. But it needs to be recognized that the payments under any approach would be independent of the actual use of the resources. Most current farm price and income programmes require that the recipients continue to utilize their resources in agriculture even when this means adding to already excessive supplies. Decoupled payments are not intended to influence farm production. The payments are designed to aid people in their roles as resource owners to adjust to changes in their economic environment.

Farm people have resisted the concept of decoupled payments since they believe such payments are too similar to welfare payments. There is a deep-seated desire among farm people to earn what they receive. Payments not associated with worthwhile productive activity make them uncomfortable. The irrationality of this position is evident from two facts. First, in most industrial countries, farmers receive subsidies for producing products that are an economic burden on their government – they are paid to produce a product that has a much smaller value than what they receive for producing it. Second, increasingly they are being paid to leave some of their valuable land idle or are required to leave resources idle if they are not to be subjected to heavy penalties. Leaving land idle is an element of the United States farm programmes while the European Community dairy quota requires idling resources to avoid punitive taxation on output.

Decoupled payments are not unknown. Participants in the United States supply-management programmes receive deficiency payments on the basis of their acreage base and the normal yield. Thus if a farmer has a base or allotment of 100 hectares for maize and is required to leave 20 per cent of the land idle, his deficiency payment is based on normal rather than actual output from the 80 hectares. In the past the farmer was required to plant all or nearly all of the 80 hectares to receive the deficiency payment. In addition, unless the farmer actually planted maize on the area permitted, he could lose part or all of his base and thus his rights to payments in future years. Thus farmers were encouraged to produce whether or not it was in the national interest to do so. Under legislation enacted in 1987 the farmer in our example could plant none of his maize allotment and still receive deficiency payments on 92 per cent of his allotted area. Thus if his marginal cost of production exceeded the anticipated market price, it was in his interest not to plant and to leave his land idle. This is a form of decoupled payment.

13 Negotiations for Freer Trade in Agricultural Products

Major progress in reducing levels of agricultural protection will be made as a result of multilateral actions. Very few countries have been or will be willing to reduce their levels of protection unilaterally as a result of deliberate action. The recent examples of New Zealand, Chile and Australia seem to be isolated ones for the twentieth century.[1] Given the degree to which international market prices have been depressed by domestic farm programmes, it is understandable why in most countries there would be resistance to unilateral reductions in protection. It has become popular to argue for 'a level playing field' – the terms of entry for a country's exports should be as favourable as the terms it provides for imports. This idea is presumably derived from the concept of reciprocity. The 1930s legislation in the United States that led to the important post-Second World War trade agreements and to the GATT was called the Reciprocal Trade Agreements Act. Thus even when it can be shown that unilateral reductions in protection have positive welfare effects, it is difficult to convince those who are required to adjust that they are being treated fairly.

The pattern of international trade in agricultural products during the 1970s and 1980s can be described as chaotic without serious exaggeration. Import levies or tariffs of 50 per cent and more are quite common; in fact, a significant amount of the world's imports of agricultural products pass over barriers of this magnitude. Nor are export subsidies of similar or greater relative magnitude unknown. In fact, the experience of recent decades has indicated that there is no degree of nominal protection of an agricultural product that can be called unimaginable. One can make a case that it is surprising that there is such a large volume of trade in agricultural products rather than that there is so very little. Obviously there would be more trade with less protection, but agricultural products seem to be able to pass over barriers that are prohibitive when applied to manufactured products. To some degree the large volume of exports is due to the payment of subsidies by the exporting countries.

302

Effects of Continuing Present Policies

In the original edition of this book (Chapter 12) it was stated that if the then-current agricultural and trade policies of the major industrial countries were continued, several undesirable consequences were highly probable:

(a) The level of costs of the farm policies in the industrial countries to taxpayers and/or consumers would continue to increase.
(b) A substantial and probably increasing fraction of the world's agricultural output would be produced under high-cost conditions.
(c) The percentage of the world's trade in agricultural products that was managed and manipulated through the use of export subsidies would increase.
(d) The developing countries would face increasing difficulties in obtaining markets for farm products that were directly competitive with farm products grown in temperate zones.
(e) The degree of effective protection provided agriculture would gradually increase in industrial countries.

Unfortunately these predictions were all too accurate. They were written prior to the Tokyo Round negotiations of 1973–79. Almost nothing was accomplished during that round to reduce the barriers to agricultural trade. The location of agricultural production by the principle of comparative advantage was not advanced nor was there any movement towards reducing the real costs of producing the world's food supply.

Today and Yesterday: What's New?[2]

It is a common failing of man that he so often believes that his problems are unique in history. Of course, to some extent, this is true. There is always, though, a substantial error in such a conclusion. This is particularly true in matters dealing with agriculture. The problems that we believe confront agriculture today are the same problems that have concerned policy-makers since at least the fifteenth century.

Nor are the solutions that modern-day policy-makers have 'discovered' in any way unique. The recent pattern of substantial protection of agricultural production in industrial countries is not new in the history of the modern world. It is, in fact, an old story. Anything approximating free trade in agricultural products has been the exception in the annals of history. The only major country that adhered to free trade for an extended period of time since the fifteenth century was the United Kingdom and then for rather less than a century. The abolition of the British Corn Laws in 1846 did herald a period of nearly free trade in farm products in Western Europe, but the period was a brief one of a little less than three decades.[3] War (the Franco–German War of 1870) and the depression of the last quarter of the nineteenth century induced a return to protection. Only Denmark and the Netherlands resisted the move to protectionism until the Great Depression of the 1930s when the United Kingdom also reintroduced agricultural protection.

One must also admit, even if with a degree of sadness, that the attempted solutions to the problems of agriculture that have been adopted during this century evidence almost no originality. Neither the European Community, with its variable import levies and export subsidies, nor the United States, with its import quotas and export subsidies and acreage limitations, has shown any originality in its choice of protective weapons. The only twentieth-century innovation that I have discovered in the techniques of agricultural protection is the use of direct payments to producers to meet a price or income commitment. Even this device, which was used by the United Kingdom prior to its entrance to the Community and as deficiency payments in the United States, is but a slight modification of various bounty schemes that existed, at least briefly, in a number of countries at one time or another.

Nor has our rhetoric changed very much. In each era there have been what was thought to be special reasons why the agriculture of a particular country or region faced special difficulties and required assistance and protection. At times in Western Europe it was the competition of the low-cost grains from the new lands in America and later in Australia. At other times it was the reduction in the cost of ocean transport. In recent times rapid technological change has been considered to be a major reason why special measures are required if agricultural incomes are to be acceptable. Another reason has been that there are large differences in the average size of farm or in the man/land ratio among countries. The new agricultural protectionism, which might be accurately described as the new Corn Laws, is often justified on the grounds that there is a 'built-in' ability of agriculture to produce more than can be absorbed by the available markets at remunerative prices. And lurking in the background has long been the viewpoint that a large and profitable agriculture was an essential national priority; agricultural fundamentalism has had a long and active career.

For those among us who think that the problems of the day are new, and newly discovered by us, and that our arguments for doing something about these problems are original, or that our methods of solving the problems are unique, two brief quotations from an act of the British Parliament in 1663 ...ay be both enlightening and sobering:[4]

Forasmuch as the encouragement of tillage ought to be in an especial manner regarded and endeavoured; and the surest and effectual means of promoting and advancing any trade, occupation or mystery being by rendering it profitable to the users thereof; ... and great quantities of land within this kingdom for the present lying in a manner waste, and yielding little, which might thereby be improved to considerable profit and advantage (if sufficient encouragement were given for laying out cost and labour on the same), and thereby much corn produced, great numbers of people, horse and cattle employed, and other lands also rendered more valuable.

Whereas a great deal of the richest and best land of this kingdom is and cannot so well be otherwise employed and made use of as in the feeding and fattening of cattle, and that of the coming in of late of vast numbers of cattle already fatted, such lands are in many places much fallen, and likely daily to fall more in their rents and values, and in consequence other lands also, to the great prejudice, detriment, and improvement of this kingdom.

This act was one of the numerous legislative enactments of what became known as the British Corn Laws, which had their origin as early as the fifteenth century. While controls over international trade in corn (grain) had been imposed before, this was apparently the first act that specifically protected the production of cattle and sheep. The provision of the act with respect to cattle had a modern flavour – relatively high import duties imposed only during the first six months of the calendar year when British fat cattle were marketed and the number of cattle that could be imported from the Isle of Man was limited to 600 per year. This was an early use of an import quota.

Neither the British Corn Laws nor the protectionist policies followed by other governments, were successful in solving the problems of agriculture. The inevitable adjustments, such as the transfer of labour to the rest of the economy, were barely affected. Nor, as I hope I have been successful in showing, have the new Corn Laws been any more successful in providing farm families with approximately the same incomes as families not dependent on agriculture. The success that there has been in narrowing the gap between the welfare of farm and non-farm families has been due to factors other than farm price and income policies. The mobility and migation of labour, the gradual though not everywhere complete equalization of educational opportunities, improvements in communication and transport, the mechanization and commercialization of farming have far outweighed the quite minimal effects of governmental farm programmes. Ricardo and other classical economists told us that one of the main consequences of the Corn Laws was to increase land rent; and so it is today. Why is it that we have not yet understood the validity of a conclusion reached almost two centuries ago?

Two quotations from Adam Smith are appropriate at this point.[5] The first quotation requires no comment or introduction. In the second Smith is comparing a 1746 modification of the Corn Laws with the general structure of import duties and export duties prior to that year.

1. The laws concerning corn may everywhere be compared to the laws concerning religion. The people feel themselves so much interested in what relates either to their subsistence in this life, or to their happiness in a life to come, that government must yield to their prejudices and, in order to preserve the public tranquility, establish that system which they approve of. It is upon this account perhaps, that we so seldom find a reasonable system established with regard to either of these two capital objects.

2. So far, therefore, this law seems to be inferior to the ancient system. With all its imperfections, however, we may perhaps say of it what was said of the laws of Solon, that, though not the best in itself, it is the best which the interests, prejudices, and temper of the times would admit of. It may perhaps in due time prepare the way for the better.

Unfortunately, two centuries later, we can't say that we have found the better way. Adam Smith was right about so very many things, but as of the late 1980s he missed this one.

Ending the Disarray

While there are numerous steps that individual governments can take to reduce the adverse impact of their domestic farm policies on international trade, as noted earlier it is unlikely that major steps will be taken except as a part of a general international agreement. This is particularly true of two major participants in disrupting international trade, namely the United States and the European Community. Neither has any particular trust in the other and it would seem that nothing short of binding agreements would induce one to act on the basis of commitments made by the other. As this chapter was being written, the Uruguay Round negotiations were proceeding. Consequently most of the following discussion relates to those negotiations and what may be required during the last decade of the twentieth century.

In the first edition of this book it was noted that there were three main strategies for negotiations that could lead to the relaxation of controls on international trade in farm products. The three strategies were: (i) a general round of negotiations within the GATT; (ii) negotiation of a series of commodity agreements for the major farm products and (iii) negotiations on domestic agricultural policies to achieve agreed limits to the degree of protection provided agriculture in the industrial countries.

The Tokyo Round negotiations were formally started in late 1973 and concluded in 1979 with no significant progress having been made in reducing agricultural trade interventions. Then as during the early stages of the Uruguay Round negotiations there was a major conflict between the positions taken by the European Community and the United States. T. K. Warley, of the University of Guelph, has described the conflict and its outcome as follows.[6]

> The onset of substantive negotiations on agriculture was delayed for almost four years by a dispute between the US and the EEC on whether agriculture should be negotiated in a separate group or merely be included in agreements negotiated elsewhere, particularly on tariffs and subsidies. Procedure was substance, for whereas the US was demanding that agricultural trade be treated the same as trade in other goods, and subject to the disciplines of new codes on non-tariff measures, the EEC was both philosophically persuaded that agriculture was different and politically determined that the CAP (which had finally been put in place) would not be

Word Agriculture in Disarray

308

undermined by the imposition of multilateral constraints on its operation and instrumentation. The EEC won the procedural and substantive points. The negotiations on agriculture were separated from the negotiations on other topics and specifically from the discussions which led to a new code on the use of subsidies and the response to them.

While there was no assurance that if agricultural trade had been included in the general negotiations that there would have been some success in liberalizing agricultural trade, the actual outcome of the Tokyo Round negotiations has been described by Professor Warley quite graphically:[7]

And so, at the end of yet another GATT round, the international community had again come up short in liberalizing agricultural trade and disciplining agricultural subsidy practices. Agriculture emerged as it entered, the most highly protected major sector in national economies, the most undisciplined area of international commerce and the cause of some of the most fractious and dangerous frictions in international economic relations.

The unwillingness of the United States in the Uruguay Round negotiations, as of early 1989, to compromise on its apparently extreme objective of the elimination of all trade-distorting measures within a decade may be related to the lack of response to its modifying its position during the Tokyo Round negotiations. When the Carter Administration took over from the Ford Administration in 1977, the United States agreed to accept separate agricultural negotiations. Nothing was gained from the compromise that accepted the European Community's position since the Tokyo Round negotiations achieved nothing with respect to agricultural trade. In late 1989 the United States put forward a revised proposal that did not explicitly call for the elimination of all agricultural subsidies.

Agriculture and GATT Negotiations

As the Uruguay Round negotiations got underway, the levels of protection for agricultural products were greater than when the first of the three rounds, the Dillon Round negotiations, started. This is, I fear, an accurate measure of the failures of the three rounds. Any claim that in the absence of the negotiations protection levels would now be higher is suspect. The current levels of protection are about as high as the political processes permit due to the high budgetary costs and the resistance of consumers.

Some of the important reasons for the failure of the last three GATT rounds of agricultural negotiations were historical. The Kennedy and Tokyo Rounds came at critical stages in the creation, development and consolidation of the European Community and its common agricultural policy. As Professor Warley has noted about the negotiations during the Kennedy Round:[8] 'For its part the Community was not ready to accept external constraints on its emerging common agricultural policy.' But in no way can the responsibility for the failure of the Kennedy Round negotiations be placed solely on the Community. While the negotiations were underway the United States passed legislation that provided for import quotas on ruminant meat and Canada put in place the foundations of her very protectionist dairy policy.

During the Kennedy Round negotiations the European Community put forth two related proposals which were rejected by the other parties. One was a proposal on margins of support or '*montant de soutien*' and self-sufficiency norms. With the apparent advantage of hindsight, many have argued that it was a mistake to have rejected these proposals. But the *montant de soutien* proposal was not as forthcoming as it has been depicted in some quarters. As Professor Warley has noted, it was always a concept and never a specific proposal.[9] There were serious limitations to the *montant de soutien* concept. One was that it was to obtain approval, not for a given margin of support or protection, but for international acceptance of the minimum import prices that the Community was in the process of establishing. The commitment was to last only three years. Insofar as there was an implied commitment on the margin of support, it was to be in reference to artificially established international reference prices. The proposal would have put no limit on the actual margin of support as measured by the difference between the Community import prices and the international market prices that prevailed at a given time. As Robert Paarlberg has argued, in a study for the Council on Foreign Relations, New York, the Community 'was in effect trying to secure, through the GATT, international legitimacy for its own increasingly illiberal agricultural trade policies'.[10] This included obtaining acceptance and legitimacy for the use of variable import levies.

The self-sufficiency norms proposal was also limited to three years and was to be applied only in conditions 'of global surplus', however that might be defined. The proposal was far from a simple one. It involved all countries accepting what amounted to a cartelization of international trade and agreeing on market shares for both exporters and importers. Implicit in the proposal was acceptance of the French viewpoint expressed in 1961 at a GATT ministerial meeting:[11] 'It is obvious that we must adopt a new policy, and try to reconcile the aspirations of each country by looking for solutions based not on Free Trade – which is impracticable – but on the principle of market organisation.' The European Community's proposal to the GATT during the Kennedy Round negotiations on market organization called for a World Commodity Agreement that would cover cereals, beef and veal, some dairy products, sugar and perhaps oilseeds with the objectives of stabilizing prices at 'fair and remunerative levels' and to require countries to take steps to avoid surplus production.

The failure of GATT negotiations to reduce barriers to trade in agricultural products is due, at least in part, to the exceptions to the basic GATT rules for trade that have been made for trade in agricultural products. The six basic principles underlying GATT rules are:

(a) Non-discrimination – all contracting parties should give most-favoured-nation (MFN) treatment with respect to their tariffs or other policy measures affecting trade.
(b) Protection to domestic industries is to be by tariffs only and not by quantitative restrictions.
(c) No prejudice by direct or indirect subsidies, including price or income support, to the interests of other countries.
(d) Negotiations as the basis for reducing tariff and other trade barriers.
(e) Consultations for the purpose of avoiding harm to the trading interests of other contracting parties.
(f) Compensation if benefits of GATT concessions are withdrawn.

These principles are meant to apply to all trade, with some limited exceptions. There are general exceptions, such as the right to impose import restrictions because of balance-of-payment difficulties. But there are also special exceptions that apply primarily to agricultural products. When these exceptions are added to certain ambiguities in the general principles, it is not surprising that it is so difficult to undertake general negotiations on agricultural trade under GATT rules. In effect, current GATT articles do not provide for appropriate guidelines for negotiating on agricultural trade.

To a very considerable degree, the United States is responsible for this state of affairs. American responsibility goes back to the origins of the GATT and to American insistence on exceptions from the general trade rules for agricultural trade. The basic conflicts of the rules for agricultural trade and the general liberal trade principles of the GATT are found primarily in Articles XI and XVI.

The thrust of Article X1 is to prohibit all restrictions on imports other than duties or taxes. But paragraph 2 of the article provides for certain exceptions to this general rule. With particular reference to agriculture, sub-paragraph (c) permits 'import restrictions, including quantitative restrictions, on agricultural or fishery productions, imported in any form, that is required for the enforcement of governmental measures which operate to restrict domestic production or to remove a temporary surplus by making the surplus available to certain groups free of charge or at prices below the current market level'.[12]

The intention, however, was not to permit the unrestricted use of import quotas to abet a domestic output control programme, but the imposition was to follow a specific guideline: 'Moreover, any restrictions applied ... shall not be such as will reduce the total imports relative to the total of domestic production, as compared with the proportion which might reasonably be expected to rule between the two in the absence of restrictions.' The purpose of this exception was to permit countries that restricted domestic farm production and thus increased domestic market prices from having to accept a larger volume of imports that would have negated the effect of the output reduction. But the country imposing a quantitative restriction was not to reduce imports by more proportionately than domestic output was reduced. If import quotas are to be permitted under these circumstances, the guideline for their use is a reasonable one.

The exceptions for agricultural trade permitting the use of import quotas were inserted in the original draft of the GATT to placate the United States Congress. Without the exceptions Congress would not have approved the negotiations based on the GATT articles. But these exceptions were not enough to permit the United States to carry out some of its farm programmes. Congress not only insisted on the exception in GATT Article XI but also passed an amendment to Section 22 of the Agricultural Adjustment Act of 1933 which included the following: 'No trade agreement or other international agreement heretofore or hereafter entered into by the United States shall be applied in a manner inconsistent with this section.' Section 22 required the Administration to impose quantitative restrictions or special fees (above and beyond customs duties) whenever 'any article or articles are being or are practically certain to be imported into the United States under such conditions and in such quantities as to render or tend to render ineffective, or materially interfere with' any United States farm programme or 'to reduce substantially the amount of any product' subject to such a farm programme. After the passage of this amendment, quotas were imposed on cotton, wheat, peanuts, oats, rye, barley and manufactured dairy products.

For all of the products except the manufactured dairy products there were farm programmes that limited domestic production, and the effects on imports were probably consistent with the provisions of Article XI, at least during the 1950s and 1960s. There was no effort made though to restrict dairy production and imports were restricted to a very small percentage of United States consumption. In 1951 the GATT Contracting Parties found the United States import restrictions on dairy products constituted an infringement of Article XI. The United States was subjected to retaliation provisions under Article X-XIII. It was subsequent to this action that Congress amended Section 22 as described above. In 1955 the United States Administration obtained a GATT waiver from the provisions of Article XI, not just for dairy products, but for all agricultural products. This meant that the United States was free to use quantitative restrictions on imports on any farm product, whether it had a programme that limited domestic production or not. The waiver was broad, without time limit, and its continuation required no justification by the United States.

Kenneth Dam, the American legal authority on the GATT, evaluated the effect of the waiver on the atmosphere for trade liberalization:[13]

> The breadth of the waiver, coupled with the fact that the waiver was granted to the contracting party that was at one and the same time the world's largest trading nation and the most vocal proponent of freer international trade, constituted a grave blow to GATT's prestige. The waiver, coming as it did at the same time as the unusually limited grant of authority by the United States Congress for the 1955 trade-negotiations round, was profoundly

discouraging for many GATT supporters, and the United States was accused of hypocrisy.'

The unwillingness of the United States in the late 1940s and early 1950s to subject its domestic farm programmes to the discipline of international trade resulted in the inclusion in the GATT of exceptions for agriculture with respect to subsidies, including export subsidies. As noted earlier, Article XVI of the GATT includes a general provision concerning subsidies of any form, including price and income supports, that may result in increasing exports or reducing imports. The anti-subsidy provision was not to be fully effective until 1 January 1958 when all subsidies were to have been prohibited unless specific action was taken to reduce the article's applicability. Such action was taken on the initiative of the United States to include the exceptions for primary products. The article included what turned out to be a totally meaning-less provision that the export subsidies were not to be used to achieve 'more than an equitable share of world trade in that product'. An effort was made during the Tokyo Round negotiations to devise a subsidies code that could be enforced, but without any greater success.

Obviously the United States has paid a high price for its unwilling-ness to bring its farm programmes within the discipline provided by international trade. Had these exceptions to GATT principles on import quotas and export and other subsidies not been made – and used by the United States for many years – the shape of the European Community's common agricultural policy might now be quite dif-ferent.[14] The exception for export subsidies and quantitative restric-tions on imports were crucial to the functioning of the CAP. As long as the GATT exception for import quotas for agricultural products existed, combined with the United States waiver, it was impossible for the Contracting Parties to effectively oppose the illiberal aspects of the CAP.

It was against the background of Articles XI and XVI, the United States waiver from Article XI, the institutionalization of variable import levies, which are similar in their effects to quantitative import restrictions, and export subsidies by the European Community and the domestic and export subsidies by the United States that the Uruguay Round negotiations were embarked upon in 1987. It was hardly an auspicious setting for serious negotiations. The remainder of this chapter discusses the possible approaches for achieving some reduction in the levels of protection for agricultural products in the industrial market economies.

Commodity Agreements

There are some who believe that international commodity agreements provide a useful transition from the present state of disarray to an 'agricultural trade regime with significantly lower levels of protection'. This is, I believe, a reasonably literal interpretation of part of the stage 1 of the European Community's 26 October 1987 proposal for the Uruguay Round negotiations. What is called for in the case of cereals are measures that 'could include an undertaking on prices and/or quantities placed on the market during the period under consideration (i.e. a marketing year)'. The objective of these agreements is that of 'improving international trading conditions, in particular as regards pricing'.[15] This was a distinctly less ambitious proposal than was made during the Kennedy Round negotiations under the *montant de soutien* and the self-sufficiency norms which called for establishing world reference prices and agreement on market shares that would have carried forward for at least three years. But the proposal was nonetheless a form of a commodity agreement since it implied that at least the major industrial market exporters agree both on prices and market shares in export markets.

Related proposals were made for application to cereal substitutes, sugar and dairy products. It should be made clear that these proposals for the equivalent of commodity agreements were meant to be applied for a limited period of time to 'ease the situation on worst-affected markets' while providing time for 'a concerted reduction of support aimed at the rising trend in existing imbalances and thereby initiating the process of restoring healthy market conditions'.

The trade problems are quite similar for a considerable number of farm products. It is difficult to imagine the negotiation of many commodity agreements simultaneously. The negotiation of a small number of commodity agreements for major farm products is likely to shift production adjustment problems to other commodities. But it is also true that commodity agreements have not been known for providing for adjustment for the particular commodity to changes in demand and supply. This point was well made by the OECD group of experts in their report *Agriculture and Economic Growth*, in 1965, which is as pertinent today as then: 'Experience to date with international agreements suggests that they can play a useful role in promoting short-term stability. A danger exists, however, that they can be used to inhibit long-term adjustments required to bring overall agricultural resource use into line with market requirements and to promote appropriate international balance of resource use.'[16]

There is no evidence to support the position that commodity agreements for agricultural products represent an effective approach to liberalizing agricultural trade. I do not reach this conclusion because of the limited success of the few such commodity agreements that have been negotiated.[17] The commodity agreements that have been negotiated have not had trade liberalization as an important objective. Primary emphasis has been on limiting price variations; while this may be a worthy objective, the contribution to trade liberalization is limited.

As of the late 1980s, there does not appear to be significant support for the negotiation of commodity agreements as a long-run solution for trade liberalization. While my personal experience is that there are many agricultural policy-makers in the European Community who long for negotiated stable world prices at reasonable levels and agreed shares of the available markets for the major exporters – what the ideal commodity agreement is supposed to achieve – the official Community proposal was for a very limited and temporary set of agreements.

But the most important consideration is that cartels, whether organized by private or governmental agencies, have never been known to favour liberalization of trade. The primary objectives are high and stable prices; volume of trade becomes important only as too small a volume of actual trade becomes a threat to the stability of the cartel arrangements by encouraging free-riders.

Negotiations on Agricultural Policies and Agreed Limits on Protection

As noted above, the first edition of this book suggested that there were three possible approaches to liberalizing agricultural trade. One – commodity agreements – has been briefly discussed and dismissed. The second approach, namely that of including agriculture in the general framework of GATT negotiations, generally has been rejected by the Contracting Parties. The Tokyo Round negotiations foundered over this issue with the United States arguing that agriculture should be on the same footing as manufacturing in the negotiations, with the European Community refusing to accept that approach. In the end, the agricultural negotiations were separated from the general negotiations.

The outcome, as recorded by history, was that no significant liberalization of agricultural trade occurred.

The Uruguay Round negotiations are based on the third approach, namely negotiations on domestic agricultural policies to achieve agreed limits to agricultural protection in the industrial countries. This approach was implicit in the declaration of the seven heads of government at the end of the Tokyo Summit in 1986 and in the ministerial statement at Punta del Este in 1987. The approach was very explicit in the several proposals submitted to the GATT in 1987 by the United States, the European Community, Japan, the Cairns Group and Canada. The Cairns Group consists of thirteen countries that include Australia, Canada and New Zealand plus a group of developing-country exporters that have been adversely affected by the agricultural and trade policies of the major industrial countries.

Some of the proposals, specifically those of the Cairns Group, Canada and the European Community call for strengthening and clarifying GATT rules and regulations on agricultural trade. In particular, there was emphasis on the rules governing subsidies and non-tariff barriers, which were defined by the Cairns Group to include variable import levies and minimum import prices as well as import quotas. The Japanese proposal not only called for review of Article XI on import restrictions but also called for a reconsideration of the exception to the general prohibition against quantitative export restrictions permitted for foodstuffs at times of critical shortages.

While there has been interest in revising and strengthening the special GATT rules that provide exceptions for agricultural trade, it is not obvious what revisions can be negotiated. Nor is it obvious that, once quantitative import restrictions and export subsidies are permitted, rules can be written that could eliminate the adverse effects that these instruments have on international trade in agricultural products. For this reason, the long-term objective stated in the Cairns Group and United States proposals to eliminate all trade-distorting interventions has substantial appeal. The Cairns Group's proposal stated: 'GATT rules and disciplines should be agreed upon to prohibit the use of all subsidies and other governmental support measures, including consumer transfers, having an effect on agricultural trade.' By implication, their proposal called for tariffs as the sole measure of protection and there should be 'a binding of all tariffs on agricultural products at low levels or zero'. The United States proposal, which has been called unrealistic in most quarters, called for 'a complete phase-out over 10 years of all agricultural subsidies which directly or indirectly affect trade' as well as a 'phase-out of import barriers over 10 years'. While neither the Cairns Group nor the United States proposed solutions to the problems presented by Articles XI and XVI have a significant chance of full acceptance, it is not obvious what modifications of these two articles would be acceptable.

Clearly the lower the level of prevailing protection, the less important would be the failure to modify Articles XI and XVI so that they effectively limited the adverse effects of the measures involved. If the average nominal level of protection of sugar in the United States were 25 per cent instead of several times that, the sugar import quotas would have much less adverse effect than has been the case during the 1980s. Consequently, if there is significant success in reducing levels of protection, the GATT exceptions for agriculture become less of a barrier to a liberal trading regime.

Nevertheless there are some modifications in the rules that should be considered. Article XIII states that when quantitative import restrictions are applied, they should follow the principle of most-favoured-nation treatment – the quotas must apply to all imports from all sources and should attempt to achieve a distribution of trade as close as possible to what would occur in the absence of the quotas. Once a quota regime has been in effect for many years, as is true of the United States sugar and dairy import quotas, it is not possible to determine what the distribution of trade would be in the absence of the quotas. On this score, variable import levies are clearly superior to import quotas, for import shares do change in response to the offer prices by the various exporters. Import quotas do not provide such flexibility unless the quotas are auctioned off periodically. Then the import quotas become the equivalent of the variable levies. The country that wishes to increase its share in the restricted market can do so by offering a higher price for the quota just as under the variable import-levy system, offering a lower price for the product increases market share.

There does not seem to be a specific requirement that export subsidies should abide by MFN treatment, although one could argue that since there is not a specific exception to the general MFN principle for export subsidies, they are covered. It is clear, however, that neither the European Community nor the United States believes it is bound to MFN treatment in its use of export subsidies. In fact, the United States export enhancement programme (EEP) is deliberately designed to be contrary to MFN treatment, for one of its objectives is to gain entry to markets that it had not had in recent years or presumably would not have without special tailoring of the export subsidies to particular market situations. The EEP has, in effect, been used to compete against the Community for markets.

While it is not possible to imagine how import or export quotas can be made fully consistent with MFN treatment, it is possible to have export subsidies that are. All that would be required is that export subsidies be announced and the same subsidy be available to all comers. The subsidy would need to be uniform for a given port or point of export and not be specific to particular destinations. Except for the export subsidies related to food aid, United States export subsidies paid during the 1960s and early 1970s did follow the MFN principle. Thus in the case of export subsidies, a rule requiring consistency with MFN treatment is possible and if export subsidies cannot be prohibited, then Article XVI should be amended to make them subject to the MFN rule.

As noted, the Japanese proposal referred to the desirability of modifying the exception in Article XI that permits export embargoes and restrictions to prevent or relieve critical shortages of foodstuffs in the exporting country. In my view, this should be eliminated and severe penalties should be provided for any country that imposes export restrictions on any agricultural product. The effect of the present exception in Article XI is that there is no explicit restraint on the use of export restrictions other than the commercial one that their use makes the country an unreliable supplier. But there should be specific provision for loss of trade benefits for any contracting party to the GATT using export embargoes or quotas except as required to enforce internationally imposed sanctions. A penalty such as loss of MFN treatment on its exports of agricultural products for a specified period or the imposition of an import tax by all importers for a similar period would not be too severe. Export restraints impose a heavy cost on the international trading system. The cost is a loss of confidence in the trading system and the support that embargoes give to those in importing countries who wish to follow protectionist policies.

An issue that is perhaps even more difficult to resolve is that of 'voluntary' export restraints (VERs), such as the United States has negotiated several times with countries that export beef to it and that the European Community has for cassava. It is a misuse of language to call the VERs voluntary; exporters accept them because they anticipate a more stringent unilateral action if they do not do so. As the United States has used the VERs for beef, it becomes necessary for the exporting country to intervene in their beef exports in order to ensure that the terms of the VER are met. Thus the VER is a source of illiberal actions in international trade; it is obvious that the VERs do not promote liberal trade. The interventions that may be made by the exporter can have negative effects on producers in third countries. One effect of the United States VER is to raise the value of an export to the United States above the value to alternative markets. One government has handled this problem by requiring a tied arrangement; for example, to export a ton of beef to the United States, the exporter had to export 200 kilograms to a third market.

A further rule-change that should be made is that there cannot be a waiver of the rules and regulations such as was granted to the United States in 1955. This does not mean that the United States or any other country would be prohibited from taking actions contrary to their obligations under the GATT. What it would mean is that when they did so, there would be some price to pay in terms of demands for compensation by other GATT contracting parties.

The granting of an indefinite waiver to the United States was an error that did great damage to the role of the GATT in agricultural trade. Given the existence of the waiver, it was difficult to take seriously any concession made by the United States. The concession could be withdrawn with impunity. Unfortunately it appears that some GATT contracting parties have not been displeased with this barrier to success in previous negotiations because they did not wish to subject their farm programmes to the discipline of the international market and to negotiations in an international forum.

Conditions for a Successful Negotiation

In the first edition of this book I offered for consideration two criteria to serve as the basis for meaningful negotiations that could lead to liberalization of agricultural trade. The first criterion was that governments should negotiate on the rate of *effective* protection provided to agriculture. The second criterion was that whatever degree of protection was agreed, governments should give careful consideration to the effects of the particular price-support and income-support measures on output and consumption and thus on trade. I added that the second criterion had no more content than the GATT principle that domestic farm policies should not be used to harm the interests of other countries, but it did have the advantage of emphasizing those aspects of domestic programmes that harm others.

Because of the ambiguities in categorizing measures in terms of their harm to others, including the now-popular idea of decoupled subsidies, the first criterion is clearly the critical one. The effect of domestic farm programmes on the volume and value of trade and the fraction of that trade that is determined by the principles of comparative advantage is the important consideration and not the particular trade-restrictive and interfering devices that are applied. It is not variable import levies or variable export subsidies *per se* that are more serious impediments to trade than fixed import duties; it is the degree of protection, however achieved, that primarily limits and distorts international trade. This is not to say that the form of protection is without importance. Clearly it is to be preferred if subsidies are unrelated to current production. Stable domestic prices, even with low average levels of protection over time, result in unstable international market prices compared with what would be the case with an *ad valorem* tariff of the same low level. Thus I do not wish to minimize the importance of emphasizing the forms of protection that have the fewest adverse effects but only to make clear that with high levels of protection the form of protection is far less important than the level.

In the first edition it was urged that prior to negotiations there should be competent analyses of the output and trade effects, the distribution of costs and benefits among consumers, taxpayers and farmers and the determination of the level of protection.

In the intervening fifteen years, some of these analyses have been undertaken, but much remains to be done. The OECD studies of agricultural protection and trade emphasized measuring the rate of protection, the costs to consumers and taxpayers of that protection and the effects of the protection on output, trade and international market prices.[18] There were no studies of the distribution of either the costs among consumers and taxpayers by income level or of the benefits to farm families. Thus while the OECD study advanced knowledge of agricultural protection and its effects, it left unstudied many important issues. But one should applaud what was done. A similar effort was not possible during the Tokyo Round negotiations and could probably not have been done at any time before the early 1980s.

The measure of protection used in the OECD study, based on earlier work done for the Food and Agriculture Organization by T. E. Josling, was the producer subsidy equivalent.[19] The PSE is the percentage of the total producer value that was due to government-induced transfers. The transfers as measured included a wide range of subsidies including not only those related directly to prices and output but credit and input subsidies, the costs of grading and inspection and of research and extension, and the administrative costs of the programmes. A related measure called the consumer subsidy equivalent (CSE) was estimated, which for the industrial economies is misnamed because it measures the effects of agricultural protection on costs borne by consumers. In the industrial economies these costs are positive numbers, but in the CSE they are negative, for what is being measured is a negative subsidy.

In the text above there are references to effective protection; the PSE is not a measure of effective protection. Should the OECD study have used a measure of effective protection and should negotiations be guided by that measure of protection? The purist in me says the answer is in the affirmative while the more practical side of me says that it has been difficult enough to obtain grudging acceptance of the PSE estimates and it would be much more difficult to get negotiators and policy-makers to accept the concept of effective protection. It is not only that the data needed is much greater for measuring effective protection, but much of the required data is not available on a timely basis in most countries. The measurement of effective protection requires an estimate of the protection afforded the inputs used in agriculture and of the importance of those inputs in the production process. To make this calculation requires a current and very detailed national input–output table or highly disaggregated production functions for farm production. Except for Australia among the industrial countries, the level of protection of farm inputs is generally low enough, so that measures of nominal protection are probably adequate for use in negotiations. In Australia, protection of the non-agricultural sector is relatively high; and therefore if there were free trade in farm products, the effective rate of protection for agriculture would be negative.

The most serious limitation of the PSE or nominal protection rates may be in giving a misleading impression of the disparity in effective protection among farming activities in a given economy. As discussed in Chapter 6, effective protection is a measure of the protection of the value added in the production of a commodity, while nominal protection refers to the protection of the final product to whether the input is of non-farm or farm origin. If all non-farm inputs have the same degree of nominal protection, the magnitude of the effective protection for farm products will vary according to the percentage of the value of the final product that went to the purchased inputs from the non-farm sector.

Assume the nominal protection rates are the same for two farm products, say 40 per cent, and inputs from the non-farm sector have nominal protection rates of 10 per cent. One of the products has inputs from the non-farm sector equal to 60 per cent of the value of the output and the other has 30 per cent. The effective protection of the value added by agriculture is 76 per cent in the first case and 51 per cent in the second. Even at very low rates of nominal protection, such as 10 per cent when the inputs are available at international market prices, there will be significant differences in the effective protection depending upon the importance of purchased non-farm inputs. Thus while it is desirable to move toward uniformity in nominal rates of protection, doing so is not enough to provide uniform rates of protection for the farm productive activity. But it is probably true that moving the disparate rates of nominal protection towards a more uniform level would generally reduce disparities in effective protection rates.

The Uruguay Round negotiations hopefully represent a first step towards serious negotiations about domestic agricultural price-support and income-support programmes. The previous negotiations have floundered because none of the participants was able and willing to enter into such discussions. While the United States during both the Kennedy and Tokyo Rounds professed its willingness to negotiate seriously about all aspects of its farm programmes, my personal belief, based on some involvement in both negotiations, was that the United States Administration was not prepared to respond to a serious proposal by other countries that would have required the elimination of import quotas on dairy products and sugar and the substitution of some alternative protective device providing a significantly lower level of protection.

Decoupled Payments

As noted in Chapter 12 there is a long history of proposals for decoupling farm subsidy payments from current production activity. In terms of the current trade negotiations, the primary objective of decoupled payments is to have production decisions made on the basis of current market prices that reflect world supply and demand conditions, while providing for compensation for the losses that would result from the transition from the current policies. The transition would result in major losses to owners of fixed assets, especially land and buildings, that cannot be shifted to other uses. There would also be losses to farm workers and operators, especially the older ones, who have few non-farm employment opportunities and whose best alternative would be to stay in agriculture even at a substantially lower rate of return for their effort until the farm labour supply has adjusted to the change in output prices. It is not clear how long this would be, since we have little historical experience to guide us. It appears reasonable to assume, however, that the period of full adjustment in the labour market would occur within five to ten years. The adjustment would occur more rapidly the greater the confidence that the policy changes were irreversible.

Various proposals have been made for decoupled payments. In the United States, Senators Boschwitz and Boren have proposed a programme of decoupled payments for the grains, cotton and oilseeds. In the proposal made in 1988, payment rates were established for the following year that used the base acreages and yields assigned to each farm for 1989. The amount of the payment per unit of hypothetical production was based on the level of anticipated deficiency payments, except for oilseeds, for which there were no deficiency payments. In the case of oilseeds the payment per unit of output was based on the anticipated decline in market price that would result from the elimination of the supply management programmes. After the first year, the payments would decline by 10 per cent annually, except that for the oilseeds the decline would be 20 per cent annually. The payments would be independent of what was actually produced in any year or what actual market prices were. The payments are decoupled because they are related to past production, not present or prospective. If the land were left idle or if the farmer moved out of agriculture, the payments would be continued.

The Boschwitz–Boren proposal emphasizes the significant point that, if decoupled payments are not to have an influence on production decisions, the payments should be temporary or transitional and that the payments are independent of the actual use of the resources. It is important that the payments not be dependent on the resources, especially labour, continuing to be employed in agriculture.

A very effective decoupled payment would be a lump-sum payment that represented the anticipated future value of the price and subsidy programmes. An example of such a decoupled payment would be if the Canadian Government purchased the production quotas for milk and poultry products and then permitted free trade in those products. The payment could be based on the recent market values of the quotas, where there has been an active market, or on a formula derived from situations where the quotas have been for sale. There have been other suggestions for decoupled payments, such as assuring farm operators of their recent level of net income for a period of years, say a decade. Such a scheme would reduce the possibility of major financial stress arising from the transition to freer trade, although perhaps it would not entirely eliminate it. None of the proposals that I have seen would protect the interests of hired farm workers, many of whom would suffer losses during a transition period. One possibility would be to make a lump-sum payment to hired farm workers employed in agriculture at the time of the announcement of the programme related to the number of years of full-time employment as a hired worker and the anticipated reduction in farm wage rates over the next several years. The payment would be larger for older farm workers who would probably be the largest losers because of their difficulties in finding employment outside of agriculture. The payment might cover the present value of the anticipated losses for a decade.

It is important that the decoupled payments be seen as transitory or for a limited period of time. Otherwise it becomes difficult if not impossible to divorce such payments from current production. If the payments are permanent, it is highly probable that there will be some relationship to how resources are used. Consequently people will either stay in agriculture or enter agriculture based, at least in part, on the continuation of the payments. It is absolutely essential that the payments not be available to new entrants into agriculture. Otherwise the payments will influence the amounts of resources engaged in agriculture.

In spite of the dangers indicated in the previous paragraph, governments will almost certainly argue for permanent programmes to meet at least some of the problems of instability in agriculture. The emphasis on stable prices, even though such prices don't provide for much stability of income, is too ingrained in the thinking of farmers and policy-makers in several industrial countries that there will be strong pressure to have some insurance against sharp declines in farm prices and incomes. It is important that such programmes be evaluated in some international forum so that there will be at least an understanding of their potential effects on agricultural production.

It is not my intention to make detailed suggestions for the conduct of trade negotiations. Several such suggestions or proposals have been made by responsible individuals or groups.[20] I have noted some of the changes in GATT rules that seem essential, not so much for the negotiations but for the maintenance of a liberal trading regime in agriculture once that objective has been achieved.

There seems to be agreement that the negotiations should tackle both short-run measures for significantly reducing the degree of agricultural protection over a reasonable period of time, such as five to ten years, and then to negotiate concerning the long-run objective. Some GATT contracting parties have argued for the eventual elimination of all trade-distorting price interventions and subsidies while others believe such a long-run objective is neither desirable nor feasible. The art of negotiation is to achieve an acceptable compromise among the conflicting objectives.

Notes and References

1 Politics and Economics and Farmers

1. *Labour Force Statistics, 1964–1984* (Paris: OECD, 1986).
2. *World Development Report 1986* (New York: Oxford University Press, for the World Bank, 1986), chs 4 and 5.
3. Rodney Tyers and Kym Anderson, *Price, Trade and Welfare Effects of Agricultural Protection: the Case of East Asia*, Pacific Economic Paper No. 109 (Canberra: Australia–Japan Research Centre, Australian National University, 1984), p. 8.
4. Ibid.
5. Ibid.
6. *World Development Report 1986*, op. cit., ch. 6.
7. D. Gale Johnson, 'World Agriculture, Commodity Policy and Price Variability', *American Journal of Agricultural Economics*, December 1975, pp. 823–8, for an early discussion of the effect of domestic farm policies that stabilize domestic prices through varying net agricultural trade on international market prices. The Organisation for Economic Cooperation and Development (OECD), while rather slow in accepting the analysis that farm price policies are important sources of world price instability, stated the following as the introductory sentence to a chapter with the title 'Implications of Agricultural Policies for Market Stability': 'The implementation of governmental policies can both augment and attenuate instability in national and international markets . . . . Moreover . . . various measures taken for strictly domestic or interior motives can result in an international situation that is less stable.' *The Instability of Agricultural Commodity Markets* (Paris: OECD, 1980), p. 48.

2 Farm and Trade Policies of the Industrial Countries

1. The most complete and definitive reports on the agricultural policies of the industrial countries are those started by the Organisation for European Economic Cooperation (OEEC), the predecessor to the OECD, the fifth in the series being *Trends in Agricultural Policies Since 1955* (Paris: OEEC, 1961), and *Agricultural Policies in 1966: Europe, North America and Japan* (Paris: OECD, 1967).

   The OECD continued the surveys of agricultural policies in *Review of Agricultural Policies: General Survey* (1975) and in a series of annual publications under the title *Review of Agricultural Policies in OECD Member Countries*. The first in the series covered 1974–76. The links between domestic agricultural policies and international trade policies are emphasized in *OECD Problems of Agricultural Trade* (1982). In 1987, the OECD published the results of its large-scale study, *National Policies and*

Agricultural Trade. In addition to the overall report that presented estimates of the degree of protection of agriculture in OECD countries, budgetary and consumer costs and trade effects of national farm policies, there were national reports describing the farm policies that were in effect for 1970–82. These detailed reports were published for the United States, the European Community, Austria, New Zealand, Australia, Japan and Canada. Subsequent national reports have covered Sweden and Finland.

An excellent presentation of the historical development of agricultural and trade policy in Western Europe may be found in Michael Tracy, *Agriculture in Western Europe: Challenge and Response 1880–1980*, second edition (London: Granada, 1982). A short and highly useful summary may be found in David L. MacFarlane and Lewis A. Fischer, 'Prospects for Trade Liberalization in Agriculture', in Gerald I. Trant, MacFarlane and Fischer, *Trade Liberalization and Canadian Agriculture* (Toronto: University of Toronto Press, for the Private Planning Association of Canada, 1968). Also see Brian Fernon, *Issues in World Farm Trade: Chaos or Cooperation?*, Atlantic Trade Study No. 13 (London: Trade Policy Research Centre, 1970).

2. *Agricultural Policies in 1966*, op. cit., p. 59.
3. The continuing discussion (ibid.) is of interest:

In several cases these income objectives are qualified or accompanied by references to the need for a satisfactory level of productivity in agriculture, and sometimes they relate specifically to farms meeting certain standards of efficiency: thus in Belgium the aim is to ensure the profitability of holdings which are well managed and whose existence is economically and socially justified; in Finland, farms with a 'satisfactory degree of rationalization' should have incomes corresponding to those of other economic groups; in Sweden the size of farm to be used in income comparisons is laid down; in Switzerland a fair remuneration for farmers is to be ensured through prices covering average production costs on rationally operated farms; in the United States the objective is to provide opportunity for the efficient family farmer to earn 'parity of income from farming operations' and to provide 'parity of opportunity' for all rural people, including small farmers; in some cases income comparisons are made with specified non-farm groups (wage-earners in comparable non-agricultural occupations in West Germany, certain groups of industrial workers in low-cost living areas in Sweden, non-farm workers in rural and semi-urban districts in Switzerland).

4. The original act gave the Secretary of Agriculture authority to spend funds 'for expansion of markets and removal of surplus agricultural products'. Section 32, enacted in 1935, authorized the use of funds to 'encourage the exportation of agricultural commodities and products thereof by payments of benefits in connection with the exportation thereof or of indemnities for losses incurred in connection with the production of that part of an agricultural commodity required for domestic consumption, and reestablish farmers' purchasing power by making payments in connection with the normal production of any agricultural product for domestic consumption'.

See D.G. Johnson, *Trade and Agriculture: a Study of Inconsistent Policies* (New York: John Wiley, 1950).

5. *Trends in Agricultural Policies Since 1955*, op. cit., pp. 48–9.

6. The nominal rate of protection is a measure of the difference between the return to domestic producers and the border price, with the latter adjusted to reflect quality differences and relevant transport – and marketing costs to make it comparable with the price received by domestic producers. The domestic return is the price received by farmers plus any direct payment, such as a deficiency payment, that is related to the level of output. The nominal rate of protection is calculated as (domestic return – border price) divided by the border price and subtracting one from this result. The figure obtained is multiplied by 100 if it is wished to convert the rate to a percentage. The 1956 estimate is from Gavin McCrone, *The Economics of Subsidizing Agriculture* (London: Allen & Unwin, 1962), p. 51, and the 1965–67 estimate is from Richard W. Howarth, *Agricultural Support in Western Europe*, Research Monograph No. 25 (London: Institute of Economic Affairs, 1971), p. 29. The other estimates are from Kym Anderson and Yujiro Hayami, *The Political Economy of Agricultural Protection: East Asia in International Perspective* (London: Allen & Unwin, 1986), p. 26. Masayoshi Honma assisted with the estimates of protection levels.

7. Anyone who is interested in detailed and authoritative summary and analysis of United States farm programmes since the Second World War will be rewarded by study of Willard W. Cochrane and Mary E. Ryan, *American Farm Policy 1948–1973* (Minneapolis: University of Minnesota Press, 1976).

8. Two excellent analyses of the price divergencies that have occurred within the European Community may be found in Theodor Heidhues, T.E. Josling, Christopher Ritson and Stefan Tangermann, *Common Prices and Europe's Farm Policy*, Thames Essay No. 14 (London: Trade Policy Research Centre, 1978) and Josling, Mark Langworthy and Scott Pearson, *Options for Farm Policy in the European Community*, Thames Essay No. 27 (London: Trade Policy Research Centre, 1981), especially pp. 12–15 and 26–35.

9. *Trends in Agricultural Policies Since 1955*, op. cit., p. 35.

10. Albert Simantov, 'Agricultural Developments in OECD Countries and Implications for Trade', speech given at the United States National Agricultural Outlook Conference, Washington, 17 February 1969.

11. An indication of the disparities in educational opportunities is provided in Chapter 11.

3 Present State of Disarray

1. See Chapter 10.

2. Vladimir G. Treml, *Agricultural Subsidies in the Soviet Union*, Foreign Economic Report No. 15 (Washington: Bureau of the Census, United States Department of Commerce, 1978), p. 8.

3. Rodney Tyers and Kym Anderson, of the University of Adelaide, have produced a substantial volume of research on the effects of agricultural trade restrictions on international market prices and the welfare costs of those restrictions. Among their studies the following may be noted: 'Global Interactions and Trade Liberalisation in Agriculture', mimeograph, Department of Economics, University of Adelaide, April 1987; 'Liberalising OECD Agricultural Policies in the Uruguay Round: Effects on Trade and Welfare', *Journal of Agricultural Economics*, May 1988, pp. 197–216; and *Global Effects of Liberalizing Trade in Farm Products*, Thames Essay No. 55 (Aldershot, Brookfield and Sydney: Gower, for the Trade Policy Research Centre, 1989). Reference should also be made to Anthony H. Chisholm and Tyers, 'Agricultural Protection and Market Insulation Policies: Applications of a Dynamic Multisectoral Policy', in John Piggott and John Whalley (eds), *New Developments in Applied General Equilibrium Analysis* (Cambridge: Cambridge University Press, 1985).

4. *Grain in the European Community: Rising Protection and Falling Imports* (Washington: United States Department of Agriculture [USDA], 1970).

5. Ibid., and Presidential Commission on International Trade and Investment Policy, *United States International Economic Policy in an Interdependent World*, Williams Report (Washington: US Government Printing Office, 1971).

6. *Wheat Situation and Outlook Report*, United States Department of Agriculture, Washington, July 1969, pp. 21, 22 and 24; and *Review of the World Grains Situation, 1968/69* (London: International Wheat Council [IWC], 1969), p. 77.

7. *Trade yearbook*, Food and Agriculture Organization (FAO), Rome, various issues.

8. *The State of Food and Agriculture, 1965* (Rome: FAO, 1966), pp. 250 and 253.

9. *Agricultural Statistics, 1955–1968* (Paris: OECD, 1969), pp. 106–9.

10. D.G. Johnson, 'World Agriculture, Commodity Policy and Price Variability', op. cit.

11. For an excellent analysis of the Soviet wheat purchases in the 1970s and of the overall impact of governmental price and trade policies on the variability of international wheat prices, see Maurice W. Schiff, *An Econometric Analysis of the World Wheat Market and Simulation of Alternative Policies, 1960–80*, Economic Research Service Staff Report No. AGES 850827 (Washington: United States Department of Agriculture, 1985), especially pp. 28–30.

12. Martin E. Abel and Anthony S. Rojko, *World Food Situation: Prospects for World Grain Production, Consumption and Trade* (Washington: United States Department of Agriculture, 1967), p. 19.

13. Ibid., p. 26.

14. *Provisional Indicative World Plan for Agricultural Development* (Rome: FAO, 1969), ch. 14, pp. 113–14.

15. *Agricultural Projections for 1975 and 1985: Europe, North America, Japan and Oceania* (Paris: OECD, 1968), pp. 57–8. The commodities included in the projections are all grains, sugar, beef and veal, mutton and lamb, pigmeat, poultry-meat, eggs and dairy products. The projected estimates of

330   *Notes and References*

net exports or of grain exports do not include Australia and New Zealand. In 1961/63 Australia exported 6.7 million tons of grain (6.0 million tons of bread grains) and 1975 exports are projected to be 10.2 million tons (ibid., p. 22). New Zealand is an unimportant contributor to grain trade. The adjustments referred to in the last paragraph of the quotation assume that part of the projected deficit in the supply of beef and veal within the OECD area would be met by increased production of beef and veal within the area (in excess of the increase expected with current prices and policies) by increased feeding of grain. The estimated reduction in grain exports due to the expansion of meat production is estimated to be from 4 to 9 million tons, depending on the distribution of increased meat output by type of meat animal. The projected net exports of grain from the OECD area in 1975 are 79.6 million tons.

16. Tyers and Anderson, 'Global Interactions and Trade Liberalisation in Agriculture', op. cit., p. 16.

4 Agricultural Change

1. See *The Growth of Output, 1960–1980* (Paris: OECD, 1970), p. 35.
2. *Output, Expenses and Income of Agriculture in European Countries, Sixth Report* (New York: United Nations, for the Economic Commission for Europe and the FAO, 1969) pp. 330 and 336.
3. See Table 4.3 for sources.
4. *Changes in Farm Production and Efficiency, 1986* (Washington: United States Department of Agriculture, 1986), p. 56.
5. *Agricultural Statistics, 1952* (Washington: United States Department of Agriculture, 1953), pp. 455, 637, 644 and 651.
6. *Economic Indicators of the Farm Sector: Farm Sector Review, 1985* (Washington: United States Department of Agriculture, 1987), p. 11. The calculation in the text indicates how lacking in realism is the view that agriculture in the industrial countries should turn from mechanical power to animal power due to the high energy prices. Farm production would be drastically reduced if even a fifth of the current power provided by tractors were replaced by animals. The actual production of food in the United States (and in other industrial countries) uses but a tiny fraction of the fossil fuel energy consumed – approximately 3 per cent of the total. More energy is used in home food preparation, in food processing and in restaurants – not in total but in each category – than for farm food production in the United States.
7. *Economic Indicators of the Farm Sector: National Financial Summary, 1986* (Washington: United States Department of Agriculture, 1987), p. 51, and *Statistical Abstract of the United States 1987* (Washington: Department of Commerce, 1987), pp. 512 and 723.

For a discussion of the valuation of investment, see Allen G. Smith, 'Comparative Investment per Worker in Agriculture and Manufacturing Sectors of the Economy', *American Journal of Agricultural Economics*, February 1971, pp. 101–2.

8. *US Population Mobility and Distribution: Charts on Recent Trends* (Washington: United States Department of Agriculture, 1969), pp. 31–2.
9. Ibid.
10. *Labour Force Statistics* (OECD), various issues.
11. *Production Yearbook 1981* (Rome: FAO, 1982).
12. *Economic Indicators of the Farm Sector: National Financial Summary, 1986*, op. cit., pp. 8 and 10.
13. Calculated from *Production Yearbook* (FAO), for 1968 and 1985.
14. *OECD Agricultural Review*, OECD, Paris, No. 3, 1970, p. 97. In 1967/68 over 60 per cent of all commercial fertilizer used in the world was used in the OECD countries. New Zealand was not an OECD member at the time. In 1984, according to World Bank estimates, New Zealand used more than a ton of plant nutrients per hectare, well in excess of the 788 kilograms used in the Netherlands.
15. Data are for the industrial market economies as designated by the World Bank and based on fertilizer use per hectare of arable land. *World Development Report 1987* (New York: Oxford University Press, for the World Bank, 1987), p. 213.
16. Over the subsequent decade (1968 to 1978), the use of nitrogen increased by 6 million tons and grain production by 100 million tons. Consequently farmers were making very effective use of fertilizers as the rate of growth of fertilizer use slowed down. Data from *Agricultural Statistics, 1955–1968* (OECD), op. cit., and *Production Yearbook* (FAO), for 1970 and 1980. New Zealand and Australia are not included.
17. Hayami and Vernon W. Ruttan, *Agricultural Development: an International Perspective* (Baltimore: Johns Hopkins Press, 1971), ch. IV. Farm employment includes only male workers and the measure of land is all agricultural land.
18. Unfortunately some of the differences between the agricultures of the United States and Japan, on the one hand, and India, on the other hand, grew during the 1960s and the 1970s. For example, farm output per farm worker in 1960 in the United States was 43 times that in India in the same year; Table 4.6 indicates that in 1980 the ratio was 90 times. The difference in the amount of agricultural land per worker in the United States also grew during the 1960s and in the 1970s while declining in India.
19. *Production Yearbook 1985* (Rome: FAO, 1986).

5 Agriculture Must Change

1. C.H. Shah, in his presidential address at the Thirty-ninth Conference of the Indian Agricultural Economics Society presented evidence that even at the very lowest levels of income in India food tastes or preferences were substitutes for calories. In other words, even very poor people spent additional income to achieve variety and taste even when by traditional measurements their food intake was deficient in calories. Among his conclusions are: 'Emergence of food taste as an important element to reckon with in the food demand below the calories-based poverty line has

... implications relevant for policy purposes .... [I]t weakens the claim of calories as a criterion for measuring the extent of poverty. We have already seen that even with rising income there may be a possible increase in the number of persons with calorie intake below the recommended level. While this may not be welcome, it need not be frightening. The improved "taste" content (which may include increased consumption of even vegetables and fruits and milk, besides pulses), may add to quality of life.' C.H. Shah, 'Food Preferences and Nutrition: a perspective on Poverty in Less Developed Countries', *Indian Journal of Agricultural Economics*, Bombay, January–March 1980, p. 35.

2. *Agricultural Statistics* (USDA), various issues.
3. *Agricultural Commodities: Projections for 1970* (Rome: FAO, 1962), pp. 11–67.
4. The conditions under which agriculture's share of total employment would increase are quite restrictive. One condition is that farm prices relative to all other prices increase continuously over time. The slow growth of farm output is due to a failure to increase resource productivity as rapidly in agriculture as in the rest of the economy. Assume this is due to a fixed supply of land and rapidly diminishing marginal returns to all other resources. While the marginal physical productivity of labour would be increasing in the rest of the economy, as it must if real income growth occurs, the marginal physical productivity of labour in agriculture would be either stable or declining. Thus real farm prices would have to increase at a rate at least equal to the difference in the annual rate of growth of the marginal physical product of labour in the rest of the economy and in agriculture. This would be necessary if the returns to labour in agriculture were to increase at the same rate as the returns to labour in the rest of the economy.
5. *Economic Report of the President 1988* (Washington; US Government Printing Office, 1988), p. 361.
6. Hayami and Ruttan, op. cit., ch. 4.

6 Agricultural Prices and the Use of Resources

1. Estimates of variable import levies for maize are derived from *Agricultural Situation in the Community: 1978 Report* (Brussels: Commission of the European Community, 1979), p. 202 for 1968/69 and from *Yearbook of Agricultural Statistics, 1977–80* (Luxembourg: Statistical Office of the European Community, 1980), p. 261 for 1978/79. Estimates for 1986 are derived from a comparison of threshold prices and Rotterdam prices for United States maize.
2. W.E. Pearson and R.E. Friend, *The Netherlands Mixed Feed Industry* (Washington: United States Department of Agriculture, 1970), p. 36, and *The Agricultural Situation in the Community: 1987 Report* (Brussels: Commission of the European Community, 1988), pp. 245–46.
3. During the 1980s, the amount of manioc that could be exported to the European Community was controlled by import quotas. This step was

taken by the Community to minimize further substitution of non-grain materials for grain. Efforts to stem the flow of oilmeal imports by taxes or similar devices were not successful, although the large subsidies given for the production of oilseeds in the Community increased the production of the three major oilseeds – rapeseed, sunflower and soyabeans by nearly five-fold between 1973 and 1986. *The Agricultural Situation in the Community: 1986 Report* (Brussels: Commission of the European Community, 1987), pp. 150–51, and *The Agricultural Situation in the Community: 1987 Report*, op. cit., p. T/193.

4. James P. Houck and Abraham Subotnik, 'The US Supply of Soybeans: Regional Acreage Functions', *Agricultural Economics Research*, United States Department of Agriculture, Washington, October 1969, p. 105. The elasticity of soya-bean acreage with respect to the price of corn was −0.65.

5. Marc Nerlove, *The Dynamics of Supply: Estimation of Farmers' Response to Price* (Baltimore: Johns Hopkins Press, 1958), ch. VIII.

6. Luther Tweeten, *Foundations of Farm Policy*, second edition (Lincoln: University of Nebraska Press, 1979), p. 274. The long-run elasticity of crop production was estimated to be 1.56 for the United States; the acreage elasticity was 0.10 and the yield elasticity was 1.5.

7. Tyers and Anderson, 'Global Interactions and Trade Liberalisation in Agriculture', op. cit., p. 13.

8. Ibid., p. 18.

7 World Prices for Farm Products: Real or Fictitious?

1. Interestingly enough the low-wage argument is seldom if ever used to justify agricultural protection. The argument has no apparent validity because several of the most competitive exporters are high-income (high-wage) countries.

2. *France and Agriculture* (New York: Service de Presse et d'Information de France, 1963), p. 48.

3. Denis Bergmann et al., *A Future for European Agriculture*, Atlantic Paper No. 4 (Paris: Atlantic Institute for International Affairs, 1970), pp. 14–15.

4. John R. Block, *Speeches* (Washington: United States Department of Agriculture, 1983), p. 21.

5. *Farm Product Imports, Present State of Agriculture and Direction of Agricultural Policy* (Tokyo: Ministry of Agriculture, Forestry and Fisheries, 1982).

6. *Wheat Situation and Outlook Report* (USDA), July 1969, p. 13.

7. From 1967/68 to 1971/72 soft wheat prices in the European Community averaged 1.98 times import prices. See Brian E. Hill, *The Common Agricultural Policy: Past, Present and Future* (London: Methuen, 1984), p. 87. It is tempting to utilize the price elasticities of supply for wheat given in Table 6.6 to arrive at an estimate of the relative contribution of wheat protection to wheat output in the major exporting countries and in Western Europe, including the European Community. Any results that

might be obtained from such an exercise need to be interpreted with a great deal of caution. There are at least two reasons for this. One is that the nominal protection of wheat in Western Europe was so large – the variable import levy on wheat imposed by the Community from 1967/68 to 1971/72 was nearly equal to the import cost – that it cannot be assumed the elasticities of supply would be valid for the very large reduction of price if it were reduced to world market levels. The other is that most, although not all, of the estimated elasticities were based on changes in the price of wheat relative to other competing products. Thus it cannot be said that the price of wheat in the Community has increased by 90 per cent or even 50 per cent relative to farm products that compete for the same resources. In fact, since the adoption of the common agricultural policy the price of wheat has fallen relative to the price of feed-grains in the Community.

8. In this discussion the production and trade policies of the developing importing countries have been ignored as well as the policies of the centrally-planned economies. During the 1960s the centrally-planned economies imported about the same amount of wheat as they exported, while the developing countries imported substantial quantities of wheat, but much of it on a concessional basis.

9. *Grain in the European Community: Rising Protection and Falling Imports*, op. cit., p. 3.

10. John E. Hutchison, James J. Naive and Sheldon K. Tsu, *World Demand Prospects for Wheat in 1980 with Emphasis on Trade by Less Developed Countries* (Washington: United States Department of Agriculture, 1970), p. 49; *Grain in the European Community: Rising Protection and Falling Imports*, op. cit., p. 20; and *Wheat Situation and Outlook Report* (USDA), November 1970.

11. *Review of the World Grains Situation, 1968/69* (IWC), op. cit., p. 33.

12. The statement assumes that all of the wheat and flour of the developing countries from 1949/50 through 1953/54 of 8.7 million tons was on commercial terms. As used in this context, the developing countries exclude the centrally-planned economies. For 1959/60 through 1963/64 the developing countries imported 17.7 million tons of wheat and flour, of which 10.6 million tons was through some type of concessional terms and 7.1 million tons was on commercial terms. For the years from 1964/65 through to 1968/69 total imports ranged from 21.1 to 26.6 million tons and commercial imports averaged 12.3 million tons and concessional imports 12.0 million tons. Thus it does not appear unreasonable to assume that at least 6 million tons of the concessional exports represented additional trade in wheat and flour. For data on trade, ibid., p. 30, and *Trends and Problems in the World Grain Economy* (London: International Wheat Council, 1966), Appendix Table V.

13. *1969 Feed Grain and Wheat Programs* (Washington: United States Department of Agriculture, 1970), pp. 2–3.

14. Ibid.

15. The national feed-grain base was determined by acreage planted in 1959 and 1960 plus land in the Conservation Reserve programme during those years on farms that produced feed-grains. Generally the feed-grain programme has not included oats; the area of oats harvested has declined by

half in fifteen years. The total area of corn (for grain), sorghum and barley harvested in 1959 and 1960 was 41.1 million hectares; the feed-grain base for these three grains is about 54 million hectares. *Feed Statistics through 1966* (Washington: United States Department of Agriculture, 1967), pp. 6 and 46–47.

16. *1969 Feed Grain and Wheat Programs*, op. cit., pp. 2–3.
17. *Grain in the European Community: Rising Protection and Falling Imports*, op. cit., p. 30.
18. *Agriculture Abroad*, Canadian Department of Agriculture, Ottawa, December 1970, p. 15.
19. *Grain in the European Community: Rising Protection and Falling Imports*, op. cit., p. 20.
20. Ibid., p. 2.
21. *1970 Handbook of Agricultural Charts* (Washington: United States Department of Agriculture, 1970), p. 106.
22. Ibid., p. 105. Production total for 1969.
23. *Production Yearbook, 1969* (Rome: FAO, 1970), pp. 229–57.
24. In 1969 the cash income from cottonseed was 16 per cent of the total income from the sale of cotton lint and seed in the United States. *Farm Income Situation and Outlook Report*, United States Department of Agriculture, Washington, July 1970, p. 38.
25. *Production Yearbook, 1969* (FAO), op. cit., pp. 229–57.
26. *Foreign Agricultural Trade of the United States*, United States Department of Agriculture, Washington, July 1970, p. 7.
27. *Agricultural Statistics, 1970* (Washington: United States Department of Agriculture, 1971), p. 135.
28. Houck and J.S. Mann, *An Analysis of Domestic and Foreign Demand for US Soybeans and Soybean Products* (Minneapolis: Agricultural Experiment Station, University of Minnesota, 1968), p. 26, estimate that a reduction of 225 million kilograms in PL 480 shipments of soyabean oil would reduce the price of soyabeans by about 6 per cent. In 1968/69 PL 480 shipments of soyabean oil were about 360 million kilograms. It is my opinion that the price elasticity of demand found in the analysis is too low and that the American surplus disposal of soyabean oil is given too much 'credit' for maintaining the world market price for vegetable oils. Soyabean oil constitutes only 30 per cent of total vegetable oil production in the world and only 16 per cent of the total of vegetable oil, palm oil, marine oils, butter and lard. The price elasticity of −0.15 for American soyabean oil export seems too low given the relative importance of soyabean oil and the substitution possibilities that exist.
29. The price of feed-grains received by farmers was $88 per ton in the European Community and $42 in the United States in 1968.
30. William F. Roenigk, *Agriculture in the European Community and the United States, 1958–1968* (Washington: United States Department of Agriculture, 1971), pp. 2 and 8. Population data for 1969; consumption data for 1966/ 67 through 1968/69.
31. *Agricultural Projections for 1975 and 1985*, op. cit., pp. 18–19.
32. *Agricultural Policies of Foreign Governments* (Washington: United States Department of Agriculture, 1967), p. 13.

336 Notes and References

33. From 6 750 000 million bales in 1955–59 to 9 600 000 million bales in 1968–69. See *Cotton Situation*, United States Department of Agriculture, Washington, November 1966, p. 39, and January 1971, p. 31.
34. See D.G. Johnson, 'Soviet Agriculture Revisited', *American Journal of Agricultural Economics*, May 1971. In 1967 the cotton price paid to farms in the Soviet Union was about $1.43 per kilogram of lint cotton. The price of one grade of Soviet Union cotton in the London market was $0.69 per kilogram in the same year. See *Cotton Situation* (USDA), August 1968, p. 32.
35. See an excellent analysis by George E. Dudley, James R. Donald and Russell G. Barlowe, 'Yield and Acreage Implications for US Cotton', *Cotton Situation* (USDA), August 1970, pp. 17–23.
36. It might be argued that the large payments that have been made have induced farmers to remain in cotton production primarily to earn the payments (in 1969 almost 80 per cent of the cash receipts from the sale of cotton lint and seed). There have been very liberal provisions for transfer of cotton allotments within counties and states; thus a farmer who did not wish to produce cotton could lease his allotment to another farmer and in this way capture most of the payment.
37. Alberto Valdés and Joachim Zietz, *Agricultural Protection in OECD Countries: Its Costs to Less-developed Countries*, Research Report No. 21 (Washington: International Food Policy Research Institute, 1980).
38. Valdés, 'Agriculture in the Uruguay Round: Interests of Developing Countries', *The World Bank Economic Review*, Washington, September 1987, pp. 571–93.
39. Tyers, 'Effects on ASEAN of Food Trade Liberalization in Industrial Countries', a paper presented to the Second Western Pacific Food Trade Workshop, Jakarta, 22–23 August 1982.
40. Ibid., p. 26.
41. Ibid., p. 30.
42. Ulrich Koester, *Policy Options for the Grain Economy of the European Community: Implications for Developing Countries*, Research Report No. 35 (Washington: International Food Policy Research Institute, 1982).
43. Schiff, op. cit.
44. Tangermann and Wolfgang Krostitz, *Protectionism in the Livestock Sector with Particular Reference to the International Beef Trade* (Göttingen: Institut für Agrarökonomie der Universität Göttingen, 1982).
45. Roy Allen, Claudia Dodge and Andrew Schmitz, 'Voluntary Export Restraints as Protection Policy: the US Beef Case, *American Journal of Agricultural Economics*, May 1983, pp. 291–95.
46. In *Guidelines for European Agriculture*, the Commission of the European Community stated the following position:

Comparisons with world market prices may easily lead to misleading conclusions. It is highly unlikely that European consumers could be supplied for long at low and stable world prices if Community supply, because of reduction in production, would depend to a greater extent on imports. World market prices are notoriously volatile because the quantities involved in international trade are often marginal in relation to total production (e.g. sugar, cereals, dairy products) and may reflect short-term fluctuations in production. For several products (e.g. beef, wine, tobacco) there is no real world market and prices vary according to the destination of exports. Therefore the Commission is convinced that a generalized and systematic alignment to world market prices would not be a practical policy guideline.

(*Guidelines for European Agriculture*, COM(81) 608 final (Brussels: Commission of the European Community, 1981), pp. 8–9.)

47. Anderson and Tyers, 'European Community Grain and Meat Policies: Effects on International Prices', *European Review of Agricultural Economics*, Amsterdam, Vol. 11, no. 4, 1984, pp. 367–94.
48. Alexander H. Sarris and John Freebairn, 'Endogenous Price Policies and International Wheat Prices', *American Journal of Agricultural Economics*, May 1983, pp. 214–24.
49. Ibid., p. 223.
50. For example, the large-scale study undertaken at the International Institute for Applied Systems Analysis in Laxenburg, Austria, of the effects on international market prices of moving from the 1978–80 levels of protection by all market economies would result in an increase of 9 per cent in world market prices by 1990. The largest price changes were projected by dairy products and bovine and ovine meat. See Kirit S. Parikh, Gunther Fischer, Klaus Frohberg and Odd Gulbrandsen, *Towards Free Trade in Agriculture* (Dordrecht: Martinus Nijhoff, for the International Institute for Applied Systems Analysis, 1988), p. 194.
51. Tyers and Anderson, 'Distortions in World Food Markets: a Quantitative Assessment', a background paper for the World Bank's *World Development Report 1986*.
52. D.G. Johnson, 'Are High Farm Prices Here to Stay?', *Morgan Guaranty Survey*, New York, August 1974, pp. 9–14.
53. Ibid., p. 10.
54. D.G. Johnson, 'World Agriculture, Commodity Policy and Price Variability', op. cit.
55. Schiff, op. cit.
56. Shei Shun-yi and Robert L. Thompson, 'The Impact of Trade Restrictions on Price Stability in the World Wheat Market', *American Journal of Agricultural Economics*, November 1977, p. 637.
57. Paul R. Johnson, Thomas Grennes and Marie Thursby, 'Devaluation, Foreign Trade Controls and Domestic Wheat Prices', *American Journal of Agricultural Economics*, November 1977, pp. 619–27.

8 World Food Adequacy and Security

1. See, for example, Barbara Huddleston, *Closing the Cereals Gap with Trade and Food Aid*, Research Report No. 43 (Washington: International Food Policy Research Institute, 1984), especially ch. 7.
2. See Peter Svedberg, 'Food Insecurity in Developing Countries: Causes, Trends and Policy Options', UNCTAD/CD/301, GE.84-51933, UNCTAD, Geneva 6 June 1984, for a reference to an unpublished report

by S.J. Maxwell and H.W. Singer, p. 65. The study indicated that 25 per cent of food aid was provided for work programmes and special nutrition programmes. About 7 per cent of the food aid was for emergencies – earthquakes, floods and wars. Dr Huddleston (ibid., p. 69) reports the conclusion by the Food and Agriculture Organization 'that less than one-third of the 17.0 to 18.5 million tons of food aid it thinks will be needed by 1985 can be used in targeted food aid projects. Most of the rest will have to be sold on the open market and used for general budget support, with a small amount designated for genuine emergency relief ... the small proportion FAO allocates to targeted projects indicates how difficult it may be to expand direct distribution programs significantly, despite their attractive demand-creating features.'

3. In 1981 feed use of grain was estimated to be 534 million tons out of a total use of 1.451 million tons in 1980/81. Estimates by the United States Department of Agriculture.

4. The deviations of annual grain production were estimated from a regression of the logarithm of world grain production on time for 1960/61 through 1985/86. The data used were the United States Department of Agriculture estimates and include rice as milled rice. The annual compound growth rate of grain production for the world was 2.82 per cent.

5. See D.G. Johnson, 'Grain Insurance, Reserves and Trade: Contributions to Food Security for LDCs', in Valdés (ed.), *Food Security for Developing Countries* (Boulder: Westview Press, 1981), p. 261.

6. See ibid., p. 260.

7. I owe the calculations to Anjini Kochar, although I am responsible for the particular interpretation of the data.

8. At the World Food Conference in Rome in 1974 there was a call for annual commitments of a minimum of 10 million tons of grain as food aid with the desired level being 14–15 million tons to reach the levels of the 1960s. See 'The World Food Problem: Proposals for National and International Action', United Nations World Food Conference, Rome, 5–16 November 1974, E/CONF. 65/4, pp. 189–93.

9. This idea was presented in *Food Reserve Policies for World Food Security: a Consultant Study of Alternative Approaches*, ESC:CSP/75/2 (Rome: FAO, 1975). The consultants also included Jimmye Hillman and Roger Gray. Needless to say, the insurance proposal was given little attention at the subsequent meeting of the FAO Committee on Commodity Problems held in Rome in February 1975.

10. The accuracy of grain production data in many developing countries is subject to substantial error. The existence of the insurance programme could provide an incentive to a government to minimize its estimates of grain production in a given year in order to increase the grain actually transferred. Over time, this practice would be self-defeating, for estimates of trend production for future years would be affected by such under-estimates. Since many governments may have a brief expected life, however, the self-correcting feature may not be of much value in some cases. It might be necessary for the insurance agency to have the right to obtain grain production estimates from an organization that was independent of both the agency and the developing country.

11. The estimate of famine death losses is from Basil Ashton, Kenneth Hill, Alan Piazza and Robin Zeitz, 'Famine in China: 1958–61', *Population and Development Review*, New York, December 1984, p. 619. Chinese grain and food crops were sharply lower in 1959, 1960 and 1961 than in earlier years. Gross agricultural output in 1961 was some 26 per cent below 1958. But poor crops can be due to factors other than climatic conditions. Liang Wensen, a senior member of the Chinese Academy of Social Sciences, after noting the decline in farm output, wrote: 'Although natural disasters and the scrapping of contracts by the Soviet Government played a role in these setbacks, the major cause was the miscalculation in our economic planning which led to serious imbalances between industry and agriculture and in the economy as a whole.' Liang Wensen, 'Balanced Development of Industry and Agriculture', in Xu Dixin et al., *China's Search for Economic Growth: the Chinese Economy since 1949* (Beijing: New World Press, 1982), p. 60.

12. David Bigman and Shlomo Reutlinger, 'Food Price and Supply Stabilization: National Buffer Stocks and Trade Policies', *American Journal of Agricultural Economics*, November 1979, p. 664.

13. Ibid., p. 666.

14. Huddleston and Panos Konandreas, 'Insurance Approach to Food Security: Simulation of Benefits for 1970/71–1975/76 and for 1978–1982', in Valdés (ed.), *Food Security for Developing Countries*, op. cit., pp. 241–54.

15. Valdés and Konandreas, 'Assessing Food Insecurity Based on National Aggregates in Developing Countries', in Valdés (ed.), *Food Security for Developing Countries*, op. cit., p. 36.

16. See D.G. Johnson, 'International Prices and Trade in Reducing Distortions in Incentives', in Theodore W. Schultz (ed.), *Distortions of Agricultural Incentives* (Bloomington: Indiana University Press, 1978).

17. See Svedberg, op. cit., pp. 24–35.

18. Peter B.R. Hazell, *Instability in Indian Grain Production*, Research Report No. 30 (Washington: International Food Policy Research Institute, 1982).

19. *World Development Report 1986*, op. cit., chs 4 and 5.

20. Schultz, *Transforming Traditional Agriculture* (New Haven: Yale University Press, 1964), now available from the University of Chicago Press.

21. The new varieties of rice and wheat were introduced into South and Southeast Asia in 1966–67. By 1972–73, 53 per cent of all wheat in this area was sown with new wheat varieties and 20 per cent of all rice. Five years later the percentages were, respectively, 74 and 35. While the new varieties have been adaptable to a wide variety of growing conditions, they are not adapted to every situation. Dana G. Dalrymple, *Development and Spread of High Yielding Wheat Varieties in Developing Countries* (Washington: Agency for International Development, 1986), p. 87.

22. *Production Yearbook*, FAO, Rome, for 1980 and 1985.

9 Who Gains from Agricultural Protection?

1. Such comparisons should not be accepted uncritically. There are many differences in the composition of the labour forces in agriculture and non-

agriculture with respect to age, education, skill and degree of participation in the labour force. See Chapter 11 for a fuller discussion of the problems of making such comparisons.

2. Colin Clark, *The Conditions of Economic Progress*, second edition (London: Macmillan, 1951), p. 531. Data are given for five periods between 1860 and 1944. In the latter year land rent was 15 per cent of net product.

3. G.A. MacEachern and Ruttan, 'Determining Factor Shares, in *Farmers in the Market Economy* (Ames: Iowa State Center for Agricultural and Economic Development, 1964), p. 208. The factor shares as percentages of value added in 1957–59 were estimated to be: land, 22; buildings, 12; non-real-estate capital, 28 and labour, 38.

4. Kazushi Ohkawa, Bruce F. Johnston and Hiromitsu Kaneda (eds), *Agriculture and Economic Growth: Japan's Experience* (Tokyo: University of Tokyo Press, 1969).

5. This statement is not absolutely certain since the elasticity of supply of land is lower than for any other input used in agriculture. As more of all other inputs would be used in agriculture, the value of the marginal product of land would increase both because of the higher output price and the rise in the marginal physical product due to the greater amount or other inputs used per unit of land. But in a modern agriculture the higher rent or price of land leads to the search for new knowledge and new inputs that will substitute more effectively for land and tends to hold land's factor share at a constant or declining fraction.

6. In 1986 approximately a seventh of the farms in the United States accounted for 70 per cent of cash receipts from farming. This included all farms with sales of $100 000 or more. The average family income, including both farm and non-farm incomes, for these 276 000 families was $132 000. This compares with a mean family money income in the United States of about $31 000 in the same year. See *Economic Indicators of the Farm Sector: National Financial Summary, 1986*, op. cit., pp. 40, 46 and 48; and *Economic Indicators of the Farm Sector: Farm Sector Review, 1986* (Washington: United States Department of Agriculture, 1988), p. 51.

7. *Economic Indicators of the Farm Sector: National Financial Summary, 1985* (Washington: United States Department of Agriculture, 1986), p. 58; and *Agricultural Resources: Agricultural Land Values and Markets Situation and Outlook Report* (Washington: United States Department of Agriculture, 1987), p. 8. It may be noted that while many farmers were subjected to foreclosure or bankruptcy, the percentage who were so affected was about 0.5 to at most 1.0 each year from 1983 to 1987.

8. Edward W. Tyrchniewicz and G. Edward Schuh, 'Econometric Analysis of the Agricultural Labor Market', *American Journal of Agricultural Economics*, November 1969, pp. 770–87.

9. *Economic Indicators of the Farm Sector: National Financial Summary, 1985*, op. cit.

10. The reciprocal is relevant because what we are interested in is the price of labour as a function of the quantity of labour. In other words, we want to know how much the price of labour will change when the quantity of labour changes, while the elasticity of demand for labour with respect to its price tells us how much the quantity of labour changes when the price of

labour changes. The elasticity of price with respect to quantity, sometimes called the elasticity of price flexibility, is simply the reciprocal of the elasticity of the quantity demanded with respect to the price.

11. Demand: $Q_l^* = -0.261P_l^* + 3.10$
    Supply: $Q_l^* = 0.649P_l^*$.
    When supply equals demand:
    $$0.649P_l^* = -0.261P_l^* + 3.10$$
    $$0.910P_l^* = 3.10$$
    $$P_l^* = 3.4$$
    $$Q_l^* = 2.21.$$

    P^* and Q^* represent percentage changes in each of the variables due to the 10 per cent increase in real farm product prices resulting from a government programme. The shift in the demand function is 3.10, which means that if the price of labour remained unchanged the quantity of labour demanded would increase by 3.10 per cent.

12. See the previous note for definition of variables.
    Demand: $Q_l^* = -0.492P_l^* + 5.85$
    Supply: $Q_l^* = 1.545P_l^*$.
    When supply equals demand:
    $$1.545P_l^* = -0.492P_l^* + 5.85$$
    $$2.037P_l^* = 5.85$$
    $$P_l^* = 2.87$$
    $$Q_l^* = 4.44.$$

13. The estimates were calculated as follows:
    Demand: $Q_L^* = -0.492P_L^*$
    Supply: $Q_L^* = 1.545P_L^* - 3.38$
    $$-0.492P^* = 1.545P^* - 3.38$$
    $$-2.037P^* = -3.38$$
    $$P^* = 1.66$$
    $$Q_L^* = 0.82.$$

14. The estimate was derived from state data in 1950 and 1960; thus it reflects changes or variations from state to state as well as between 1950 and 1960.

15. Micha Gisser, 'The Pure Theory of Government Aid to Agriculture', *American Journal of Agricultural Economics*, December 1969, p. 1513.

16. Ibid., p. 1514.

17. Gisser, 'Schooling and the Agricultural Labor Force', unpublished thesis, University of Chicago, 1962.

18. Gisser, 'Schooling and the Farm Problem', *Econometrica*, London, July 1965, p. 591.

19. John E. Floyd, 'The Effects of Farm Price Supports on the Returns to Land and Labor in Agriculture', *Journal of Political Economy*, Chicago, April 1965, p. 156.

20. In the discussion of the value of tobacco allotments I have relied on the excellent summary article by James A. Seagraves, 'Capitalized Values of Tobacco Allotments and the Rate of Return to Allotment Owners', *American Journal of Agricultural Economics*, May 1969, pp. 320–34.

21. J.L. Hedrick, 'Factor Returns Under the Tobacco Program', in George S. Tolley (ed.). *Study of US Agricultural Adjustments* (Raleigh: State University of North Carolina, 1970).

342 Notes and References

22. Ibid., pp. 264–66.
23. Summarized by Tweeten, *Foundations of Farm Policy*, op. cit., pp. 260–62.
24. Cochrane, *The City Man's Guide to the Farm Problem* (Minneapolis: University of Minnesota Press, 1965).
25. Tweeten, *Foundations of Farm Policy*, op. cit., p. 270.
26. Earl O. Heady and Leo V. Mayer, 'Opportunities and Alternatives in Program Modifications', in *Farm Program Choices* (Ames: Iowa State Center for Agricultural and Economic Development, 1970), p. 99.
27. Richard R. Barichello, *The Economics of Canadian Dairy Industry Regulation*, Technical Report No. E/12 (Ottawa: Economic Council of Canada, 1981), p. 45.
28. Barichello, 'Analyzing an Agricultural Marketing Quota', a paper presented at the IVth Congress of Agricultural Economists, Kiel, Federal Republic of Germany, 3–7 September 1984, p. 46.
29. Peter L. Arcus, *Broilers and Eggs*, Technical Report No. E/13 (Ottawa: Economic Council of Canada, 1981), p. 49.
30. Ibid., pp. 54–5.
31. Ibid., pp. 69–70.
32. Barichello, 'Recent Canadian Agricultural Policy and its Relevance for the United States', a paper prepared for the Agricultural Trade Project of the American Enterprise Institute, Washington, April 1986, p. 42.
33. Daniel A. Sumner and Julian M. Alston, *Consequences of Elimination of the Tobacco Program*, Bulletin No. 469 (Raleigh, North Carolina Agricultural Research Service, North Carolina State University, 1984), p. 12.
34. John Rosine and Peter Helmberger, 'A Neo-classical Analysis of the US Farm Sector, 1948–1970', *American Journal of Agricultural Economics*, November 1974, pp. 717–29.
35. Ibid., p. 725. It was noted that during the 1950s when land diversion payments were relatively unimportant, about two-thirds of the benefits accrued to land.
36. Andrew Barkley, 'The Determinants of Off-Farm Migration and Agricultural Investment in the United States: 1940–1985', unpublished doctoral dissertation, Department of Economics, University of Chicago, 1988, pp. 90–91.
37. Philip Ehrensaft, Pierre LaRamee, Ray D. Bollman and Frederick H. Buttel, 'The Microdynamics of Farm Structural Change in North America: the Canadian Experience and Canada–USA Comparisons', *American Journal of Agricultural Economics*, December 1984, p. 826.
38. Ibid., p. 827.
39. Ibid., p. 826.
40. Tweeten, 'The Microdynamics of Structural Change in Agriculture: Discussion', *Amrican Journal of Agricultural Economics*, December 1984, p. 844.
41. Ibid.
42. *Agricultural Statistics, 1980* (Washington: United States Department of Agriculture, 1981).
43. See Table 6.10 where it is shown that only Japan and France achieved increases in real farm prices in the 1960s.

44. Much of what is often described as an increase in efficiency in production is a result of inaccurate measurement of inputs such as tractors, implements and perhaps fertilizer. Thus large measured increases in output per unit of input should be viewed with suspicion. But some gains can occur due to farm reorganization and high pay-off new inputs. When such gains occur, net farm income will be increased if there is no effect on output prices as a result of expanded output. If output prices are reduced because of greater output, income gains to farm people are quite conjectural.
45. The statement that a 5 per cent reduction in the farm labour force would increase the return to labour by 5 per cent is not meant as a prediction, although it is approximately congruent with the experience in the United States during the 1960s. The assumption underlying such a statement is that the long-run elasticity of demand for farm labour is unity and that the demand curve for farm labour does not shift either due to a change in farm product prices or to the introduction of new inputs that substitute for labour. In any concrete situation product prices can change or substitutions can occur.
46. It should not be inferred that a 5 per cent increase in product prices would result in a 5 per cent increase in the return to labour. The earlier discussion implies that the long-run increase in the return to farm labour would be much smaller than 5 per cent. The 5 per cent increase in product prices is used to indicate how difficult it would be to use continuous increases in product prices, with a constant labour force, to achieve a continuous increase in the return to farm labour.
47. While not directly relevant to the present discussion it may be noted that between 1960 and 1970 the cost of living in farm areas in the United States increased by 24.5 per cent. Thus the increase in real farm wages during the decade was 37 per cent or an annual rate of increase of 3.2 per cent.
48. The increase in the marginal physical product was derived by dividing 110, the output level in 1970 relative to 1960, by 63 or the labour input index in 1970 relative to 1960.
49. It is quite unlikely that government programmes increased farm prices by as much as 15 per cent during the decade. Much of the increase in prices received was due to higher prices for animal products and oil-bearing crops. The prices received for crop products covered by governmental programmes actually declined.
50. See *The Agricultural Situation in the Community: 1986 Report*, op. cit., p. 39.

10 What Difference Does Trade Make?

1. Assume that at world prices consumption was 60 000 million units. At a price of one, the price elasticity of demand is −2 and price is increased by 10 per cent by the imposition of a tariff. Consumption falls to approximately 48 000 million units and the value of the area F is 12 000 million. But

consumer expenditure on food falls from 60 000 million to 52 800 million. The net value of the change in consumer expenditure and F is 4 800 million. The loss in consumers' surplus (the triangle E) is 600 million monetary units so that the total cost to consumers is 5400 million.

2. Arnold C. Harberger, 'Using the Resources at Hand More Effectively', *American Economic Review*, May 1959, p. 135; and Harry G. Johnson, 'The Gains from Free Trade with Europe: an Estimate', *Manchester School*, Manchester, September 1958.
3. J. Wemelsfelder, 'The Short-run Effects of the Lowering of Import Duties in Germany', *Economic Journal*, London, March 1960, p. 100.
4. Josling, *Agriculture and Britain's Trade Policy Dilemma*, Thames Essay No. 2 (London: Trade Policy Research Centre, 1970).
5. The estimates of the real cost of protection that have been presented are under-estimates of the actual costs, although the magnitude of the under-estimate is not known. Three sources of under-estimation may be noted: (i) all of the examples assume that there are no intermediate products or that a protected product is not used as an input; (ii) the elasticities of supply and demand that have been used are generally for the short run; if the long-run elasticities, especially of supply, are substantially higher than in the short run the real losses are increased significantly; and (iii) the estimates generally assume a single rate of protection and if there are varying degrees of protection the real costs become higher. The first point is another way of saying that protection is likely to move an economy away from its production possibility curve to an inferior position.
6. Kenneth W. Clements and Larry A. Sjaastad, *How Protection Taxes Exporters*, Thames Essay No. 39 (London: Trade Policy Research Centre, 1984).
7. Hugo Dicke, Juergen B. Donges, Egbert Gerken and Grant Kirkpatrick, 'The Economic Effects of Agricultural Policy in West Germany', *Weltwirtschaftliches Archiv*, Kiel, Vol. 124, no. 2, 1988, pp. 301–20. The full CIE studies have been published in A.B. Stoeckel, David Vincent and A.G. Cuthbertson (eds), *Macroeconomic Consequences of Farm Support Policies* (Durham, North Carolina: Duke University Press, 1989).
8. *Macro-economic Consequences of Farm-support Policies*, Overview of an International Program of Studies (Canberra: Centre for International Economics, 1988), pp. 25–30.
9. Ibid., pp. 31–6.
10. Ibid., pp. 38–44.
11. Ibid., pp. 18–24.
12. See H.G. Johnson, *Economic Policy Towards Less Developed Countries* (Washington: Brookings Institution, 1967), ch. 3.
13. An assumption concerning the relative importance of the factors of production is required. The following factor shares have been assumed: labour, 0.35; land, 0.20; all other inputs, including current purchases and reproducible capital, 0.45.
14. Josling and Donna Hamway, 'Distribution of Costs and Benefits of Farm Policy', in Josling et al., *Burdens and Benefits of Farm-support Policies*, Agricultural Trade Paper No. 1 (London: Trade Policy Research Centre, 1972), p. 79.

15. Data on 1966 distribution of direct payments from *Economic Indicators of the Farm Sector: National Financial Summary, 1985*, op. cit., p. 46.
16. *Economic Indicators of the Farm Sector: Farm Sector Review, 1985*, op. cit., p. 46.
17. D.G. Johnson, 'Agriculture and Foreign Economic Policy, *Journal of Farm Economics*, December 1964, pp. 926–7.
18. *World Development Report 1986*, op. cit., pp. 64–5.
19. The findings of Joachim Zietz and Alberto Valdés are summarized and updated in Valdés, 'Agriculture in the Uruguay Round: Interests of Developing Countries', op. cit.
20. For the Tyers–Anderson results, see ibid. The 1980 Zeitz–Valdés estimates are set out in *World Development Report 1986*, op. cit., Table 6.6.
21. I.M. Roberts, *European Community Sugar Support Policies and World Market Prices: a Comparative Static Analysis*, Working Paper No. 8213 (Canberra: Australian Bureau of Agricultural Economics, 1982), p. 40.

11 Limited Achievement of Farm Policy Objectives

1. See Vernon O. Roningen and Praveen M. Dixit, 'Economic Implications of Agricultural Policy Reform in Industrial Market Economies', a paper presented at the symposium of the International Agricultural Trade Research Consortium, Annapolis, Maryland, on 19–20 August 1988; and Tyers and Anderson, 'Liberalising OECD Agricultural Policies in the Uruguay Round: Effects on Trade and Welfare', op. cit.
2. Simantov, 'Agricultural Surpluses: an International Responsibility', in *OECD Agricultural Review* (Paris: OECD, 1970) pp. 35–6.
3. *National Policies and Agricultural Trade: Country Study, European Economic Community* (Paris: OECD, 1987), pp. 59–60.
4. *The Agricultural Policy of the EC* (Brussels: Commission of the European Community, 1979), p. 20.
5. Ibid.
6. *The Agricultural Situation in the Community: 1980 Report* (Brussels: Commission of the European Community, 1981), p. 52; and *The Common Agricultural Policy and Its Reform* (Brussels: Commission of the European Community, 1987), p. 74.
7. Koester et al., *Disharmonies in EC and US Agricultural Policy Measures* (Brussels: Commission of the European Community, 1988).
8. *The Agricultural Situation in the Community: 1980 Report*, op. cit., p. 52.
9. *Agriculture Statistical Yearbook 1988* (Luxembourg: Statistical Office of the European Community, 1988), pp. 44 and 226–7.
10. The estimated net agricultural income per full-time farm worker, derived from the source indicated in Note 8, for 1985 were as follows (in ECUs): West Germany, 6704; Spain, 6737; Belgium, 15 351; and Greece, 5822.
11. The survey of existing data on off-farm incomes of farm families was undertaken by the firm Peat Marwick Mitchell and the result was published under the title *Study of Outside Gainful Activities of Farmers and*

Their Spouses in the EEC (Luxembourg: Official Publications of the European Community, 1986).

12. *Embargoes, Surplus Disposal and US Agriculture*, Agricultural Economic Report No. 544 (Washington: United States Department of Agriculture, 1986). The team of economists that wrote the report was chaired by Alec McCalla, of the University of California, Davis.

13. During 1937–39 domestic production of rice in Japan was 85 per cent of use; the remaining 15 per cent was imported from two colonies – Taiwan and Korea. By losing the war, it lost its direct control over the imports from the colonies. Consequently having been self-sufficient in rice before the war was not adequate to have prevented starvation after the war. External aid was required to prevent famine. For data on Japanese rice production and use, see Eric Saxon and Anderson, *Japanese Agricultural Protection in Historical Perspective*, Pacific Economic Paper No. 92 (Canberra: Australian National University, 1982), appendix tables.

14. See Note 10 for source for West Germany and Italy. Data for Japan may be found in Hayami, *Japanese Agriculture Under Siege* (London: Macmillan, 1988) pp. 92–3. Data for the United States and Canada may be found in publications of the United States Department of Agriculture and Agriculture Canada, respectively.

15. See Chapter 9 above for analysis that leads to the conclusion that price supports and subsidies have little long-run effect on the returns to agricultural resources.

16. Hayami, *Japanese Agriculture Under Siege*, op. cit., p. 89. The 30 per cent of the farms were the full-time farms and the part-time farms where the majority of the income came from farming.

17. Ibid., p. 93. In 1985 the average household incomes were as follows in thousand yen: full-time farmers, 4489; part-time I, 7399; part-time II, 7466; and urban worker household, 5388.

18. Ibid., p. 91.

19. Ibid., p. 89.

20. *The Agricultural Situation in the Community: 1986 Report*, op. cit., p. 120.

21. Obtained from various publications of the Commission of the European Community, including reports on *The Agricultural Situation in the Community*.

22. Data from the *Economic Report of the President 1988*, op. cit., and publications of the United States Department of Agriculture on costs of government programmes.

23. Frederick V. Waugh, 'Does the Consumer Benefit from Price Instability?', *Quarterly Journal of Economics*, Cambridge, Massachusetts, August 1944, pp. 602–14.

24. Masayoshi Honma and Hayami, 'The Determinants of Agricultural Protection Levels: an Econometric Analysis', in Anderson and Hayami, op. cit., pp. 39–49.

25. *World Development Report 1988* (New York: Oxford University Press, for the World Bank, 1988), appendix tables.

26. *Demographic Yearbook 1984* (New York: United Nations, 1986), Vol. 36. The discussion of the text of the continued viability of rural communities in

spite of the large reductions in farm employment does not imply, nor should it be so interpreted, to mean that every rural community had maintained its viability. Obviously not all have. There are many factors that influence the fate of a given community, whether it is rural or urban. Each of us who lives in cities knows that some urban neighbourhoods decay while others thrive. So it is with rural communities.

27. Tracy, op. cit., p. 344.
28. Ibid.

12 New Directions for Agricultural Policy in the Industrial Countries

1. Centre de Recherches et de Documentation sur la Consommation, *Production and Uses of Selected Farm Products in France: Projections to 1970 and 1975* (Washington: United States Department of Agriculture, 1967), p. 136.
2. Ibid. As one who attended a one-room country school for eight years, I cannot agree that such schools were all bad!
3. The conclusion is valid for North America, Japan and many Western European countries if off-farm income is included in family income.
4. Finis Welch, 'Education in Production', *Journal of Political Economy*, January–February 1970, pp. 40 and 53. Professor Welch found that the level of expenditure on agricultural research by universities and experimental stations had a major effect on the relative earnings of college graduates who farmed. Research expenditures per farm in the United States increased about six-fold between 1940 and 1959. If these expenditures had been reduced to the 1940 level, approximately a third of the income differential between college and high-school graduates would have been eliminated. In his important article, 'The Value of the Ability to Deal with Disequilibria', *Journal of Economic Literature*, September 1975, pp. 827–46, Theodore W. Schultz emphasized the role of higher education in providing better and lower-cost access to information as well as the consequent improvement of the farm operator's ability to deal with change.
5. The apparent failure of the income differential between farm and non-farm families to narrow during the 1950s and 1960s in the industrial market economies was emphasized in the first edition of *World Agriculture in Disarray*, pp. 212–13.
6. *Abstract of Statistics on Agriculture, Forestry and Fisheries, Japan, 1984* (Tokyo: Ministry of Agriculture, Forestry and Fisheries, 1985) and the first edition of *World Agriculture in Disarray*, p. 215.
7. Hayami, op. cit., p. 85.
8. Ibid., pp. 90–91.
9. Since age and education are negatively correlated, the farm labour force has a much lower level of human capital than the non-farm labour force. This is in addition to the lower earnings of females than males in Japan.

10. For data on the relative importance of farm and off-farm income for farm-operator families, see *Agricultural Outlook*, a monthly periodical of the Economic Research Service of the United States Department of Agriculture. The data given in the text was from the December 1988 issue (p. 62). During 1987 net income from farm operations was $39.3 billion while off-farm income was $46.8 billion. A new series of data on incomes of farm-operator households with comparisons to all United States households has become available from the United States Department of Agriculture (*Economic Indicators of the Farm Sector: Farm Sector Review, 1986*, op. cit.). Farm operator household incomes from all sources were the following percentages of the average incomes of all United States households for selected years for the United States: 1970, 95; 1975, 114; 1980, 88; 1984, 81; 1985, 101; and 1986, 111. These percentages are higher than the per capita income series since farm households are larger than non-farm ones.

11. From 1960 to 1987 the average farm household net income from all sources increased at a compound annual rate of 3.2 per cent. The real annual growth rate for net farm income was 2.7 per cent while off-farm income grew at an annual rate of 3.7 per cent. For the national population personal income grew at 2.2 per cent. In all cases the growth in nominal dollars was deflated by the gross national product deflator. Data are from *Economic Indicators of the Farm Sector: National Financial Summary, 1985*, op. cit.; *Economic Indicators of the Farm Sector: National Financial Summary, 1987* (Washington: United States Department of Agriculture, 1988); and *Economic Report of the President 1988*, op. cit.

12. *Economic Indicators of the Farm Sector: National Financial Summary, 1986*, op. cit., p. 47. The asset data are from the same publication, p. 84.

13. *Production Yearbook 1986* (Rome: FAO, 1987).

14. Real export prices of United States wheat and corn (maize) declined at an annual rate of approximately 1 per cent from the mid-1920s to the mid-1980s. The disruption to the international grain markets that followed from the change in United States farm price-support and subsidy policies and the large-scale exports of the European Community during 1986 and 1987 are indicated by the relationship between actual export prices in those two years and the trend prices.

15. *Trade Yearbook 1986* (Rome: FAO, 1987), Table 1.

16. *Europe Without Frontiers: Completing the Internal Market*, second edition (Brussels: Commission of the European Community, 1988), p. 13.

17. The idea of decoupled payments – payments not associated with current production – is not a new one. The idea was put forward by Theodore W. Schultz in his *Redirecting Farm Policy* (New York: Macmillan Company, 1943) ch. 6. He described the idea as follows: 'supplementary income should be tied to the farm family, the home, to consumption, which in the last analysis means relating it to the human agent. This is in contrast to supplementing income on the basis of property resources – such as farm land, the size of the farm etc. – or tying it to the farm as a business concern' (p. 68). For a brief history of decoupled payments, see J.K. Martin, 'Decoupling: the Concept and Its Future in Canada', *Canadian Farm Economics*, Ottawa, Vol. 22, no. 1, 1988, pp. 39–51, for reports from a conference on the topic.

13 Negotiations for Freer Trade in Agricultural Products

1. Both Chile and New Zealand have unilaterally reduced the protection to agriculture to very low levels. The moves to trade liberalization and some of the important consequences were discussed in papers presented at the XXth International Conference of Agricultural Economists, Buenos Aires, 24–31 August 1988. See Ralph Lattimore, Bruce Ross and Ron Sandrey, 'Agricultural Policy Reforms in New Zealand, 1984', and Pablo Barahona and Jorge Quirozz, 'Policy Reforms and Agricultural Response: the Case of Chile'. In 1988, Australia embarked on a programme of reducing her protection of agriculture, which in 1979–81 was much lower than any other OECD country. See *Farmline*, United States Department of Agriculture, Washington, November 1988, pp. 4–7.

2. This section is taken from the first edition with little change.

3. For an excellent discussion and analysis of the historical development of agricultural and trade policies in Western Europe, see Tracy, op. cit.

4. Cornelius Walford, 'The Famines of the World: Past and Present', Part II, *Journal of the Royal Statistical Society*, London, March 1879, pp. 137–8.

5. Adam Smith, *The Wealth of Nations* (New York: Modern Library, 1937), pp. 507 and 510.

6. T.K. Warley, *Agriculture in the GATT: Past and Future*, Discussion Paper Series DP88/4 (Guelph, Ontario: Department of Agricultural Economics and Business, University of Guelph, 1988), p. 5.

7. Ibid., p. 6.

8. Ibid.

9. Ibid., p. 4.

10. Robert L. Paarlberg, *Fixing Farm Trade: Policy Options for the United States* (Cambridge, Massachusetts: Ballinger, for the Council on Foreign Relations, 1987), p. 49.

11. Tracy, op. cit., p. 376.

12. Kenneth W. Dam, *The GATT: Law and Economic Organization* (Chicago and London: University of Chicago Press, 1970), p. 261.

13. Ibid.

14. See Simon Harris, Alan Swinbank and Guy Wilkinson for the development of this point in their *The Food and Farm Policies of the European Community* (Chichester: John Wiley, 1983), p. 275.

15. This is the proposal that the European Community tabled in the Uruguay Round negotiations on 26 October 1987.

16. *Agriculture and Economic Growth*, Report by a Group of Experts (Paris: OECD, 1965), p. 81.

17. For a discussion of the limited achievements of commodity agreements, see *World Development Report 1986*, op. cit., ch. 7.

18. The publications that resulted from the OECD study include *National Policies and Agricultural Trade*, op. cit. and seven country studies. The countries included were Australia, Austria, Canada, the European Community, Japan, New Zealand and the United States. A follow-up study, *Agricultural Policies, Markets and Trade: Monitoring and Outlook 1988* (1988), extended the estimates of protection through 1986; in the earlier

publications, the levels of protection had been estimated for 1979–81. The study has been further up-dated in a 1989 edition, and national reports have been published on Finland and Sweden.

19. T.E. Josling's work resulted in two FAO documents: *Agricultural Protection: Domestic Policy and International Trade* (Rome: FAO, 1973) and *Agricultural Protection and Stabilization Policies: a Framework of Measurement in the Context of Agricultural Adjustment* (Rome: FAO, 1975).

20. Some examples of such proposals include Paarlberg, op. cit.; Dale E. Hathaway, *Agriculture and the GATT: Rewriting the Rules*, Policy Analyses in International Economics No. 20 (Washington: Institute for International Economics, 1987); *National Proposals Presented to the GATT for Negotiations on Agriculture* (Washington: National Center for Food and Agricultural Policy, Resources for the Future, 1988); and Joachim Zietz and Valdés, *Agriculture in the GATT: an Analysis of Alternative Approaches to Reform*, Research Report No. 70 (Washington: International Food Policy Research Institute, 1988).

Bibliography

MARTIN E. ABEL and ANTHONY S. ROJKO, *World Food Situation: Prospects for World Grain Production, Consumption and Trade* (Washington: United States Department of Agriculture, 1967).

Agricultural Commodities: Projections for 1970 (Rome: FAO, 1962).

Agricultural Policies in 1966: Europe, North America and Japan (Paris: OECD, 1967).

Agricultural Policies in the European Community: Their Origins, Nature and Effects on Production and Trade, Policy Monograph No. 2 (Canberra: Australian Government Publishing Service, for the [Australian] Bureau of Agricultural [and Resource] Economics, 1985).

Agricultural Policies, Markets and Trade: Monitoring and Outlook 1989 (Paris: OECD, 1989).

Agricultural Policies of Foreign Governments (Washington: United States Department of Agriculture, 1967).

The Agricultural Situation in the Community, Commission of the European Community, Brussels, annual.

Agriculture and Economic Growth, Report by a Group of Experts (Paris: OECD, 1965).

Agriculture Statistical Yearbook, Statistical Office of the European Community, Luxembourg, annual.

ROY ALLEN, CLAUDIA DODGE and ANDREW SCHMITZ, 'Voluntary Export Restraints as Protection Policy: the US Beef Case', *American Journal of Agricultural Economics*, May 1983.

KYM ANDERSON and YUJIRO HAYAMI, *The Political Economy of Agricultural Protection: East Asia in International Perspective* (London: Allen & Unwin, 1986).

KYM ANDERSON and RODNEY TYERS, 'European Community Grain and Meat Policies: Effects on International Prices', *European Review of Agricultural Economics*, Amsterdam, Vol. 11, no. 4, 1984.

KYM ANDERSON and RODNEY TYERS, *Global Effects of Liberalizing Trade in Farm Products*, Thames Essay No. 55 (Aldershot, Brookfield and Sydney: Gower, for the Trade Policy Research Centre, 1989). ✓

PETER L. ARCUS, *Broilers and Eggs*, Technical Report No. E/13 (Ottawa: Economic Council of Canada, 1981).

BASIL ASHTON, KENNETH HALL, ALAN PIAZZA and ROBIN ZEITZ, 'Famine in China, 1958–61', *Population and Development Review*, New York, December 1984.

PABLO BARAHONA and JORGE QUIROZZ, 'Policy Reforms and Agricultural Response: the Case of Chile', a paper presented at the XXth International Conference of Agricultural Economists, Buenos Aires, 24–31 August 1988.

RICHARD R. BARICHELLO, 'Analyzing an Agricultural Marketing Quota', a paper presented at the IVth Congress of Agricultural Economists, Kiel, Federal Republic of Germany, 3–7 September 1984.

351

RICHARD R. BARICHELLO, *The Economics of Canadian Dairy Industry Regulation*, Technical Report No. E/12 (Ottawa: Economic Council of Canada, 1981).

RICHARD R. BARICHELLO, 'Recent Canadian Agricultural Policy and its Relevance for the United States', a paper prepared for the Agricultural Trade Project of the American Enterprise Institute, Washington, April 1986.

ANDREW BARKLEY, 'The Determinants of Off-farm Migration and Agricultural Investment in the United States: 1940–85', unpublished doctoral dissertation, Department of Economics, University of Chicago, 1988.

DENIS BERGMANN et al., *A Future for European Agriculture*, Atlantic Paper No. 4 (Paris: Atlantic Institute for International Affairs, 1970).

DAVID BIGMAN and SHLOMO REUTLINGER, 'Food Price and Supply Stabilization: National Buffer Stocks and Trade Policies', *American Journal of Agricultural Economics*, November 1979.

JOHN R. BLOCK, *Speeches* (Washington: United States Department of Agriculture, 1983).

Centre de Recherches et de Documentation sur la Consommation, *Production and Uses of Selected Farm Products in France: Projections to 1970 and 1975* (Washington: United States Department of Agriculture, 1967).

ANTHONY H. CHISHOLM and RODNEY TYERS, 'Agricultural Protection and Market Insulation Policies: Applications of a Dynamic Multisectoral Policy', in John Piggott and John Whalley (eds), *New Developments in Applied General Equilibrium Analysis* (Cambridge: Cambridge University Press, 1985).

COLIN CLARKE, *The Conditions of Economic Progress*, second edition (London: Macmillan, 1951).

KENNETH W. CLEMENTS and LARRY A. SJAASTAD, *How Protection Taxes Exporters*, Thames Essay No. 39 (London: Trade Policy Research Centre, 1984).

WILLARD COCHRANE, *The City Man's Guide to the Farm Problem* (Minneapolis: University of Minnesota Press, 1965).

WILLARD W. COCHRANE and MARY E. RYAN, *American Farm Policy 1948–1973* (Minneapolis: University of Minnesota Press, 1976).

The Common Agricultural Policy and its Reform (Brussels: Commission of the European Community, 1987).

DANA G. DALRYMPLE, *Development and Spread of High Yielding Wheat Varieties in Developing Countries* (Washington: Agency for International Development, 1986).

KENNETH W. DAM, *The GATT: Law and Economic Organization* (Chicago and London: University of Chicago Press, 1970).

HUGO DICKE, JUERGEN B. DONGES, EGBERT GERKEN and GRANT KIRKPATRICK, 'The Economic Effects of Agricultural Policy in West Germany', *Weltwirtschaftliches Archiv*, Kiel, Vol. 124, no. 2, 1988.

GEORGE E. DUDLEY, JAMES R. ROLAND and RUSSELL G. BARLOWE, 'Yield and Acreage Implications for US Cotton', *Cotton Situation and Outlook Report*, United States Department of Agriculture, Washington, August 1970.

PHILIP EHRENSAFT, PIERRE LaRAMEE, RAY D. BOLLMAN and FREDERICK H. BUTTEL, 'The Microdynamics of Farm Structural

Change in North America: the Canadian Experience and Canada–USA Comparisons', *American Journal of Agricultural Economics*, December 1984.
Embargoes, Surplus Disposal and US Agriculture, Agricultural Economic Report No. 544 (Washington: United States Department of Agriculture, 1986).
Farm Product Imports, Present State of Agriculture and Direction of Agricultural Policy (Tokyo: Ministry of Agriculture, Forestry and Fisheries, 1982).
BRIAN FERNON, *Issues in World Farm Trade: Chaos or Cooperation?*, Atlantic Trade Study No. 13 (London: Trade Policy Research Centre, 1970).
JOHN E. FLOYD, 'The Effects of Farm Price Supports on the Returns to Land and Labor in Agriculture', *Journal of Political Economy*, Chicago, April 1965.
Food Reserve Policies for World Food Security: a Consultant Study of Alternative Approaches, ESC: CSP/75/2 (Rome: FAO, 1975).
France and Agriculture (New York: Service de Presse et d'Information de France, 1963).
MICHA GISSER, 'The Pure Theory of Government Aid to Agriculture', *American Journal of Agricultural Economics*, December 1969.
MICHA GISSER, 'Schooling and the Agricultural Labor Force', unpublished thesis, University of Chicago, 1962.
MICHA GISSER, 'Schooling and the Farm Problem', *Econometrica*, London, July 1965.
Grain in the European Community: Rising Protection and Falling Imports (Washington: United States Department of Agriculture, 1970).
Guidelines for European Agriculture, COM(81) 608 final (Brussels: Commission of the European Community, 1981).
ARNOLD C. HARBERGER, 'Using the Resources at Hand More Effectively', *American Economic Review*, May 1959.
SIMON HARRIS, ALAN SWINBANK and GUY WILKINSON, *The Food and Farm Policies of the European Community* (Chichester: John Wiley, 1983).
DALE E. HATHAWAY, *Agriculture and the GATT: Rewriting the Rules*, Policy Analyses in International Economics No. 20 (Washington: Institute for International Economics, 1987).
YUJIRO HAYAMI, *Japanese Agriculture Under Siege* (London: Macmillan, 1988).
YUJIRO HAYAMI and VERNON W. RUTTAN, *Agricultural Development: an International Perspective* (Baltimore: Johns Hopkins Press, 1971).
PETER B.R. HAZELL, *Instability in Indian Grain Production*, Research Report No. 30 (Washington: International Food Policy Research Institute, 1982).
EARL O. HEADY and LEO V. MAYER, 'Opportunities and Alternatives in Program Modifications', in *Farm Program Choices* (Ames: Iowa State Center for Agricultural and Economic Development, 1970).
J.L. HEDRICK, 'Factor Returns Under the Tobacco Program', in George S. Tolley (ed.), *Study of US Agricultural Adjustments* (Raleigh: North Carolina State University, 1970).
THEODOR HEIDHUES, T.E. JOSLING, CHRISTOPHER RITSON and STEFAN TANGERMANN, *Common Prices and Europe's Farm Policy*, Thames Essay No. 14 (London: Trade Policy Research Centre, 1978).

354 *Bibliography*

BRIAN E. HILL, *The Common Agricultural Policy: Past, Present and Future* (London: Methuen, 1984).

MASAYOSHI HONMA and YUJIRO HAYAMI, 'The Determinants of Agricultural Protection Levels: an Econometric Analysis', in Kym Anderson and Hayami, *The Political Economy of Agricultural Protection: East Asia in International Perspective* (London: Allen & Unwin, 1986).

J.P. HOUCK and J.S. MANN, *An Analysis of Domestic and Foreign Demand for US Soyabeans and Soyabean Products* (Minneapolis: Agricultural Experiment Station, University of Minnesota, 1968).

JAMES P. HOUCK and ABRAHAM SUBOTNIK, 'The US Supply of Soyabeans: Regional Acreage Functions', *Agricultural Economics Research*, United States Department of Agriculture, Washington, October 1969.

RICHARD W. HOWARTH, *Agricultural Support in Western Europe*, Research Monograph No. 25 (London: Institute of Economic Affairs, 1971).

BARBARA HUDDLESTON, *Closing the Cereals Gap with Trade and Food Aid*, Research Report No. 43 (Washington: International Food Policy Research Institute, 1984).

BARBARA HUDDLESTON and PANOS KONANDREAS, 'Insurance Approach to Food Security: Simulation of Benefits for 1970/71–1975/76 and for 1978–1982', in Alberto Valdés (ed.), *Food Security for Developing Countries* (Boulder: Westview Press, 1981).

JOHN E. HUTCHINSON, JAMES J. NAIVE and SHELDON K. TSU, *World Demand Prospects for Wheat in 1980 with Emphasis on Trade by Less Developed Countries* (Washington: United States Department of Agriculture, 1970).

The Instability of Agricultural Commodity Markets (Paris: OECD, 1980).

Jaoanese Agricultural Policies: a Time of Change, Policy Monograph No. 3 (Canberra: Australian Government Publishing Service, for the Australian Bureau of Agricultural and Resource Economics, 1988).

D. GALE JOHNSON, 'Agriculture and Foreign Economic Policy', *Journal of Farm Economics*, December 1964.

D. GALE JOHNSON, 'Are High Farm Prices Here to Stay?', *Morgan Guaranty Survey*, New York, August 1974.

D. GALE JOHNSON, 'Grain Insurance, Reserves and Trade: Contributions to Food Security for LDCs', in Alberto Valdés (ed.), *Food Security for Developing Countries* (Boulder: Westview Press, 1981).

D. GALE JOHNSON, 'International Prices and Trade in Reducing Distortions in Incentives', in Theodore W. Schultz (ed.), *Distortions of Agricultural Incentives* (Bloomington: Indiana University Press, 1978).

D. GALE JOHNSON, 'Soviet Agriculture Revisited', *American Journal of Agricultural Economics*, May 1971.

D. GALE JOHNSON, *Trade in Agriculture: a Study of Inconsistent Policies* (New York, John Wiley, 1950).

D. GALE JOHNSON, 'World Agriculture, Commodity Policy and Price Variability', *American Journal of Agricultural Economics*, December 1975.

HARRY G. JOHNSON, *Economic Policy Towards the Less Developed Countries* (Washington: Brookings Institution, 1967).

HARRY G. JOHNSON, 'The Gains from Free Trade with Europe: an Estimate', *Manchester School*, Manchester, September 1958.

PAUL R. JOHNSON, THOMAS GRENNES and MARIE THURSBY, 'Devaluation, Foreign Trade Controls and Domestic Wheat Prices', *American Journal of Agricultural Economics*, November 1977.

T.E. JOSLING, *Agricultural Protection: Domestic Policy and International Trade* (Rome: FAO, 1973).

T.E. JOSLING, *Agricultural Protection and Stabilization Policies: a Framework of Measurement in the Context of Agricultural Adjustment* (Rome: FAO, 1975).

T.E. JOSLING, *Agriculture and Britain's Trade Policy Dilemma*, Thames Essay No. 2 (London: Trade Policy Research Centre, 1970).

T.E. JOSLING and DONNA HAMWAY, 'Distribution of Costs and Benefits of Farm Policy', in Josling et al., *Burdens and Benefits of Farm-support Policies*, Agricultural Trade Paper No. 1 (London: Trade Policy Research Centre, 1972).

T.E. JOSLING, MARK LANGWORTHY and SCOTT PEARSON, *Options for Farm Policy in the European Community*, Thames Essay No. 27 (London: Trade Policy Research Centre, 1981).

ULRICH KOESTER, *Policy Options for the Grain Economy of the European Community: Implications for Developing Countries*, Research Report No. 35 (Washington: International Food Policy Research Institute, 1982).

ULRICH KOESTER et al., *Disharmonies in EC and US Agricultural Policy Measures* (Brussels: Commission of the European Community, 1988).

RALPH LATTIMORE, BRUCE ROSS and RON SANDREY, 'Agricultural Policy Reforms in New Zealand, 1984', a paper presented at the XXth International Conference of Agricultural Economists, Buenos Aires, 24–31 August 1988.

GAVIN McCRONE, *The Economics of Subsidizing Agriculture* (London: Allen & Unwin, 1962).

G.A. MacEACHERN and VERNON W. RUTTAN, 'Determining Factor Shares', in *Farmers in the Market Economy* (Ames: Iowa State Center for Agricultural and Economic Development, 1964).

DAVID L. MacFARLANE and LEWIS A. FISCHER, 'Prospects for Trade Liberalization in Agriculture', in Gerald I. Trant, MacFarlane and Fischer, *Trade Liberalization and Canadian Agriculture* (Toronto: University of Toronto Press, for the Private Planning Association of Canada, 1968).

Macro-economic Consequences of Farm-support Policies, Overview of an International Program of Studies (Canberra: Centre for International Economics, 1988).

J.K. MARTIN, 'Decoupling: the Concept and its Future in Canada', *Canadian Farm Economics*, Ottawa, Vol. 22, no. 1, 1988.

National Policies and Agricultural Trade (Paris: OECD, 1987).

National Policies and Agricultural Trade: Country Study, European Economic Community (Paris: OECD, 1987).

MARC NERLOVE, *The Dynamics of Supply: Estimation of Farmers' Response to Price* (Baltimore: Johns Hopkins Press, 1958).

OECD Problems of Agricultural Trade (Paris: OECD, 1982).

KAZUSHI OHKAWA, BRUCE F. JOHNSTON and HIROMITSU KANEDA (eds), *Agriculture and Economic Growth: Japan's Experience* (Tokyo: University of Tokyo Press, 1969).

ROBERT L. PAARLBERG, *Fixing Farm Trade: Policy Options for the United States* (Cambridge, Massachusetts: Ballinger, for the Council on Foreign Relations, 1987).

KIRIT S. PARIKH, GUNTHER FISCHER, KLAUS FROHBERG and ODD GULBRANDSEN, *Towards Free Trade in Agriculture* (Dordrecht: Martinus Nijhoff, for the International Institute for Applied Systems Analysis, 1988).

W.E. PEARSON and R.E. FRIEND, *The Netherlands Mixed Feed Industry* (Washington: United States Department of Agriculture, 1970).

Presidential Commission on International Trade and Investment Policy, *United States International Economic Policy in an Interdependent World*, Williams Report (Washington: US Government Printing Office, 1971).

Production Yearbook, FAO, Rome, annual.

Proposals Presented to the GATT for Negotiations on Agriculture (Washington: National Center for Food and Agricultural Policy, Resources for the Future, 1988).

Review of Agricultural Policies: General Survey (Paris: OECD, 1975).

I.M. ROBERTS, *European Community Sugar Support Policies and World Market Prices: a Comparative Static Analysis*, Working Paper No. 8213 (Canberra: Australian Bureau of Agricultural Economics, 1982).

WILLIAM F. ROENIGK, *Agriculture in the European Community and the United States, 1958–1968* (Washington: United States Department of Agriculture, 1971).

VERNON O. RONINGEN and PRAVEEN M. DIXIT, 'Economic Implications of Agricultural Policy Reform in Industrial Market Economies', a paper presented at the symposium of the International Agricultural Trade Research Consortium, Annapolis, Maryland, 19–20 August 1988.

JOHN ROSINE and PETER HELMBERGER, 'A Neo-classical Analysis of the US Farm Sector, 1948–1970', *American Journal of Agricultural Economics*, November 1974.

ALEXANDER H. SARRIS and JOHN FREEBAIRN, 'Endogenous Price Policies and International Wheat Prices', *American Journal of Agricultural Economics*, May 1983.

ERIC SAXON and KYM ANDERSON, *Japanese Agricultural Protection in Historical Perspective*, Pacific Economic Paper No. 92 (Canberra: Australian National University, 1982).

THEODORE W. SCHULTZ, *Redirecting Farm Policy* (New York: Macmillan Company, 1943).

THEODORE W. SCHULTZ, *Transforming Traditional Agriculture* (New Haven: Yale University Press, 1964).

THEODORE W. SCHULTZ, 'The Value of the Ability to Deal with Disequilibria', *Journal of Economic Literature*, September 1975.

C.H. SHAH, 'Food Preferences and Nutrition: a Perspective on Poverty in Less Developed Countries', Presidential Address to the Thirty-ninth Conference of the Indian Agricultural Economics Society, *Indian Journal of Agricultural Economics*, Bombay, January–March 1980.

SHEI SHUN-YI and ROBERT L. THOMPSON, 'The Impact of Trade Restrictions on Price Stability in the World Wheat Market', *American Journal of Agricultural Economics*, November 1977.

MAURICE W. SCHIFF, *An Econometric Analysis of the World Wheat Market and Simulation of Alternative Policies, 1960–80*, Economic Research Service Staff Report No. AGES 850827 (Washington: United States Department of Agriculture, 1985).

JAMES A. SEAGRAVES, 'Capitalized Values of Tobacco Allotments and the Rate of Return to Allotment Owners', *American Journal of Agricultural Economics*, May 1969.

ALBERT SIMANTOV, 'Agricultural Developments in OECD Countries and Implications for Trade', speech given at the United States National Agricultural Outlook Conference, Washington, 17 February 1969.

ALBERT SIMANTOV, 'Agricultural Surpluses: an International Responsibility', *OECD Agricultural Review* (Paris: OECD, 1970).

ADAM SMITH, *The Wealth of Nations* (New York: Modern Library, 1937).

ALLEN G. SMITH, 'Comparative Investment per Worker in Agriculture and Manufacturing Sectors of the Economy', *American Journal of Agricultural Economics*, February 1971.

The State of Food and Agriculture, FAO, Rome, annual.

A.B. STOECKEL, DAVID VINCENT and A.G. CUTHBERTSON (eds), *Macroeconomic Consequences of Farm Support Policies* (Durham, North Carolina: Duke University Press, 1989).

Study of Outside Gainful Activities of Farmers and Their Spouses in the EEC (Luxembourg: Official Publications of the European Community, 1986).

DANIEL A. SUMNER and JULIAN M. ALSTON, *Consequences of Elimination of the Tobacco Program*, Bulletin No. 469 (Raleigh: North Carolina Agricultural Research Service, North Carolina State University, 1984).

PETER SVEDBERG, 'Food Insecurity in Developing Countries: Causes, Trends and Policy Options', UNCTAD/CD/301, GE.84-51933, UNCTAD, Geneva, 6 June 1984.

STEFAN TANGERMANN and WOLFGANG KROSTITZ, *Protectionism in the Livestock Sector with Particular Reference to the International Beef Trade* (Göttingen: Institut für Agrarökonomie der Universität Göttingen, 1982).

MICHAEL TRACY, *Agriculture in Western Europe: Challenge and Response 1880–1980*, second edition (London: Granada, 1982).

Trade Yearbook, FAO, Rome, annual.

VLADIMIR G. TREML, *Agricultural Subsidies in the Soviet Union*, Foreign Economic Report No. 15 (Washington: Bureau of the Census, United States Department of Commerce, 1978). Trends in Agricultural Policies Since 1955 (Paris: OEEC, 1961).

EDWARD W. TYRCHNIEWICZ and G. EDWARD SCHUH, 'Economic Analysis of the Agricultural Labor Market', *American Journal of Agricultural Economics*, November 1969.

LUTHER TWEETEN, *Foundations of Farm Policy*, second edition (Lincoln: University of Nebraska Press, 1979).

LUTHER TWEETEN, 'The Microdynamics of Structural Change in Agriculture: Discussion', *American Journal of Agricultural Economics*, December 1984.

RODNEY TYERS, 'Effects on ASEAN of Food Trade Liberalization in Industrial Countries', a paper presented to the Second Western Pacific Food Trade Workshop, Jakarta, 22–23 August 1982.

RODNEY TYERS and KYM ANDERSON, 'Distortions in World Food Markets: a Quantitative Assessment', a background paper for the World Bank's *World Development Report 1986.*

RODNEY TYERS and KYM ANDERSON, 'Global Interactions and Trade Liberalisation in Agriculture', mimeograph, Department of Economics, University of Adelaide, April 1987.

RODNEY TYERS and KYM ANDERSON, 'Liberalising OECD Agricultural Policies in the Uruguay Round: Effects on Trade and Welfare', *Journal of Agricultural Economics*, May 1988.

RODNEY TYERS and KYM ANDERSON, *Price, Trade and Welfare Effects of Agricultural Protection: the Case of East Asia*, Pacific Economic Paper No. 109 (Canberra: Australia–Japan Research Centre, Australian National University, 1984).

US Grain Policies and the World Market, Policy Monograph No. 4 (Canberra: Australian Government Publishing Service, for the Australian Bureau of Agricultural and Resource Economics, 1989).

ALBERTO VALDÉS, 'Agriculture in the Uruguay Round: Interests of Developing Countries', *The World Bank Economic Review*, Washington, September 1987.

ALBERTO VALDÉS and PANOS KONANDREAS, 'Assessing Food Insecurity Based on National Aggregates in Developing Countries', in Valdés (ed.), *Food Security for Developing Countries* (Boulder: Westview Press, 1981).

ALBERTO VALDÉS and JOACHIM ZIETZ, *Agricultural Protection in OECD Countries: Its Costs to Less-developed Countries*, Research Report No. 21 (Washington: International Food Policy Research Institute, 1980).

CORNELIUS WALFORD, 'The Famines of the World: Past and Present', Part II, *Journal of the Royal Statistical Society*, London, March 1879.

T.K. WARLEY, *Agriculture in the GATT: Past and Future*, Discussion Paper Series DP88/4 (Guelph, Ontario: Department of Agricultural Economics and Business, University of Guelph, 1988).

FREDERICK V. WAUGH, 'Does the Consumer Benefit from Price Instability?', *Quarterly Journal of Economics*, Cambridge, Massachusetts, August 1984.

FINIS WELCH, 'Education in Production', *Journal of Political Economy*, January–February 1970.

J. WEMELSFELDER, 'The Short-run Effects of the Lowering of Import Duties in Germany', *Economic Journal*, London, March 1960.

LIANG WENSEN, 'Balanced Development of Industry and Agriculture', in Xu Dixin et al., *China's Search for Economic Growth: the Chinese Economy Since 1949* (Beijing: New World Press, 1982).

World Development Report (New York: Oxford University Press, for the World Bank, annual).

'The World Food Problem: Proposals for National and International Action', United Nations World Food Conference, Rome, 5–16 November 1974, E/CONF.65/4, pp. 189–93.

JOACHIM ZIETZ and ALBERTO VALDÉS, *Agriculture in the GATT: an Analysis of Alternative Approaches to Reform*, Research Report No. 70 (Washington: International Food Policy Research Institute, 1988).

Index

Index

agricultural output and consumption
52
exports and imports 47–8
GDP per employed worker 56–8
meat importation 140
projected world price increases due to
reduction in trade barriers 143–50,
242–3
rates of protection 37
studies of agricultural protection
320–2
use of fertilizers 68
see also individual countries
Organisation for European Economic
Cooperation 20–1

Paarlberg, Robert 309
Pakistan 145–7
Philippines 145–7
Poland 3
Portugal 20, 210
price stability 8–9, 12, 13, 22–3,
25–6, 120–1
as objectives of farm policy
265–72
national price stability and international
instability 150–3
price supports
and returns to labour 192–204,
207–10
and returns to land 192–204
prices
changes in real farm prices 112–17
government influence on 17–25, 90
higher prices and returns to farm labour
185–6
increases in 49–51, 53
national differences 38–46
world market prices 120, 124–5
as guide to real costs 121–3
see also feed prices; income for
farmers; market price distortions;
price stability; price supports;
protection for agriculture
producer subsidy equivalents (PSEs)
43–6, 320–22
*Production and Uses of Selected Farm
Products in France* 282
production controls 18–19, 31, 46–8
protection for agriculture 124–5, 215–16,
218
costs to the excluded 230–3
costs to the protected 218–24
effects on less developed countries
241–4

excess capacity 247–9
export subsidies 122–3, 128–9
fixed rate of protection 210–15
history of 303–6
in EC 35–9, 107, 119, 122–3, 149
in industrial economies 117–19, 241
income transfer 219–24, 230–40,
245–6
international commodity agreements
314–15
justification for 120–4
producer subsidy equivalents (PSEs)
43–6, 320–2
reform of 297–306, 315–25
'voluntary' export restraints 318–19
welfare costs 224–30
see also farm policies; income for
farmers; market price distortions;
price supports
*Provisional Indicative World Plan for
Agricultural Development* (FAO) 51–2

Quarterly Journal of Economics 267

Reagan Administration 23
Reciprocal Trade Agreements Act (1934)
5, 302
Reutlinger, Shlomo 172–4
Rojko, Anthony S. 51
Rosine, John 202–3
rural sector, as objective of farm policy
272–7, 295–6
Ruttan, Vernon 70, 89

Sarris, Alexander 149
Schiff, Maurice 147–8, 151
Schmitz, Andrew 148–9
Schuh, G. Edward 186–7, 190, 203–4,
208, 234
Schultz, T. W. 178, 283
Seagraves, James 195–6
Simantov, Albert 248–9, 283
Singapore 145–7
Sjaastad, Larry 228
Smith, Adam 306
Smoot-Hawley Tariff 5
South Africa 133, 135
South Korea *see* Korea, Republic of
Soviet Union 151
cotton production 29–30, 142–3
economic policies 2–3, 6
feed-grain production 133
import of wheat from EC and USA
29, 50–1, 157
price subsidies 37–8